The Head Hutt

On Building the Head Hutt Mega-Sculpture

Simple Edition

In Black and White

By Gabrielle Angel Lilly

The Head Hutt,

Simple Edition in Black and White

Copyright © 2020 Gabrielle Angel Lilly

FunFast Productions, GAL Media & 1000 Words Press

All rights reserved.

ISBN-13: 978-1-7326698-4-0

DEDICATION

Dedicated to friends and family of Seth and Demian Larson, and to everyone who has ever built something with their own bare and gloved hands, and to a better and better future.

Many Thanks and Super Gratitude to all things big and small, dark and sweet, beautiful and light, knowing and unknowing, known and unknown, conspiring on my behalf.

Cheers to our evolution, baby!

This book is for you if you are interested in alternative construction, papercrete, mega-sculptures, folk art, art therapy, tire wall construction, bottle wall, recycled art, lime plaster, cob, adobe, domes, off-grid housing, tiny housing, site specific art, dig therapy, the mental health benefits of physical exercise, or creativity.

The Head Hutt Picture Book

Prelude:

This book, much like the Head Hutt project itself, is something of a loose experiment. I have chosen to include a good number of the pictures with the captions as I wrote them along the way. I have included some anecdotal stories and some personal background as well, which may or may not be of interest to you, dear reader.

You can flip through this book and get a pretty quick overview of how I built the Head Hutt. If you are interested in any particular section, I did try to include some details for each. In many cases I left the captions of pictures unedited, with the dates I recorded them, so you can get a sense of the time frame that things happened, and did not happen, in this project.

Many of my friends think of the Head Hutt as an Earthship, even though it is not. I'm sure that is largely because I was inspired greatly by Earthships and I worked two different Earthships while I was just starting this project. I like to try to educate people about the six components that make an Earthship.

A proper Earthship has the following six characteristics, of which the Head Hutt Mega-Sculpture only has one, maybe two. Those are: Thermal/Solar Heating & Cooling, Solar & Wind Electricity, Contained Sewage Treatment, Building with Natural & Recycled Materials, Water Harvesting, and Food Production. The Head Hutt is made from many natural and recycled materials, and it does use some thermal and solar heating and cooling, albeit not very efficiently. Otherwise, it does not have much in common with an Earthship.

This book is organized in three main parts. There are pictures throughout, however, the middle section has the most pictures and captions. Captions are barely edited versions of what I wrote

The Head Hutt Picture Book

at the time of posting these and other pictures online. I put the captioned bits in italics so you can tell them apart, as sometimes they are out of context with the overall story.

I started this project in response to many factors in my life. I had been contemplating a garage or workspace or greenhouse for some time. My son was starting junior high school and needing my attention much less than the years of part time home schooling in grade school. I was angry about our involvement in climate changes, frustrated by the obvious wide-spread break-down of our governing bodies and institutions, learning about desertification, food supply nightmares, and so many other things. Here is some of that story.

I welcome your questions, so feel free to look me up.

The Head Hutt Picture Book

The Head Hutt

on Building the Head Hutt Mega-Sculpture

Simple Edition

In Black and White

by Gabrielle Angel Lilly

CONTENTS

	Acknowledgments	i
1	Introduction	12
2	The Inspiration, Reasons and Seasons	15
3	I Can Do Anything & So Can You	22
4	The Dig; Tires, Tires, & More Tires	24
5	The Bond Beam	45
6	Pillars and Arches Oh My	48
7	Glass, Glass, Glass, Glass	54
8	The Dome	82
9	Infills and Plasters	90
10	PLASTERDOME!!!	111
11	Vigas and Floors	130
12	Openings Are Eyes	140
13	Cob Infill, Lime Plaster, Steps	151
14	Devil is in the Details	164
15	Closing Thoughts, Finishing the Future	234
16	About the Author/Artist	237
17	Epilogue	241

ACKNOWLEDGMENTS and GRATITUDE

To my son, who lived with me for a mother, and didn't seem to mind that I was outside playing in the dirt most of the time, and to my friends who supported me through the building and documenting of this one of a kind creation. Thank you.

Many Thanks and Super Gratitude to all things big and small, dark and sweet, beautiful and light, knowing and unknowing, known and unknown, conspiring on my behalf.

Cheers to our evolution, baby!

The Head Hutt Picture Book

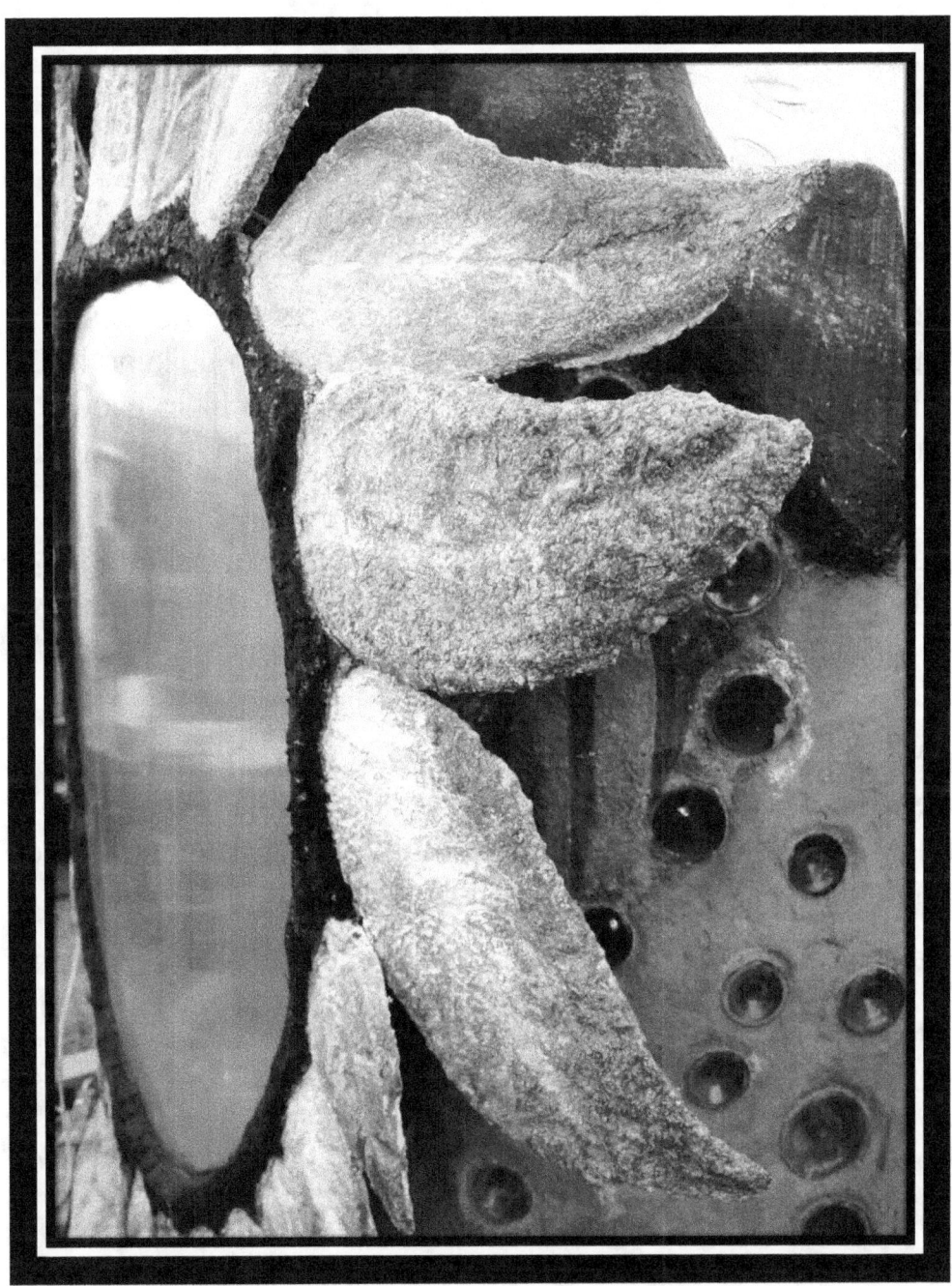

Introduction

Welcome to the story of the Head Hutt. This is an overview of the process of building it, and what inspired me to build it, and what I learned in building it. It is also a story about my vision for the future. A call to action. A call to allow yourself to dream and take action on your dreams. Support me in mine if you feel like it suits you. In any case, dream your dreams.

Bringing energy into alignment is the ultimate main objective of most things I do. My mission currently is to help people heal themselves, love themselves, forgive themselves, and find their most authentic, aligned selves, and take positive action there.

When I started the Head Hutt, my alignment was pretty far off. Or, maybe it was perfect like everything always turns out to be. In any case, I had a pretty prominent wobble going on. I was unhappy about many things. I wanted to do something to add momentum to creating a more aligned future.

I wanted to feel better. I wanted to build something. I wanted to learn. I wanted to demonstrate, explore, and encourage others. I wanted to prove to myself I could do it.

I wanted to create something unique. Explore new and old options. Learn. Make something good out of some bad feelings. Get outside and sweat in the dirt.

In my quest to find a healthy way of dealing with some anger and inner shifting that came up, I decided to build something. What it was going to be was not completely clear at any time. The ends are not always clear to me.

This project taught me what all lessons seem to return to. That life is short, time goes by more quickly than you think, and you can do more than you think if you start and keep going.

You can do it. *Will you?* That is your question.

A giant Head sculpture just seemed like a natural course for me. I made heads with many assignments in college, finding that the narrower focus helped my creativity flourish and helped me get started pronto. Also, I wanted to try a round building, at some point decided on a round dome, which is, you know, more or less head-shaped.

I gave a good deal of consideration to the details of the Head, such as the expansive star shaped pattern on the back of the 'skull', the swirling temples, the butterfly eyebrows in the dome, the mirror-eyes downstairs, and the leaf-feather-lashes on the large front eye windows. I have always been something of a philosopher, and a person who likes to explore expressions of self and Universal self through my hands, and especially with Earth and stone. In many ways building Mega-Sculptures, combining art and function through architecture, has been a natural part of my personal evolutionary process.

I have a background in ceramics, among other things. I went to college for a long time, studied many things, and spent a lot of time in the art department, mainly in studios. Ceramics was always one of my favorites. I love site specific art installations, and multi-medium large-scale sculpture. I started making clay/ceramic heads at some point early in my studies, and then continued with the theme after I graduated. The Head Hutt was a continuation of that work in many ways. That is what the Head Hutt and the Foo Dog are.

Mega-Sculptures.

The main lessons of the Head Hutt, for me, were of persistence, willingness to try, fail, learn, try again, keep going even when things get slowed down, and also to be okay with going slower than you planned. It was about transforming something impossibly terrible and wasteful into something impossibly beautiful and uniquely creative. It was about triumph over doubt. Choosing love instead of fear.

In many ways, the ten years that have passed since I started the Head Hutt went by quickly, and in other ways they took a lifetime. As I am finally finishing this book, they seem to fit neatly into a decade of my life which it feels good to be finally finishing. The entire project seems inevitable and improbable at the same time. Just like you and I, I suppose.

I don't necessarily feel like the Head Hutt was any kind of an original idea. More of a common Universal idea, a thought form that has existed for thousands or maybe millions of years, realized in my own unique way. I suspect anything we imagine already exist in the ether of evolution, just waiting for any of us to align ourselves, tune to the right frequency, and receive the idea/thought. I don't really know, of course. It's just an idea.

I do know that the idea of building a unique structure, sculpting, building living spaces and play spaces is an idea that has been on humankind's minds for some time.

You know that is true because it rhymed.

There are many metaphorical lessons that played out in building the Head Hutt, and continue to unfold, even now as I wrap up the writing and publishing of this book. I learned much about construction, about myself, and about life. How we do one thing is how we do everything.

I learned I can do things I don't know how to yet. That people love to be helpful, though they are not always good at it, and that construction can be difficult, as in, physically, emotionally, and intellectually challenging.

The Head Hutt is finished, as of the publishing of this book. I can feel my new wings unfolding. Stretching. Growing stronger. Of course, repairs, maintenance, its own evolution will continue. I am happy to be done with it in many ways, and to have a new beginning with it at the same time. As all endings are also beginnings.

The Head Hutt Picture Book

The Inspiration—Reasons and Seasons

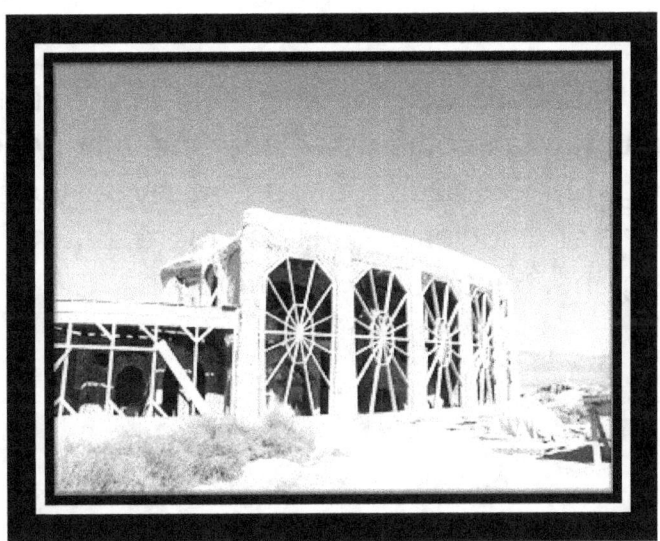

This is the E.V.E. project at Earthship Biotecture, as it was in 2010. I am sure it is looking much different today!

I highly recommend that you watch Garbage Warrior, if you are interested in the history of the beginnings of this living classroom. This structure and its history, Mike Reynolds, and all the people I worked with on the two homes I got to work on had a remarkable inspirational and motivational impact on me.

Meeting so many hard working, talented, brave, kind, loving, hard-working, people from all over the world, brought together by a common dream of building a better, more sustainable, more peaceful future, still brings tears of joy to my eyes. I hope that my story inspires you to think more about what you can do to build a better future, to dream, to try something you don't know how to do.

I also was inspired and learned from several other architects, visionaries, and builders, including Steve Kornher of Flying Concrete, the mud girls, Rob Roy and his cordwood buildings, strawbail construction by Jeff Ruppert, SunRay Kelly, CalEarth founder Nader Khalili, and numerous other greenbuilders, including but not limited to Mark Ketchum, Lloyd Turner, Fernando Martinez Lewels, Kelly Hart, Michael Collins, and Bo Atkinson.

I learned about ferrocement, adobe, straw, sand, stone, thermal mass, insulation, radiant heat, magnesium, glass, tires, and much, much, more. I studied permaculture, food forests, vertical farming, aquaponics, swales, fungus, and Hugelkultur. I put in a passive gray water system in my home and have plans in the works for solar panels on the roof.

Originally, one of my intentions was to explore off-grid building and demonstrate what one human could do without machinery or special skills. Ultimately, in the long run, I realized there are many reasons we come together in civilizations and societies. Building more thriving community in my life, and around the globe, became my bigger focus.

The Head Hutt Picture Book

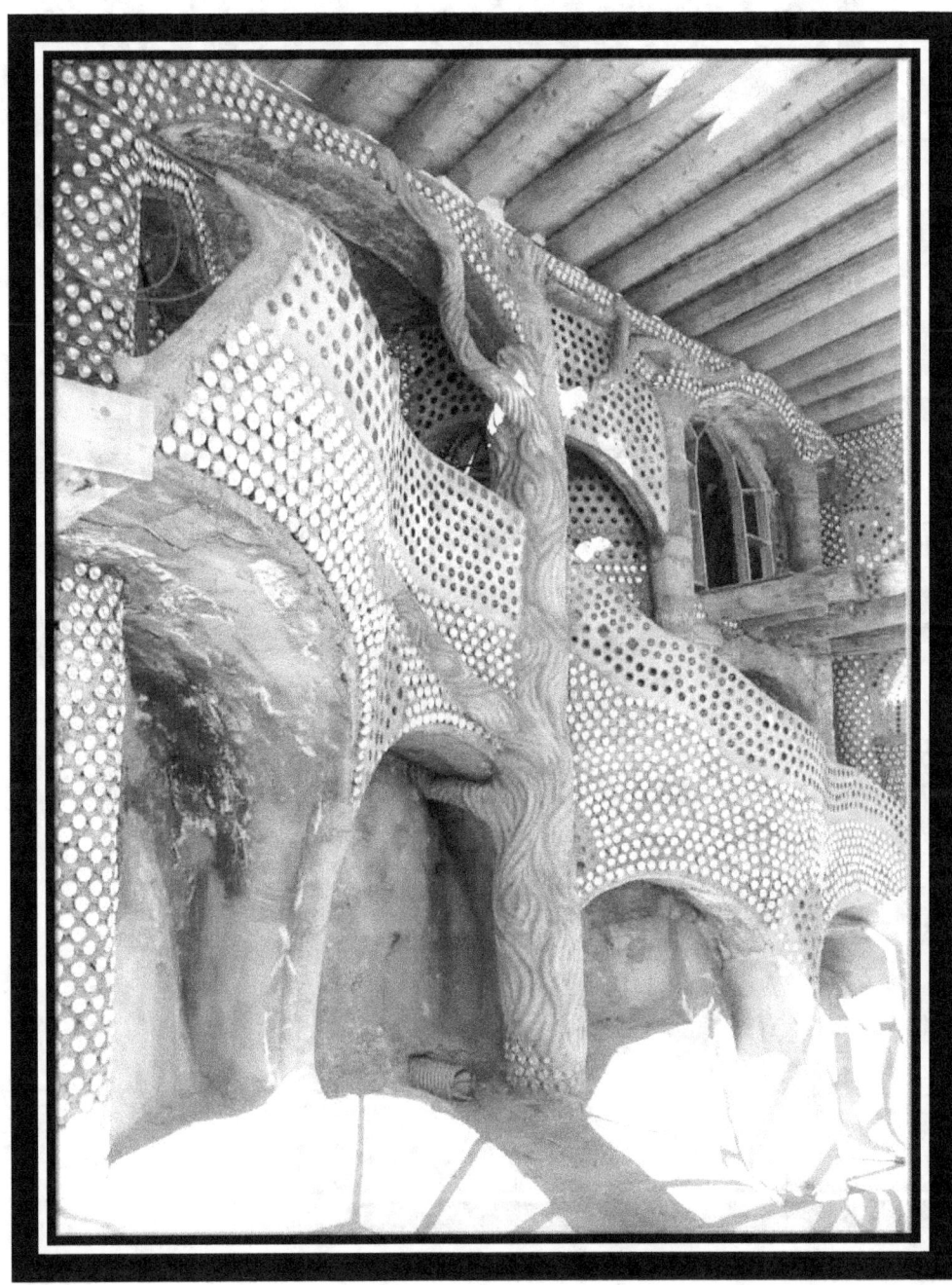

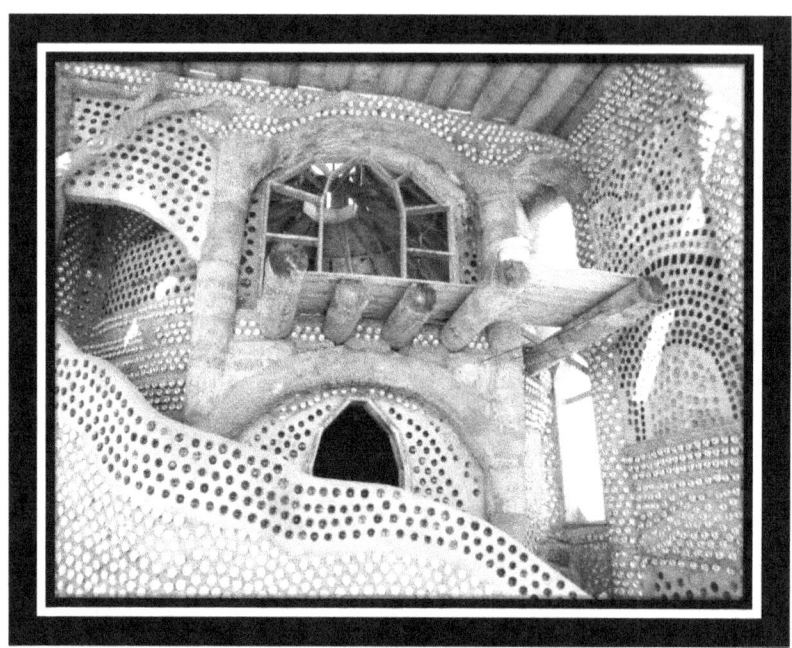

E.V.E. Project classroom, Taos, New Mexico, 2010.

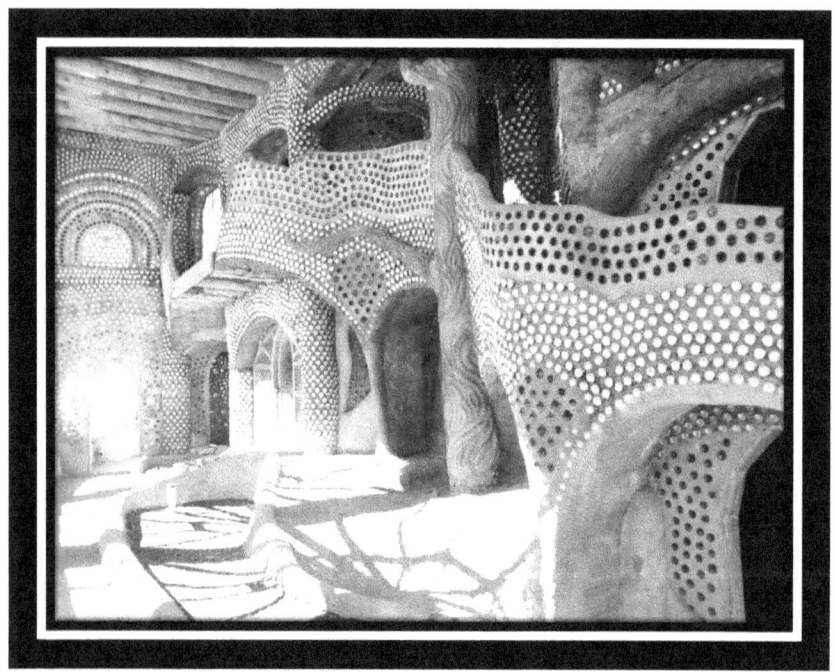

The Head Hutt Picture Book

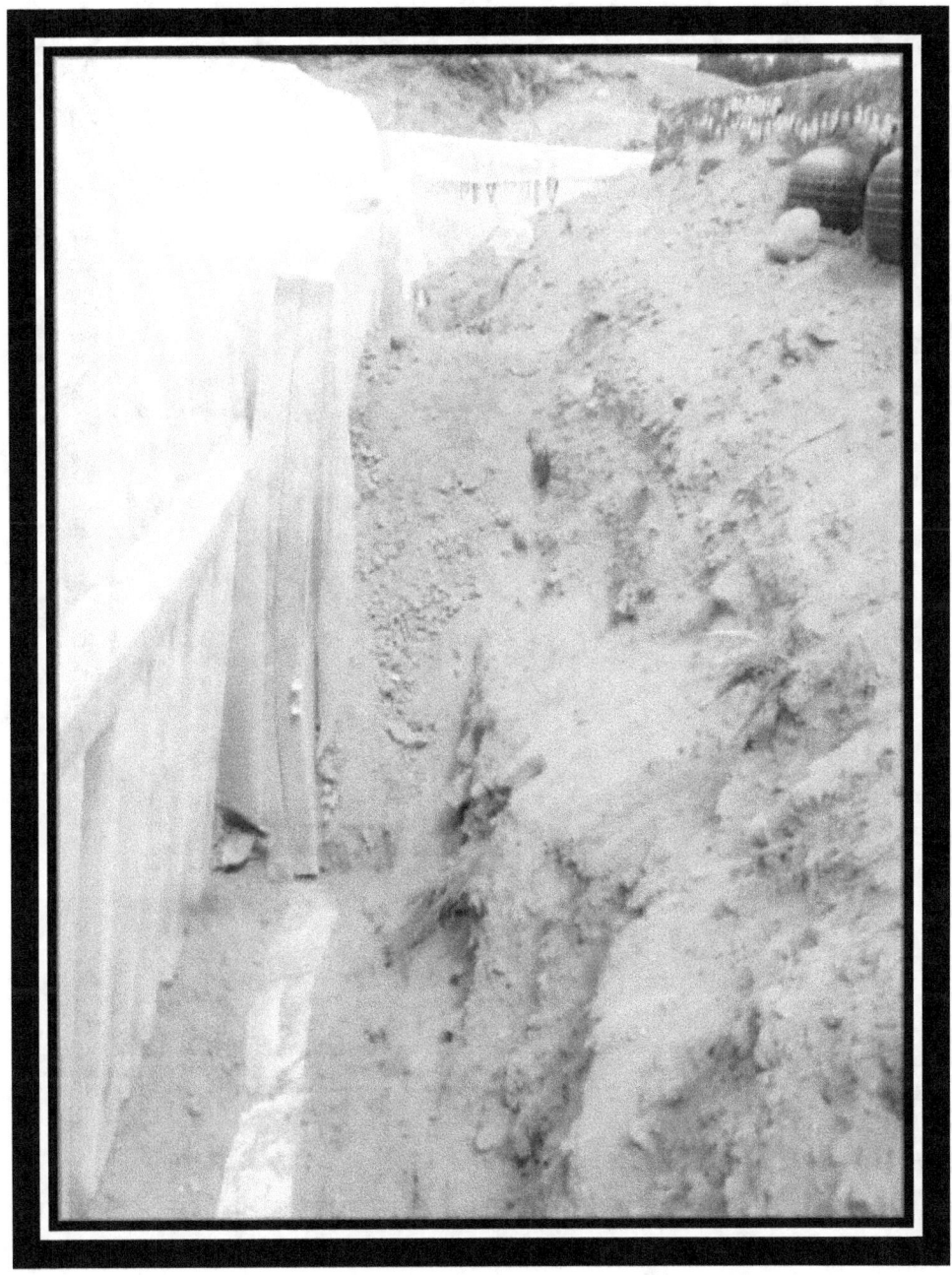

Earthship in Cerrillos, NM, outside Santa Fe. Water tanks.

I put in this layer of thermal wrap in back. I had to move the same dirt over and over and over, in a hot trench between the cisterns and the back wall--talk about an oblique workout!

The cooling tubes slope down half inch per foot from the building and go out 20' or more...and then they get buried with cool, cool earth.

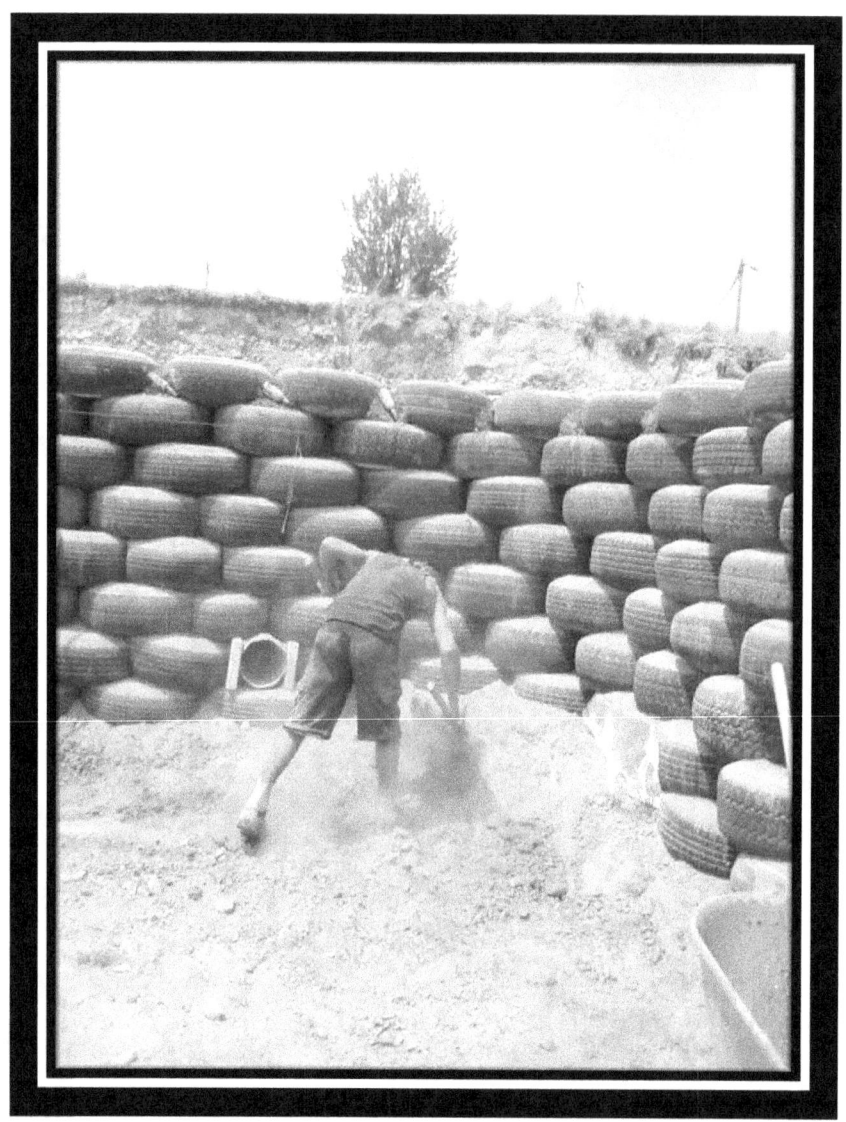

Whenever I need to muster a little more strength or stamina, I summon my 'inner Rory', and do a bit more, or go a bit faster, or harder. This is a picture of Rory in action. He was by far the quietest and hardest working person on the crew I had the pleasure of working on with him. A dozen or so interns filled and pounded the tire walls on either side, while Rory did most of the back (longer) wall himself, plus checked and finished nearly every one of ours. I was tasked with removing excess dirt that had built up on the inside floor and was picking at it and shoveling it away slowly. It was hard packed moist clay. Rory waited for me to pause briefly and then asked if he could use the pickax. He proceeded to use two pickaxes, and like some kind of machine attacked the dirt, which somehow looks loose and dry in this picture.

The Head Hutt Picture Book

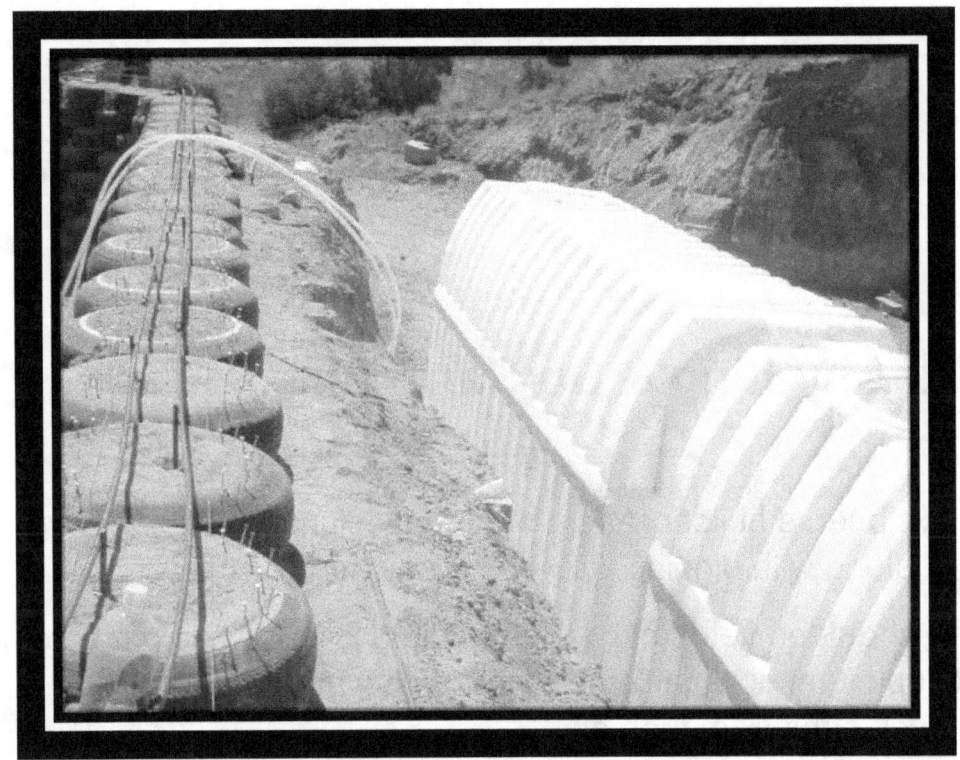

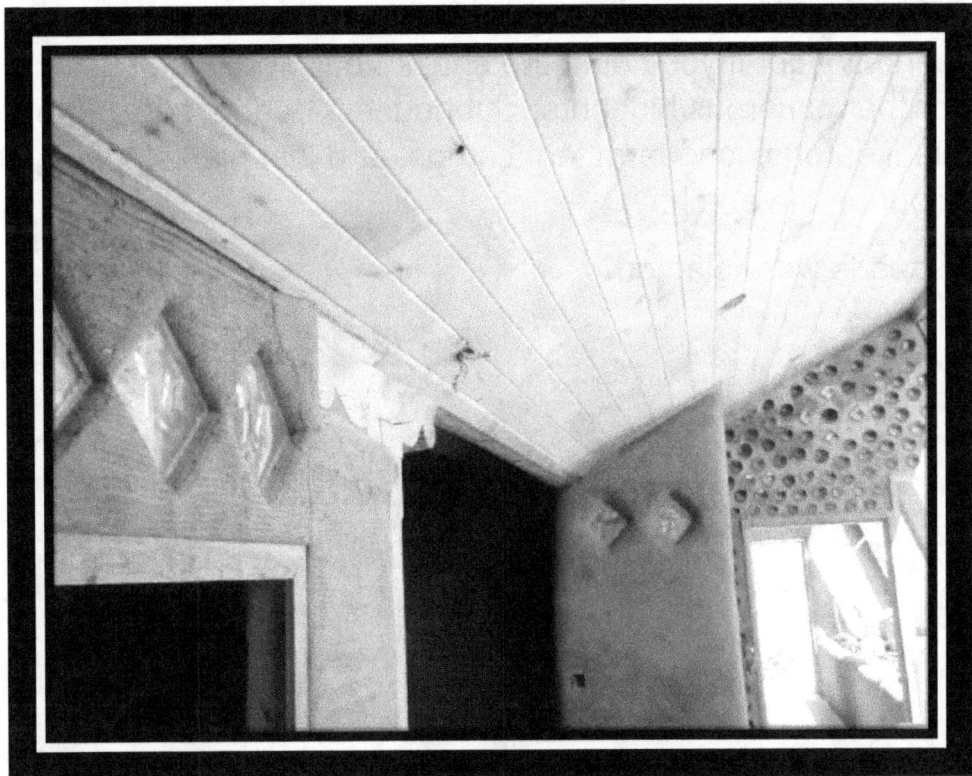

Placitas Earthship 8 2012. Corbels uncovered.

I Can Do Anything & So Can You

I have always been a builder. And a digger. Design and engineering are in my blood. Right along with digging.

When I was about ten years old, I tried to dig a kiva in our front yard. I hit caliche a couple feet down, filled the hole with water to soften it, and it became a duck pond from then on.

I had been thinking about a shed or garage or workspace/storage building for a couple years...longer if you count the shack I built for myself when I was about ten, or the numerous hideouts, clubhouses, treehouses, dig-outs, straw-bail-forts, blanket forts, long term tent camps, and just plan sleeping out under the stars or out on the porch.

And so, the seeds were planted...

Breaking ground on the Head Hut Studio Aug 8, 2010. (First take, this project was halted, moved, and majorly modified shortly after getting started.)

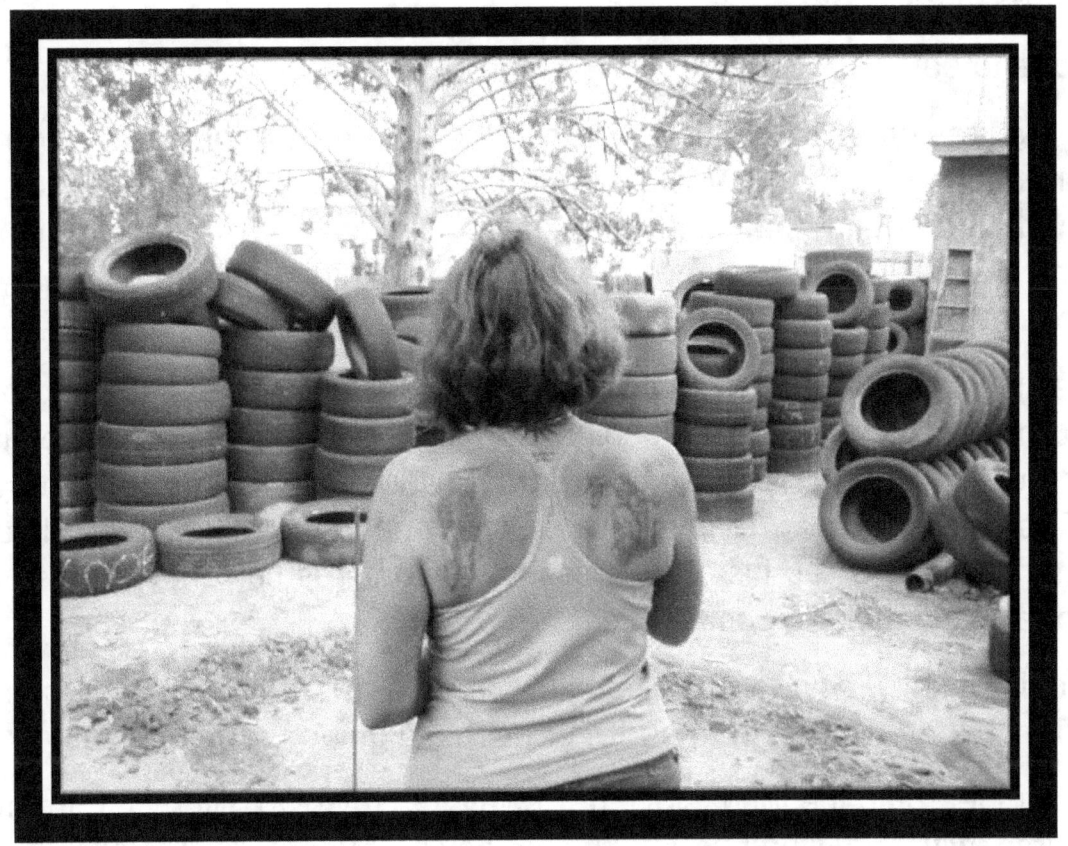

The Dig; plus Tires, Tires, and More Tires

Tires, tires, tires...

not a one to eat...

There are tires on every continent of the planet, I am told they are indigenous to every continent (Mike Reynolds says it a lot.). Stacked and piled and smashed and ground up...mostly just tossed in piles. They last a long time. Just one of so many sad examples of human wastefulness, or immaturity. We can do so much better.

The Earthship community inspired me greatly. When I was first starting out on this journey, I had heard of Earthships, and seen some of the early workings growing up in Northern New Mexico. Earth building and building with recycled materials was familiar to me, but did not know the name Mike Reynolds or Biotecture, or any of the history or mission of what has currently evolved into the global Earthship.org community.

I also did not know how to use a level to plumb a row of tires, how to compact a tire firmly and uniformly with earth, or how to dig such a large pit safely.

I set about learning the long, slow, hard way. On my own. Bit by bit. In my spare time, with very little budget. I would say no budget at all, however, I had a lot more income then, than I have now, so, yeah, a very small budget. What I could scrounge up.

Back to tires.

I figured I might need 300 or more. I only ended up using around 200 for the Head Hutt. I collected, sorted, and stacked more than 500. It took a lot of extras to make matching sets of 21-22, the number I needed for each row around the Head Hutt. I ended up getting creative with a lot of them in the end, and I have short little walls all around the perimeter of my city lot, and another one-acre project underway out of town where I took many of my excess materials.

The first place I asked for access to tires was a family run business. They took a long while to discuss it and finally said no. They couldn't risk something happening that would get them in trouble with the law. It is illegal for tire companies to dump tires, at least here, and so they could face fines if somehow they got blamed for not properly disposing of the tires.

I cried in my van on the way home, feeling discouraged. I think back on that day sometimes when I feel discouraged, to remember that it is easy to get discouraged and easy to push forward, and then try again. The next day, I mustered a trip to the tire shop up the street from my house. The owner was super friendly and happy to give me access to all the tires I need, anytime they are open, once I explained I was building with them. He was familiar with Earthships and supportive of the idea. They even let me pick through to find the sizes I need.

So after a summer or so of collecting tires, and sorting them into stacks of similar sizes, I finally had ten rows of 22-24 or so matching tires, plus the tires for the Foo Dog which had already been started at this point with super extra-large truck tires.

I don't really recommend giant tires for most projects if you can help it. They are a lot of work to fill and pack. Though there are many reasons you might decide to use giant tires; extra mass, retaining ability, and availability being three off the top of my head. I had lots of extras, which I ended up using as walls or stairs in several places. They came in handy for using up much of the excess dirt from digging the hole.

Aside from tires, there were a lot of other materials to gather, which took time, ingenuity, at times courage, and also...space...lots and lots of space.

I think one of the biggest obstacles to building a large-scale sculpture or building is where to put the materials so they will store without being damaged or deteriorating, not become a hazard to humans or animals, and be accessible when the time comes to use them. I kept materials stacked neatly and covered with tarps. My yard was still a messy construction zone of sorts, even last year. I am just getting to look like a functional yard again.

Construction sites are messy and can be dangerous. I basically turned my yard into a construction zone for 'the better part' of ten years while building the Head Hutt and Foo Dog. I also started a back-porch addition just before my business failed completely, a few years ago, which remains unfinished still. I learned a lot about the perils of digging in soft earth, the potential perils of rebar sticking out of things, the heaviness of a pallet of concrete, the sharpness of lathe, the rebound of a nail not getting hammered into a tire, and many more slightly painful lessons.

Accidents can end up costing time, money, and more. Things can change rapidly. A broken rib cost me much of a summer's work. The spring I got my vigas, I was slowed greatly by two ankle injuries from a snowboarding accident that April. Another non-building-related injury which cost me months of building time.

Tires and glass bottles were both challenges for me, as I needed specific sizes and colors/types of bottles to make the patterns I had designed, and I needed to have the entire batch of materials gathered before starting. Or at least, that is what I thought, and in many cases that was true to a large extent. Again, I over-gathered in the long run, and I still have many extra cut and uncut bottles in my life.

I collected and cut over a thousand glass bottles for each, the Head Hutt and Foo Dog Mega-Sculptures, over the course of a couple years, though the majority of it was done in one summer.

I also collected lots of shredded paper, and purchased a lot of cement, some lime, and rebar, and lathe. I bought a mixer, actually two, the first one I returned...and lots and lots of miscellaneous tools, many of them not really necessary.

I did use lots of nails, lots of wire, lots of gloves. I went through a lot of boots.

A quick side-note about shredded paper. Our city has a recycling program, as many modern cities do. A lot of energy goes into shredding preciously private, and also, often completely meaningless paper documents. A lot of that gets double or even quadruple shredded, bagged up in secure trucks, and then hauled to Phoenix, hundreds of miles away for recycling. There has got to be a better way! I think much of this paper waste could be put to good use in future dome construction and in padobe (adobe with paper added) infill.

I got interested in paper for papercrete because the cellulose in paper is similar to the cellulose in hemp core, and I think this could be a viable option for earth friendly building material in the coming decades. I was astounded to find out how much wasted energy goes into shredding and transporting paper in the city.

I also want to say some things about the fortitude it took to stick with this project, the vision of it, the dirt, the hard work, the uncertainty, the loneliness, the sore muscles, the bruised hands, the filthy van. I gave up a lot of social time. As it turns out, building a Mega-Sculpture is something of a full-time occupation, even when you are only building it in your spare time.

Once the Head Hutt and Foo Dog took shape, and I began adding color and finishing details, then people's interest peaked a bit. People could finally start to see my vision. For the first several years though, it was just a giant hole and a lot of dirt and tires and sketches. I think most of my friends and family thought I was a little 'off my rocker'. And to be fair, they were probably mostly right.

Design, planning, permitting and material gathering is enough to sway the average enthusiast. I want this book to serve as encouragement and something of a guide. Perhaps, however, it may well also be a deterrent for many. Rightfully so. The magnitude of work it took was, by most people's standards, insane. Again, I don't use that word to put myself down, I use it to mean, outside the normal parameters of what most people are willing to do.

The Head Hutt Picture Book

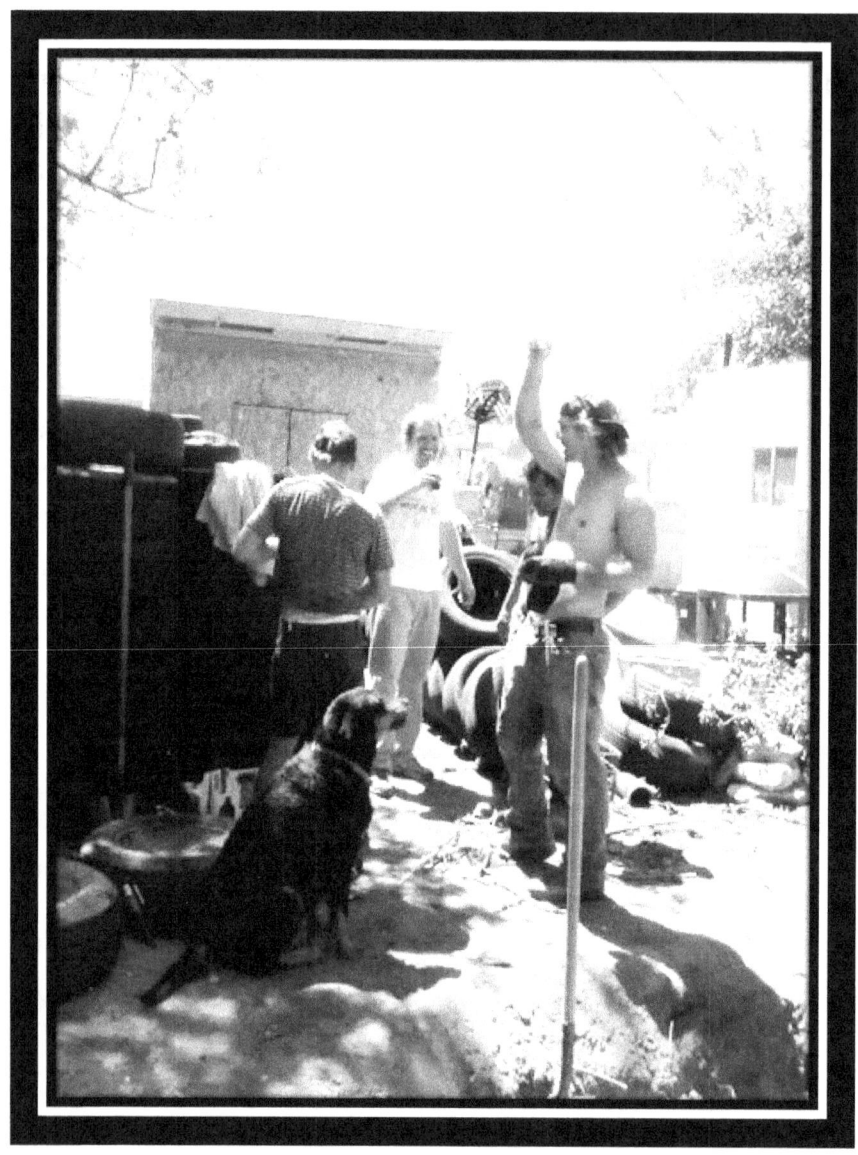

One of the only work parties I had, happened to be the day the city inspector showed up. Rockit Dog was on task, of course.

Site Specific Sculptures and The City of Albuquerque.

Early on, I started the Head Hutt (HH) in a particular spot, with lots of plans sketched out for various outcomes, and had a city inspector show up during my first work party.

I was inside, preparing some burgers for grill when the city inspector arrived. He stuck his head over the back gate in the alley and was met with the sight of several hundred tires in a maze of various stacks around my yard, five young men pounding dirt into tires in a large circle.

"What are you guys doing?" city guy asked, as my giant Rockit dog started to feel aggressive about the breached perimeter.

"We're building a shed." My brother-friend offered.

"This does not look like any shed-building operation I have ever seen." city guy tossed back.

About then I returned outside, and interjected.

"It's a rammed earth storage building and play-house." I said.

I added, "It should be less than 120sf." (that's the max shed our local county codes allow without a permit)

"It needs to be at least ten feet back from the front properly line, so even if that is true, you can't build it there."

Check.

I had checked the codes a dozen times, and I could have sworn the regulation easement was ten feet back from the alley line, five feet from the front. I was wrong. Wishful reading.

"What about all the garages in the neighborhood that are built right up on the front property line? Like that one, across the street?"

It is true, there are many garages built on the front line.

"If you want to fill out a complaint form, I will get to investigating it some months from now", he explained. "There are only two of us working this entire county."

Ah. Okay then, mate, I will have to move it.

"I came in response to a complaint about the stockpiling of tires, which are a fire hazard."

"They are building materials."

"That is fine. All building materials need to be tarped, out of sight, especially these tires. How long will you need to get them out of sight? A month?"

I agreed to get the site cleaned up and tarped before his re-inspection, and I never heard from him again.

I did try to get a permit at first. I was told that I would need engineer approval on my plans since I was using rammed earth. I was happy to find New Mexico does have a rammed-earth and adobe building code section. Building codes and procedures vary greatly from county to county, so be sure to check your local codes and get to know the people who enforce them in your area if you are planning to build something of any significant size.

I contacted a guy who worked for Mike Reynolds and the Earthship crew and talked to him about helping me. I thought he was my best bet for a quick plan approval, since he is familiar with tire wall construction and domes. He was amicable at first. I wanted to know what the largest diameter dome without a center beam that he would approve plans for would be. He did not seem to understand my vision, and eventually he told me he did not think I was actually going to build the dome. I thanked him for his time and ended our conversations.

Thank you, sir. Now I am definitely, for sure, building a dome. Good day.

I called the zoning office and asked if I needed a permit for a 15-foot-tall sculpture in my backyard. They said only if it was on a permanent foundation. I said, "and you don't consider a tire wall a permanent foundation without engineer approval, right?

Check.

"If it has walls and a door and a roof, ma'm, it is a building, and you do need a permit."

Duly noted.

The Head Hutt has openings of many different sizes, including one overhead, where the roof would be. Nothing is quite the right size to qualify as a door or a window, and since the roof is open to the sky, I am confident that it is not a building, technically.

One of my favorite things about the Head Hutt has been playing with rules, bending them to suit my needs, as rules should be. After all, we create rules to help us govern ourselves. Throughout this project I have been reminded that rules and regulations need regular upgrading, regular checks and balances, or they become stale and obsolete.

The Head Hutt Picture Book

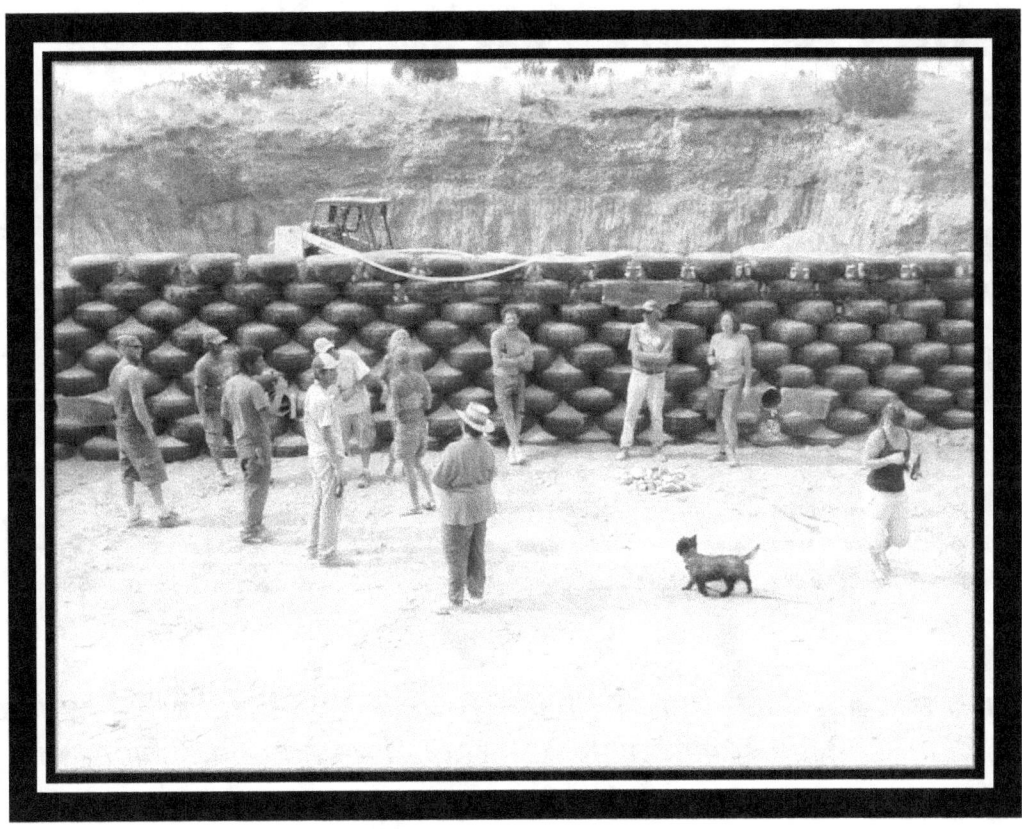

Working with the crew in Cerrillos, NM. This was my first Earthship build, proper, and I only worked on it a few days per week, as I was also going to school, running a business, and raising my teenage son. These days sit fondly in my memory as some of the hottest, hardest working days of my life. Everyone involved made it an absolute pleasure. Smiles, jokes, and lightheartedness abound, as we made mistakes and learned from them.

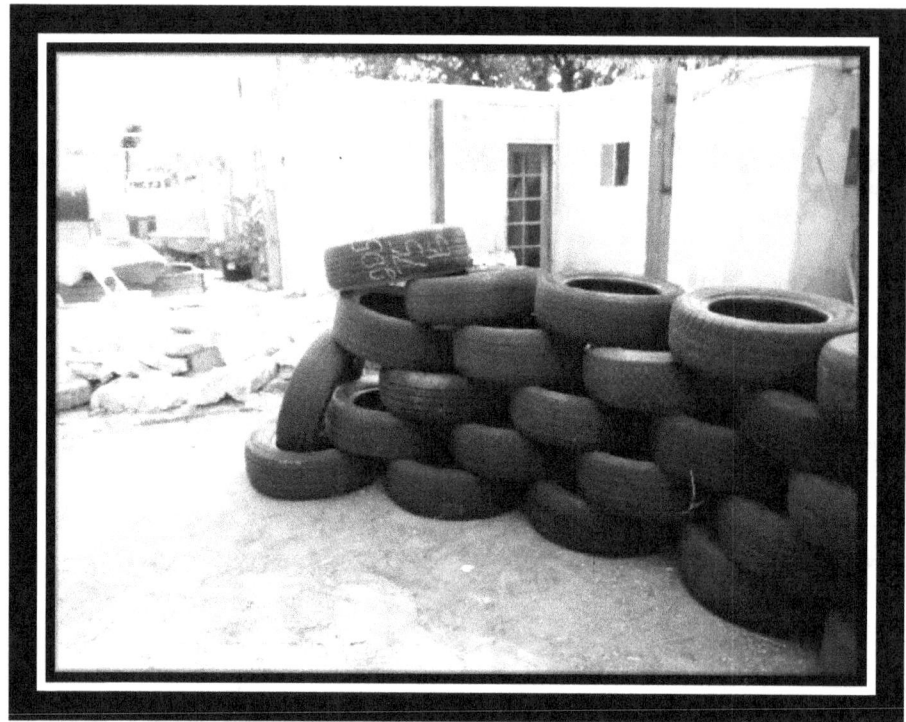

Dry run, and sorting. That's how high five rows is--the bond beam will be about this high, and the center of the loft should be around 7' high, with the dome roof.

(Actually five rows packed should be about a foot higher, as the tires really swell up several inches when packed properly!)

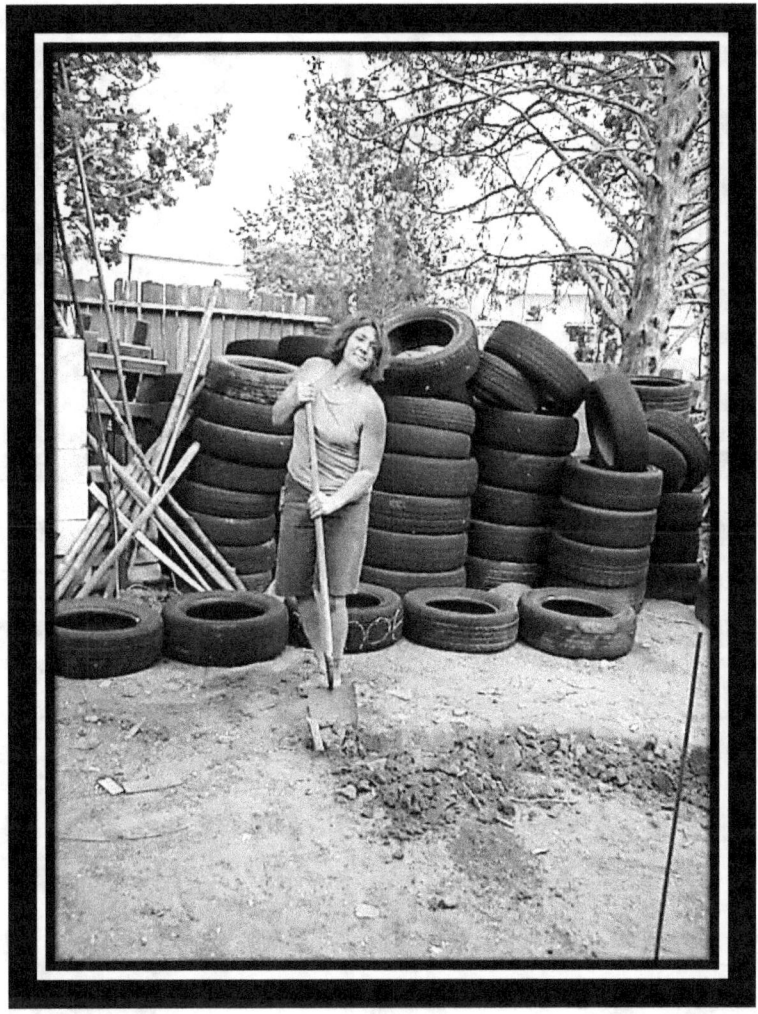

Breaking ground on the first ring. Later this dig got moved over about four feet.

After sorting and stacking hundreds of tires, I started to dig. In hindsight, I could have gathered the tires while I was digging, as it took me all summer. I used shovels and buckets, and a rope tied to a piece of rebar to mark my perimeter. Yes, I did wear the same green shirt for a couple years.

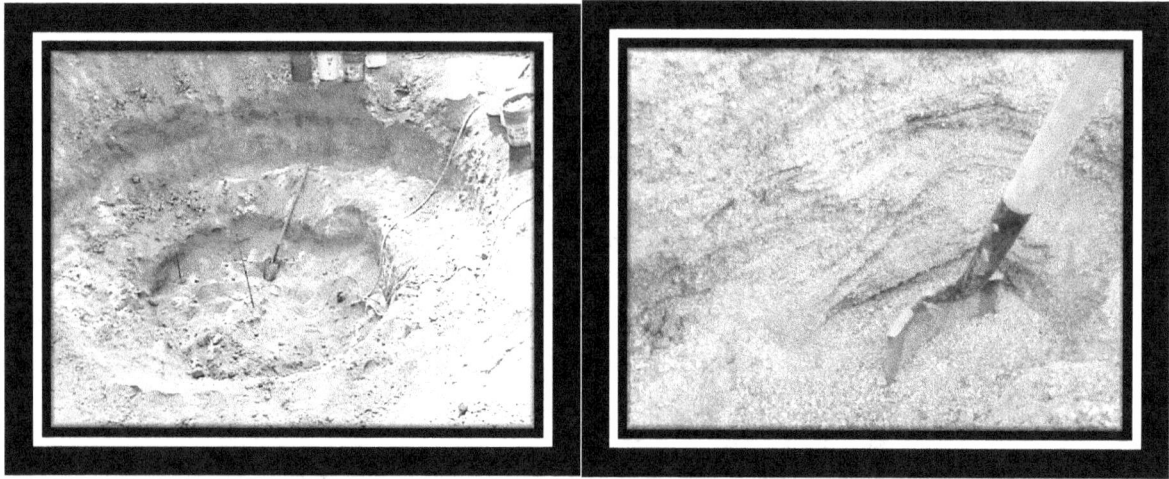

About 3-4 feet down I got under the fill dirt and hit a weak and thin layer of caliche. And then I hit scary soft sand.

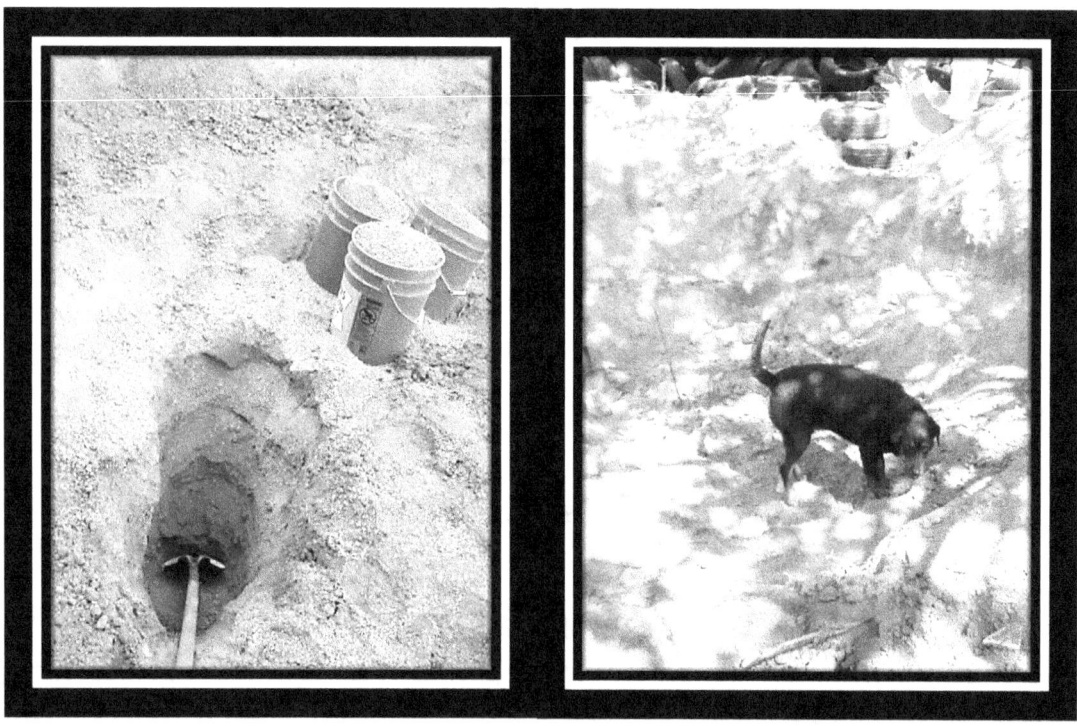

The sand seems to go on indefinitely. According to some geology reports I read, I guess it could be 3000' deep, more or less!

Rockit helped me dig often.

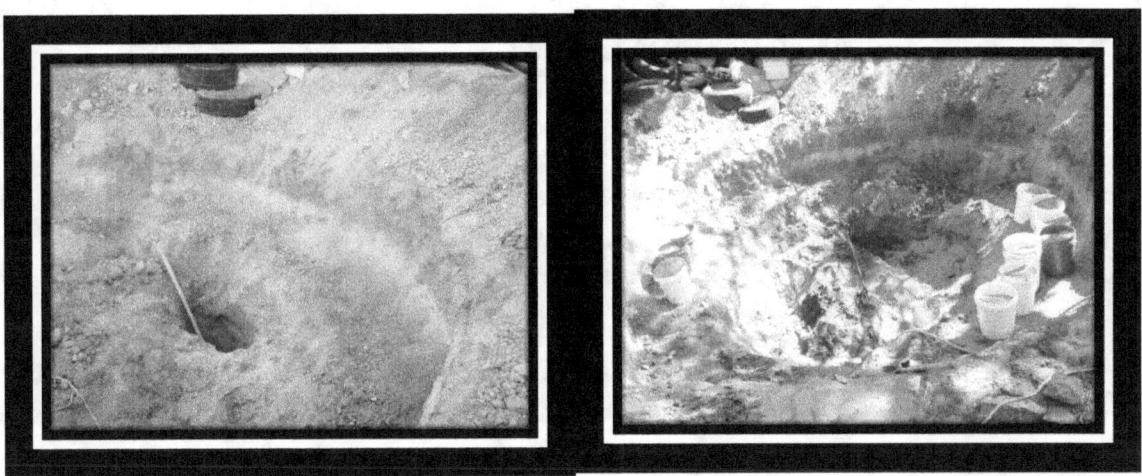

Under the fill, I hit deep sand, that clearly has had water run through it at times, perhaps annually. Eventually I could see it was an old arroyo, meandering through the yard, before it was a yard.

It got too deep to throw out by shovelfuls, so now I have to fill buckets, and lift them out, then carry them and dump them on my growing mountains of loose dirt and sand.

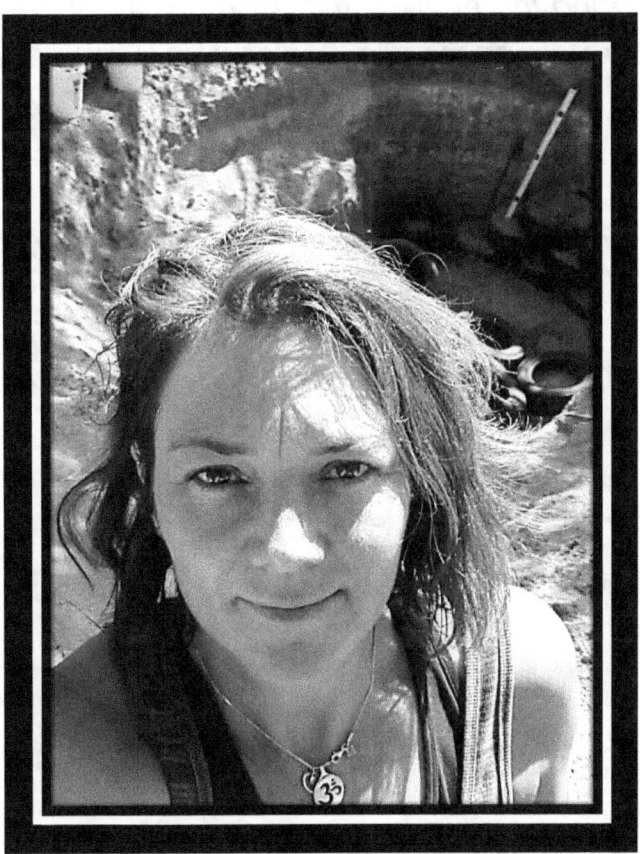

Sept 30, 2010, safety ring is 25% removed, and tires are started.

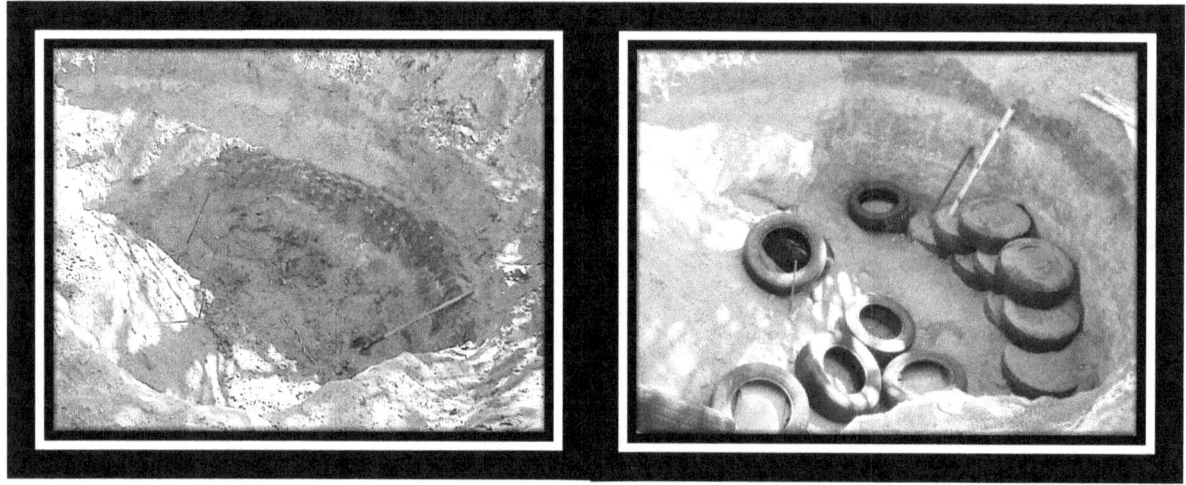

Last week of September. I dug 'the hole' in two stages, with an inner ring halfway down that gave me a sense of safety and a ledge to put my full buckets of dirt on. I would fill buckets, then lift them onto the ledge, then climb on the ledge, then lift the buckets out of the hole, then climb out of the hole and carry the buckets various places to empty them. A gross and tedious process. I decided to keep the dirt from the safety ring on the other side and start tires before clearing the entire thing. Both for safety and so I don't have to move so much more dirt so far and back again. I am about out of room for it.

Sept 30th, 2010. We have lift off! Other than the safety ring removal and setting the first tires, the others are going pretty quick! They are smaller than others I have packed, and since they won't be load bearing, I am less concerned with leveling them perfectly.

Packing tires makes digging a giant hole seem pretty easy!

Digging and Pounding. Digging and Pounding.

For a whole year. Maybe two. I dug, and pounded. I got lucky and did not hit any stone in digging out 52 cubic yards of earth for the Head Hutt, or however many I dug for the Foo Dog Root Cellar Dog Cave (RCDC), which I built alongside the Head Hutt. The two were my classrooms. I did not know how to plumb a line, especially around a round wall with round tires when I started filling tires.

After I got past the blessedly thin layer of caliche, it was easy digging. So easy that I got scared about the potential of being buried alive, and started reading up on how to dig safely. I dug an inner circle and then started removing my outer ring. I dug the entire thing with a shovel and 20 buckets. Digging this giant hole without any safety equipment was one of the most dangerous parts of this project, though I had not thought much about it before I started.

The risk of loose earth caving in and causing injury or death is very real. The two-ring system and keeping the edges curved added some peace of mind. The soft sand was alarming in a different way, and I kept getting this feeling on the bottoms of my feet that I get sometimes when I am up high and feeling some fear of height.

At one point I started tying a rope around my waist, so that if I fell into the abyss of sand, at least my son would be able to figure out what happened to me. Not that it would save me. I read that this city sits on a bed of sand and granite crumble from the mountains that is 3000 feet deep.

Part way down I hit an old arroyo bed. After I removed the fill dirt which was imported to level the neighborhood when it was developed, I hit a mild layer of caliche, and then just sand and granite crumble. I probably still should test for radon. I considered a floor plan to off-gas potential radon, since granite crumble is, I think, a prime environment for it.

I could see the edges of the arroyo, where it wound around through what is now my backyard, meandering down from the mountains. I hit part of an old roommate's buried cat, and a dog I didn't recognize. Thankfully I did not hit the sewer line or any other surprises. Of course, I had the gas and water marked off by the city some time before I started.

It took me a very long time, little by little. Some days I would fill 2-3 tires. Some days I would pack one tight and level it. I imagine it could be done in a few weeks with determination and more focus. I was working in my 'spare' time, as I was still going to school part time, being a full-time single mom, and starting to play music and feel creative again.

By the way, most Earthships are not dug into the ground like this, or if they are, only partially. In most cases they are back-buried, with an earth berm and insulation wrap added after the tire walls are built at ground level. I did not have room for the back bury on my small city lot, so down I went. It was great therapy too.

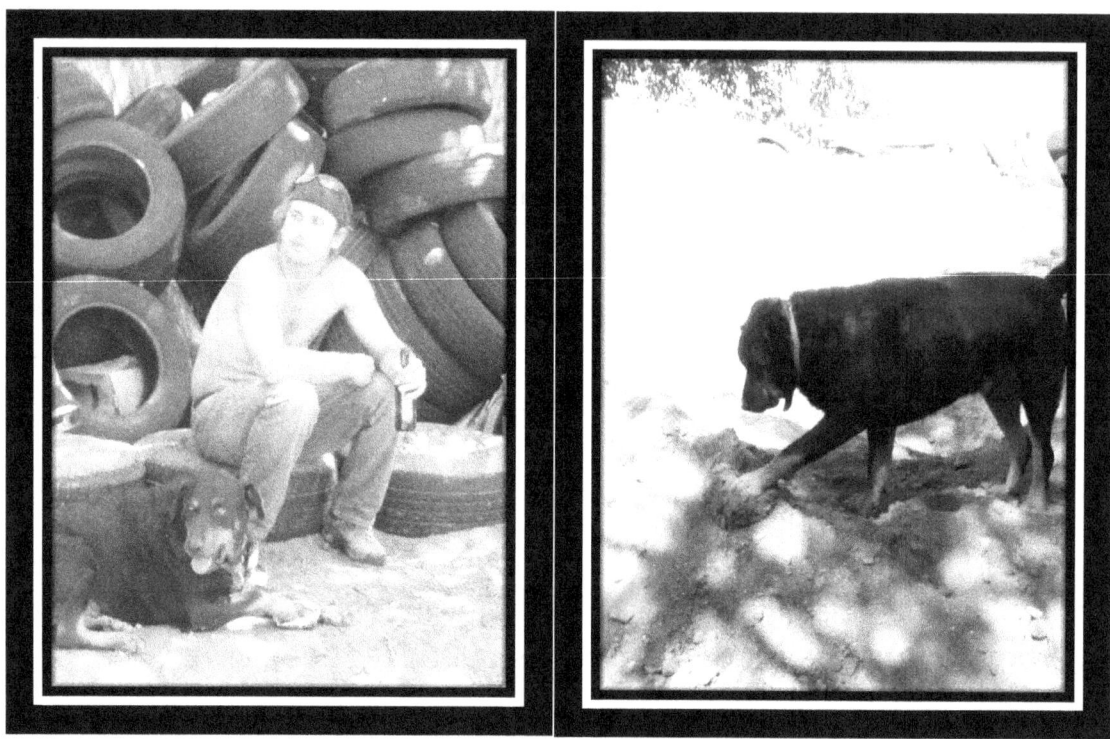

Rockit loved to hang with the work crew, and got himself an empty can to hold to show he understood what it was all about. Rockit still really tries to help!

After the city inspector stopped by and gave me a month to get my materials all consolidated and tarped, I set about getting rid of the huge mound of dirt that I was accumulating; and hiding the tires.

I spread dirt in the alley, filling potholes and raising the high end and inch or two. I was careful to pay attention to the natural slope for flooding. I have lived here a long time, and the entire city slopes downhill from the mountain to the river, so it is not difficult to know which side to add more dirt to.

I stacked many extra tires into experimental planter walls, along my existing wall and filled them with extra dirt. I began filling some of the retaining wall as soon as I could.

I filled the Foo Dog hole with stacked tires and then stacked tires on top of that and put a tarp over the giant mound.

The week of the inspection, I stacked the remaining tires inside the hole, and covered it with a giant blue tarp.

The instant I pulled the tarp over the hole, Rockit dog registered

"The hole is gone" and tried to run across it to me.

Like a cartoon, he got out past a stack or two of tires and then dropped 8 feet or so, between stacks of tires, rolled up in the blue tarp. Luckily the tarp folded his legs in nicely and he seemed unharmed. I will never forget the look on his face when he started to run across it, and how scared and confused and grateful he looked up at me when I looked down and told him he was going to be okay. I had to pull several stacks of tires out and help him out.

Rockit dog loved helping me dig that hole, and one of his favorite games for at least a year was throwing his ball down the hole and barking at me to toss it back out. The hole acted like a megaphone to his voice, amplifying his already substantial bellow to nearly a deafening level. He loved to stand on the mound on the edge of it and bark into the neighborhood.

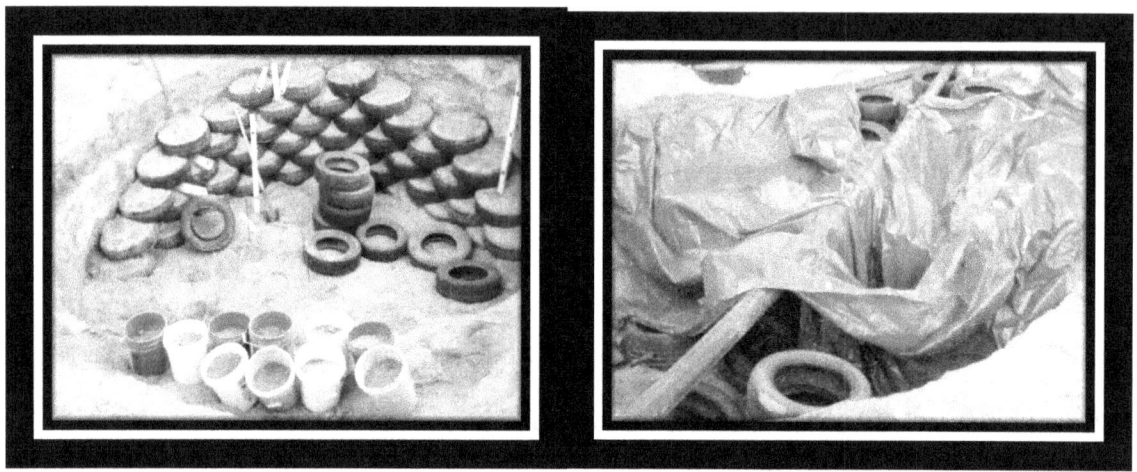

10-10-10. I am just over halfway around the bottom, and about 3/4 of my 'safety ring' is removed, one bucket--wait, make that 20 buckets at a time!

Here is where Rockit fell into the tarp.

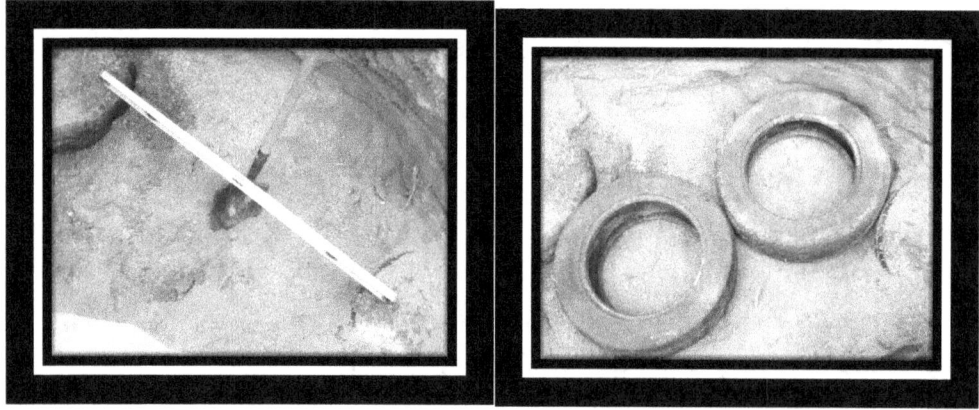

Moment of truth... .. Wow!! It is pretty level!!!

The spacing worked out perfectly for putting in a slight staircase. I pushed back the last couple tires, and pulled in the first one/s. I thought it was pretty remarkable that I came in so close to level after putting in my first row of tires around the bottom, and nervously removing my outer ring of dirt. After that I was in a bit of a hurry to get them all packed in. Once they were in, I no longer had to worry about collapse.

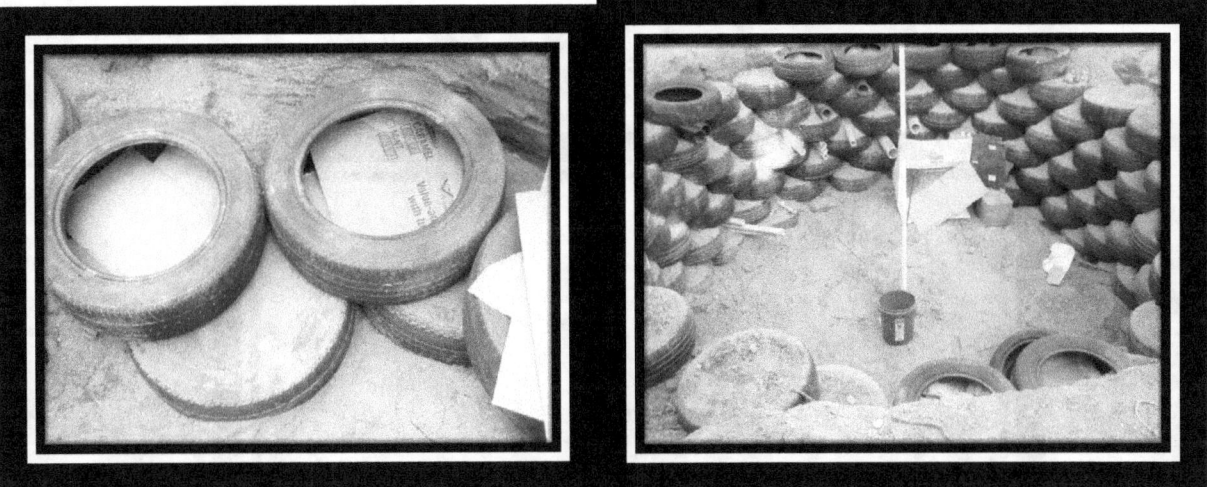

Nov 3, 2010. Almost finished with row 7--decided to go to row 9 or 10. I ended up with nine rows, and then the bond beam on top, plus the vigas, puts my floor nearly two feet about ground level, and gives plenty of head-room on the bottom floor.

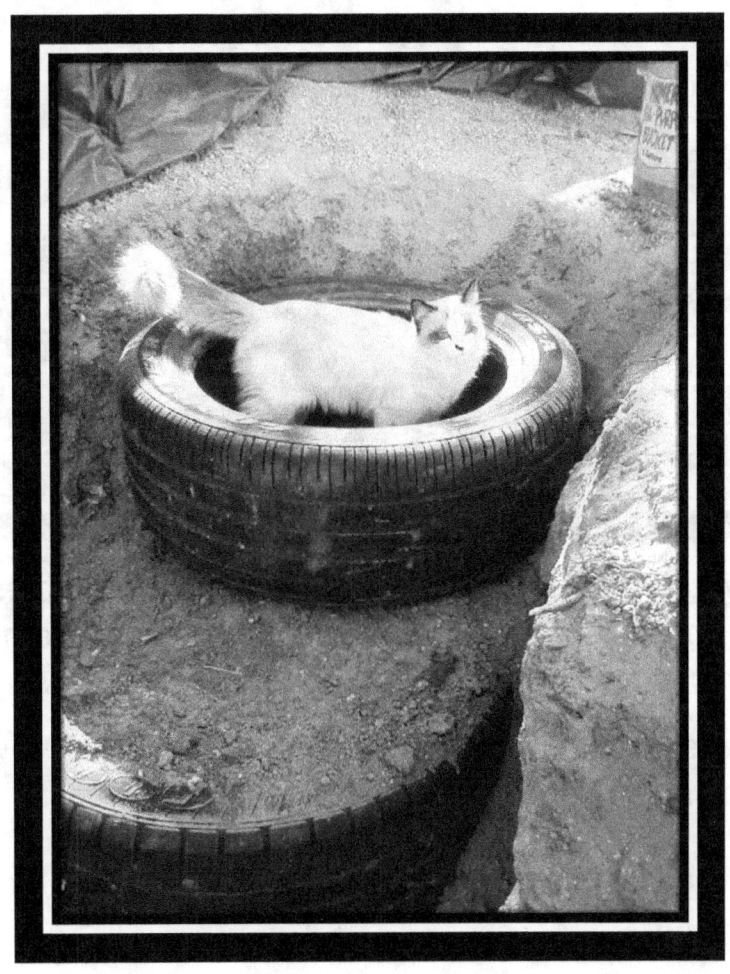

As most cats do; Sapphire likes to be the center of attention.

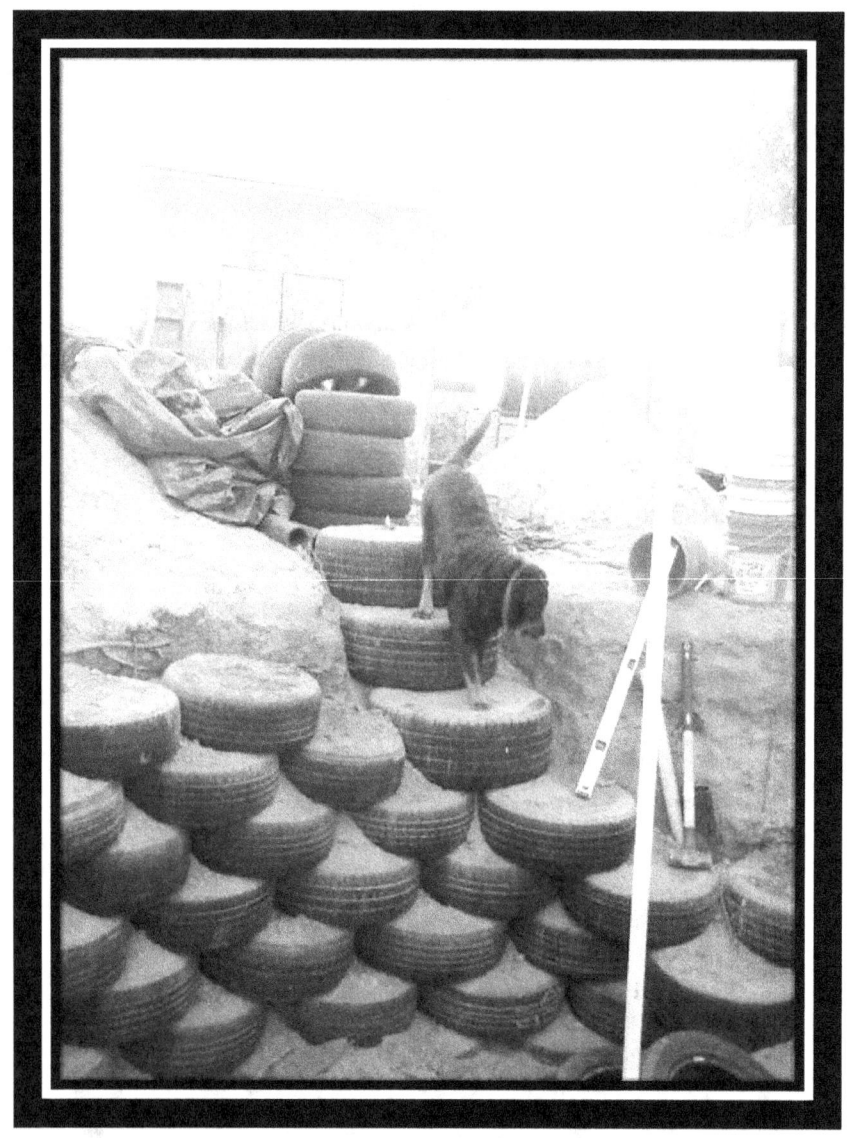

Rockit is slowly figuring out the stairs. He has fallen three times now. He loves to work with me, and especially loves to throw toys down the hole and bark for me to throw them back out for him.

January 2011. Here is ever-optimistic Rockit, hoping I will throw his bone toy or ball back out of the hole, for the umti-eth time.

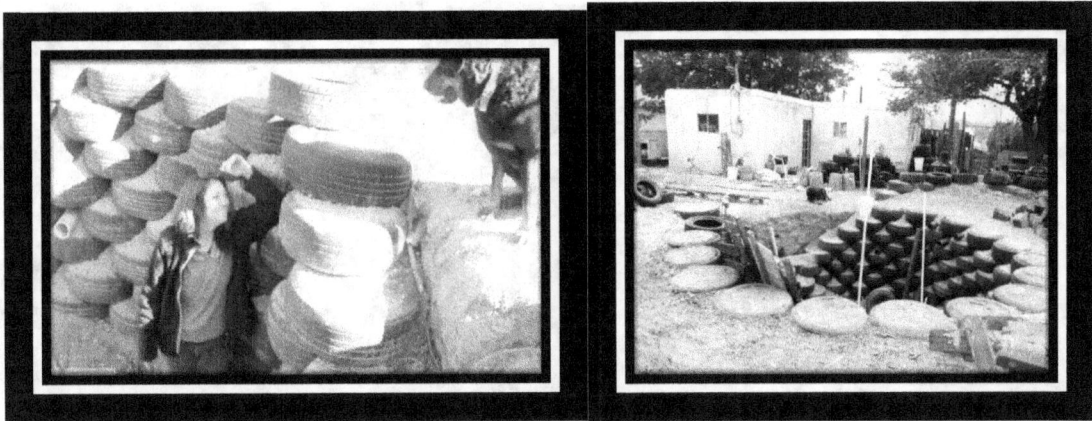

6 3 2011. Almost ready to put on the bond beam/loft floor and start the dome! Lots of small details, combined with a 60+ hour week work week and being a single mom, makes this slow going...yet, it is coming along. Now that the back yard is almost private, the dome will be underway!

Sept 2011. Playing with rebar ideas. I won't 'firm up' this part of the Head Hutt until the first phase of concrete rebar goes on in the RCDC, so I can see how strong concrete reinforced rebar really is...cans go over all rebar ends to make them more visible and save me from poking an eye in or somethin'.

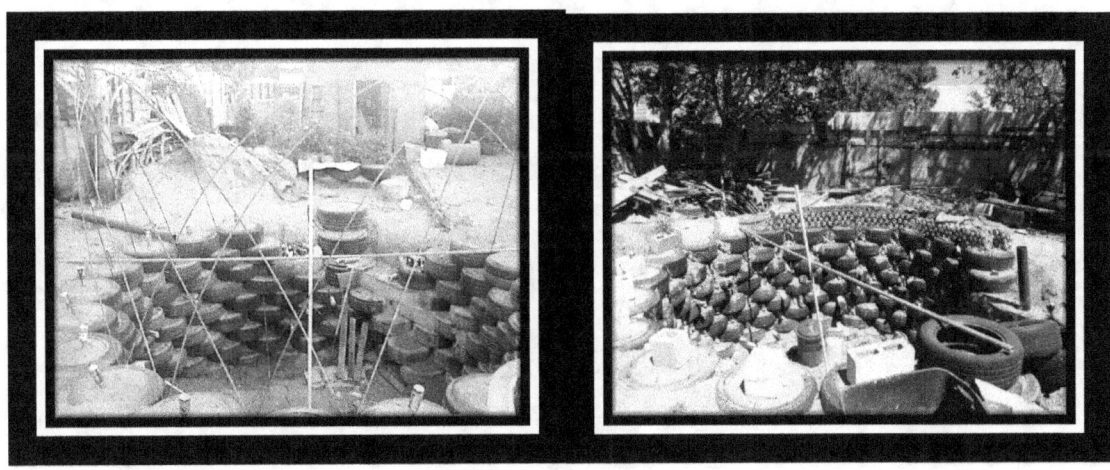

4 21 12. More progress on the retention wall for the HH bond beam, which I will be able to afford sooner than I thought!

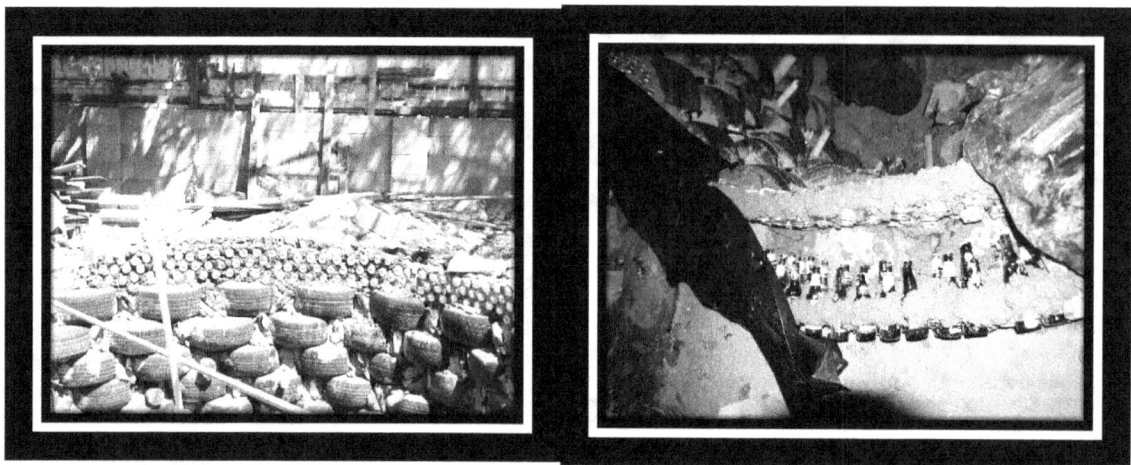

It is much harder to make a steady gradual curve come out straight (let alone plumb!), than it is to do on a straight line or a tight/short curve. Good thing I am getting some practice in. 4 21 12.

Some of you might recognize your beer bottle from last week or last year in the bond beam retention wall...I am running low on cans so am using some bottles for this part, though I would prefer cans for this part--So bring 'em on over!

The Bond Beam

The foundation is perhaps the most important part of any load bearing structure.

For the Head Hutt, I decided to build the foundation on top of the tire wall.

I made the forms for the bond beam with a can wall. This turned out to be overkill, and I would not recommend this method unless you want the experience, or like the look of it. It is a neat way to use up excess cans and bottles (though glass bottles may break, be forwarded). Can-walls are a low-tech building technique that most people can manage. Like any skill, there are some special tricks that might mark a master from a novice can wall builder. One important tip is to crunch or crush the cans just slightly so they grab onto the cement. Another is to check your plumb frequently. Also, go slow.

All that said, building the can wall forms did not take very long once all the materials were gathered.

Once the form-walls were in place, I arranged to have a pallet of Quikrete and some rebar delivered. It was an exciting day. The first delivery was the wrong type. The truck delivered a pallet of mortar mix instead of Quikrete, so I had to order a pickup and redelivery. At the time, it was an agonizing delay. In the broader picture, it was no big deal, of course.

I prepped the rebar, propping it up in spots. In hindsight I think I would not use any wire on the rebar, and I would take more care to hinder rust, just in case. I hope this turns out to be just a peace of mind thing. So far, I have not seen any problems resulting from the wire use/rust potential.

I did a lot of calculating to figure with a friend we could mix and pour all the Quikrete needed for the bond beam in one day. All advisors say it is best to pour a bond beam in one single piece, without seams between cold and hot cement in curing. However, if need be, joints can be planned out and a beam poured in sections.

This being an experimental sculpture, my bond beam was not perfectly uniform. Like many other parts of this structure, there are aspects of this I would recommend doing differently. The bond beam was satisfactory. I would have planned out my anchor bolts bit better, as I ended up going through several drill bits to anchor the vigas to the bond beam later. I did do a satisfactory job of thinking through where I wanted pillars, and I left rebar tabs sticking out of the bond beam, which I then build the pillars onto, and then the arches and dome out of.

Proper curing of cement is crucial for any parts. If you are going to use this highly polluting though ultra-convenient building material, please be sure to learn about proper setting temperatures and curing time, so that your work will not be destined to crumble after just a few decades or even just a few seasons. Properly mixed, set, and cured concrete should last many decades or even centuries.

I asked a friend to give me help for a day, and we got started before noon. My calculations were relatively close. We mixed three, 60lbs sacks at a time, in the electric mixer, dumped into the wheelbarrow, and worked around the bond beam.

As sunset approached, I wished a little I had started an hour earlier and left just a bit more extra Quikrete and daylight and energy for leveling the bond beam. Just like so many professionals say you should. In the end, as it turns out, exact leveling of this layer, as well as several others is not critical, though it is always good practice.

Cements and concretes have become something of a passion of mine through this building process. Turns out, Portland cement is the number three polluter of our atmosphere, by some calculations. It is a big contributor to the desertification.

There are many good reasons to use concrete in construction, and it is still the preferred load bearing material around the world. However, there are considerations that can make the difference between a structure that lasts dozens of years or hundreds of years. I hope you will think twice before using concrete in any project. Please do not use it frivolously, and think about how it will be disposed of, and how it will break down over time.

June 3, 2012. Markers for vigas on 30" centers.

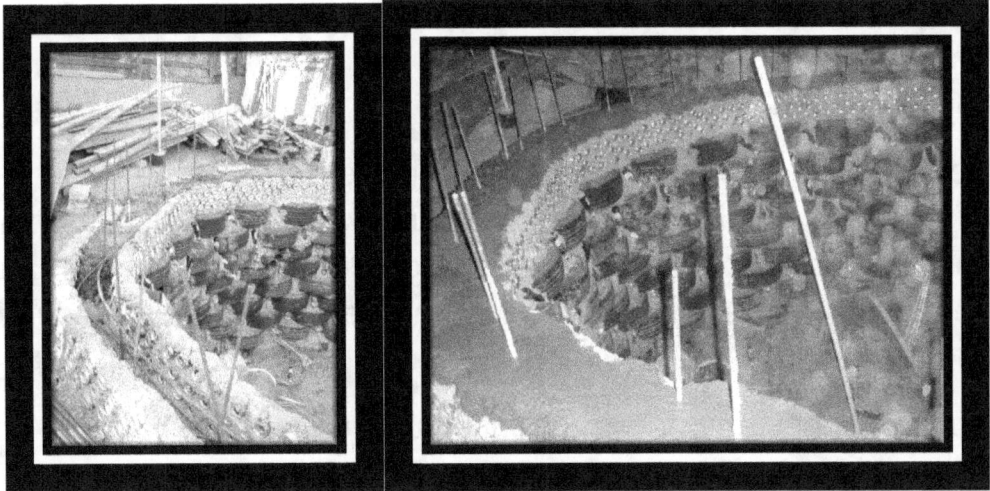

FINALLY pouring the Bond Beam. June 3, 2012.

6 3 12. Finished after sunset, and slightly off level. Leveling took longer than anticipated dt settling and not being as precise with leveling on the last row of tires. This resulted in me being a load short on concrete (because it was too dark to mix and level by the time I figured out I needed it). Lesson: Start in the morning, even if you are sure you can finish in the evening.

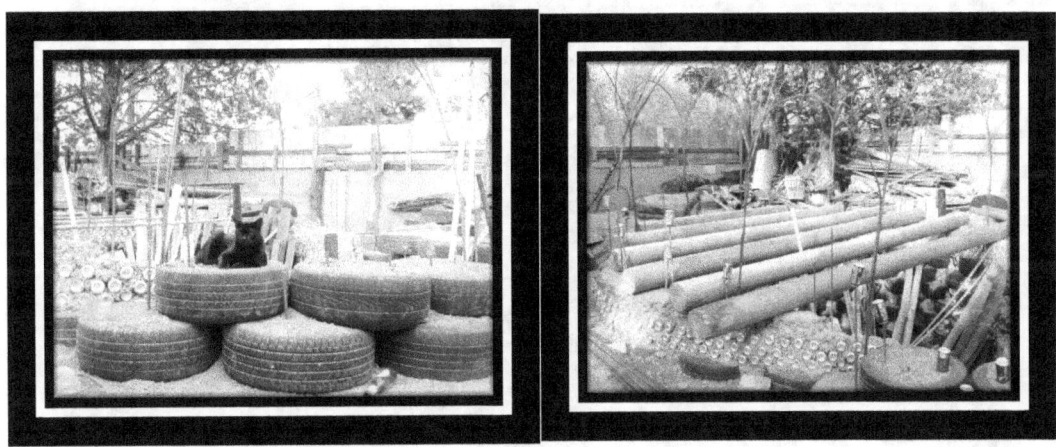

Taco tries out every new "Throne". 8 21 12.

After drying half as long as they probably should have, I sealed and moved the vigas into place...only a year or so later than I originally thought. They got a lot lighter after a week and a half in the sun, but they are still pretty heavy! My good friend Jordan helped me move them from the driveway to here. 9 12 12.

Pillars and Arches, Oh My

I used catenary arches for the overhangs and the dome of the Head Hutt, coming off of pillars of solid concrete. A catenary arch is basically an arch which a chain would make, then flipped upside down. This gives a natural, more uniform load bearing strength. These arches have been used in human architecture for hundreds or thousands of years.

If you check out nearly any ancient architecture, you will see arches and pillars holding things together over the centuries. Pillars and arches are structurally useful, and they also tend to have an aesthetic appeal. I mean, who doesn't like straight lines and curves, am I right?

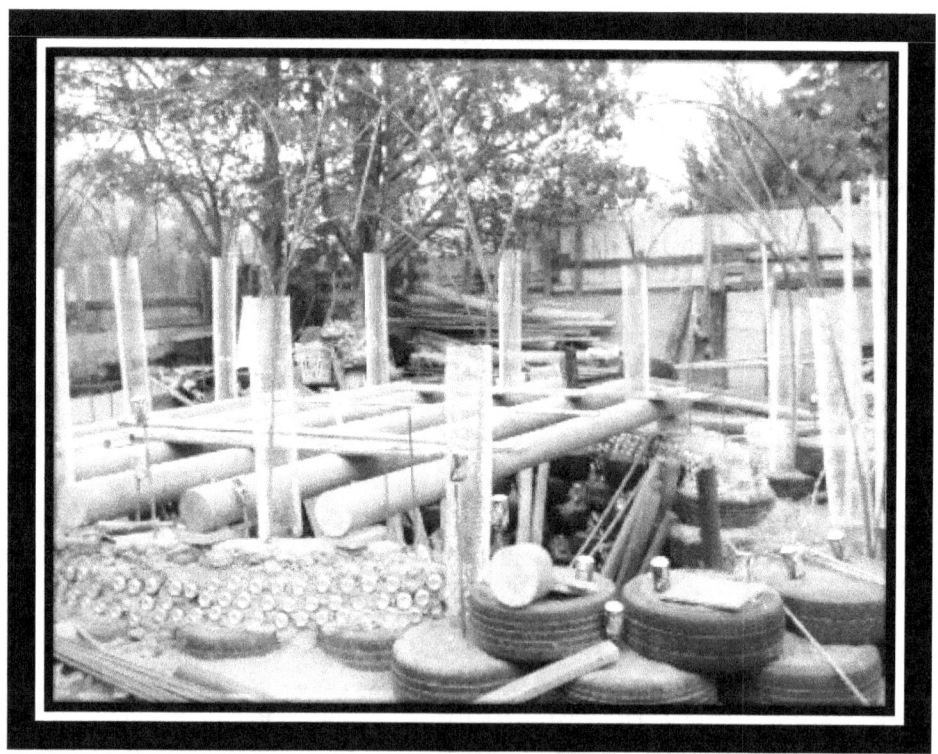

Pillars are prepped. 9 29 12

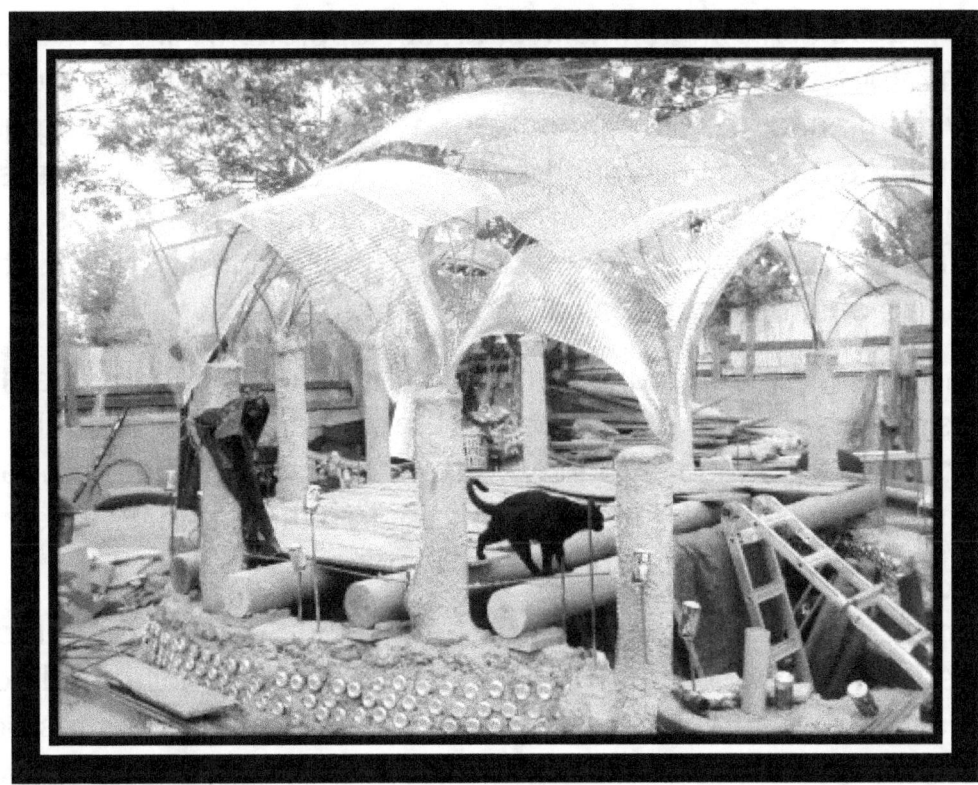

I put in little "stubs" for buttresses if I need them. They are in line with the top arc of the dome, where the load may need reinforcement (though I think I may build lightweight enough that I won't need them, and I decided that having buttress framework in before pouring the pillars/columns would make getting around my already cluttered workspace extremely challenging. I am happy with my decision, but it took an extra day for me to get there. 9 30 12.

Pillars are 'dry enough' and seem very strong. Lathe is mostly on. Now to put in some glass and start plastering! The temporary wood decking is reclaimed roofing material from a demo job some friends of mine did last summer. Eventually it will get a stronger, nicer floor. The front viga was not going to be there at all, and then went in for hanging things, but still the plan is to bring the floor/deck only to just past center to allow sunlight to hit all the way to the back of the underground portion. I did set and level the front viga to be able to bring the floor further forward if I should change my mind. 10 6 12.

Several architects and buildings inspired me to use catenary arches for the overhangs and dome, which arches over 20'.

The Head Hutt took on a more intuitive, artistic approach. All the arches were built by hand, foot, and eye. I considered putting in buttresses on the pillars, and initially did plan to do this. You can see the rebar stems sticking out of my pillars which I intended to build buttresses onto to help offset the pressure of the dome on the pillars. However, I decided not to put in buttresses by the time I got finished putting in the dome. So far, (publishing at the end of 2019), no visible signs of structural stress at these areas.

To begin the pillars, I made round forms with lathe and set them over the rebar stems I had set into the bond beam. I ran rebar arches through and out of the pillar forms and made sure they were close to plumb before pouring the pillars with Quikrete cement. I made sure to plumb them and wrapped them well in plastic and tarps to cure for several weeks.

The first three days is most critical for properly curing cement and I tool extra care to be sure these will be strong. I also put some of my pillar and bond beam mixes into core sample forms so that they can be strength tested in the future if I ever need to prove the integrity of them. If I had been working with an engineer and permitting team this would be a well-advised standard practice.

I took some extra effort putting in rebar stems to attach to buttress walls which I later decided against. A couple of the pillars had some bulging where I did not wire tie them close enough together. Everything was managed fine though, with no major concrete mishaps.

After the pillars had cured, I covered all the rebar arches with lathe in preparation for the dome. Meanwhile, I had been collecting glass and learning about how to cut it.

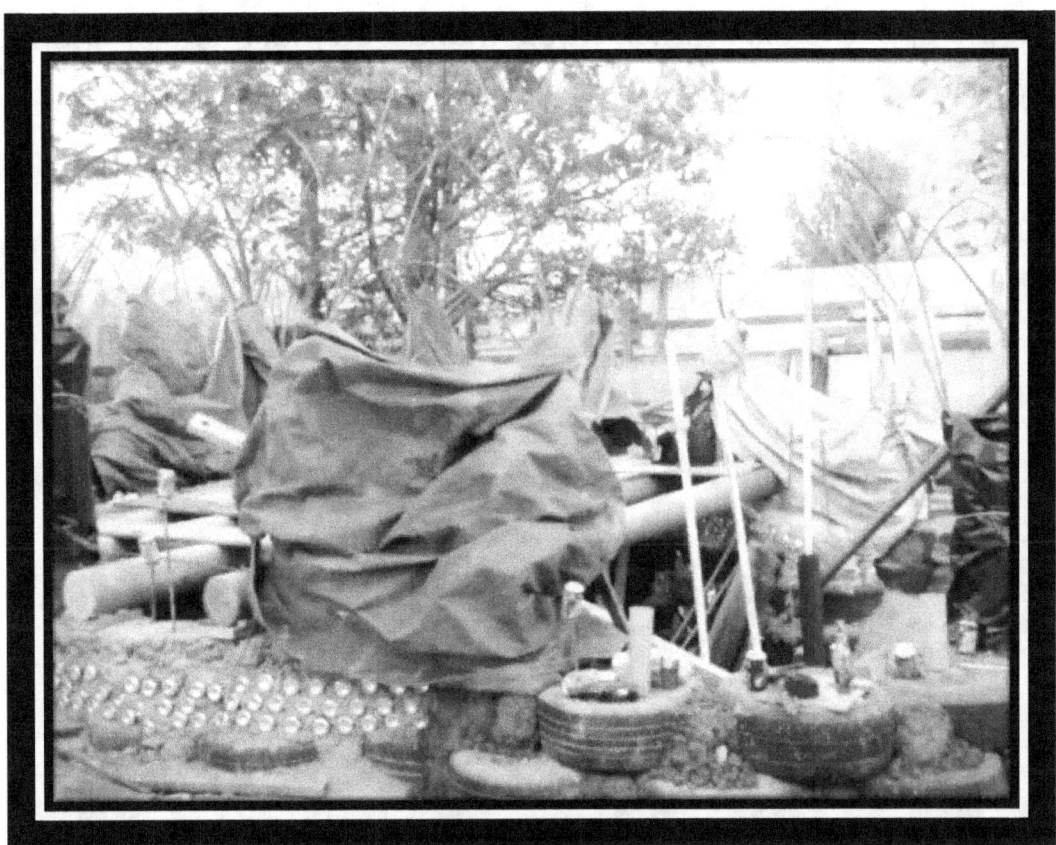

Pillars are curing nicely! 9 30 12

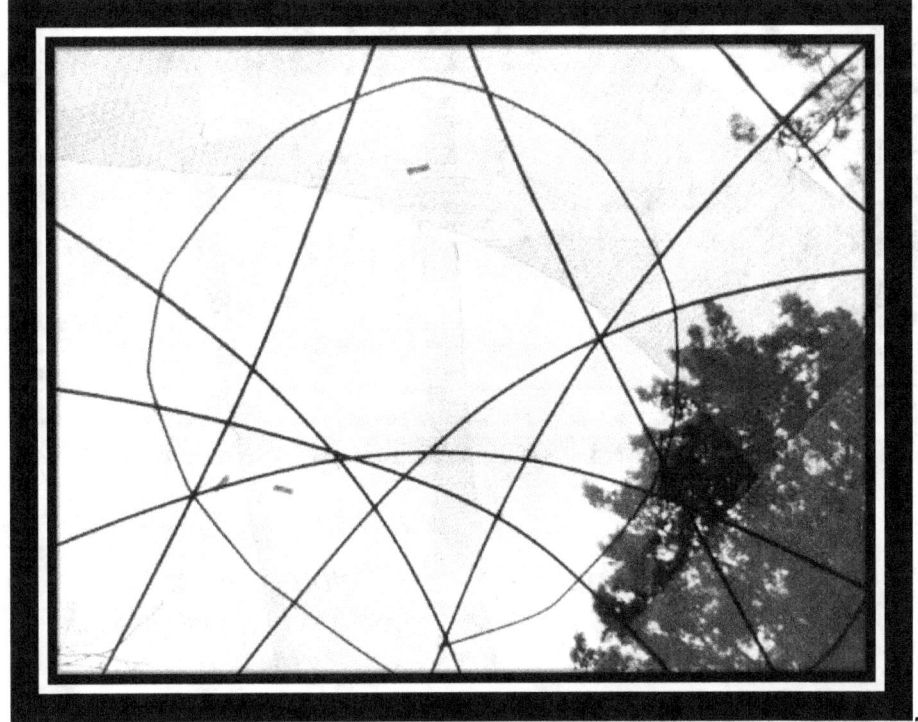

Looking up through the rebar framework on the front top. I have gotten fairly talented at tacking on lathe from one side, without an extra body & ladder to

help from the opposite side, which would make it so much easier and faster! 10 6 12.

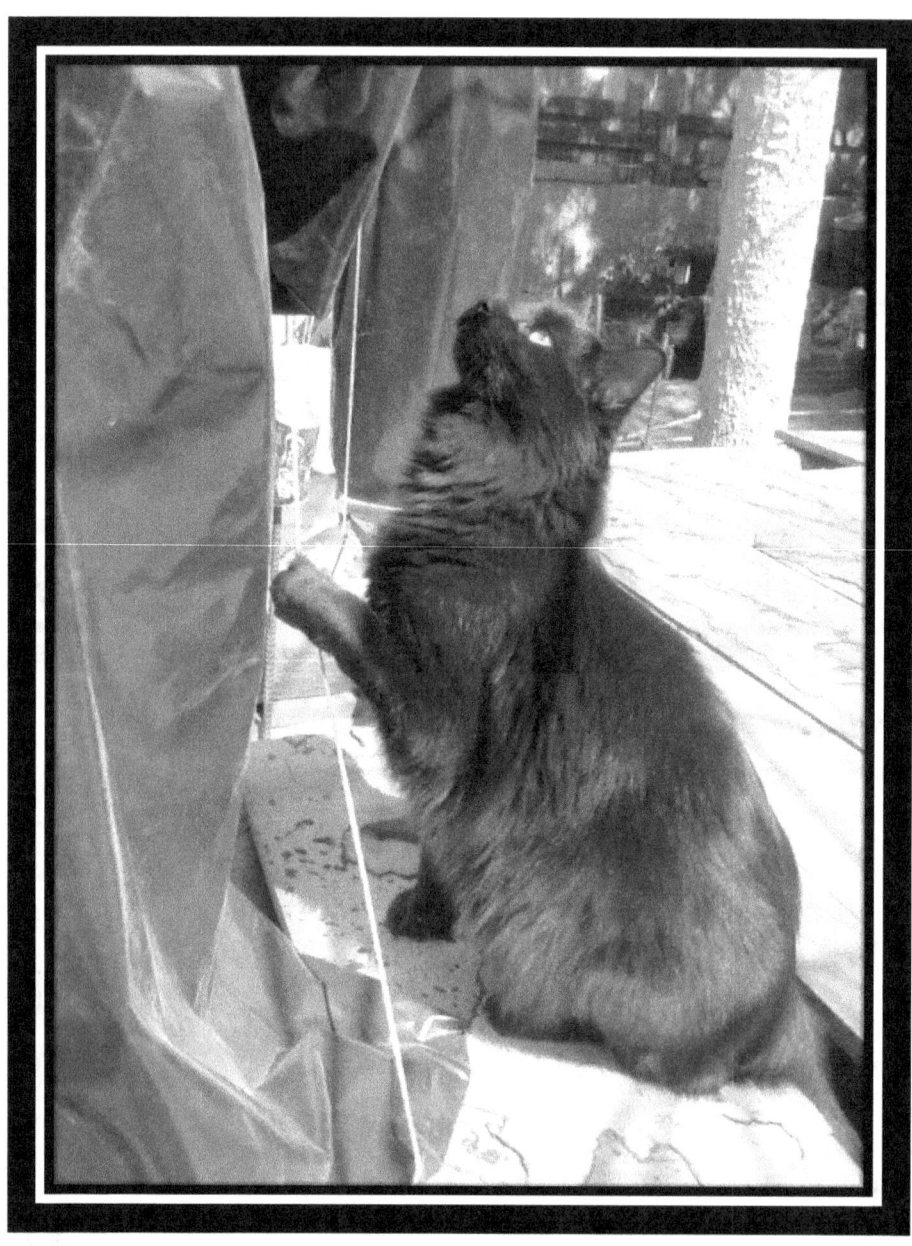

Orion cat, not helping my plumb lines.

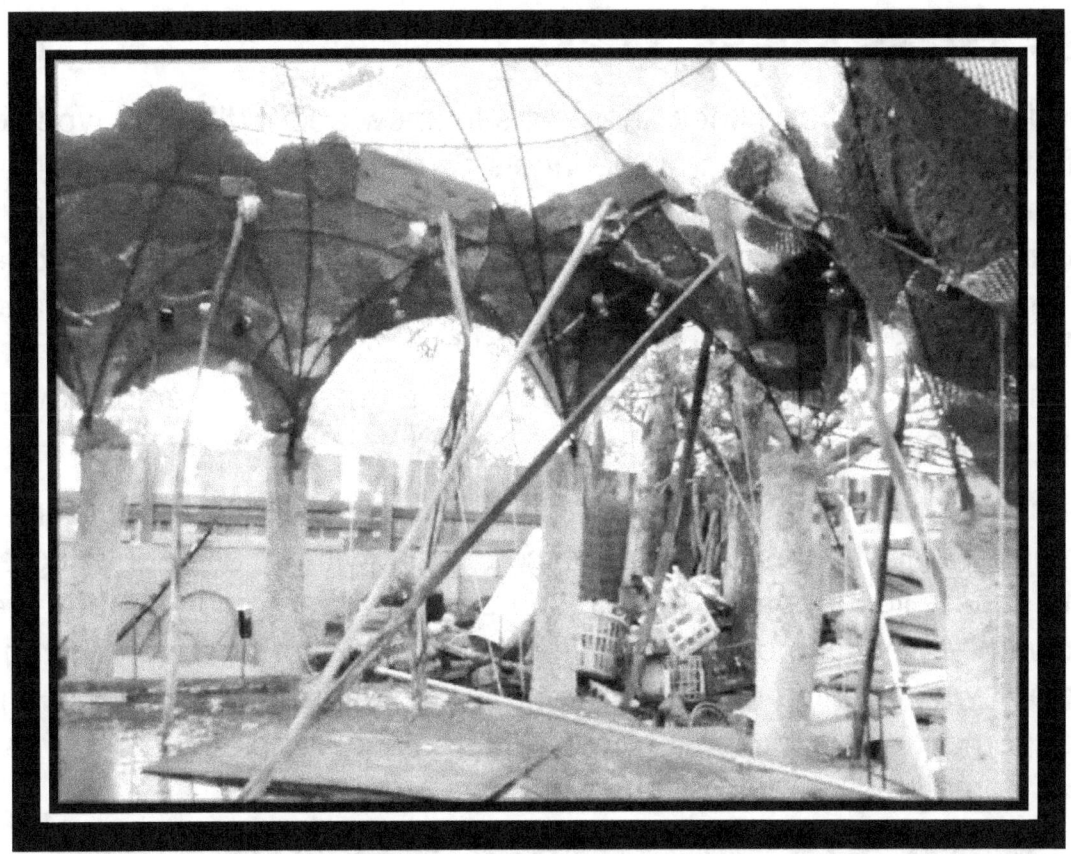

Plastering over archways. Oct 2012. I used lots of poles and various sticks to brace the lathe while the cement plaster dried/cured. It was tricky to keep it all covered to cure property, though so far it all seems to be holding up fine. Of course, this layer is completely covered with several inches of infill on both sides now.

Glass, Glass, Glass, Glass

I learned a lot more than I knew there was to know about different types of glass bottles. How they cut, how the labels come off, how easily or difficult the ends are to clean and keep clean, and which bottles pair best with which others are all factors to consider. Of course, availability is the number one factor, and that varies depending on what is near you, who you know, and/or what your friends like to drink. I had several friends drinking Bud Light Platinum beer just to donate the bottles to me (a truly hard to enjoy beverage, I should mention).

I had a couple people saving and bringing me large collections of green and blue mineral water bottles, which are nice to work with on all counts. I grew to love the square liquor bottles, though somewhat harder to cut, as they are fun to build with. At the time of building, I found them in shorter supply than most, though as I was finishing up it occurred to me that I probably could have made an arrangement with a local bar or two and had access to all the squares I needed. Something to note for future projects.

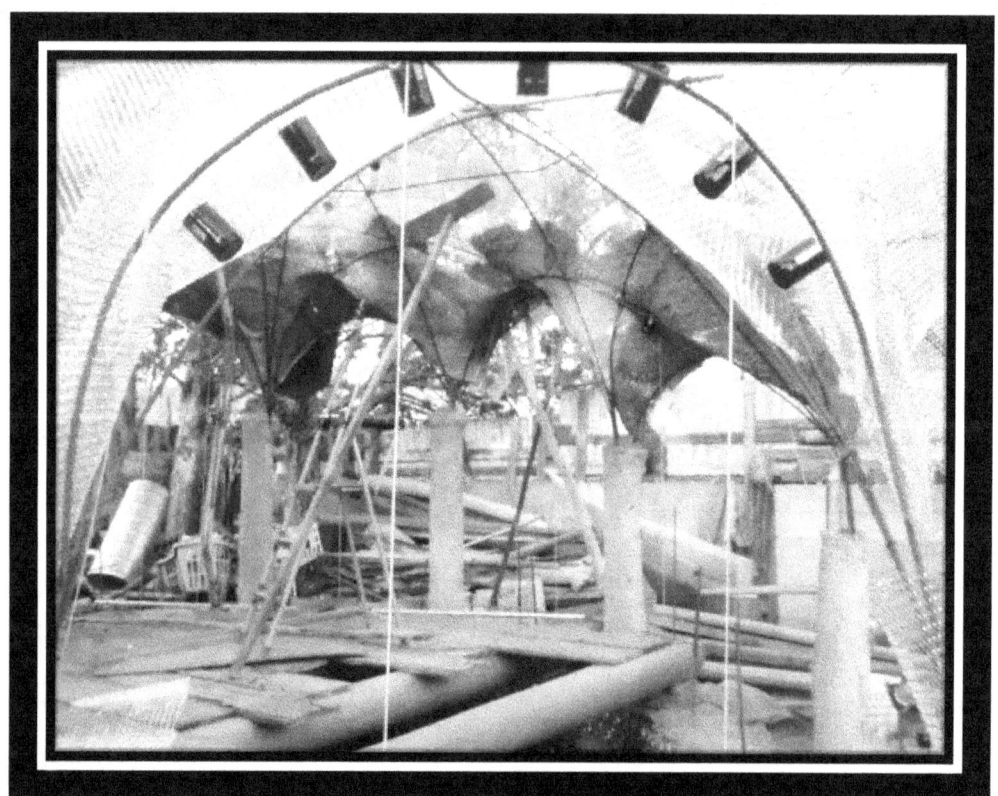

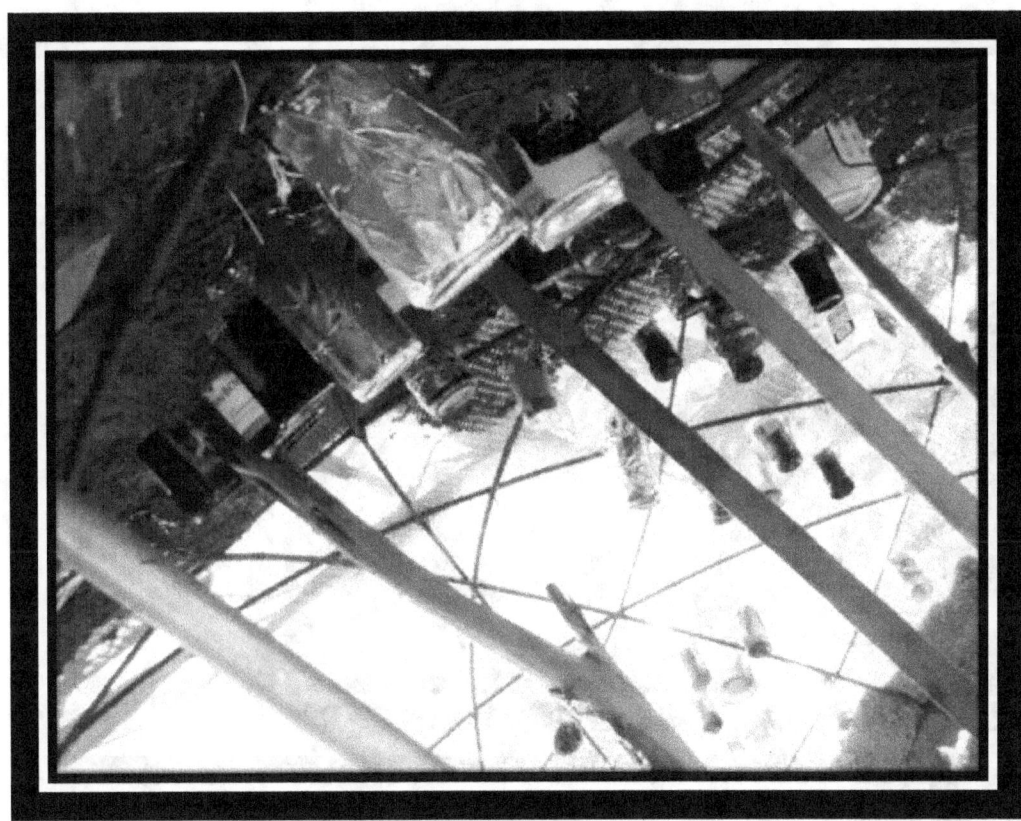

Starting to put in the front 'Eye-Window-Brows'. 10 2012.

Bracing trying to keep a rounded edge, and doing my best to keep my bottle end in roughly the same curving plane, which is just a bit tricky. End of October 2012.

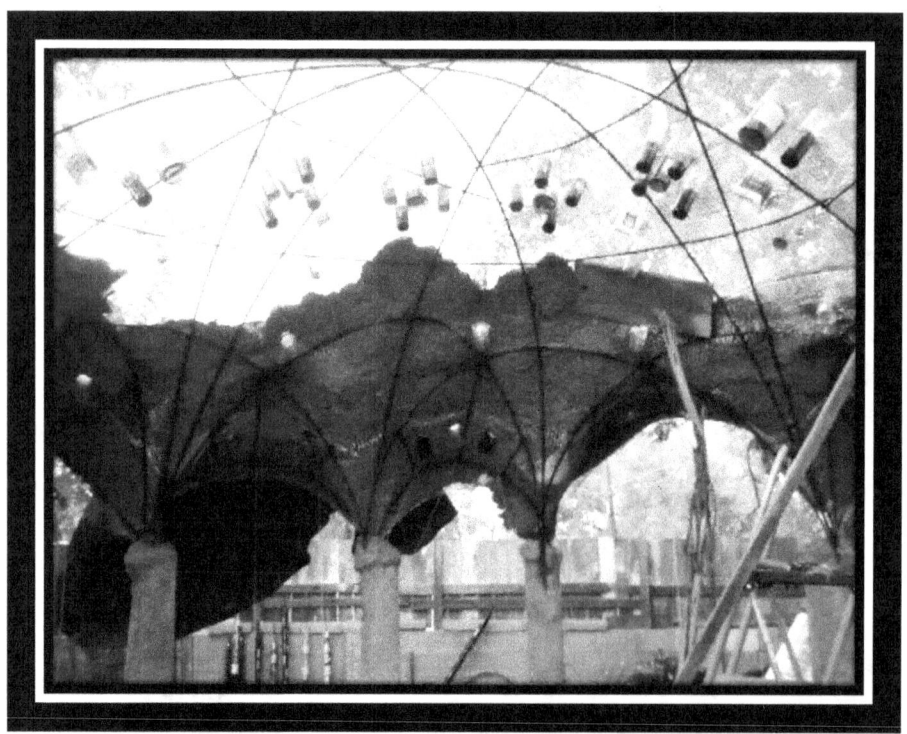

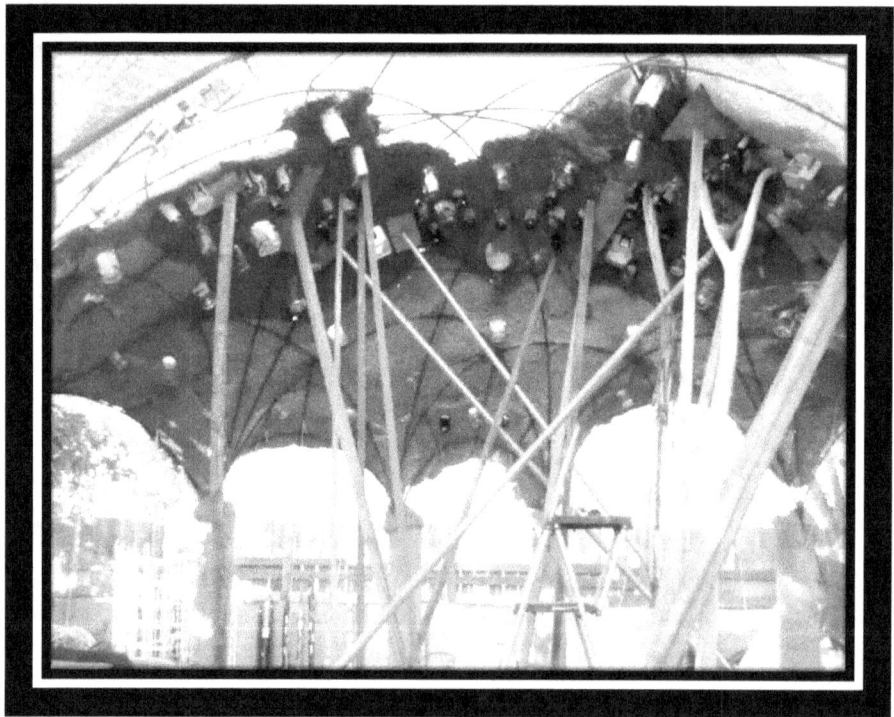

Got most of the glass in--with many tiny cuts to my hands, and MANY trips to the glass recycling bin. Oct 2012. I can't remember now exactly when I cracked a rib, reaching into a dumpster for a pretty blue glass bottle (which are harder to find than other colors, by the way). It was a minor crack so did not stop me completely, however it did make hauling heavy buckets of dirt, sand, and cement more difficult.

Custom making small LED solar lights for my sculptures. I attached the top portion of outdoor solar lights to bottles, so they can be twisted off and replaced as needed. I thought the reflective stuff might be a good idea. I don't think it had much effect though. Oct 2012.

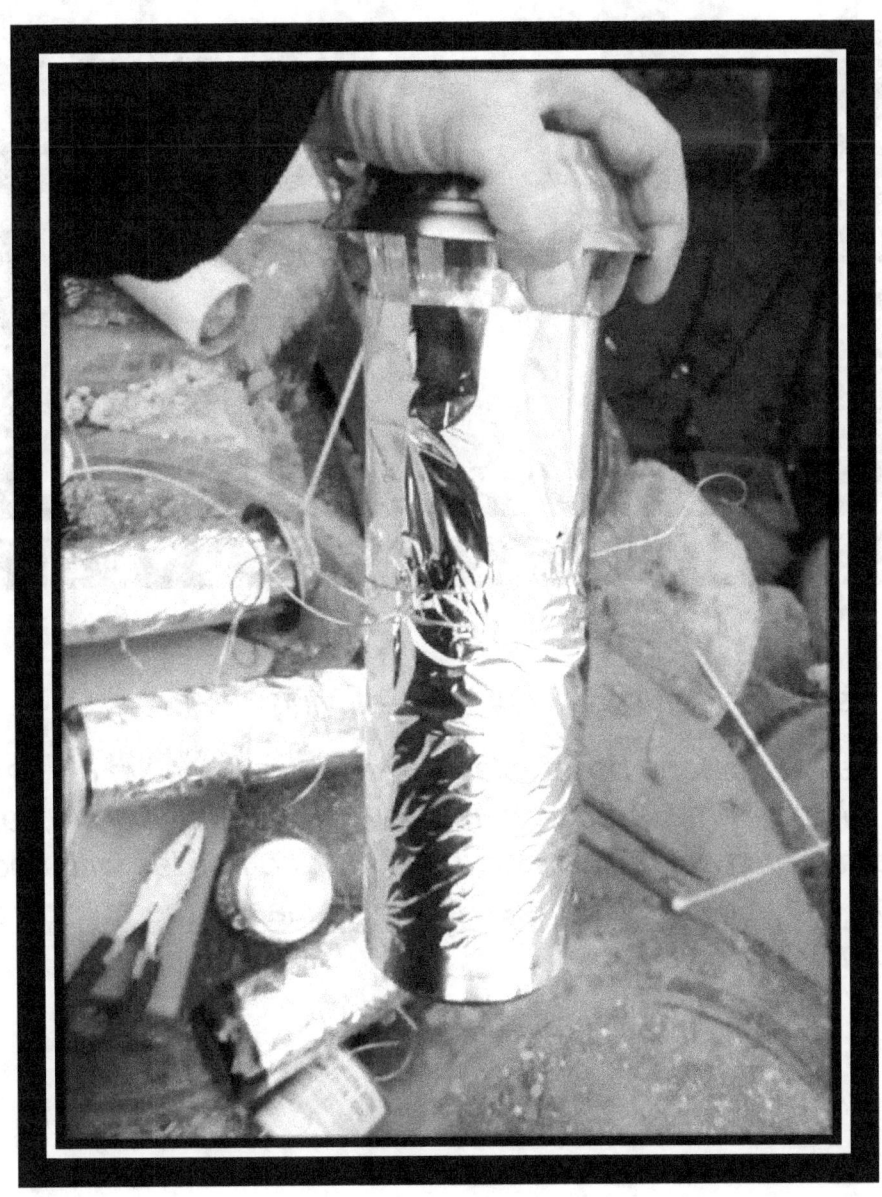

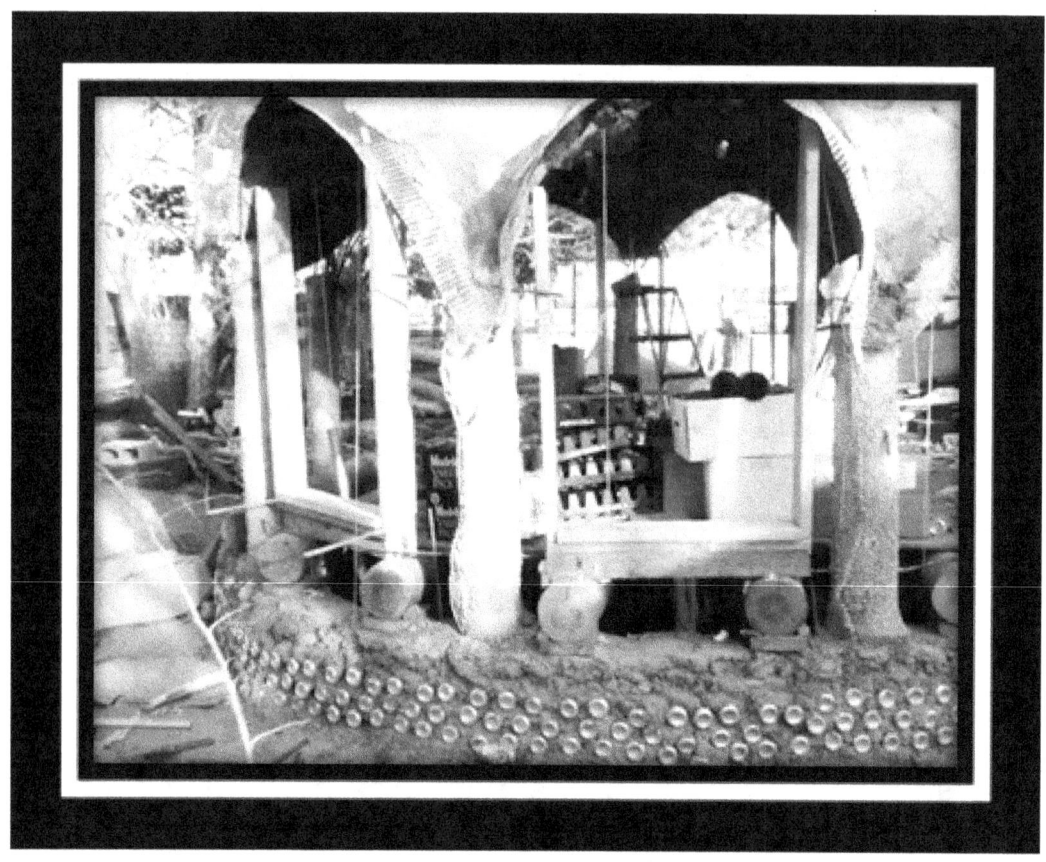

Figure it out as you go framing. Slow but gratifying. 11 12.

First coat of heavy portland based plaster going on to lock in glass and LED work before winter. Temp. bracing comes out after a day or two, but helps to keep a smoother arch shell. The plan is to finish both sides with about 4" of insulative and cheap papercrete, then probably plaster the outside after much more sculpting. 10 28 12.

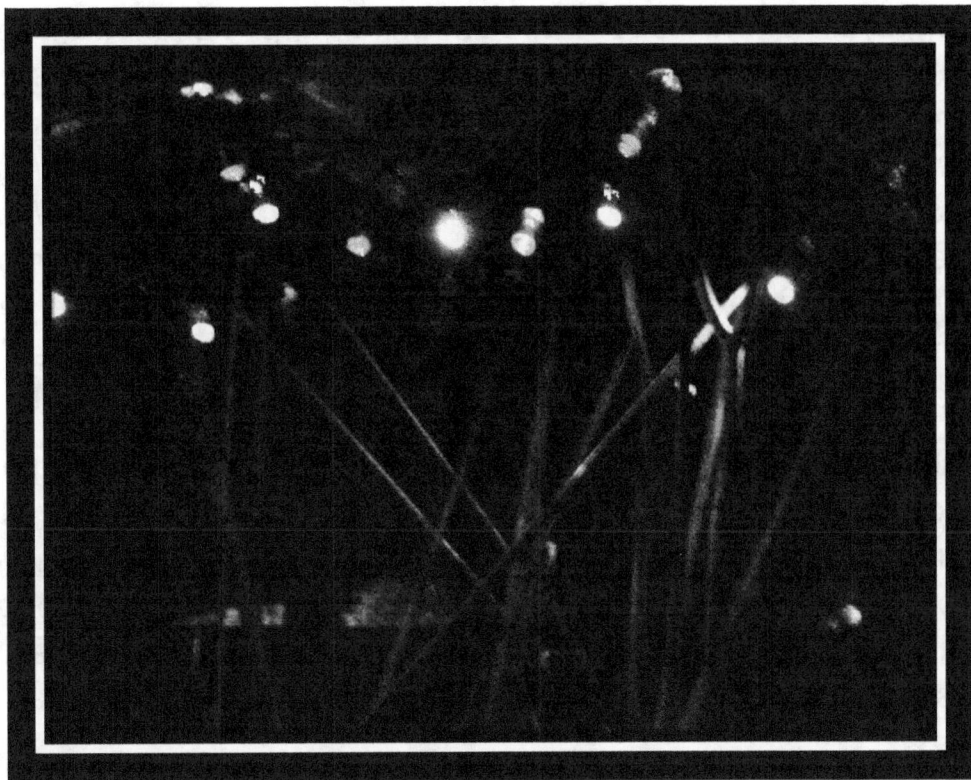

Solar LED night lights' first night in the Head Hutt Sculpture...The first ones took much longer than the next ones will...as with so many things. 10 28 12.

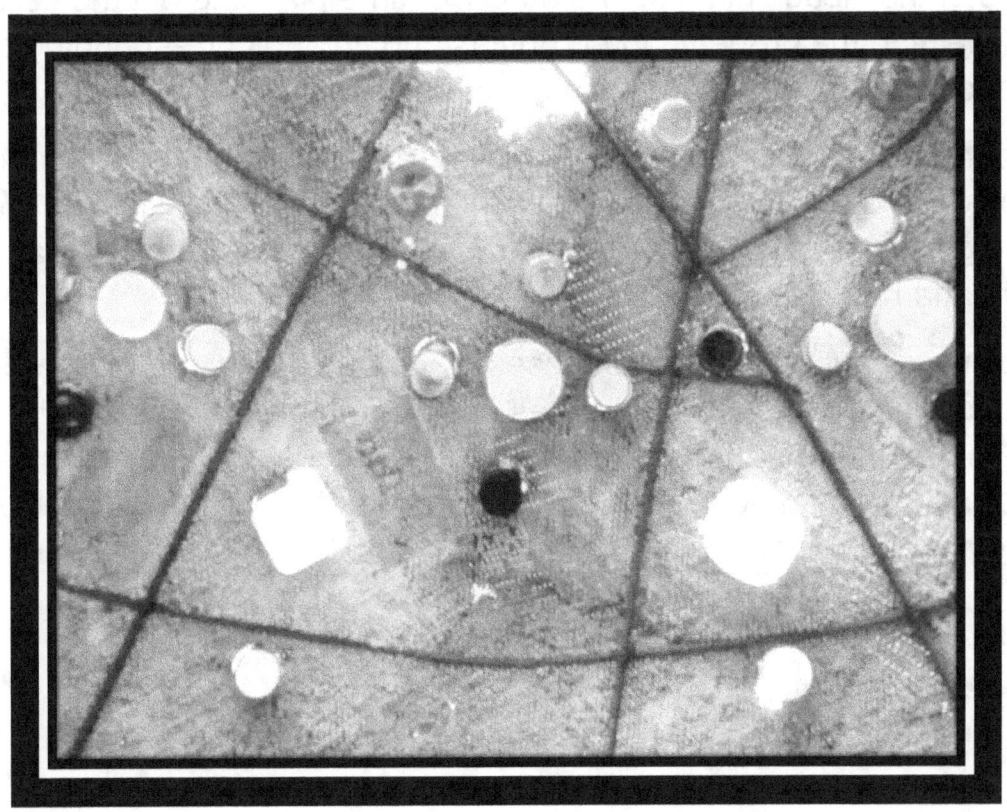

The 'Budding Brain' of the Head Hutt. I am quite happy I spent the extra time on glass work for the roof, and hoping I will not regret it later when the test of temperature control comes into play. So far I have made many mistakes and learned bunches, including: not all glass is created equal! After sorting, cutting, washing, drying, taping, and installing many hundred glass bottles, I now know about as much about the many kinds of glass and their frequencies of occurrence at the recycle depot as I learned about tires a couple years ago, when I started this project! Also, I sure have gained many great ideas already on how to do this better next time! 11 1 12.

I tried all the methods I found on the internet for cutting glass. String of fire, spinny thing...maybe that was it. I settled in on the diamond tile saw blade. Later I learned that water makes a huge difference in the dust. Initially, I cut hundreds of glass bottles without any water and it worked great, though was pretty harsh on my lungs. Always wear and SECURE your dust mask when cutting glass!

I learned the main method I used from the Earthship crew, and only later experimented with a couple other methods. I attached some to solar run LED lights, and in the front, later, I used some in other ways, without cutting them.

Initially, I was determined to have a butterfly pattern that also makes the eyebrows of the Head Hutt. I spend a LOT of time planning out the ceiling and sides. Collecting the proper colored bottles and finding corresponding clear matches took me a year or so, I think.

Towards the end of this part of the project. I realized I could have connected with a local bar owner or two and probably found a more hassle-free method of getting glass. As it was, I frequented the recycling bins so often that I did get offers and help from many people.

Friends and strangers dropped off cases of various green and blue glass. A friend tipped me off about twelve cases or so of the green water bottles. A couple I met at the recycling bins brought me six cases of blue bottles. My friends drank platinum bud light just for the blue bottles, despite it being some of the worst beer on earth.

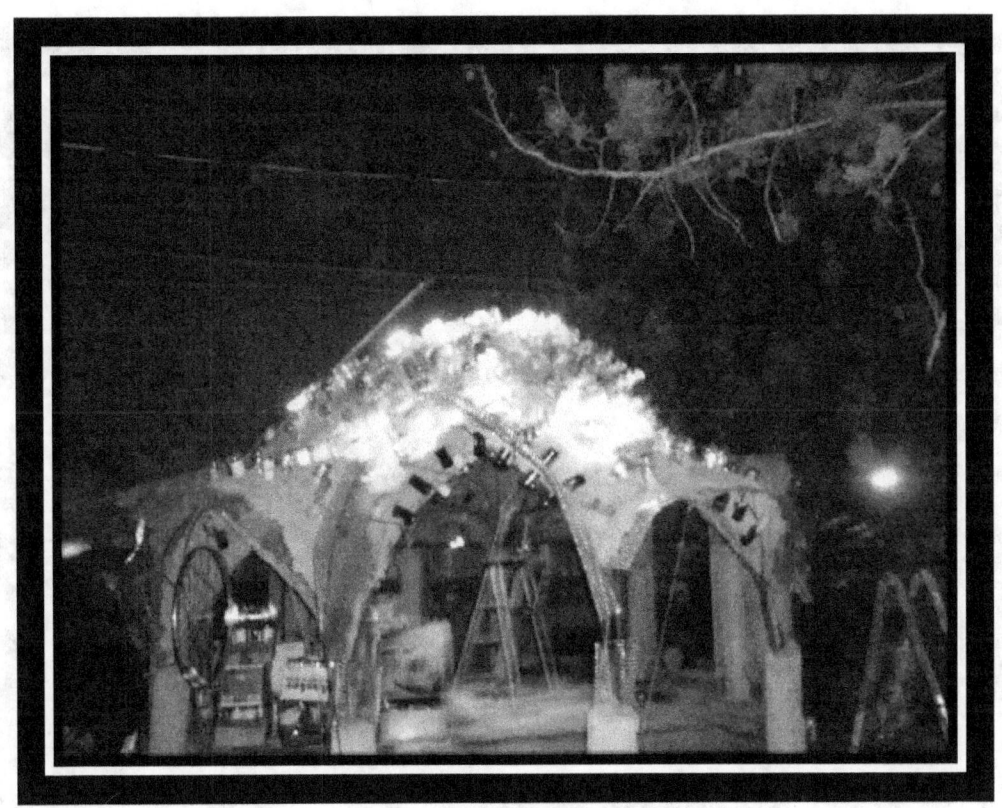

1 9 13. Slowly it comes along, at almost a dead crawl in the cold weather, but the solar LED lights are working nicely. Much more work to come!

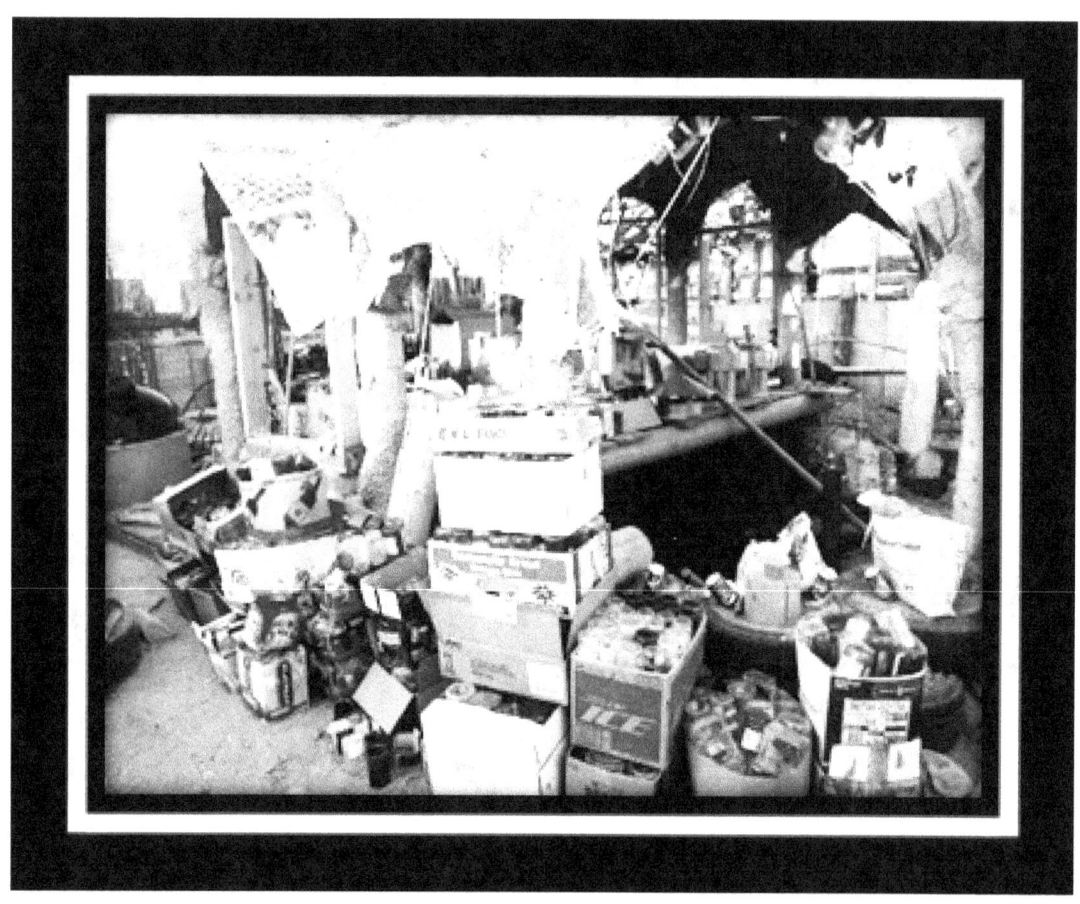

I cut this many half bottles one afternoon; like a machine! (and with a machine! MY favorite instrument of glass ripping, a diamond blade on a tile saw, with water preferably, and a good dust mask! April end 2013.

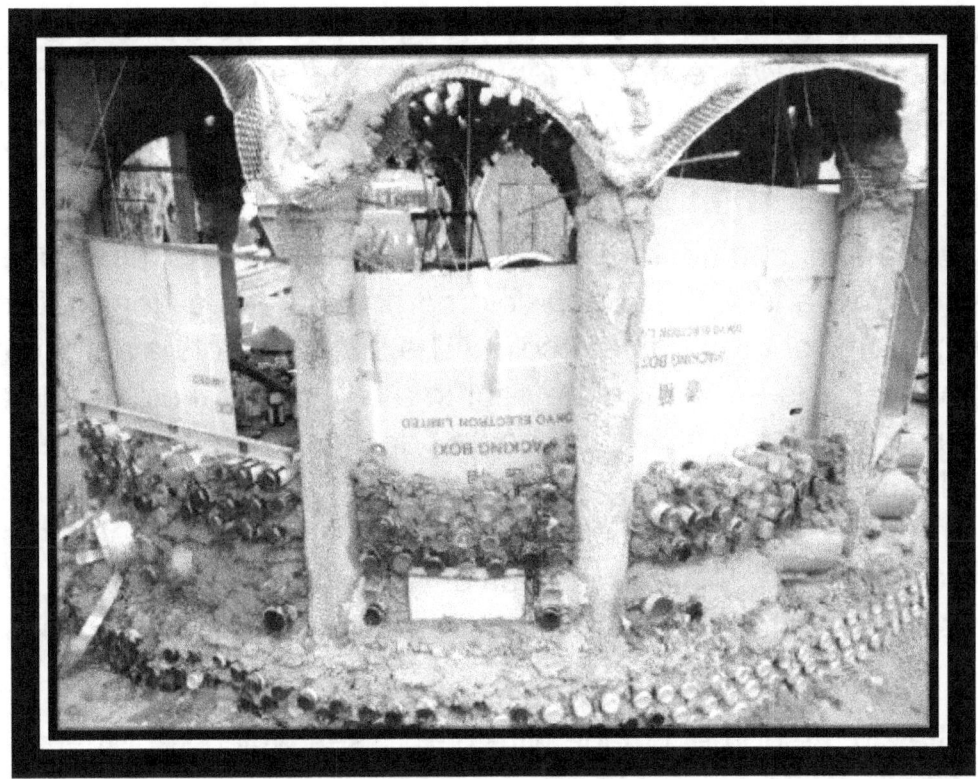

April 30, 2013. Back Panel going up. I could be more accurate in many directions, but working well with the overall structure.

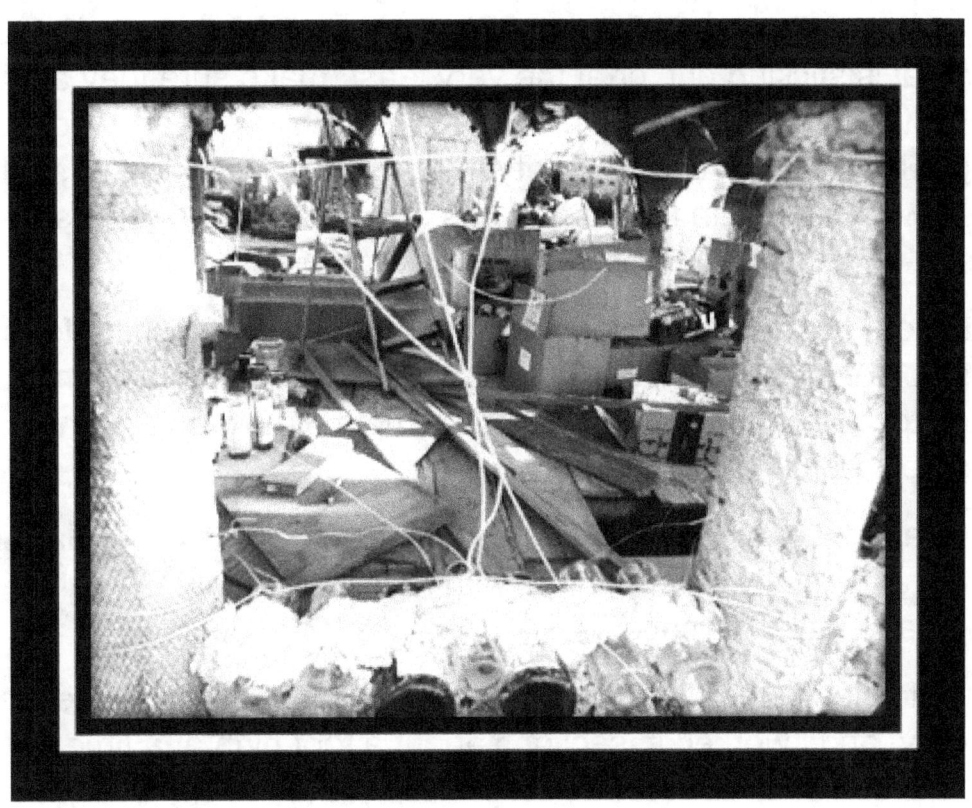

I decided to put in wire reinforcements through the bottle walls. They will also get hemp twine and wire reinforcements between the papercrete and the plaster layers. April end 2013.

Collecting, cleaning, cutting, taping, sorting the bottle bricks into boxes took a lot of time, energy, and space! Each colored brick needs a clear outside half to let in maximum light through the color. The sizes do not have to match exactly, however, it is best when they do. In a few cases, I did not do a great job of cleaning, drying, or taping the bottle bricks, and these will forever be blemishes in my work. My advice is to take time doing this part right, as it is one of the most admired parts of this type of construction, and you may notice condensation or worse, mold on the bottles you do not properly dry or seal. Of course, it is not too difficult to remove and replace them in most cases, if they really bother you.

For the bottles in the dome, I made wire harnesses which kept them propped up in the lathe. I still lost a few to gravity during the plastering process, so do be careful with workers heads and wear your hard hats!

While I am on the subject of safety, I should say a few more things. Rebar can really be a dangerous thing, especially sticking out of cement. It is easy to walk into, step on, or trip and fall onto. Please use safety covers if you can on any rebar that is sticking out, or at the very least, make sure they are visible and cover with aluminum cans to draw the eye to the ends and reduce scratching. This is not a suitable safety measure for a work crew, so do be sure to be aware of this and other hazards and take the proper precautionary measures.

As I mentioned, I cracked a rib leaning into a dumpster, reaching for a pretty blue glass bottle. This was not technically a jobsite related accident, though it was related to the project, and a perfect example of how quickly things can go wrong. Do be careful!

The interior and exterior circles are green and white glass with solar LED's, so they light up at night. I wrapped those with reflective silver lining, though I am not sure it made any difference.

I ran a few stainless-steel wires through my side panels to give them a little extra integrity, and I worked in sections about a foot high at a time. Doing my best to level each bottle, space them accurately, build in my design, and clean them after every session. Do not let cement cure onto your glass bottles! I also hung plumb lines and checked the walls frequently to be sure I was building straight up and down. My glass bottle bricks are 18" wide, so an inch of variation here or there does not make a big structural difference, though aesthetically, and for the extra infill materials, it can add up. I just did my best and did not worry much about it otherwise. I did find myself limited by the slump and weight of glass and cement.

At the start I did try to use these pieces of Lexan/polyurethane I found in a dumpster to help keep them plumb and to help me with the side spirals designs.

This is the back of that big panel, outside, before plaster and infill. I used yellow and amber glass on both sides, and matched green and blue bottles with clear or light blue glass to let in more light. I spend a lot of time collecting and matching the bottles I came to prefer, which was the result of availability, strength, and ease of cutting.

In front (facing South), I used all clear and light blue glass, except for a row of dark blue eyebrows. I left giant openings for the eyes, which I was still designing at the time.

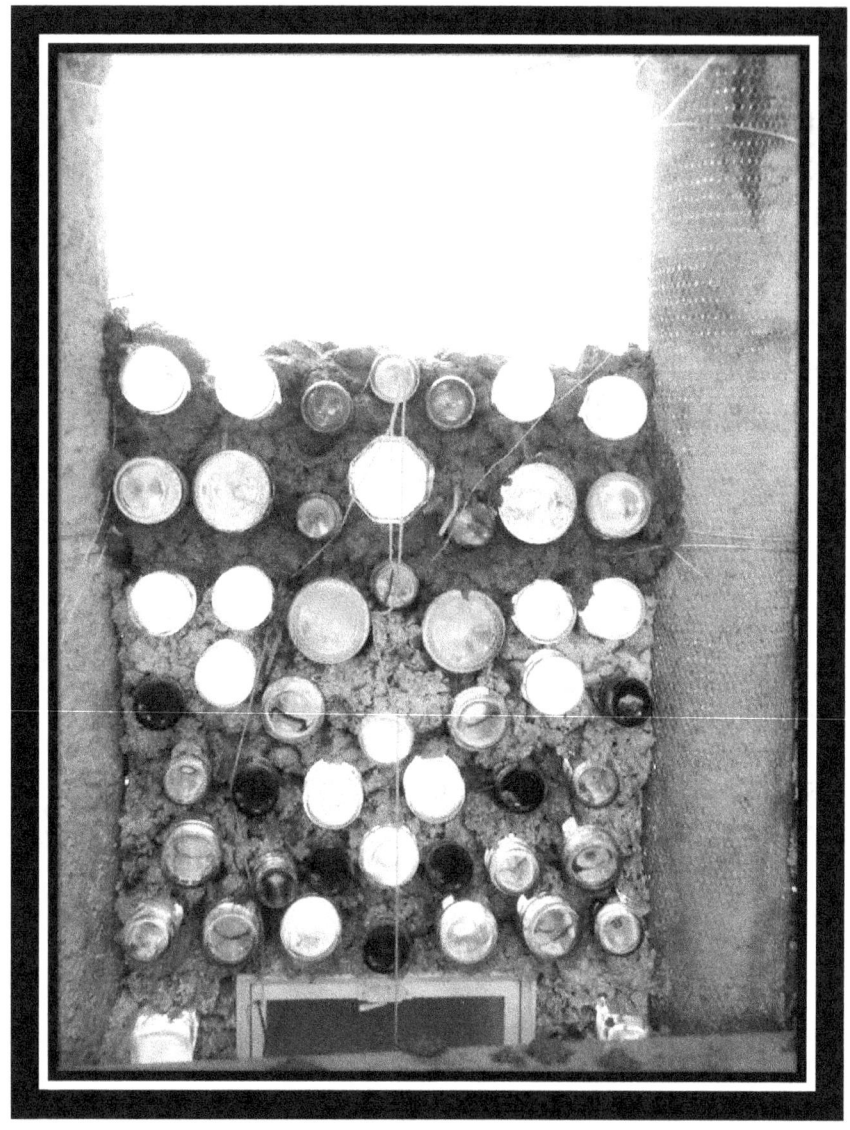

I put three pretty yellow star patterns in the back of the skull, which took some doing to collect just the right bottles.

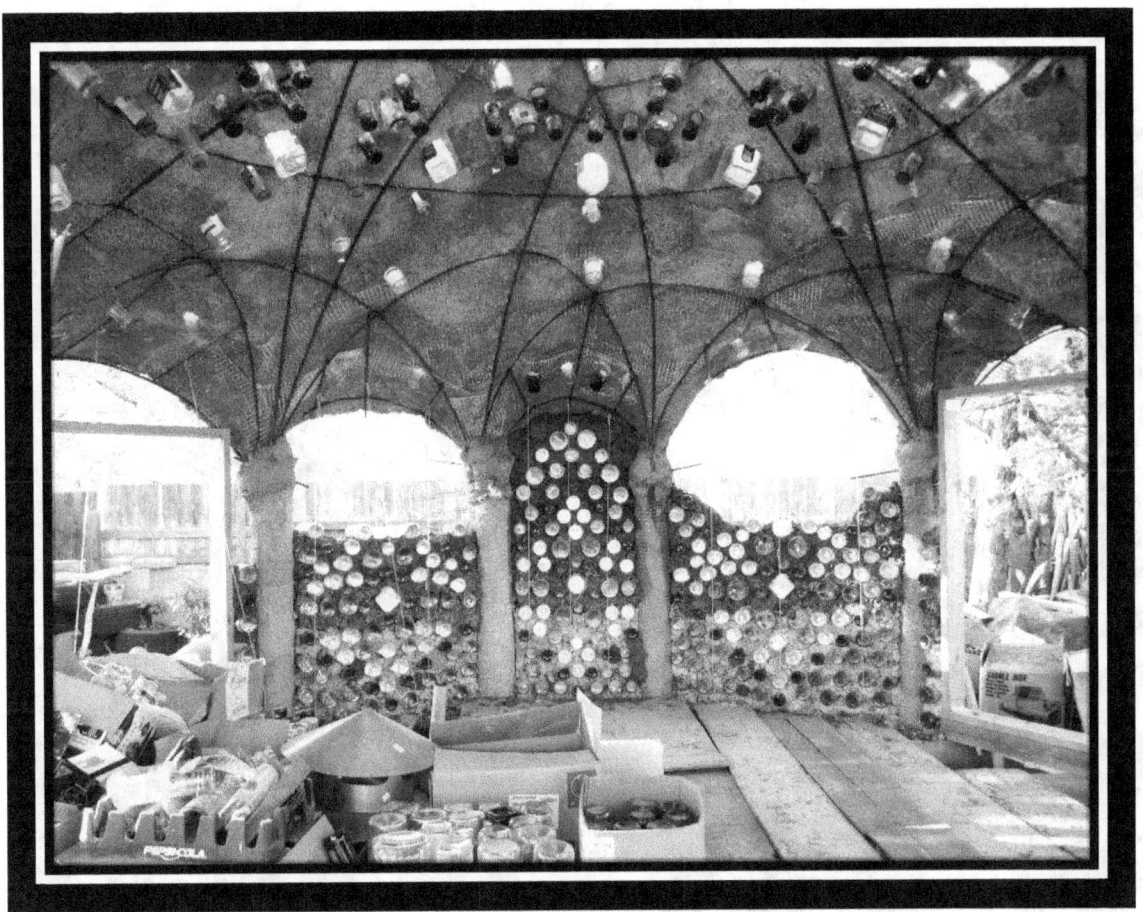

May 2, 2013. From the front. Lots more to do, then lots more finish work...in case you wonder, for example, the flooring is temp. scrap. After I finish papercretting or whatever messy-else-work inside, then I plan to install a nice floor. :)

The Head Hutt Picture Book

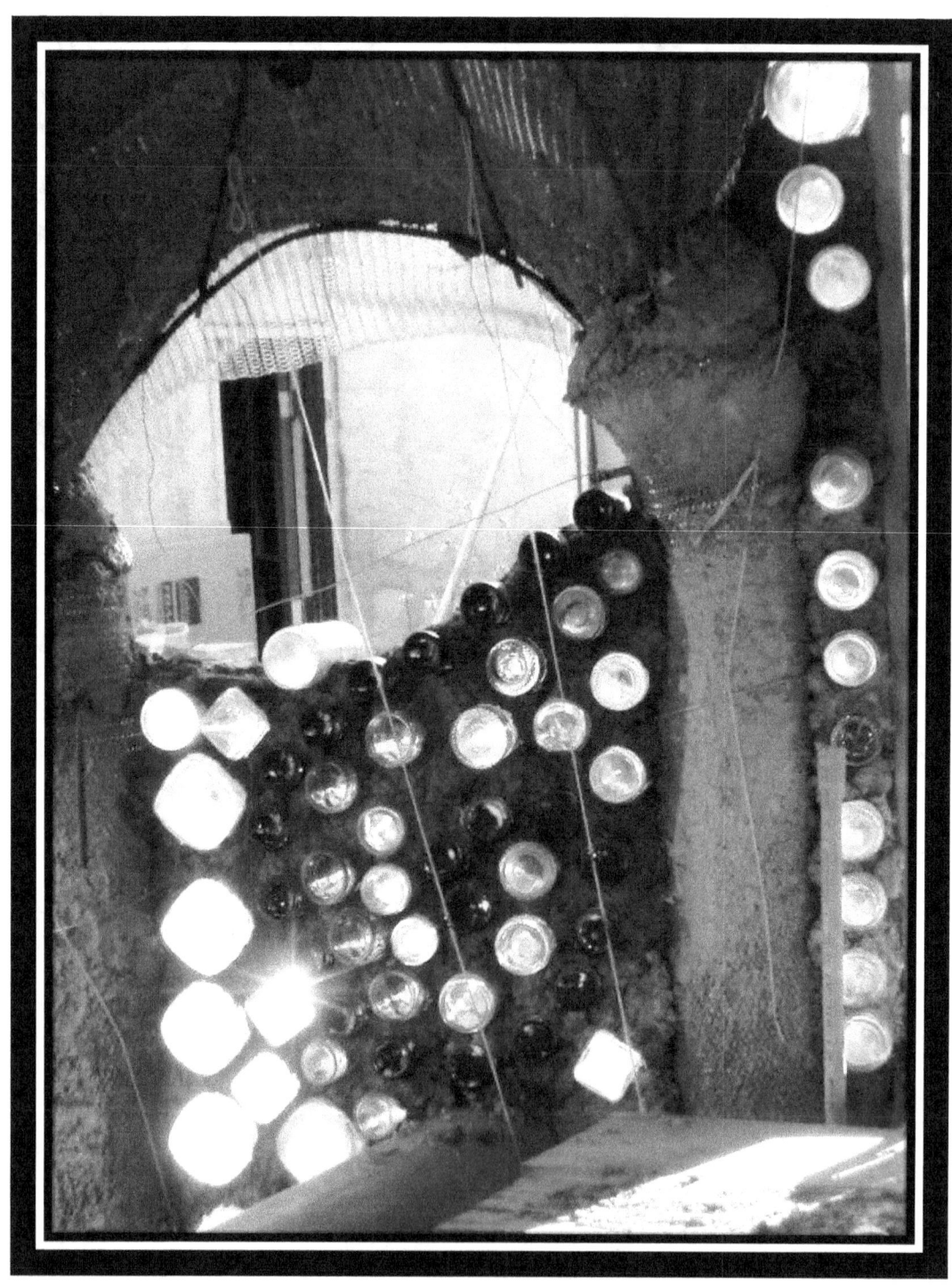

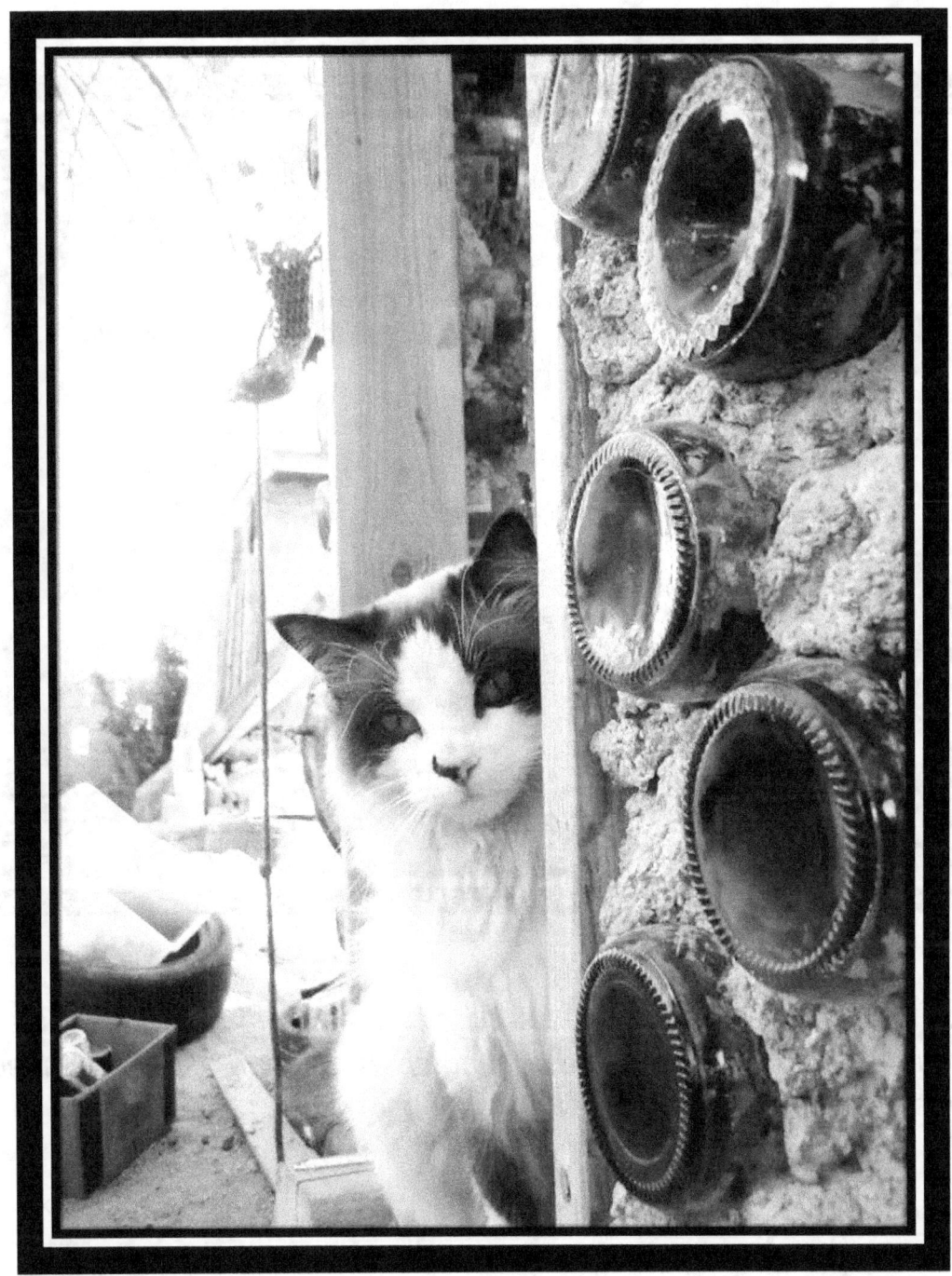

Sapphire Cat believes this is her castle, rightfully so!

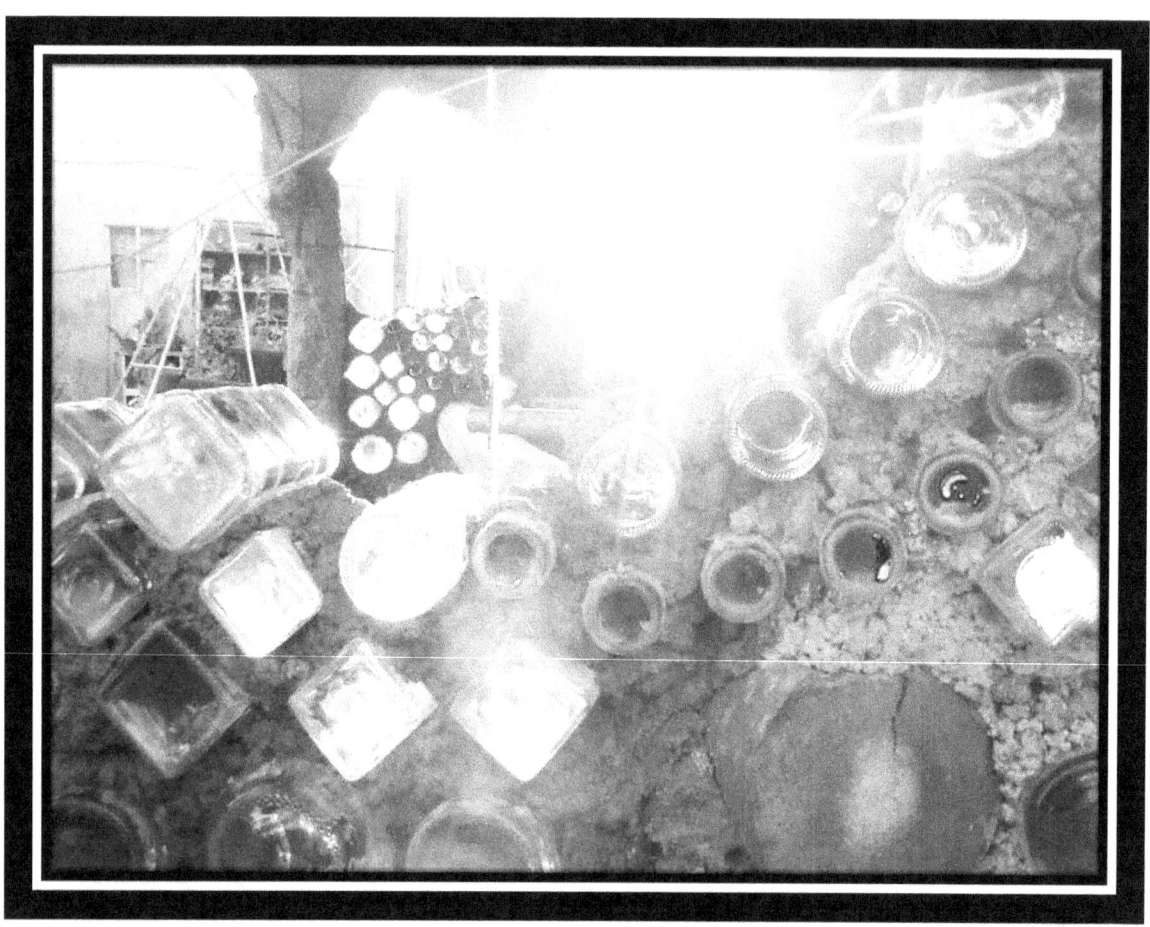

I still absolutely LOVE watching the sunlight glisten in through the bottle walls. Throughout the day the colors and lighting changes, and especially at sunsets and sunrises, they just glow so beautifully.

The Head Hutt Picture Book

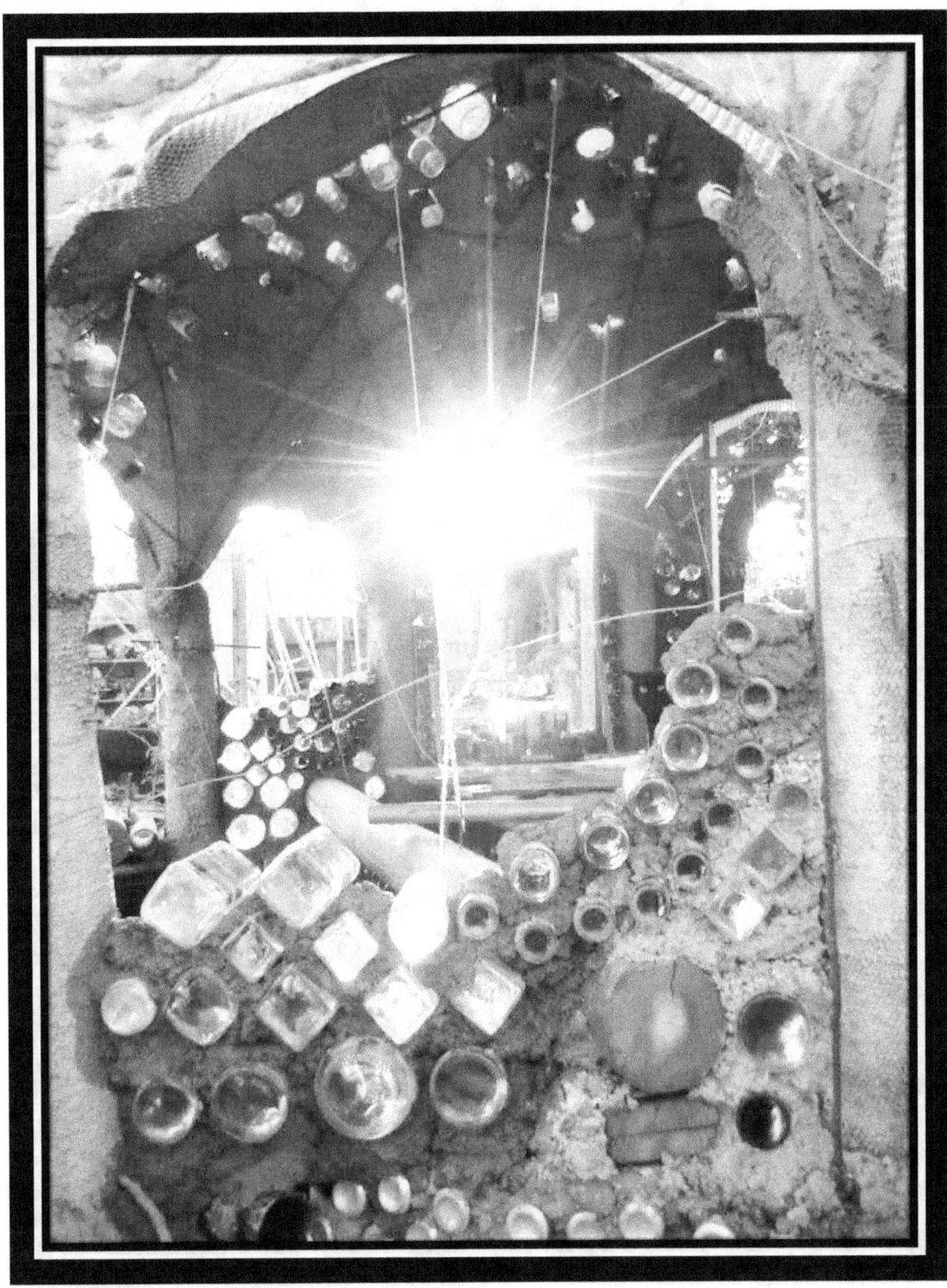

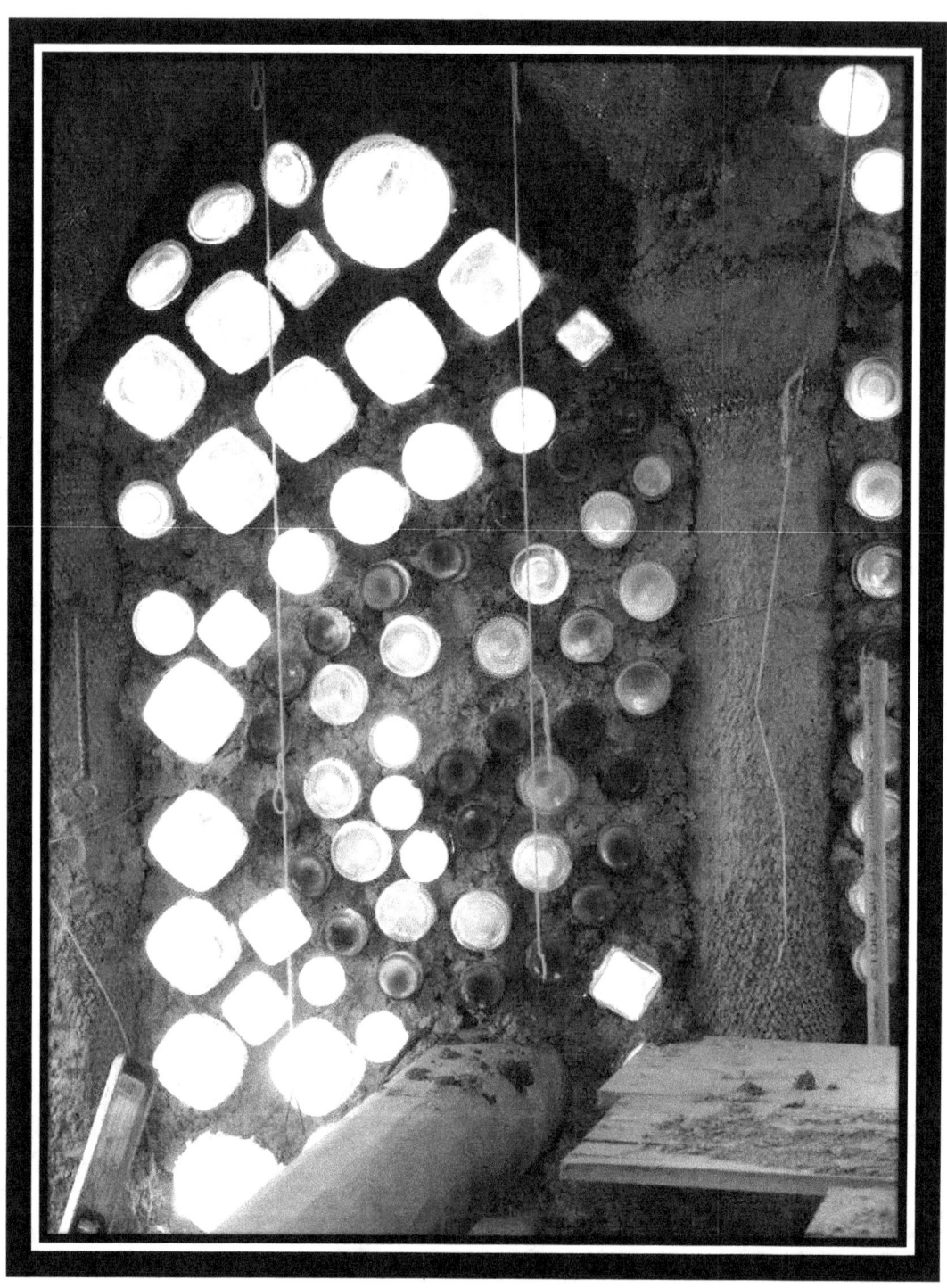

The Head Hutt Picture Book

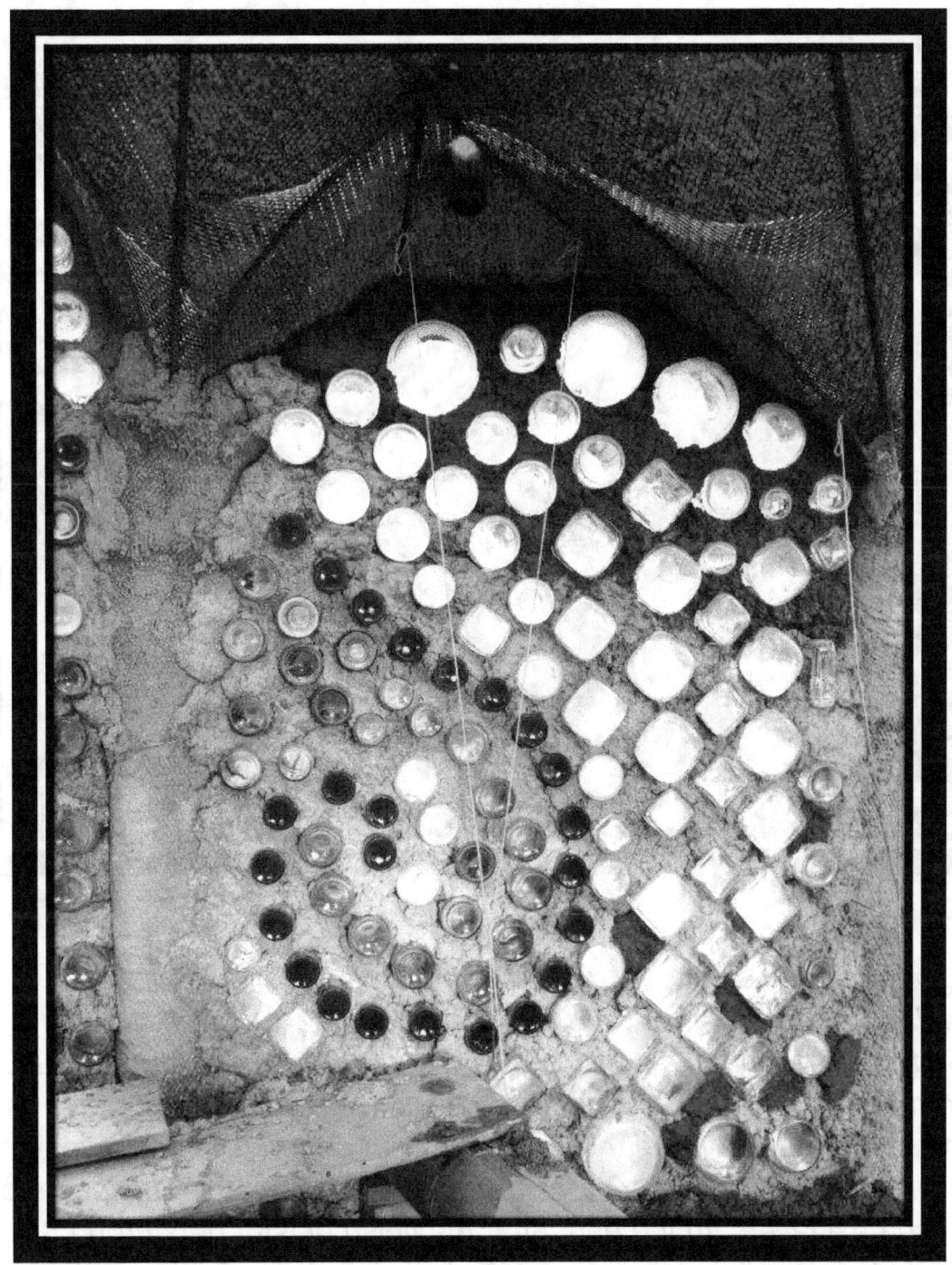

East side/left temple May 19, 2013. About 250 glass bottles repurposed-- cut, washed, dried, taped, and installed for this panel. You can't see my color schemes in this black and white print version, but, rest assured, they are fun, and colorful!

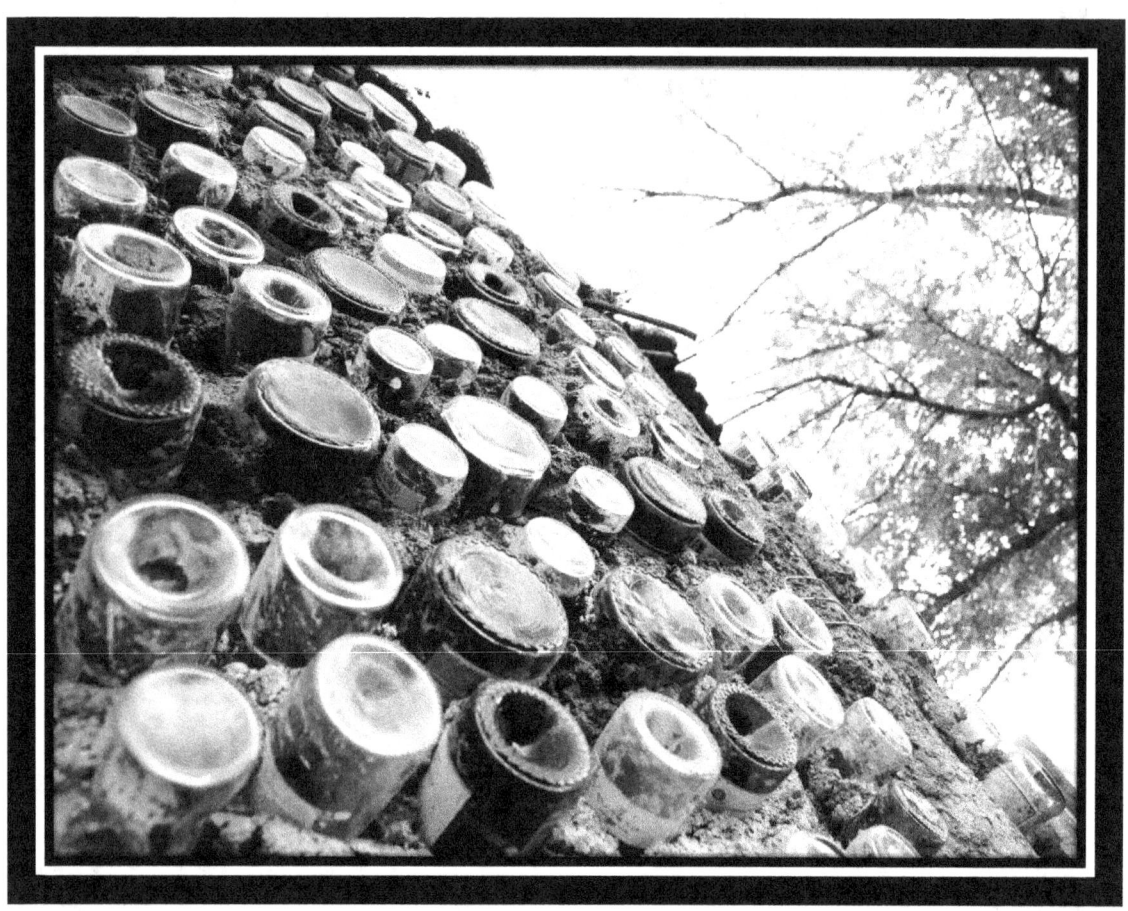

"The ugly side of a bottle wall" You can see why you might want all smooth/flat bottomed bottles, and to plumb them more perfectly than I have. It is my first attempt though, and on a curve, so I am kind of proud of it. LOL FAR from perfect, but the bottle end relations could be worse, given how close they are, and that I am 'freehanding it', and with papercrete. I will weave hemp-twine and wire reinforcements through the inside and outside before adding the next layers. In the end, after the finish plaster gets brought flush with the ends, it won't look half bad, I think. This is the outside, back, Northside. May 2, 2013.

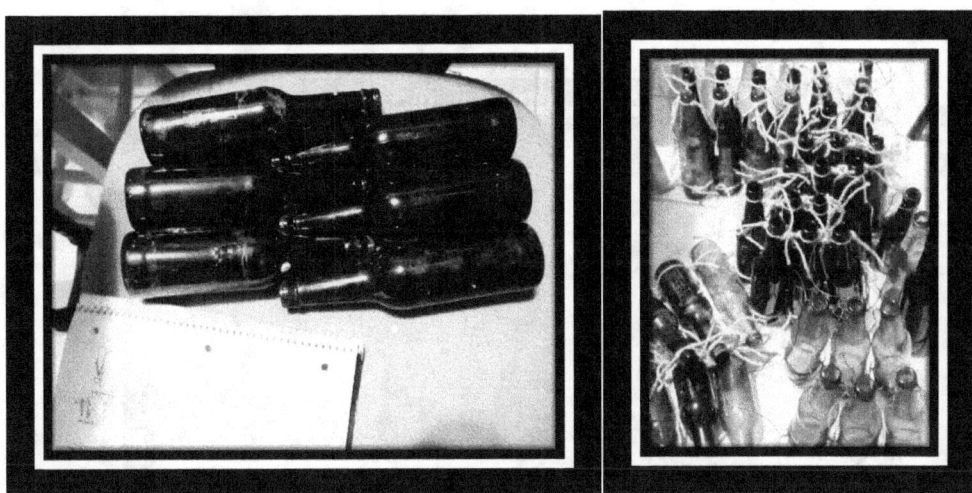

6 26 14. Somebody's playing with glass bottles again.

I finally settled on tying them with hemp rope...turns out, sometimes wire is better, sometimes hemp twine. 6 25 14.

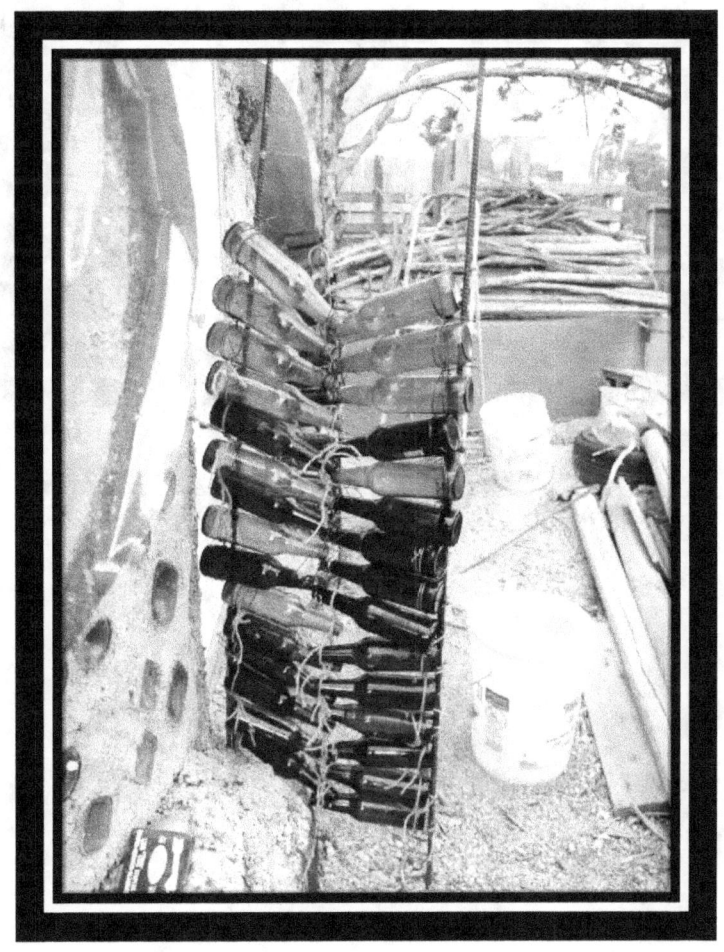

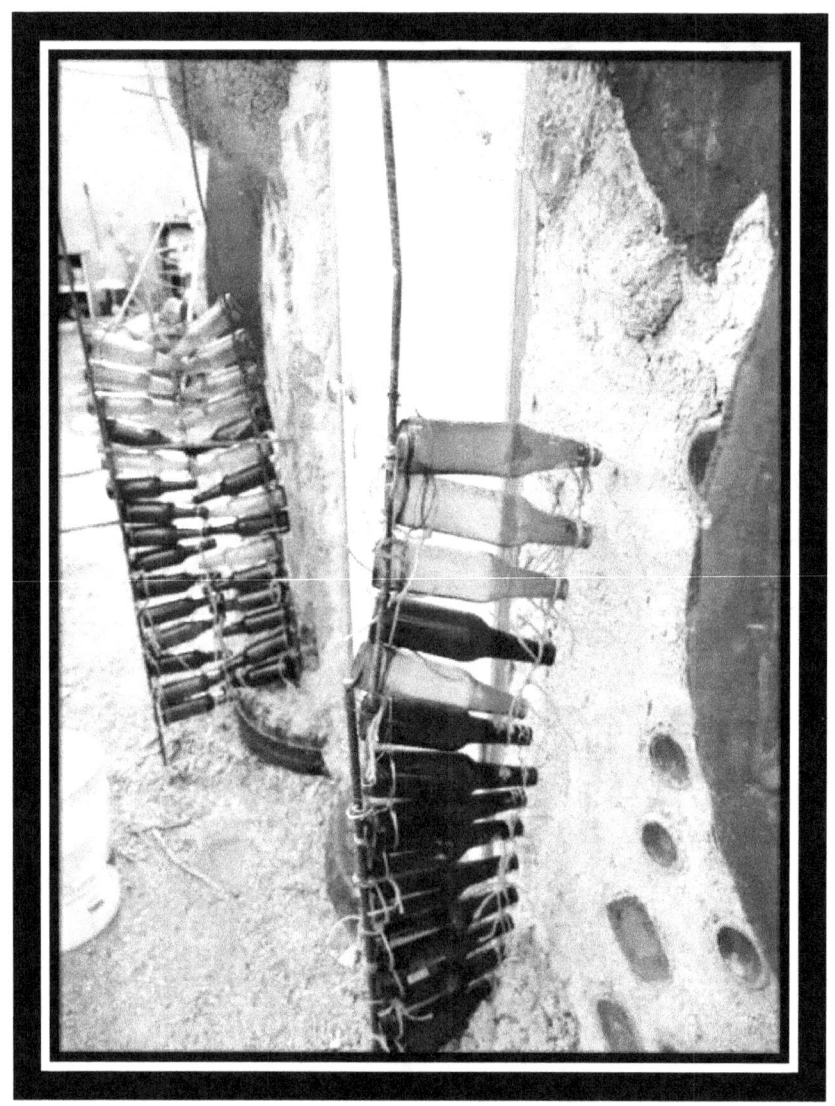

Finally getting them in! 6 27 14.

The Head Hutt Picture Book

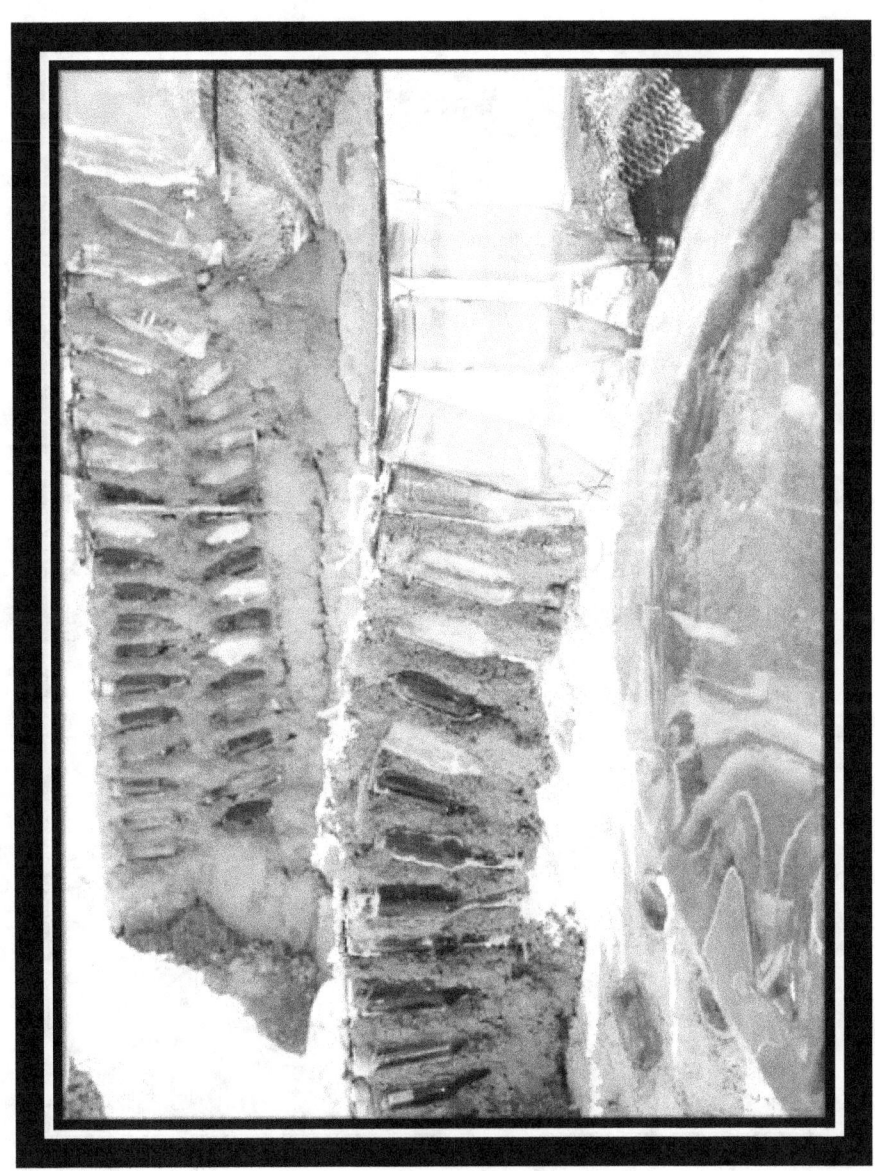

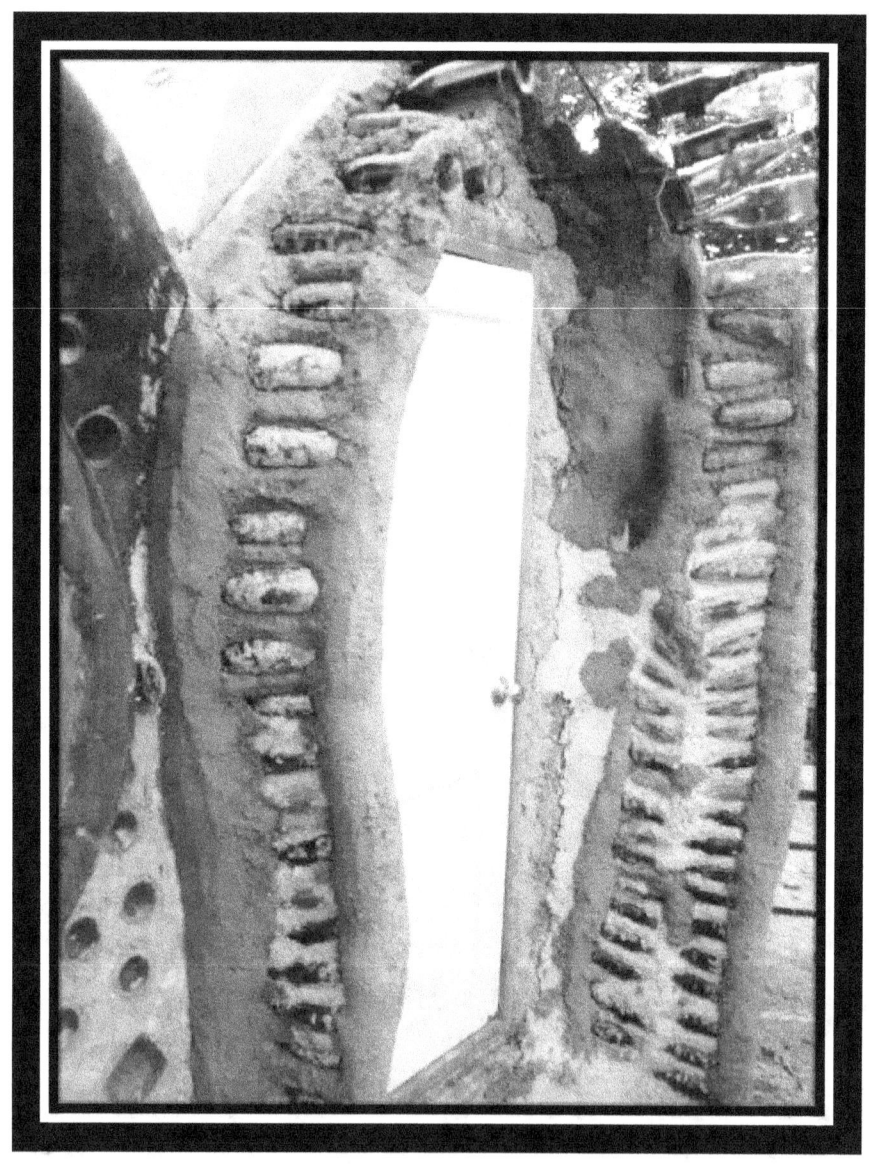

Finally getting them implanted! Still a ways to go but getting happier with this bit. 6 28 14.

Slowly, slowly, it comes along. I ran out of daylight today before cleanup-- hoping it is not too bad in the morning. Luckily, paper-pumi-crete is easily to cleanup than regular cement or mortar, by far! 6 30 14.

The Head Hutt Picture Book

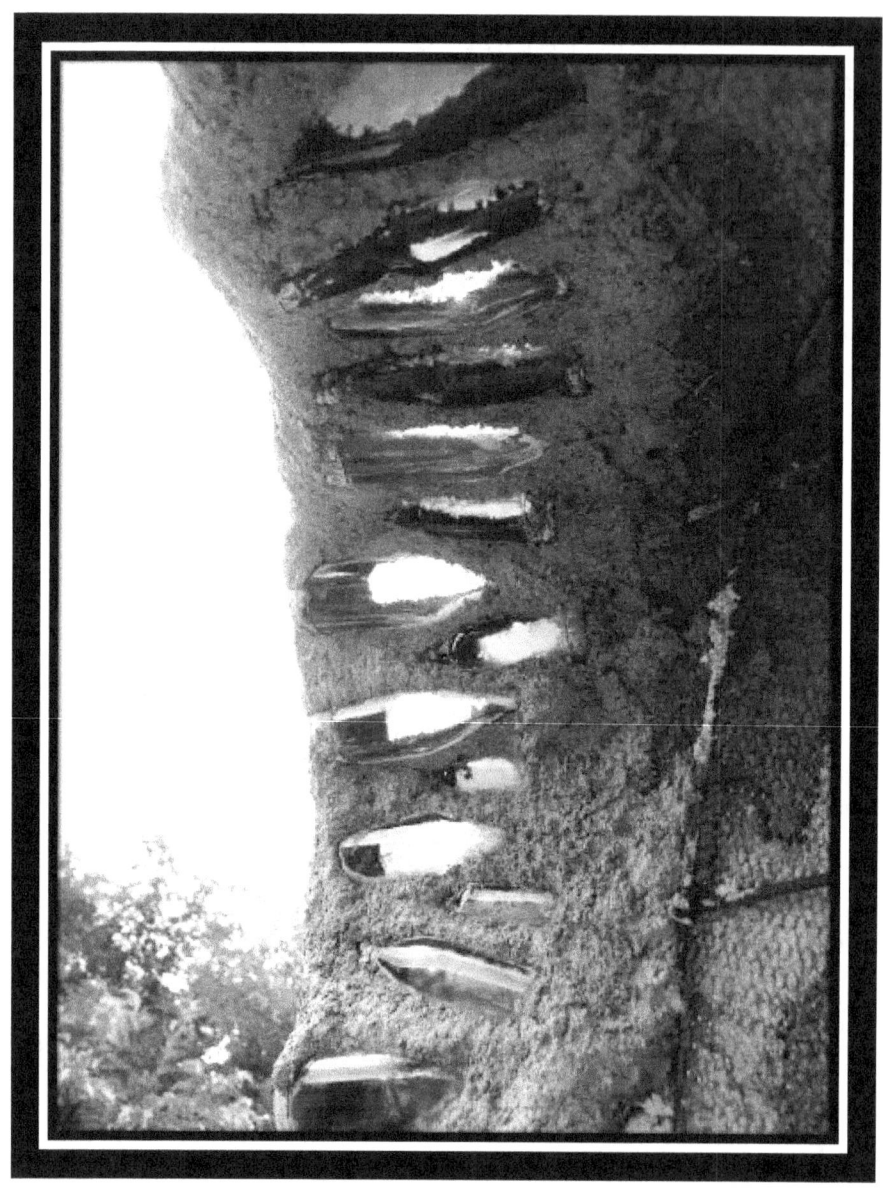

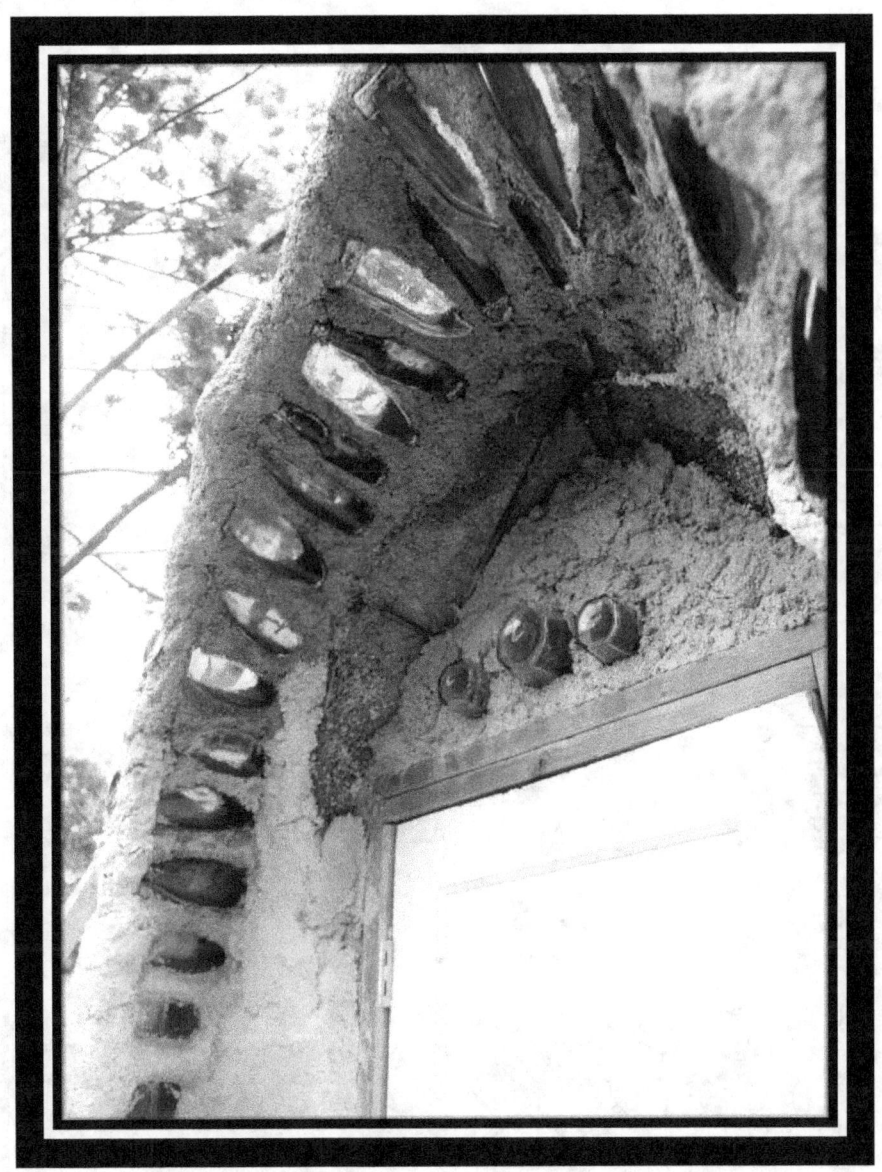

7 10 14. Front Beak-Entrance almost completely in. Just a bit more filling and smoothing and it will be ready for color/final coat.

Temp door in. Later this is replaced with Lexan shutters.

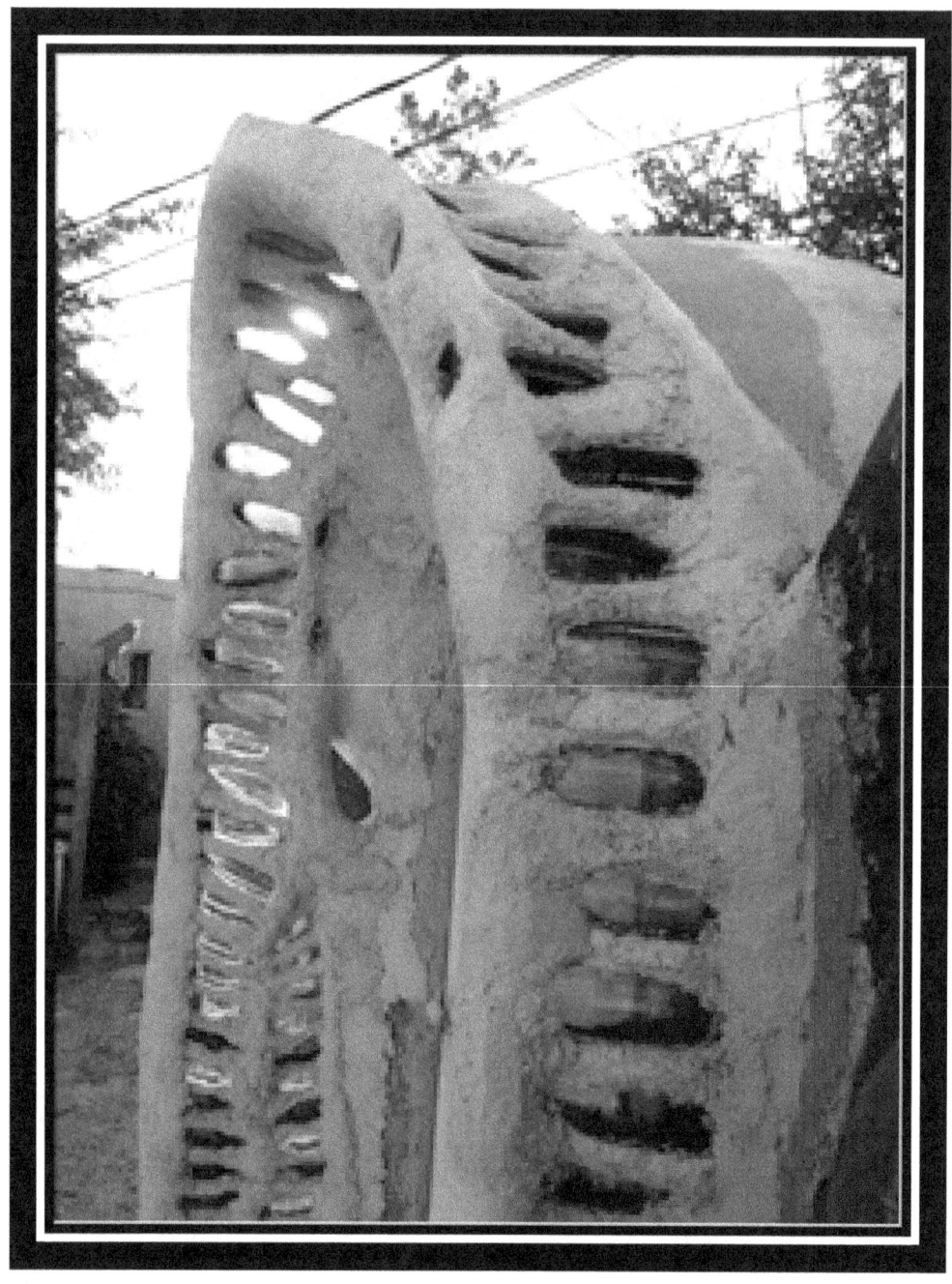

Entryway/front beak is about finished, minus polishing details and door redux. Lines are not quite where I tried to get them, and some chunks of infill will need at least one more round to get them to stick...I am finding some challenges to not-so-sticky, moderately heavy sculpting medium, especially when working directly against gravity with only air support. I will get it done though, "don't you worry". 7 15 14.

The Dome

The infrastructure of the dome was made with rebar arches, wired together with lathe. I prepared the entire dome before I began plastering and infilling. I started by putting bottle bricks in the lathe dome in preparation for first covering. In hindsight, I would not recommend ever putting glass through your ceiling at an angle like this. This is one of those things which a knowledgeable builder would never do, and I only got to do because of the sculptural aspects of this project. Still, it remains one of my favorite parts of this one-of-a-kind structure.

Initially I thought the clear glass would let in enough light to grow more plants in the center/bottom/front. However, after the dome was put on it became apparent that it was not quite enough light for food production. Houseplants love it in here though, and I do get some flowers in the front eye-windows.

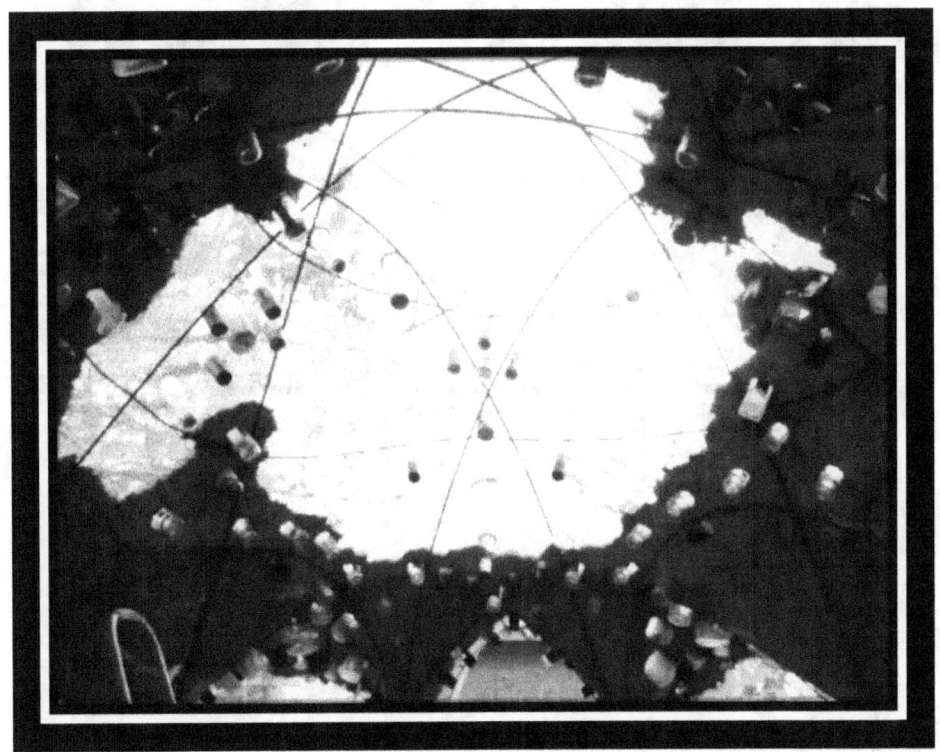

Nov 8, 2012. Still working out the last of the glass for the top before first coat. Slowed by another injury, I am not sure if I will get the entire first coat on before the weather makes me stop for a while.

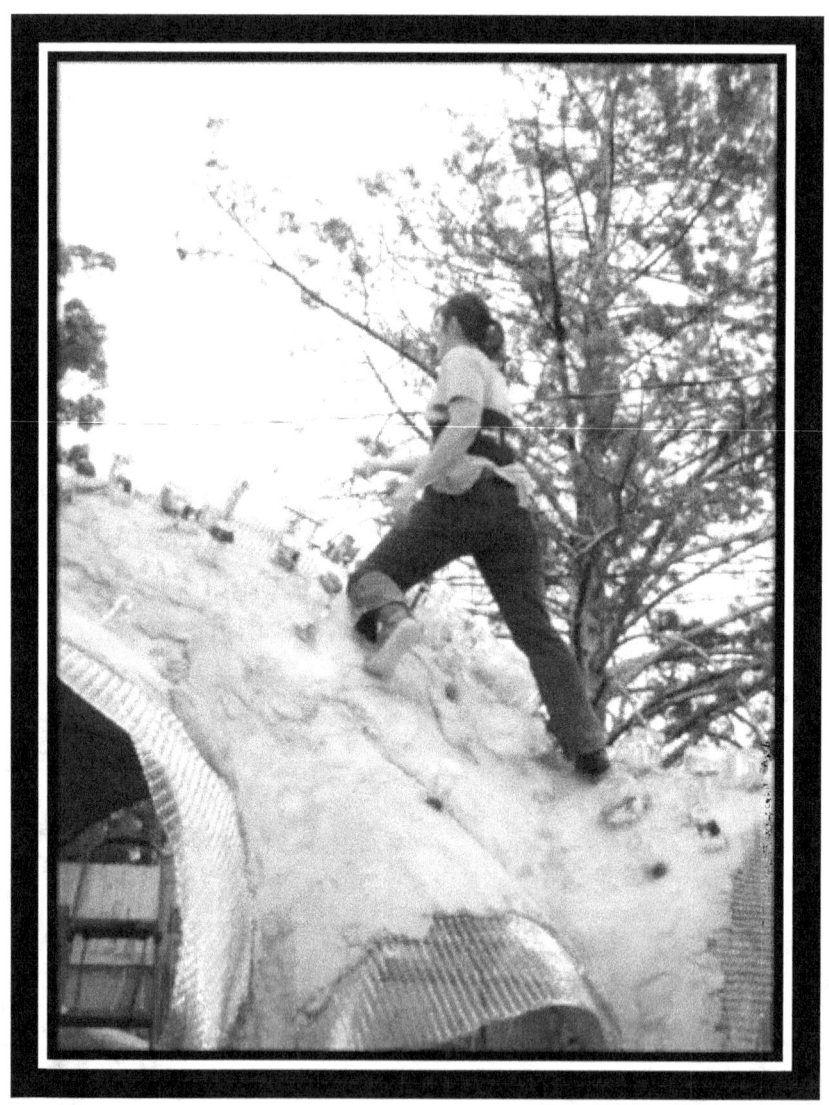

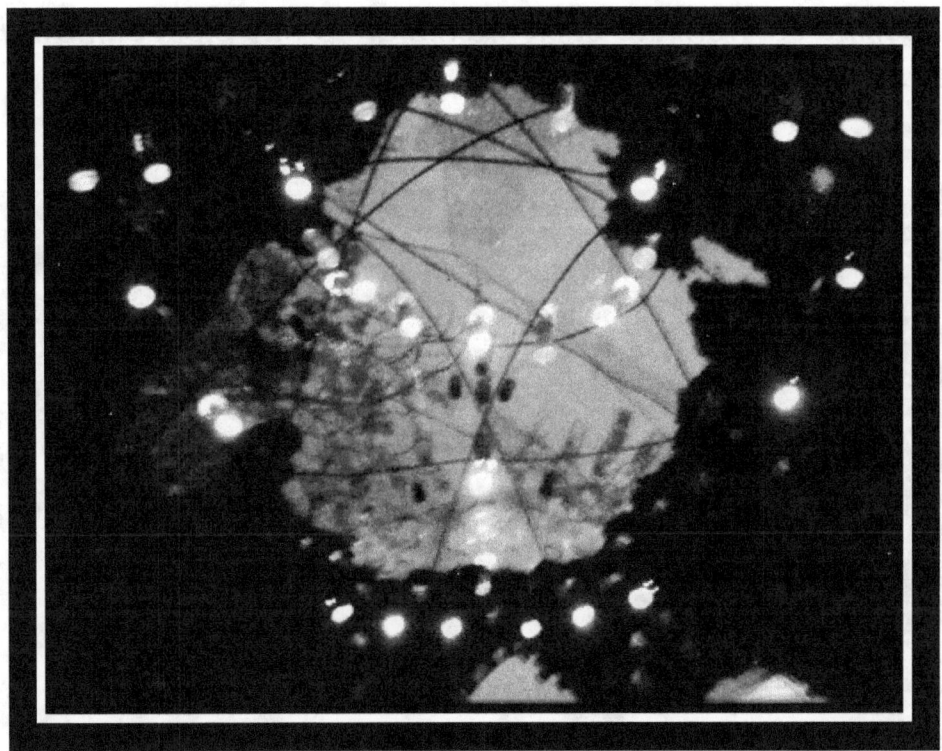

It's lookin pretty space-shipy when the solar LEDs light up at night. I love it more and more! Nov 8, 2012.

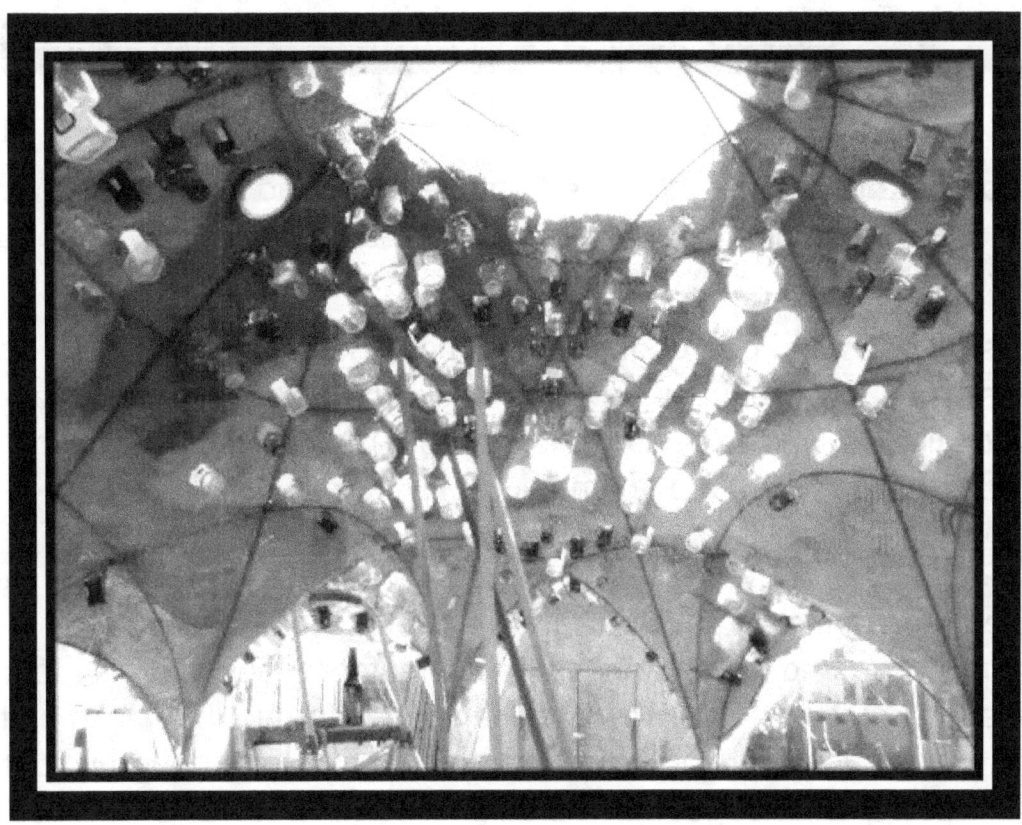

11 20 12. Looking out from the back/brain. I am pretty pleased now that I get to see what it might look like!

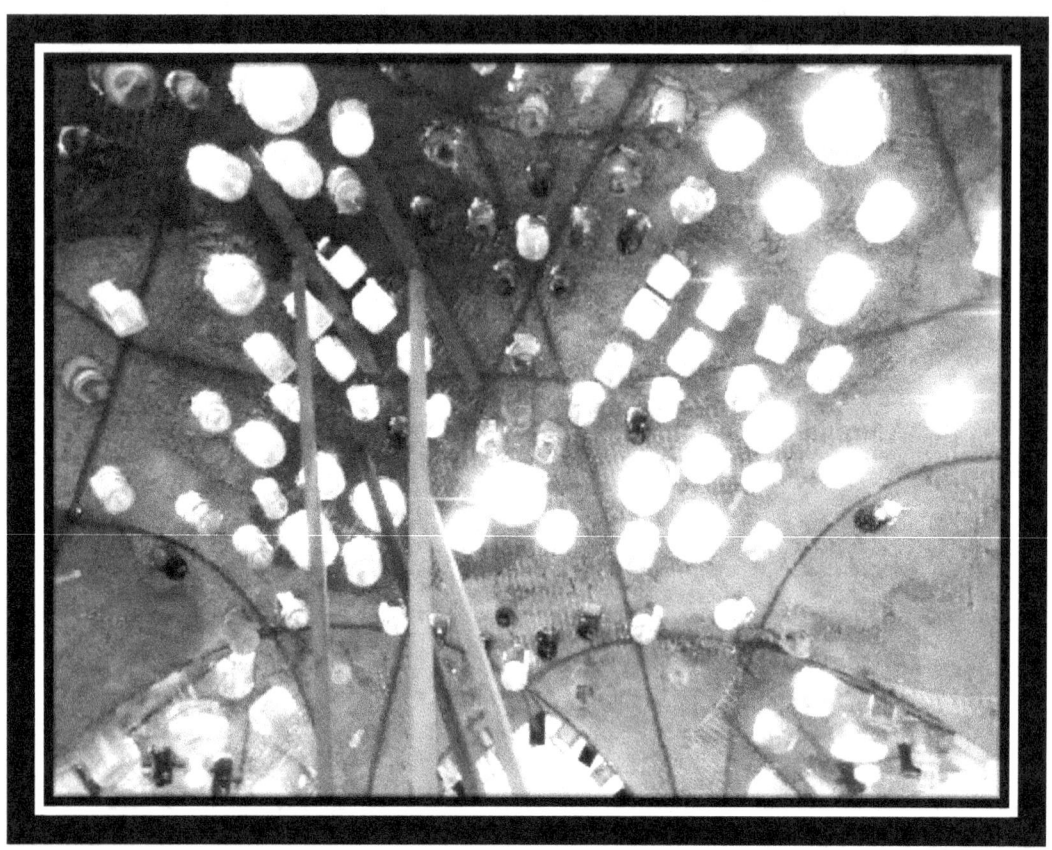

The dome was a priority for me once I got the overhead bottle bricks wired in place. I started with a high strength cement plaster mix, applying it about an inch or two thick.

I used lots of sticks and boards to prop up the lath between rebar, as it started to sag in some spots. Keeping the bottle bricks 'plum' on a curving plane proved a challenge, and I definitely did not do a masterful job of it, though over all I am thrilled with the outcome.

It took some days or weeks.

The angle of the dome and overhead wires proved challenging, and I worked my way up and around, doing my best to use safety ropes and also to cover my work and cure it well. The New Mexican sun is formidable much of the year, and it was a challenge to keep it tarped and misted, though I did the best I could and overall did not get much cracking, so I feel it was a success.

After that layer cured it felt fine to crawl on and I pouring on the middle layers.

On the top outside, I added 4-8" (about 6) of pumice mixed with a cement slurry. This was/is quite heavy, though not nearly as heavy as solid cement, and much more insulating.

The outside skin was a pumice, paper, cement skin, which I did not put on until after I got the bottle walls put in, a year or more*check later.

The inside infill is one of a few 'flaws judgement' which I do think may have structural consequences. Okay, I pretty much know it does.

I used padobe (paper and adobe and lime) infill the inside. I did put a lot of lime in it, and at the time I think I thought that would give it enough structural integrity. In hindsight, directly overhead with lots of weight and some tendency to leak moisture because of the glass intrusions was probably not a well thought out idea. I did use engineering fibers throughout my roof mixes, which does bring me some additional peace of mind.

A 'saner', or less creatively inclined person might have used a machine or one of many different methods for putting the infill up. I used my hands. One handful at a time. Schlep. Schlep. Schlep. It was messy. Tedious. Kinda fun. It took a long time.

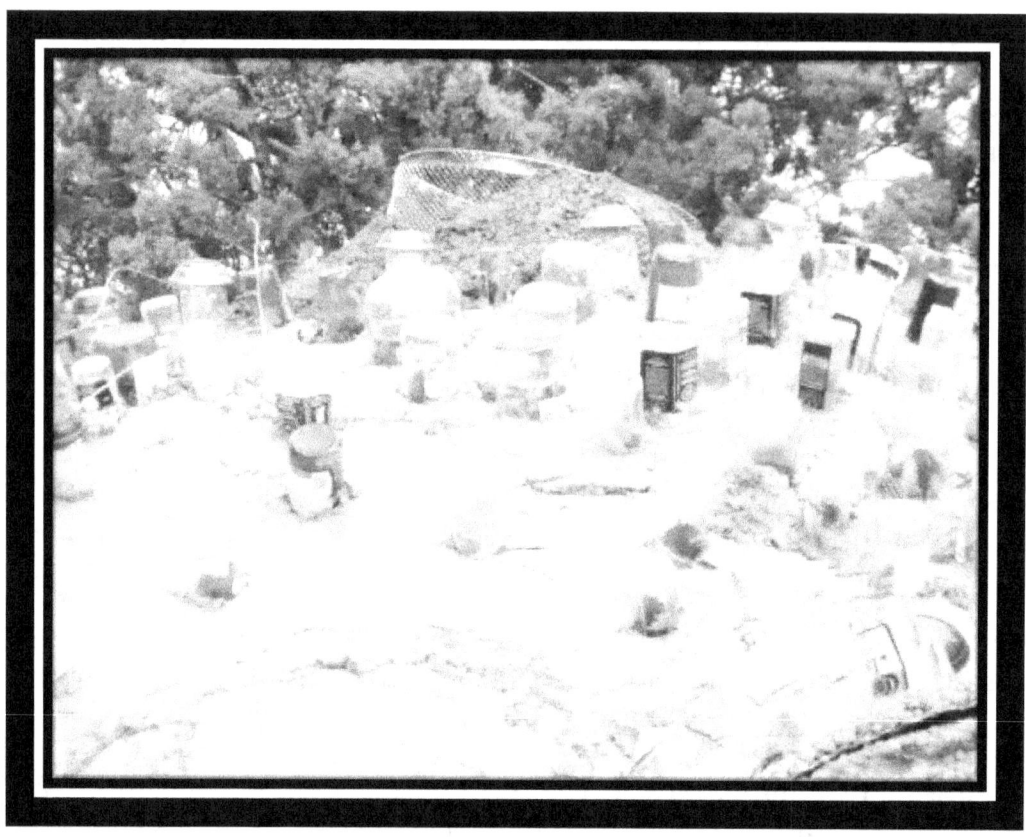

Finally setting in the top vent...a metal frame bike wheel, tilted SE--to be open sometimes, and 'plugged' with an insulated reed 'hair piece' other times.

7 20 13.

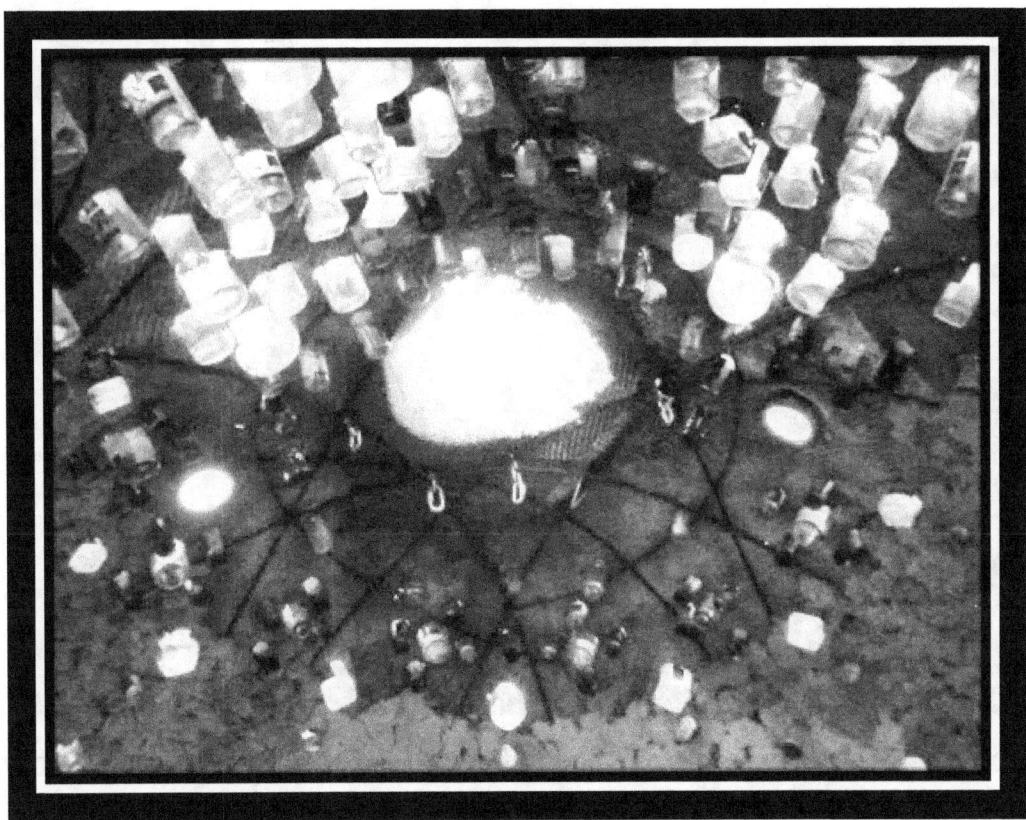

I put in some steel for hanging a swing or bed from later. All ready for infilling! 7 21 13.

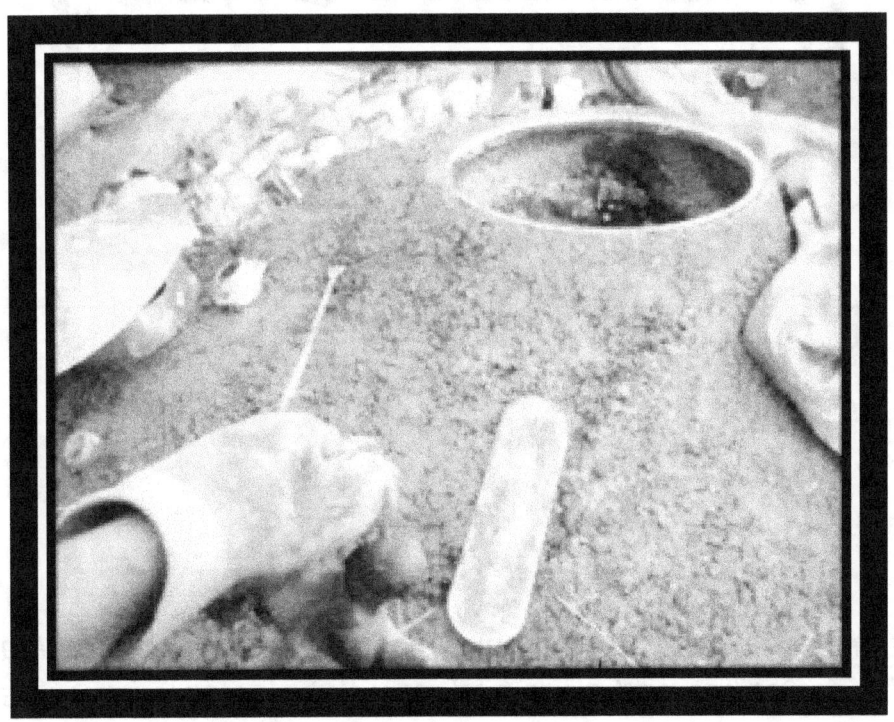

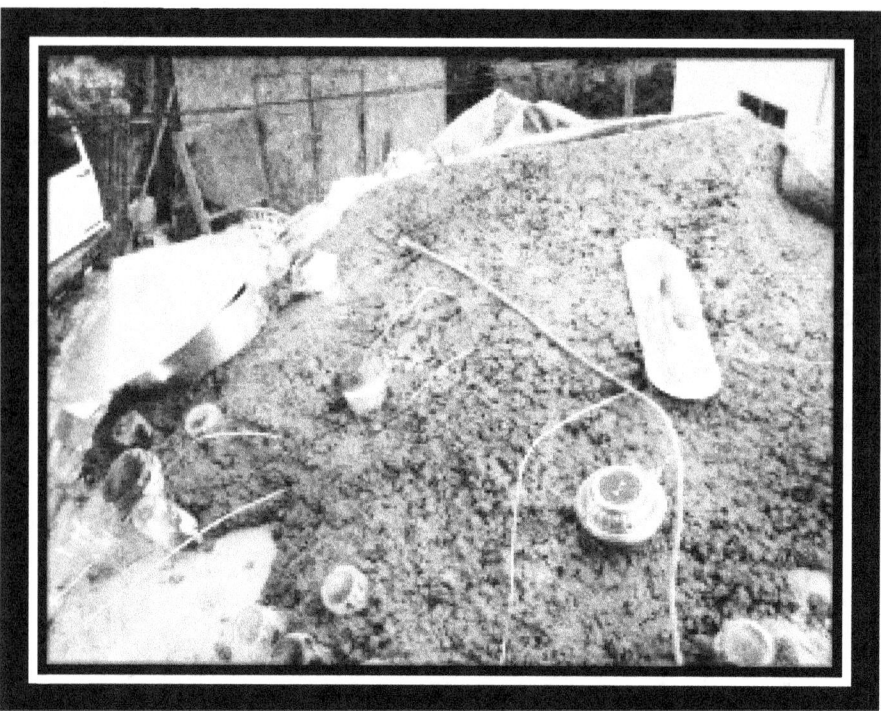

My support and aid for climbing up with buckets of pumicrete is this rope, which I hooked to steel and to strongest rebar spot....and which gave me a couple little blisters today, even through the rubber gloves. :) 7 21 13.

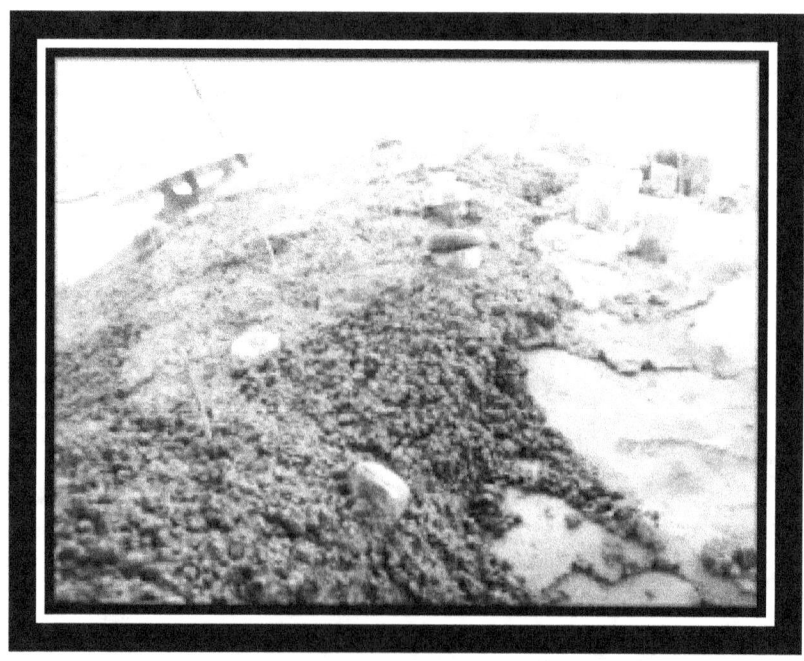

Going in rough, as usual, but I still have plaster to go...trying to balance myself and avoid the power line and glass and form the plaster is proving a challenge. I would not recommend putting glass in a curving dome like this

unless it is sealed up better and faster than I have done here. I DO love my solar LED light though! 7 21 13.

Pumicrete infill going in--3-6" deep. You can see my most crooked vent, and my much less than perfect bottle alignment and flush ends...you can also see the wires I am putting in for vines to grow on, some of my LED's, and how close the power and cable lines are to the top of the dome, which does make it a bit trickier in some spots. Also, you get a sense of how steep it is up here. 7 25 13.

Infills and Plasters

I gathered the adobe soil from the mountains nearby, in my van. I sifted it and mixed it with building sand and paper mash, and lime putty. It did make a pleasant mixture, and so far I have not seen any problems from it.

However, I changed my plans to hang a round swinging bed from the ceiling, something I put in a lot of planning to put in supports for, after thinking through the potential weaknesses. I would love to get to do some testing on padobe recipes and papercrete to see how they might stand up to high vibration domes, as I want to build play areas on the ceilings of larger scale play structures in the future.

The pumice is volcanic material mined from the nearby Jemez mountains. Making it a fortuitously accessible building material for me. I drove to Espanola several times in my van and loaded a cubic yard or two into the back of my van with snow shovels.

I would show up on my way to the lake, with my kayaks tied on top, and the back tarped off like an interior truck bed. The men that work there were happy to help me load it up, though they are used to loading trucks with tractors, and I don't think see many women in the loading yard.

The initial warm red-brown color of the infill changed the way the bottle walls looked when I came around them, and I still am not sure if i like the cool gray, the warm red or yellow, or the cold white finish best.

5 7 13. All three back panels are up! Many, many lessons learned so far. In hindsight, I would have started my pattern a row or two further up, and been more diligent with plumbing and leveling each bottle brick to every other along the way. It takes a fair amount of patience to do that in the first place, especially with 9" long bricks, then factor in slumping, which goes on longer with papercrete than regular plaster, and you see where it is easy for things to get a bit crooked. I am still pretty happy with it overall. My next two side panels are a bit more intimidating for me, but I should be starting them very soon!

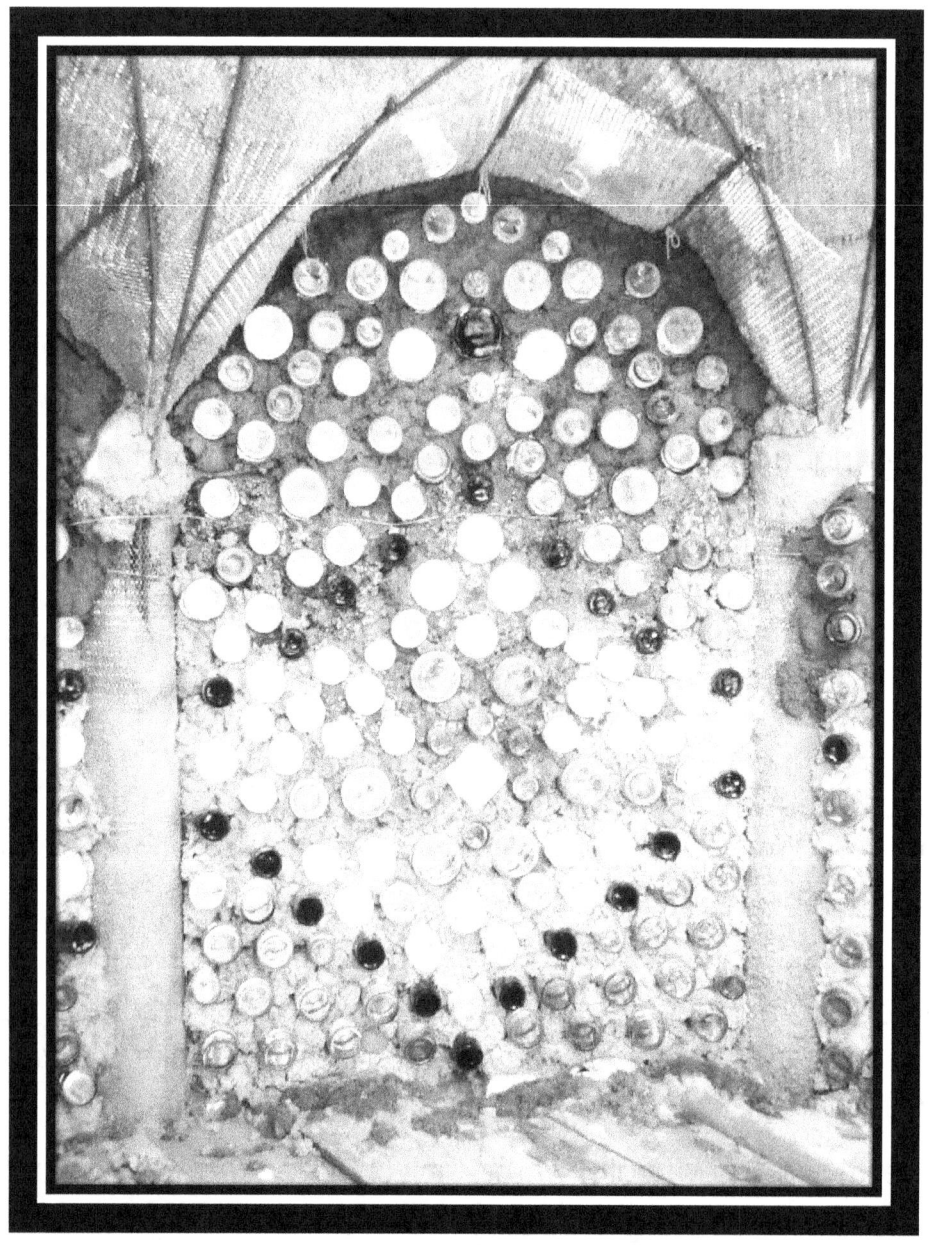

The largest of my 3 back panels. I 'accidentally' crowded my top line in a couple spots (mainly because I forgot to mark or note where it was until after I passed it), which will present plastering/finishing challenges in the near future. They should fit right in! 5 7 13.

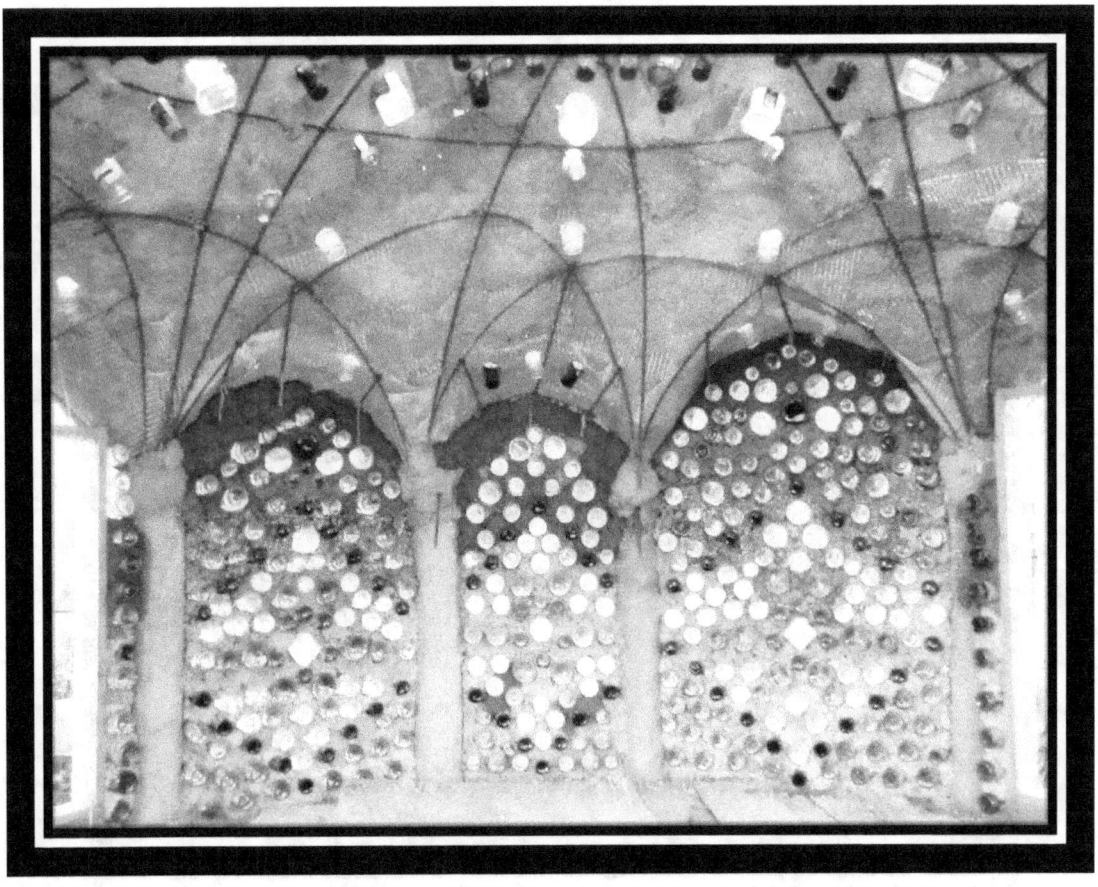

5 7 13. Trying to decide what color my plaster infill should be. Thinking I like the look for the wet/darker infill better. I could go dark red, green, yellow, gray, brown. Any thoughts on dark or light? Warm or cold?

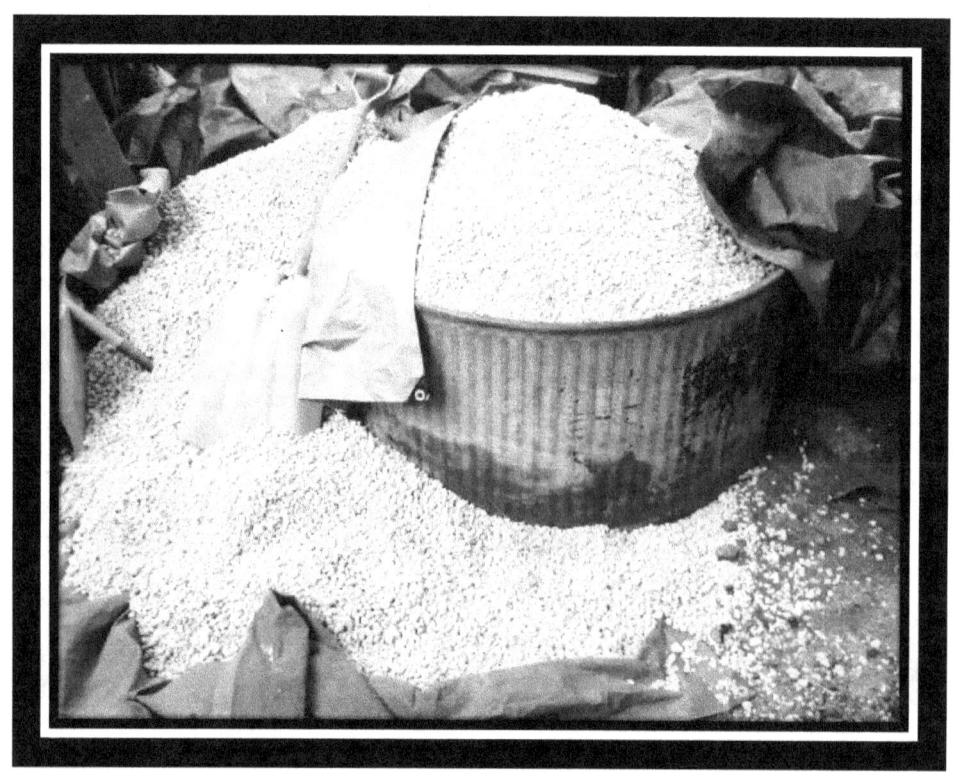

Pumice! I think this might be enough to finish my dome! 7 12 13.

(Update--had to get another load, used about 3cy altogether for infill, plus sculpting and plaster yet to come. 9 10 13.)

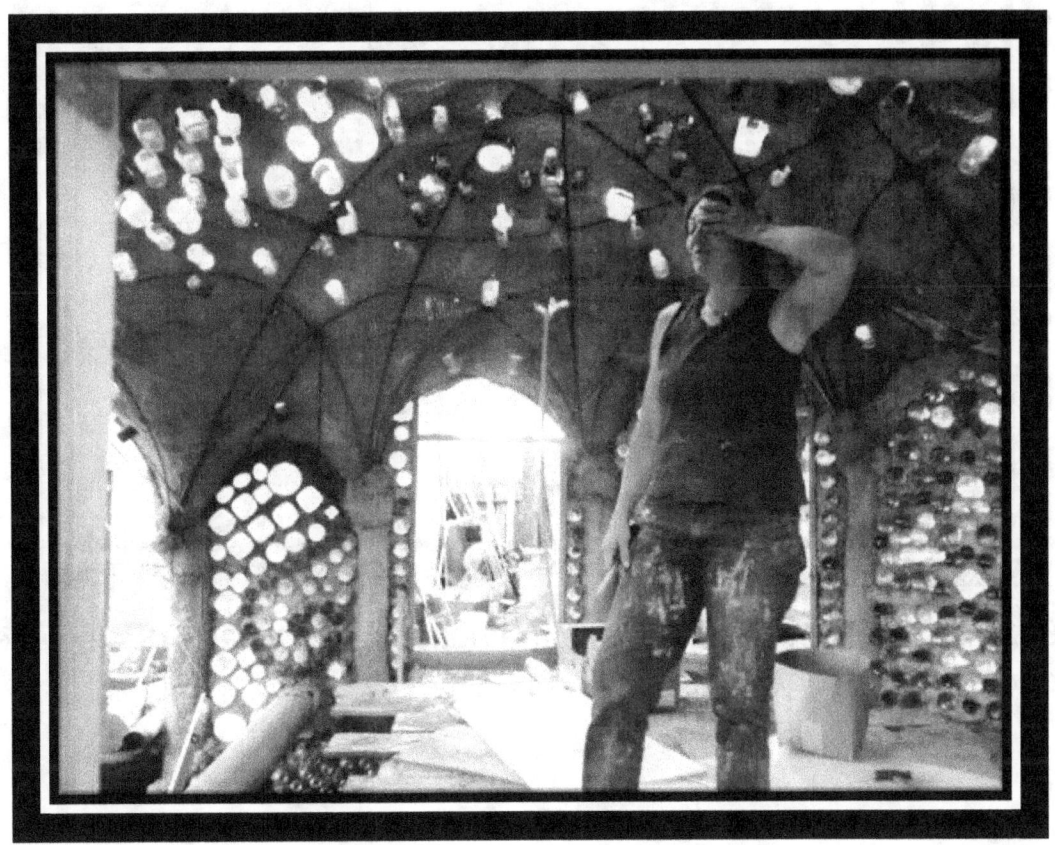

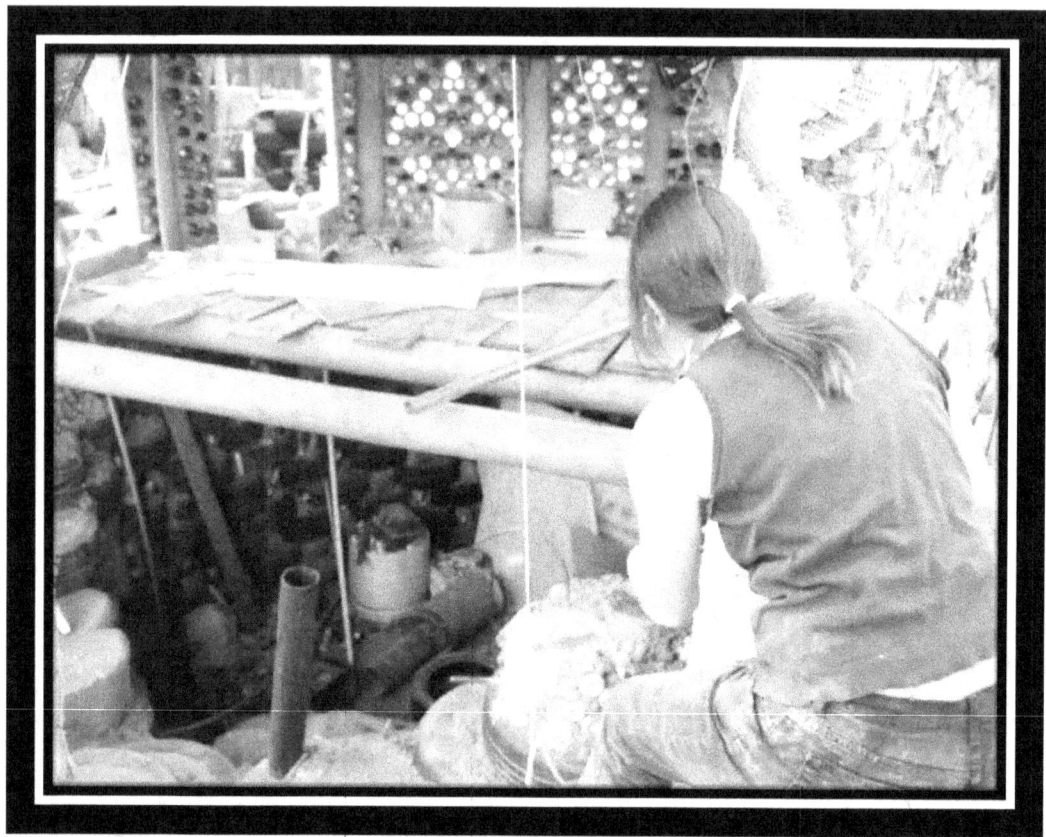

May 19, 2013. I still have to 'pack out' the bottom and plaster. It may take all summer or longer to dry if I use clay, so I may end up doing all but the last layer in Quikrete.

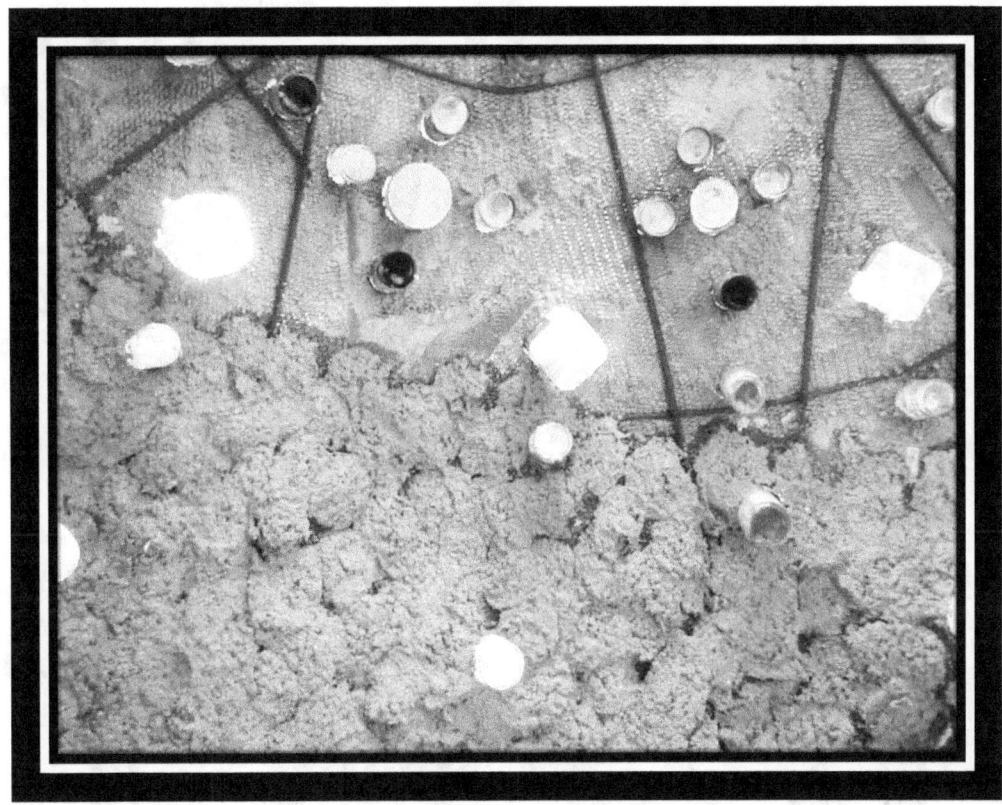

PaperAdobe infilling on the ceiling, one 'spitwad/handfull' at a time. Still a couple more layers to go. 6 12 13.

PaperAdobe infill drying nicely...remind me never to do this many bottles in one wall again, as the cleaning and pointing and plastering and infilling is pretty tedious--not to mention there is so much room for error. It should be ready for plaster on the next round. 6 13 13.

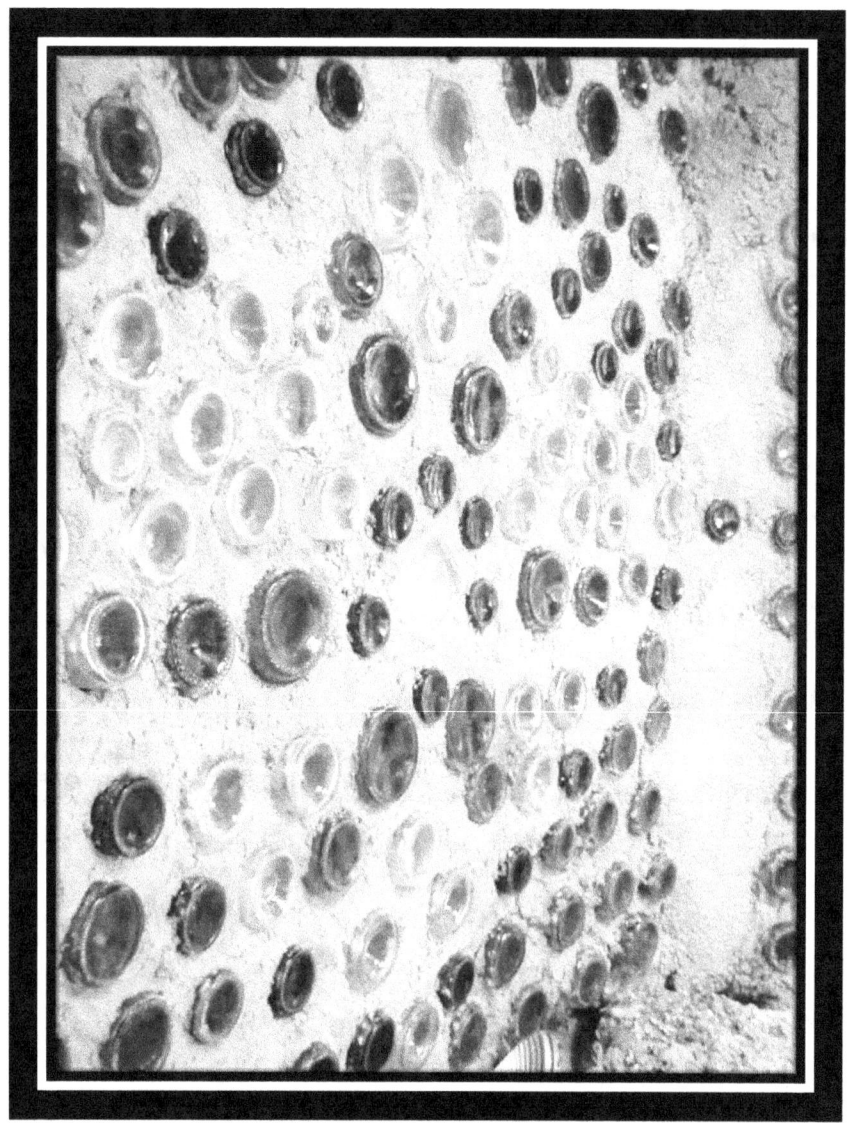

6 13 13. PaperAdobe infill going in. I must come up with some better method of spacing the ends if I do anything patterned like this again. I already knew this, but 'braved' it anyway, and now will get to look at the very imperfect results as they are locked in. I am still happy with it, but I did make plenty of mistakes.

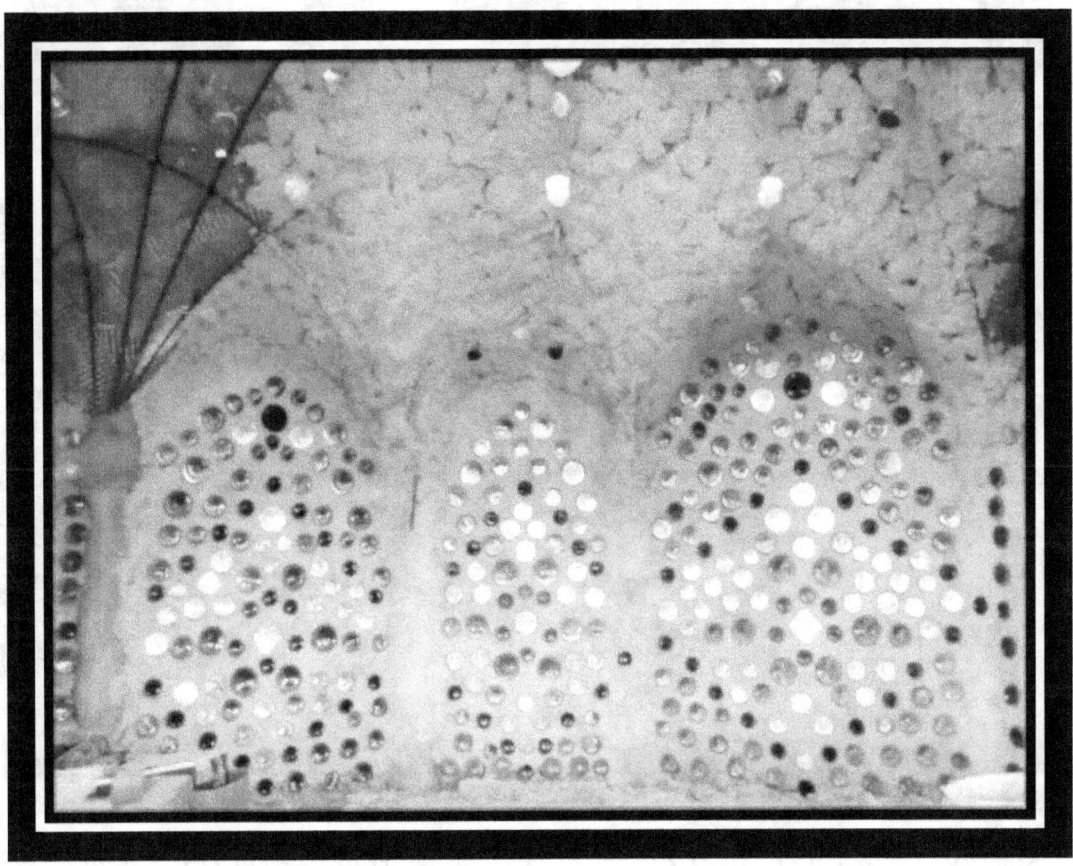

Paperadobe infill going in inside. Still much more and another layer to do on the dome, and then, plaster! 6 19 13.

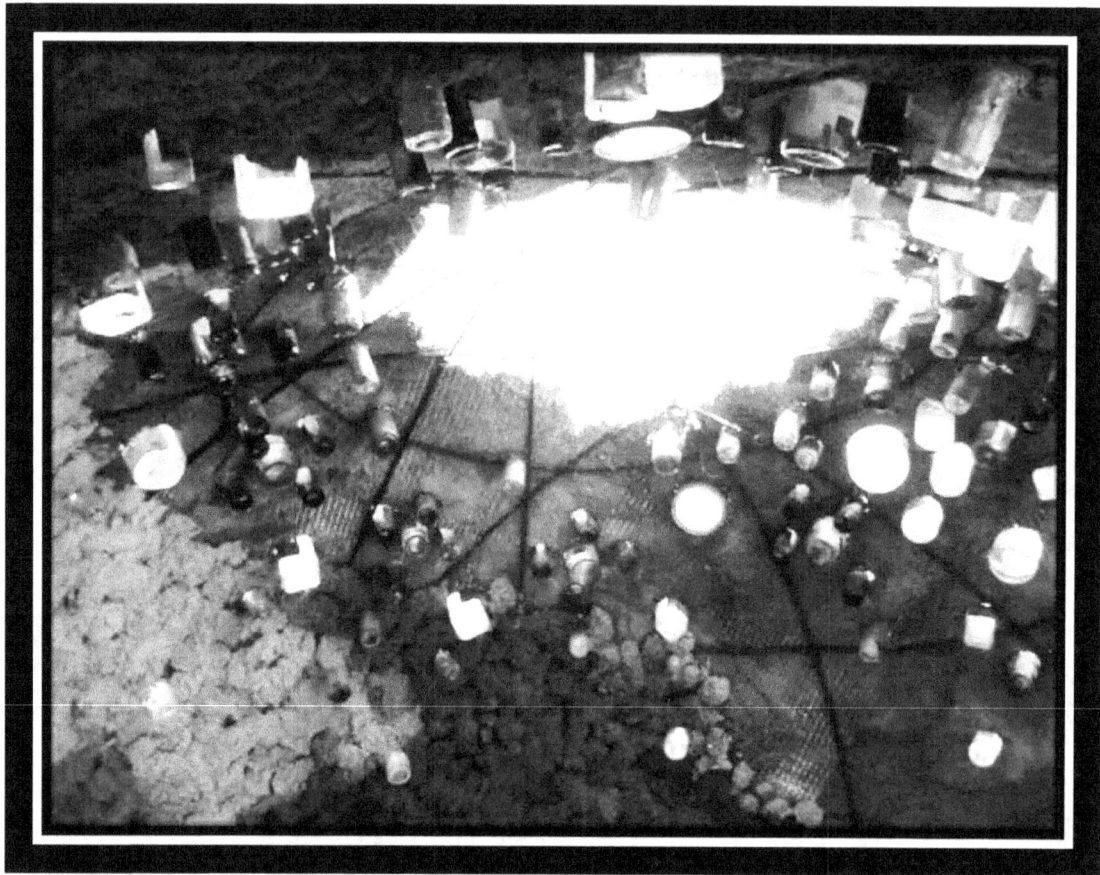

Slowly, slowly; handful by handful. PaperAdobe infill is going in. Still gotta do some framework for a window/opening up there before I can finish plastering then infilling the top. Check out the new red clay! 6 30 13.

I used many different variations of infills and plasters. I experimented, based on notes from other builders and my own, growing body of experience.

I continued to use papercrete when I was building the glass walls, in the style of cordwood buildings (Ref Rob Roy*) and using what I learned working with the Earthship Biotecture crew on the second build I got to work on with them.

Papercrete is basically paper pulp, lime powder, portland cement, and sand. The amounts of each can vary quite a bit, depending on the strength or insulative properties you want to end up with. I also added engineering fibers to many of my batches of papercrete and pumicrete.

I got a couple loads of pumice in my van for this project. It happens to be mined in some mountains nearby, so picking it up and loading it myself made it an affordable option. It is a volcanic product, so it bonds with the lime and the cement very well. I used large chunks for the outer infill on the dome, and smaller pieces, all the way to a fine dust, for different mixes of infill and plaster.

I made it a fun excursion most of the times, loading up the kayaks,, lining the back half of my van with tarps, shoveling it in, or watching the guys who worked there doing it (they usually just dump a tractor load, but since it was going in my van, and I was willing to shovel it in myself, they often ended up doing it for me, somewhat begrudgingly.

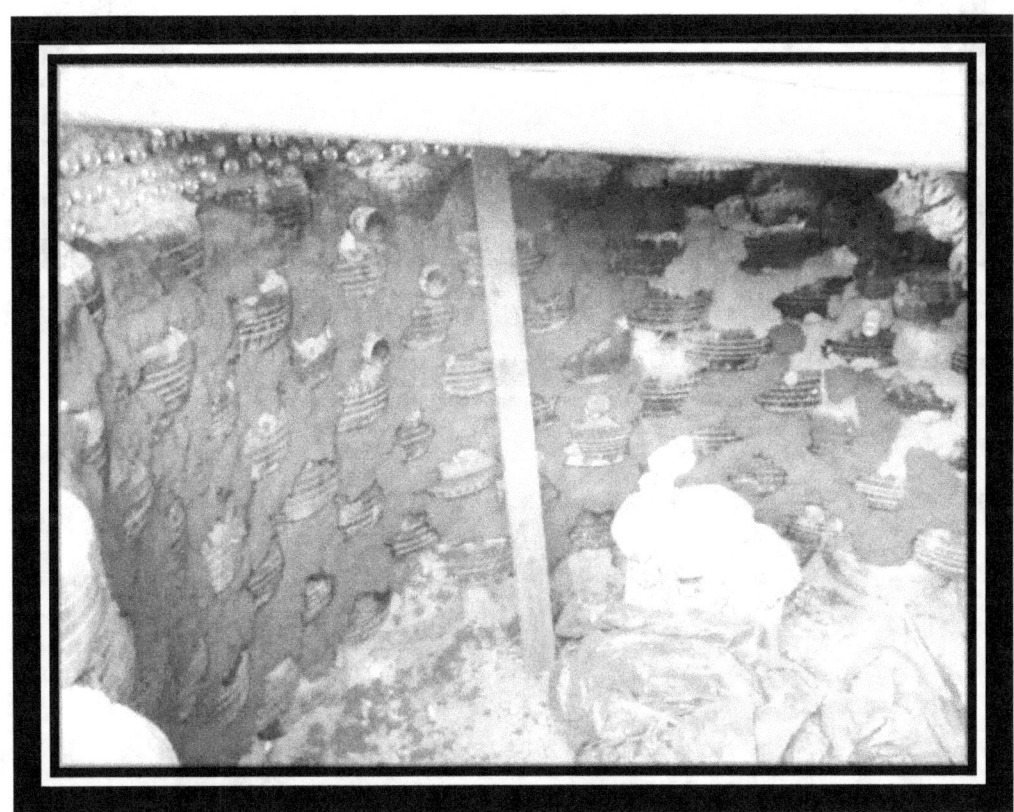

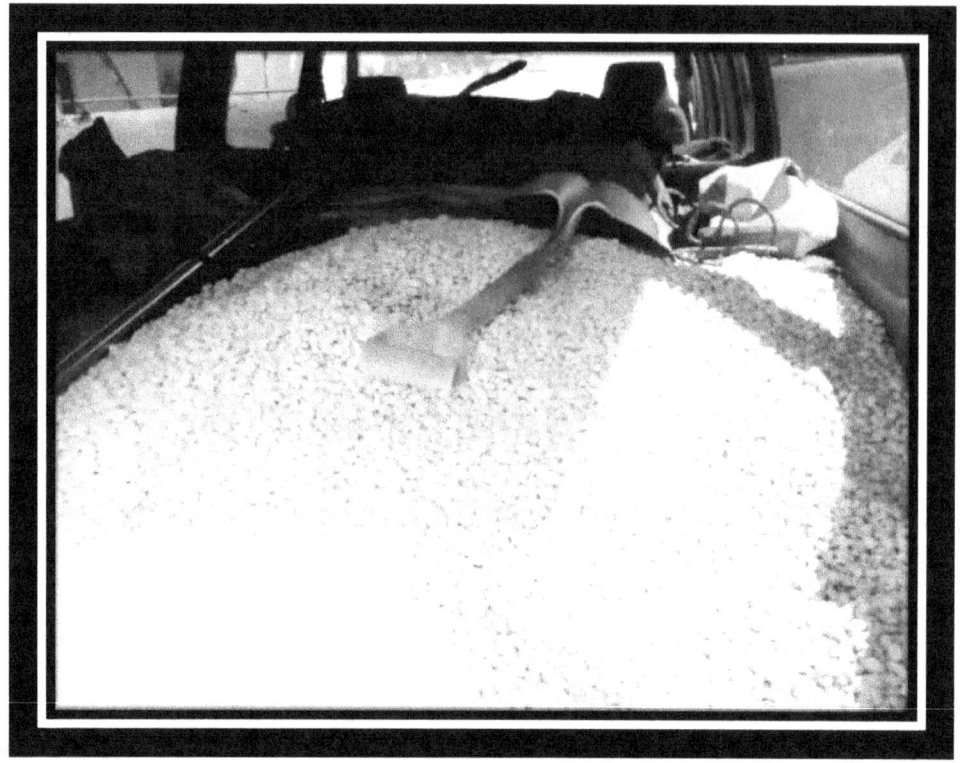

8 13 13. Van half-full of pumice. 9 7 13.

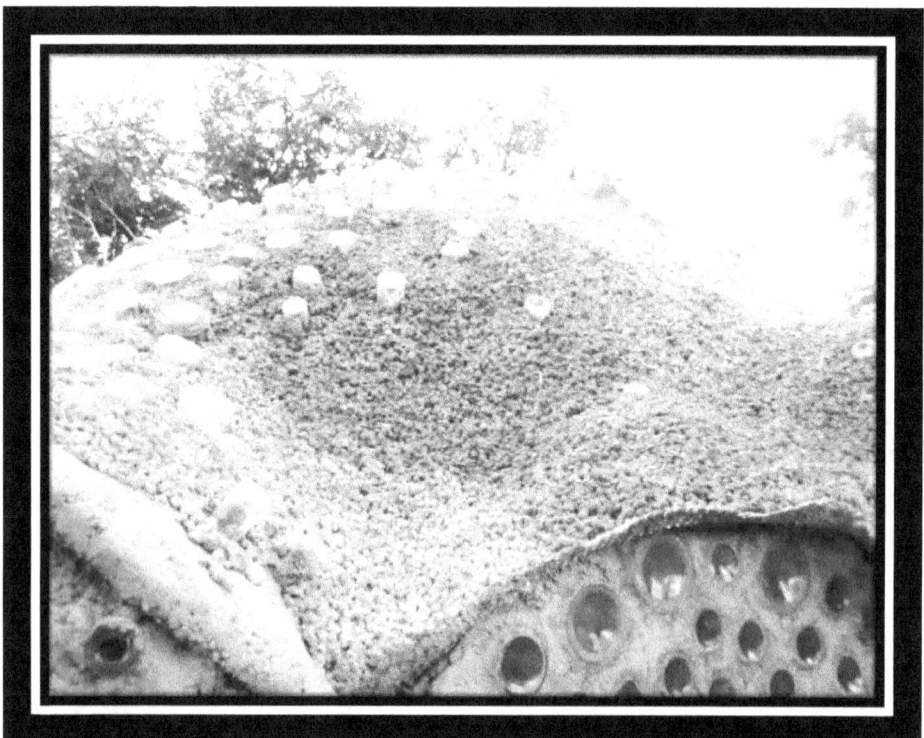

9 9 13. Pumice infill roughed in.

The Head Hutt Picture Book

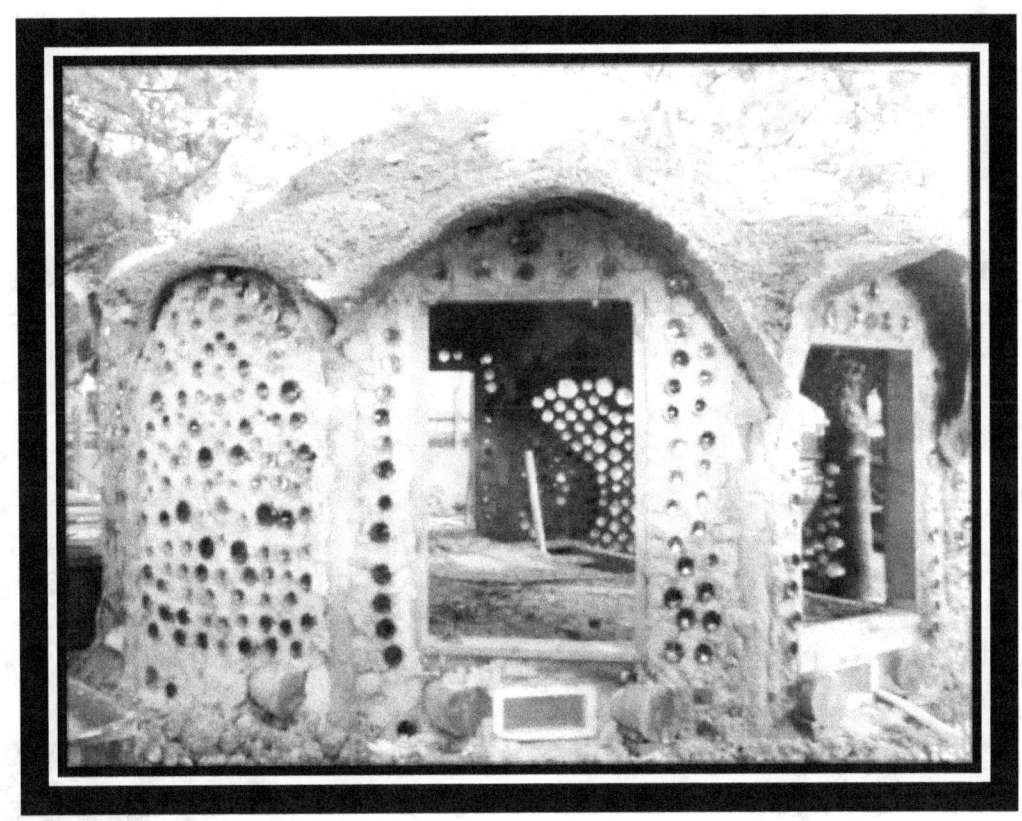

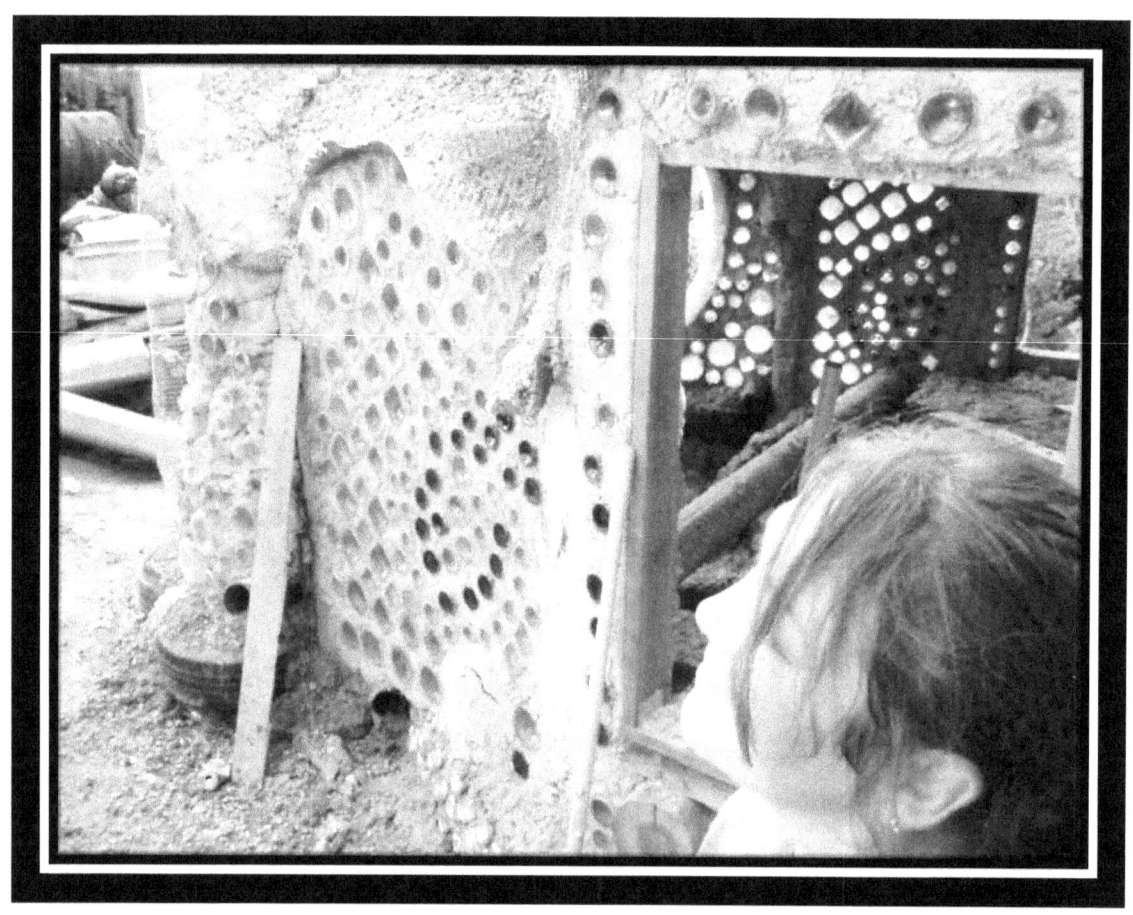

9 9 13. Pumice infill roughed in. Still needs shaping and plastering/finishing.

The Head Hutt Picture Book

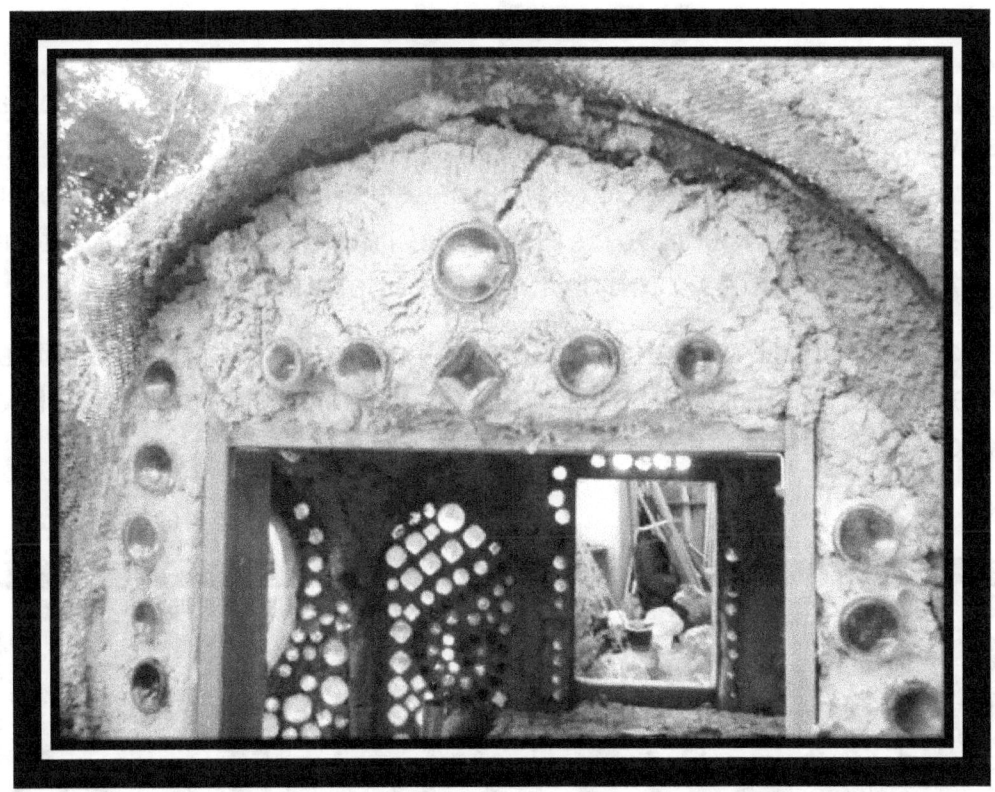

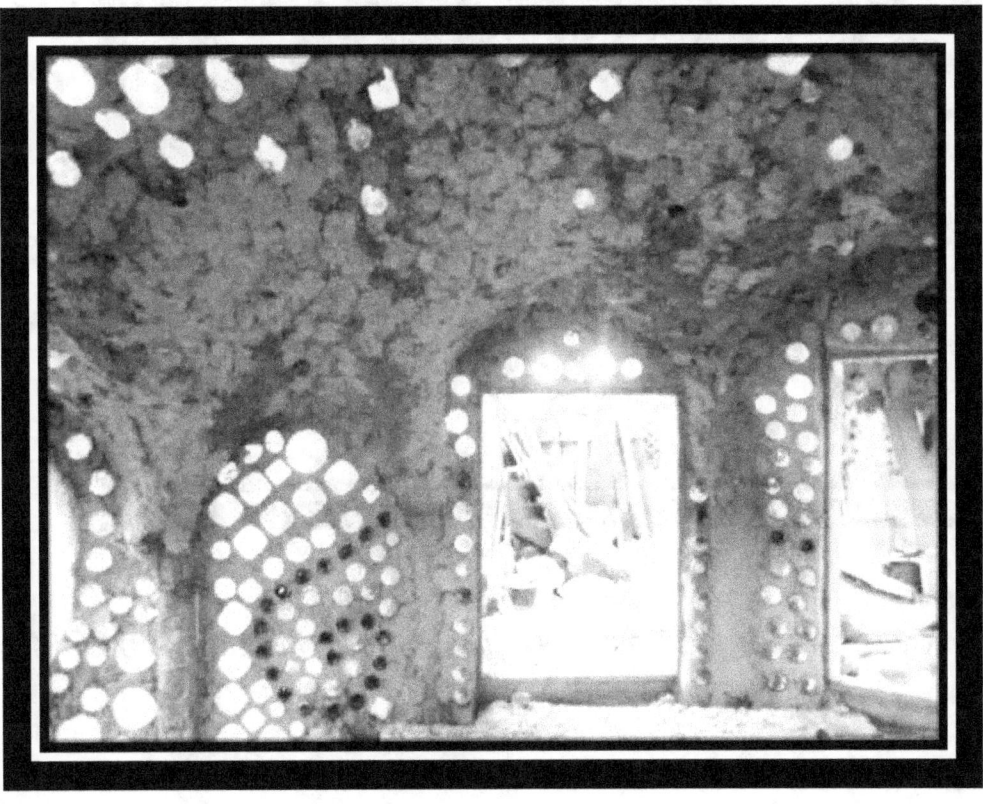

I found a pocket of high clay content earth in some mountains nearby and brought several loads of it in my van also. I screened it and mixed it with sand, straw, and of course, water, and in some cases paper pulp (the difference between padobe and adobe/cob). I also used lime in most of my batches of padobe, adobe, papercrete, pumicrete, and paperpumicrete.

I used padobe for some of the inner dome (a decision I regret more than any other, if there even are any other regrets), and cob/adobe for the bulk of the infill between tires in the bottom floor.

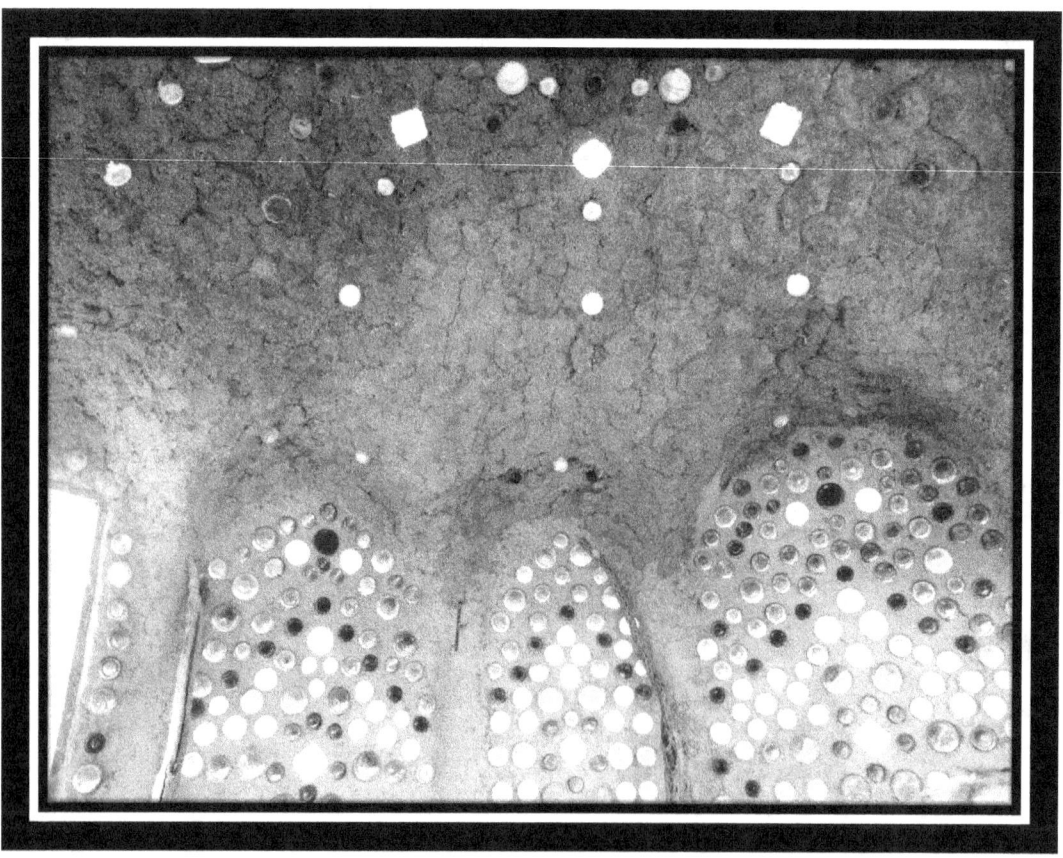

Getting closer to ready to plaster, against seemingly so many odds. 5 5 2014.

Infilling approaches finished. Against seemingly so many odds. I can hardly believe I plastered over one of my squares, given the amount of effort I spent attempting this 'pattern'. I may have to chisel it out.

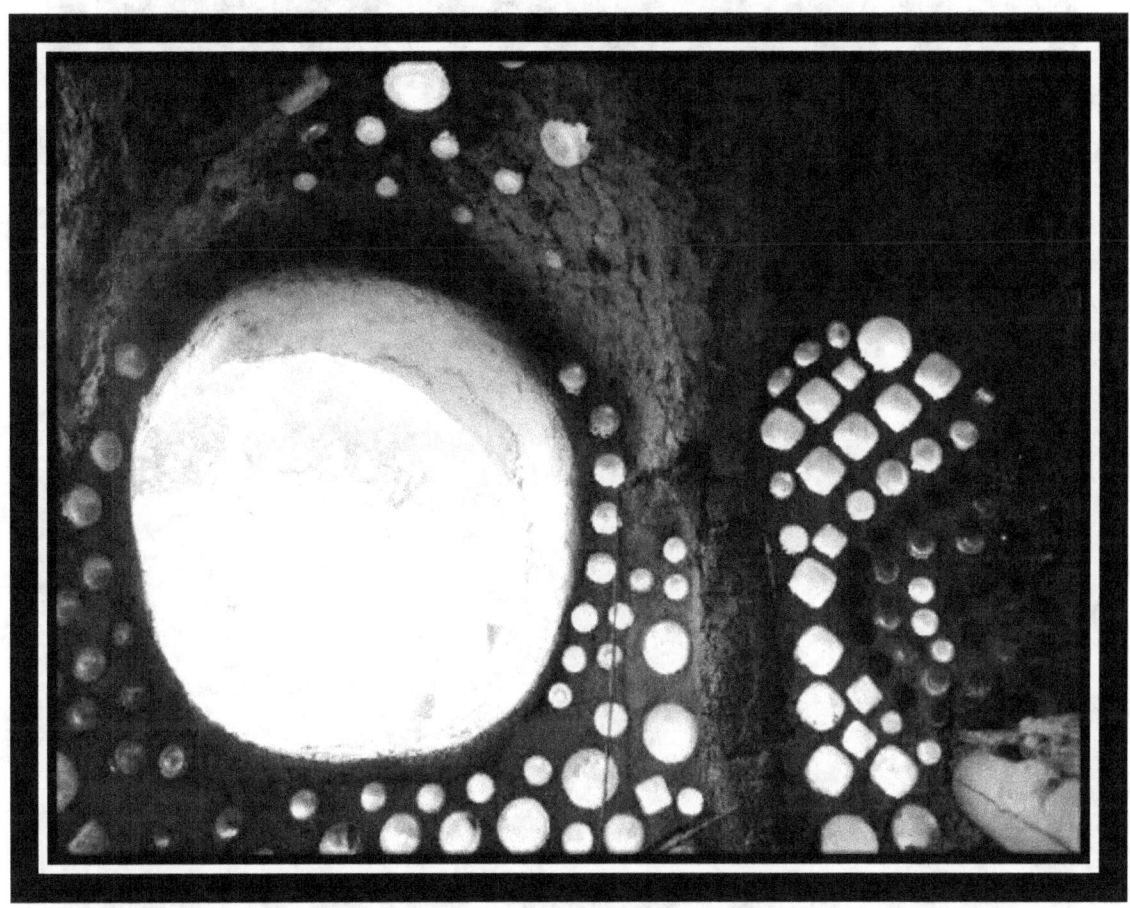

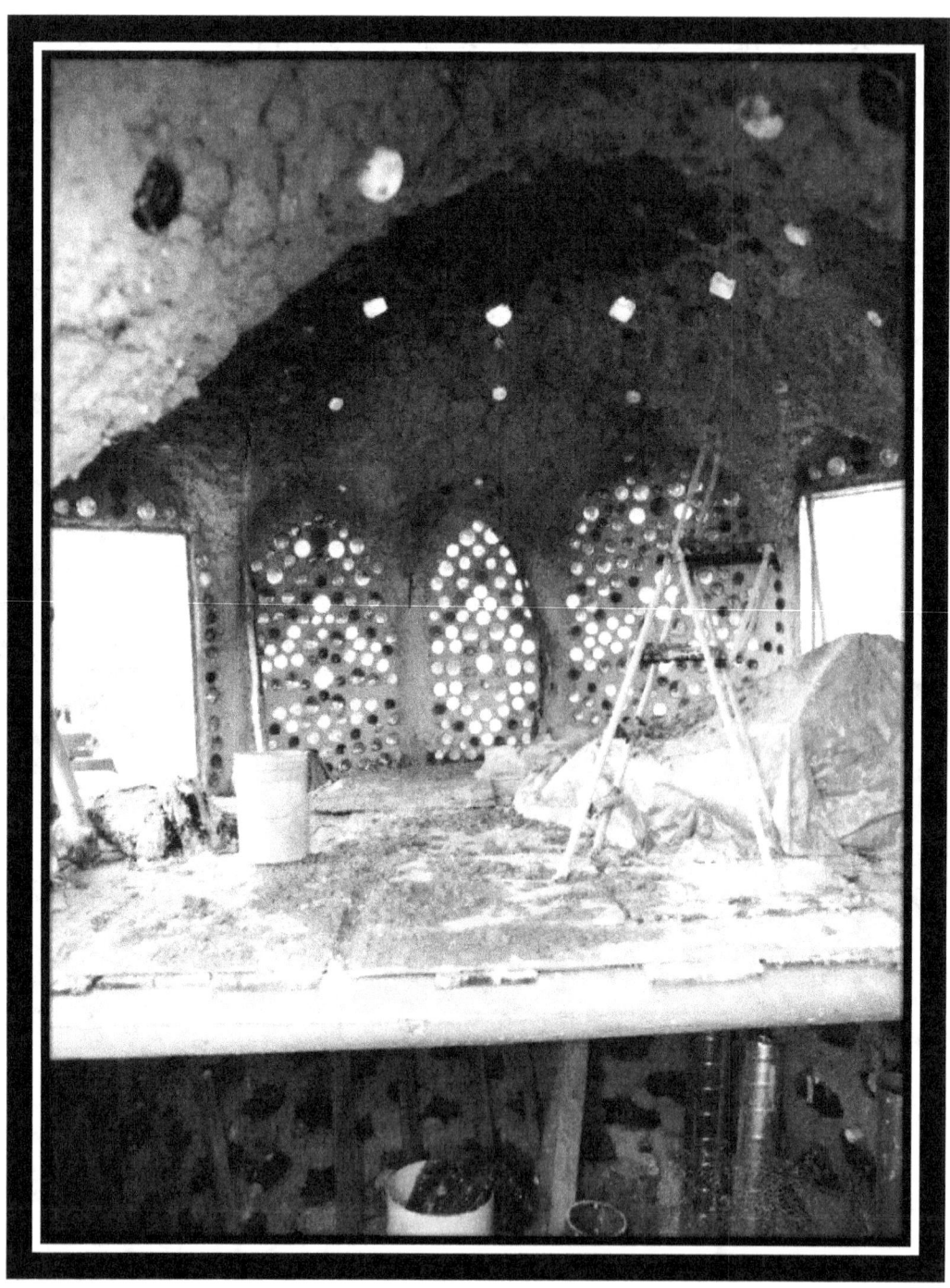

After almost a 10 months break. Infilling almost complete. Then comes plastering. 5 5 14. Infilling approaches finished...against seemingly so many odds.

5 5 2014.

Prince Orion Loving the Sun.

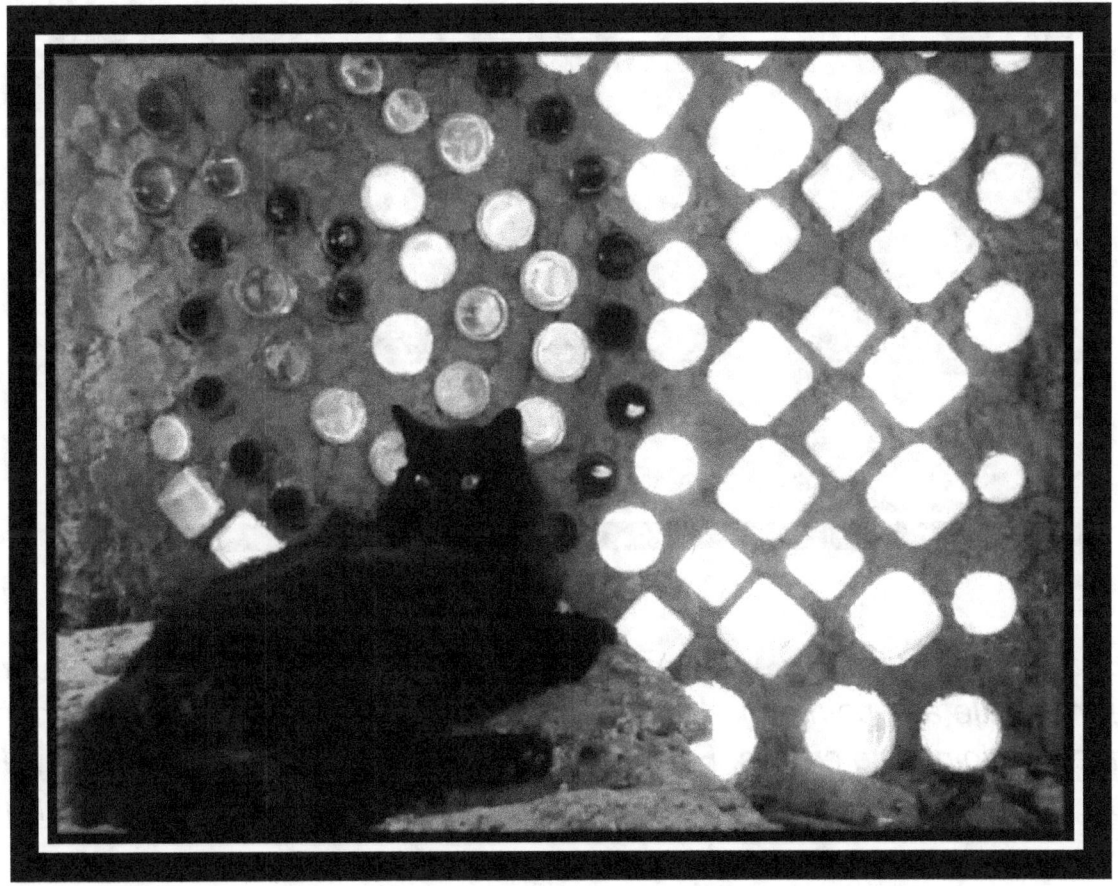

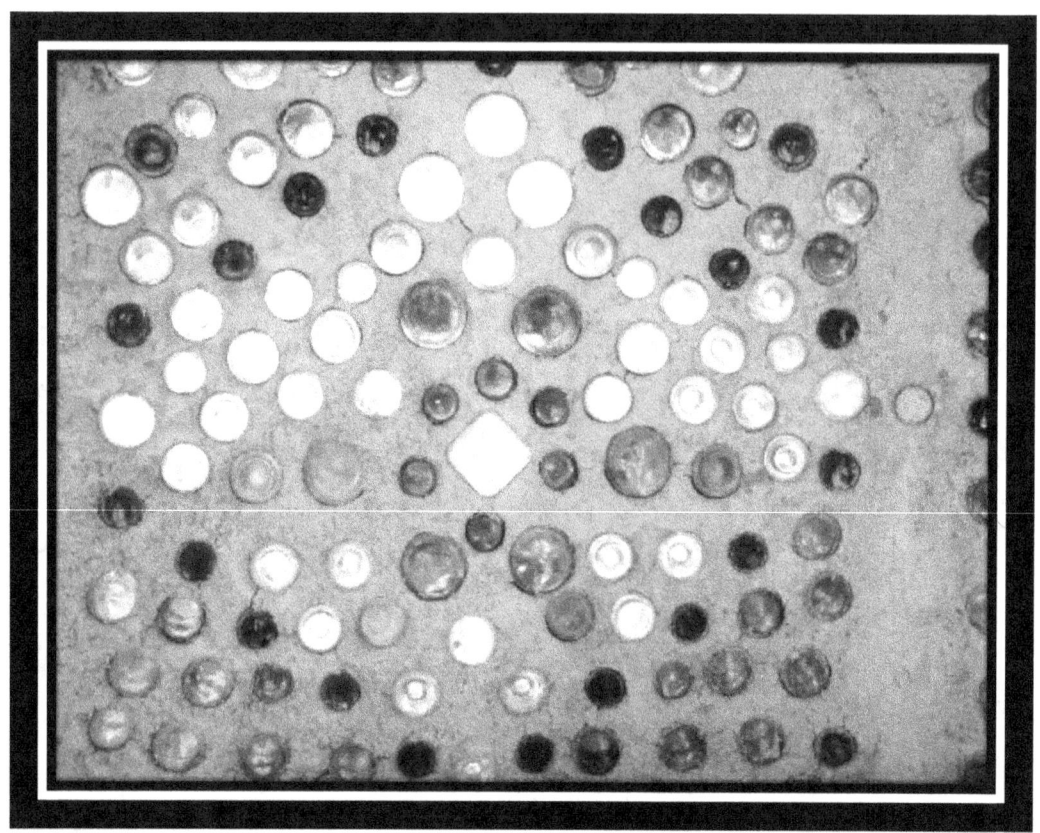

About a year after infilling, you can see some cracking in the padobe, but not bad for as little as I pointed it. I will be plastering over this, so I get another chance at minimizing cracks. For the curious, this infill is made from recycled paper, lime, clay-rich earth, and a little borax. Great stuff for indoor infilling! 6 21 14.

The Head Hutt Picture Book

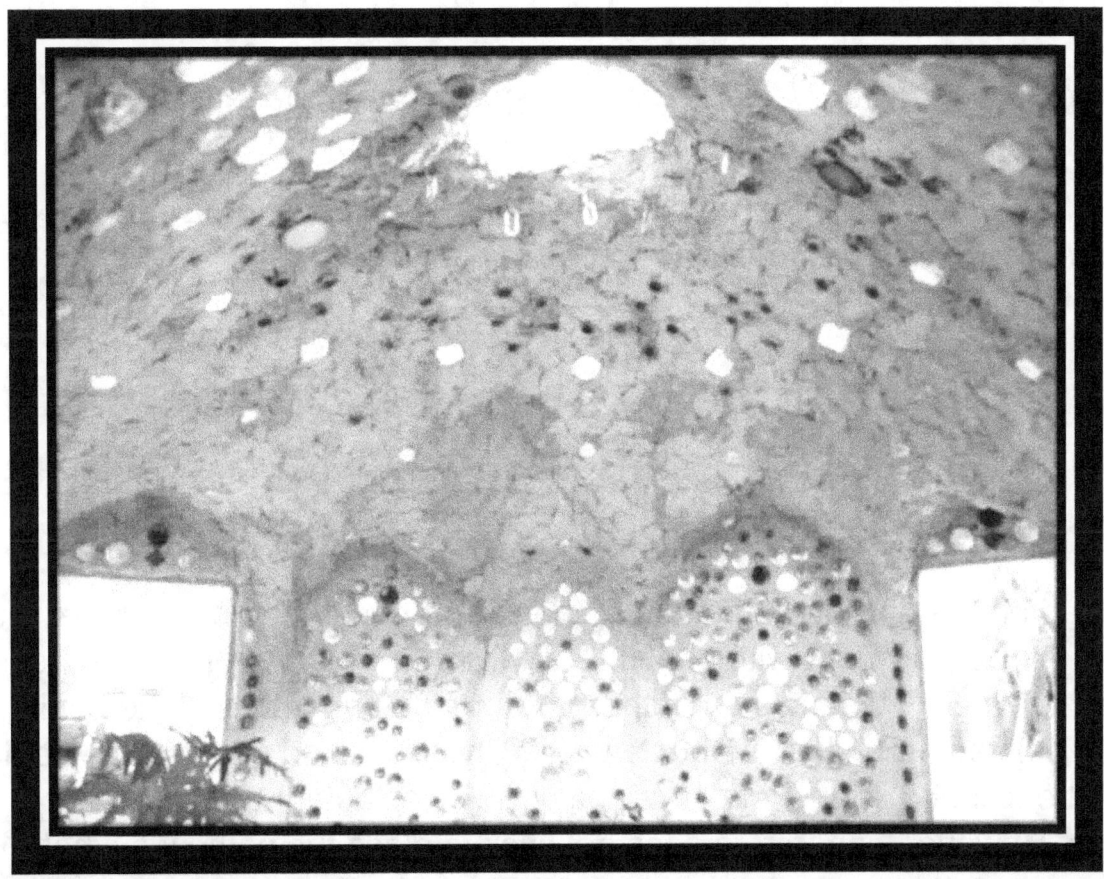

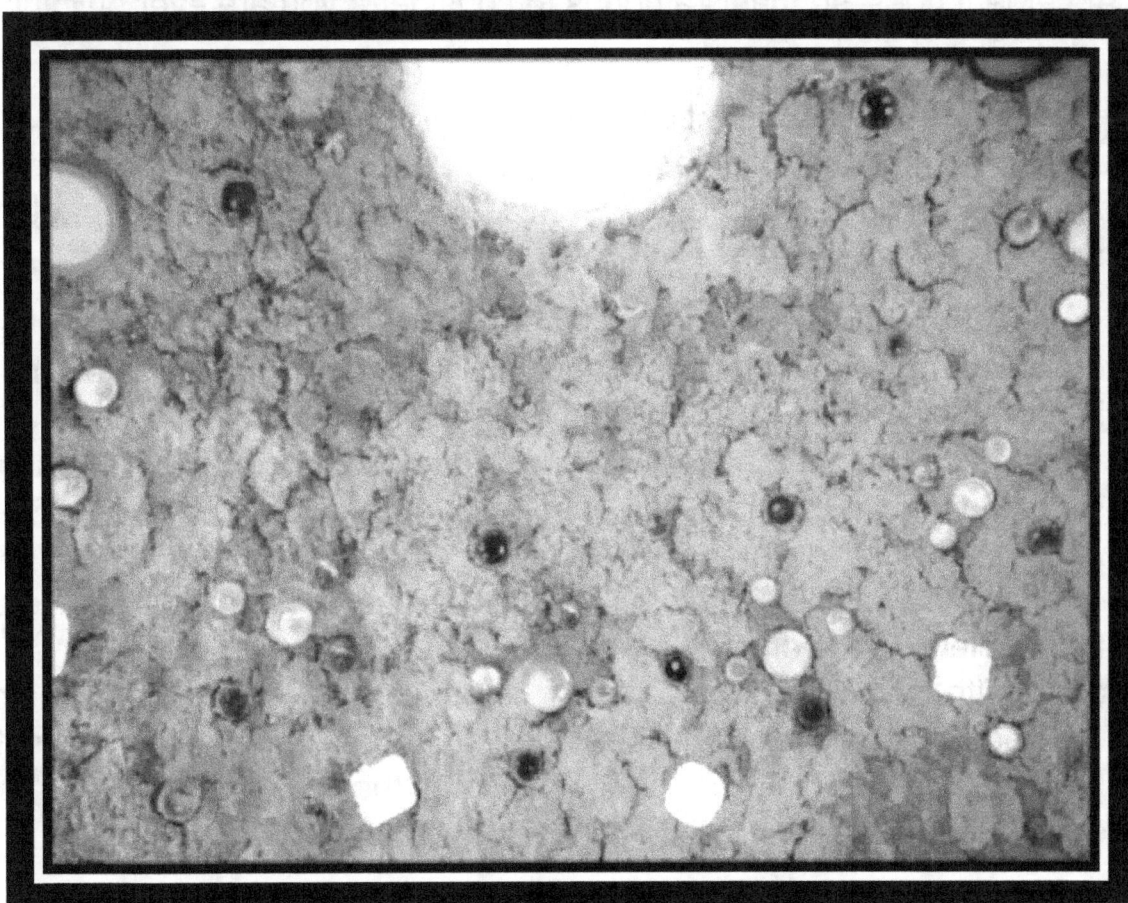

Looking up. Ready for plaster. Just waiting for more materials to gather. 6 21 14.

7 10 14. Waiting for a bit more paper and then starts interior. Dear Shredded Paper Fairy: More Shredded Paper Please!

PLASTERDOME!!!

I finished off the outside of the dome, the overhangs, the decorative details, and all the outside walls with papercrete, with some pumice in some cases (paperpumicrete). I made a smoother mix for plastering around the bottle ends. I pointed around all the bottles carefully, with good results. The bottles can to be cleaned after every round of infilling or plastering, which was tedious. However, papercrete does not stick to glass the same way that regular cement does, so that is a bonus to consider if you are ever building a bottle wall.

Papercrete is pretty neat stuff. It can be made in variety of strengths and consistency. It is not used for load bearing structures, generally, though it can be made quite strong. With lime, and pumice or any volcanic ash product, it gets harder over time.

In case you are wondering, it does take in moisture a bit if it is soaked in water and not sealed, but it does not break down. I made more than 25 different experimental mixes when I was building the Foo Dog Mega-Sculpture, alongside and just before the Head Hutt, and dried a ball or cup full of each one as I did, then I left the collection of them out for years. None of them have decomposed so far. A few of them, which I used natural herb powders in and no lime, did get some spots of mold. In a damp climate this might become a potential problem. In the dry southwest where I am currently building, it is not a concern. With the addition of even 10% cement, there is no mold. Some of the more papery mixes, with just lime and/or diatomaceous earth do get soft when wet, though still hold their shape so long as they are not pressed/gouged/put under pressure while they are soft or wet.

The final layers outside were finer, and pressed firmer. If I got cracks from shrinkage during drying, then I went over it again. I over-lapped my cold seams as best I could, an tried to hide them in a zig-zag, triangular-petal pattern. I also did this inside, with a paper-pumice-lime (no cement) mix. It was difficult to do the infilling and especially the plastering on the top of the dome. I kept a safety rope on myself, it felt more steep from up there than it looked from below, it was somewhat slippery, I had power lines to navigate, and lots and lots of bottles. And again, all needing cleaned off after every pass.

I dub thee: Ready for plaster!!! 5 25 14.

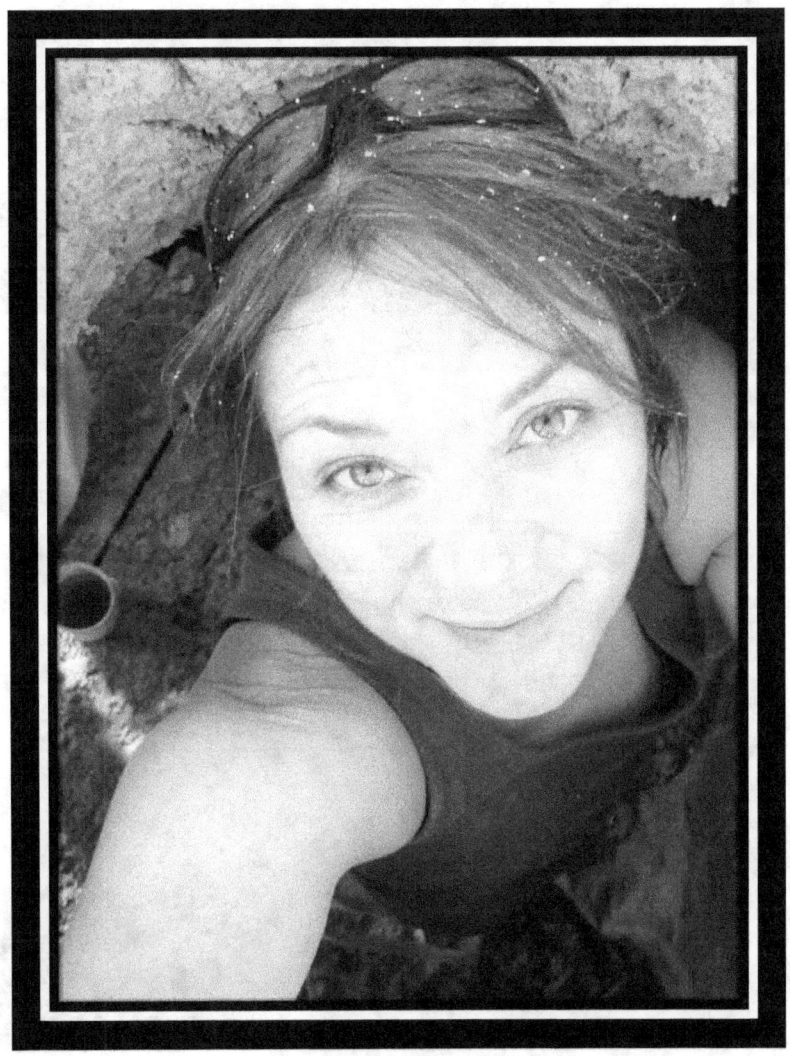

Looking in from the top of the HH. Getting ready to plaster this bitch! 5 27 14.

Plastering begins! It is slow going overhead, and my plaster is not as smooth as one might like...but, I am thrilled to be at this stage! 7 30 14.

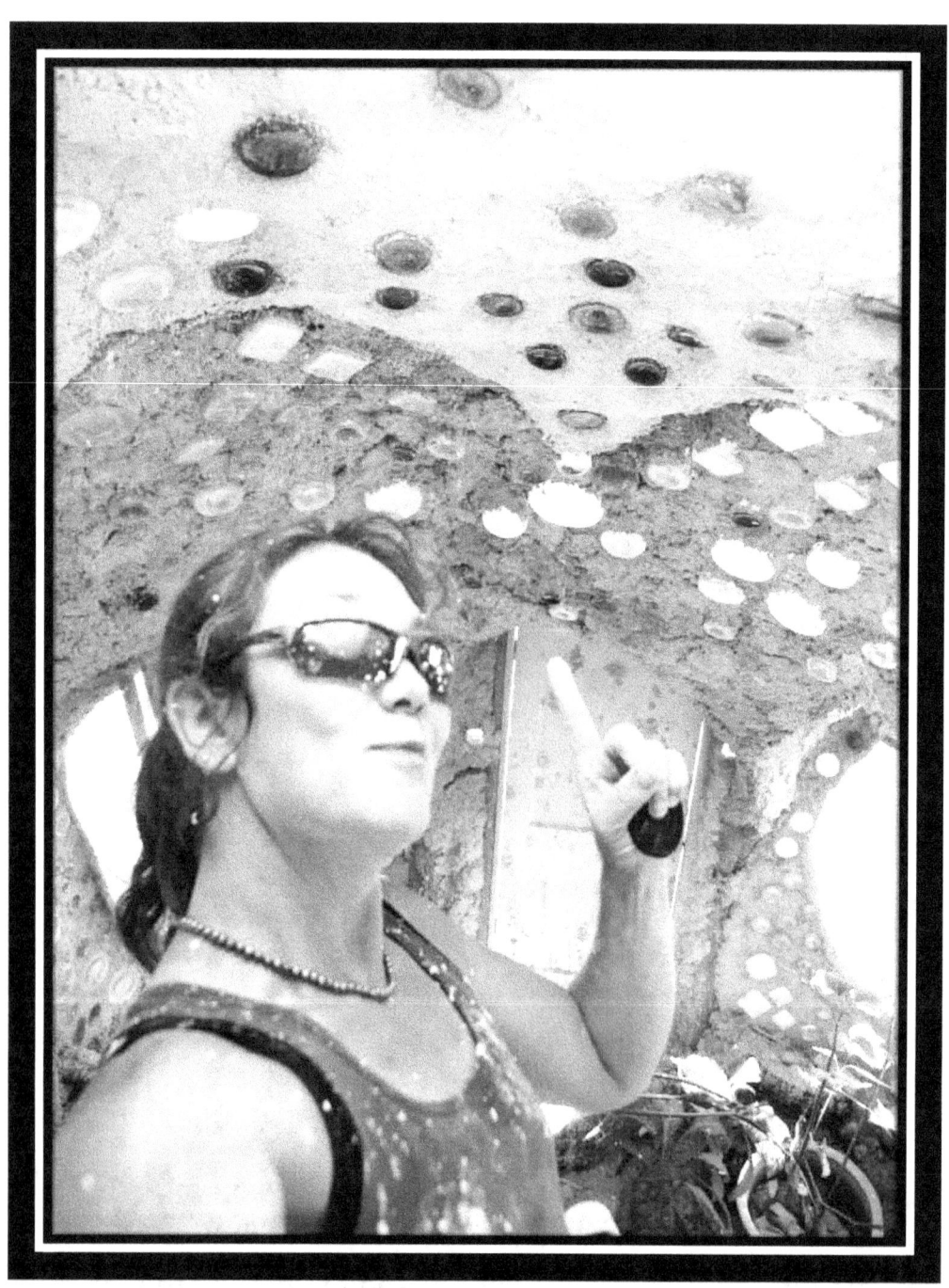

The Head Hutt Picture Book

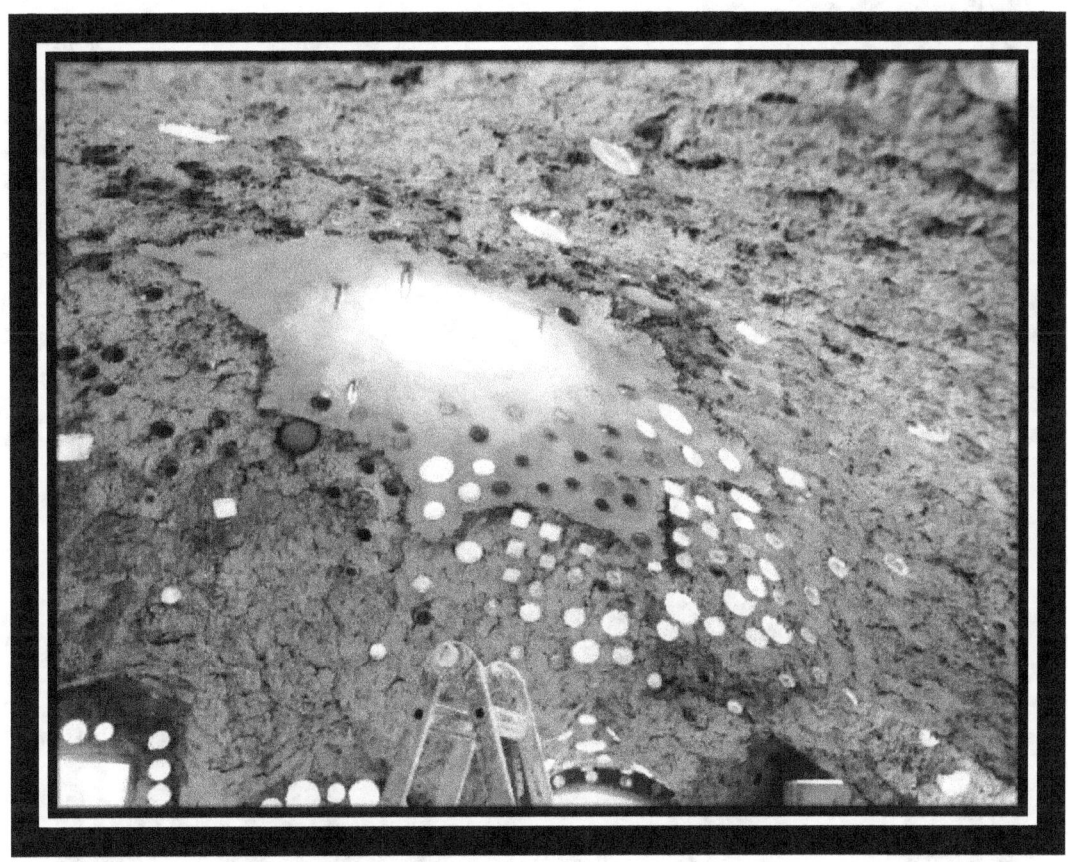

The Head Hutt Picture Book

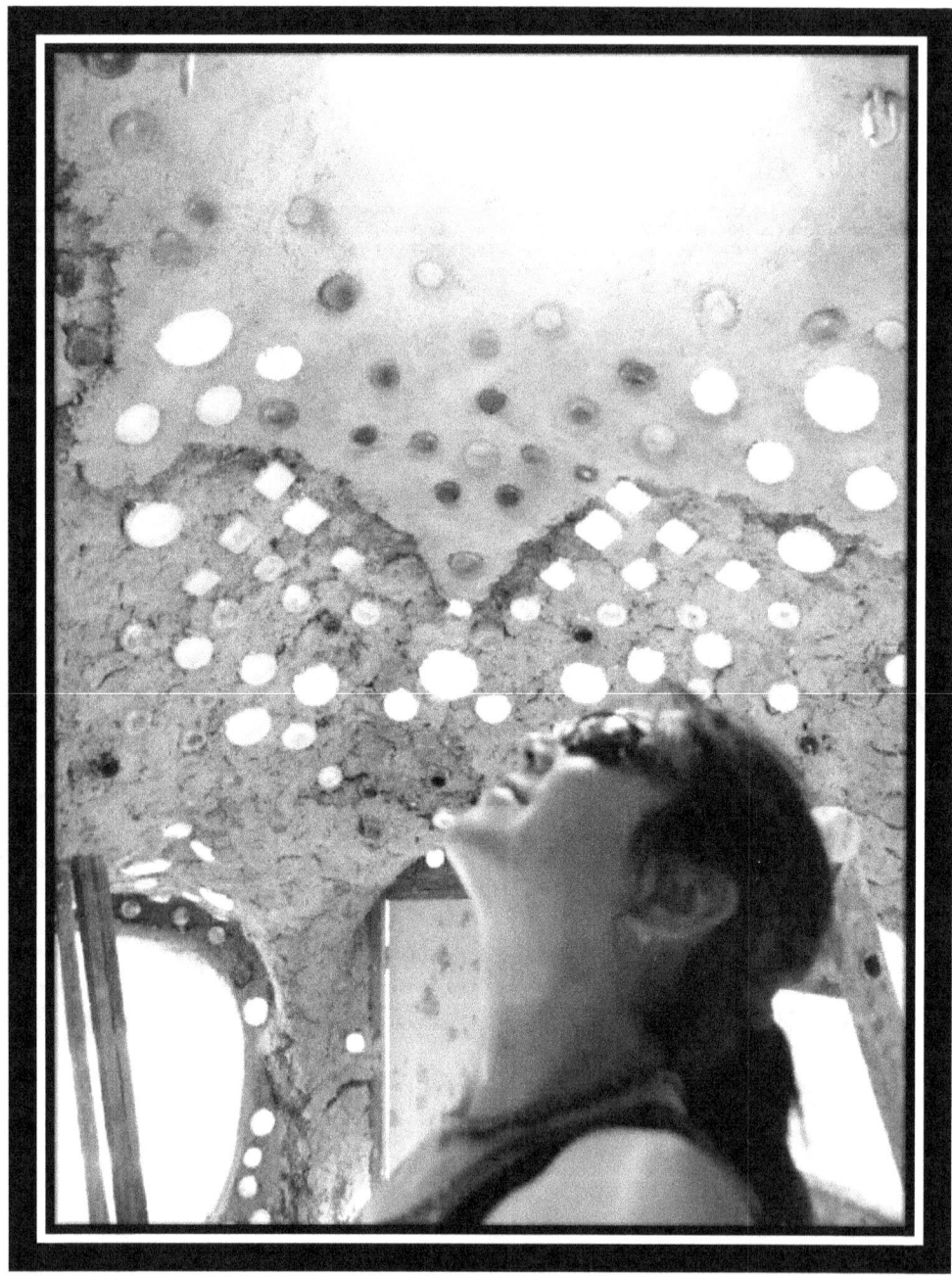

I am going yellow! ...and white....and maybe green... =P It is slow going overhead, and my plaster is not as smooth as one might like...but, I am thrilled to be at this stage! 7 30 14.

As challenging as the outside was, the inside was even more challenging. Reaching up there, pressing overhead with enough force, and all the pointing and cleaning. Again, quite possibly the work of a madwoman.

The padobe infill I put in one handful at a time, thrown up overhead. Definitely one of the things I would do differently, though I am glad I didn't know better for so many aspects of this, as it made it the great learning experience and uniquely one of a kind Mega-Sculpture artwork that it is.

Downstairs, I made a lime-putty plaster, with putty and sand, and fibers. Then I made lots of bright paints with lime putty and pigments. So far, they are all holding up beautifully.

Outside and on the upper dome, I sprayed and painted on yellow and green and red and black oxides. I had ideas for tree details over the pillars. I considered cholla cactus, mosaic glass and stones, and also more papercrete and more natural paints. I still dream of putting some mosaic pieces in sometimes.

One of my favorite things about this kind of construction is that it is easy to repair, easy to customize, easy to change many things about it. The concrete bond beam and pillars are fixed, and the dome, for the most part, though the bottles are replaceable, the center layer is lathe and cement plaster. Don't misunderstand though, papercrete and pumicrete are really durable, tough, and getting tougher with time, as the lime pulls CO_2 from the atmosphere to bind with.

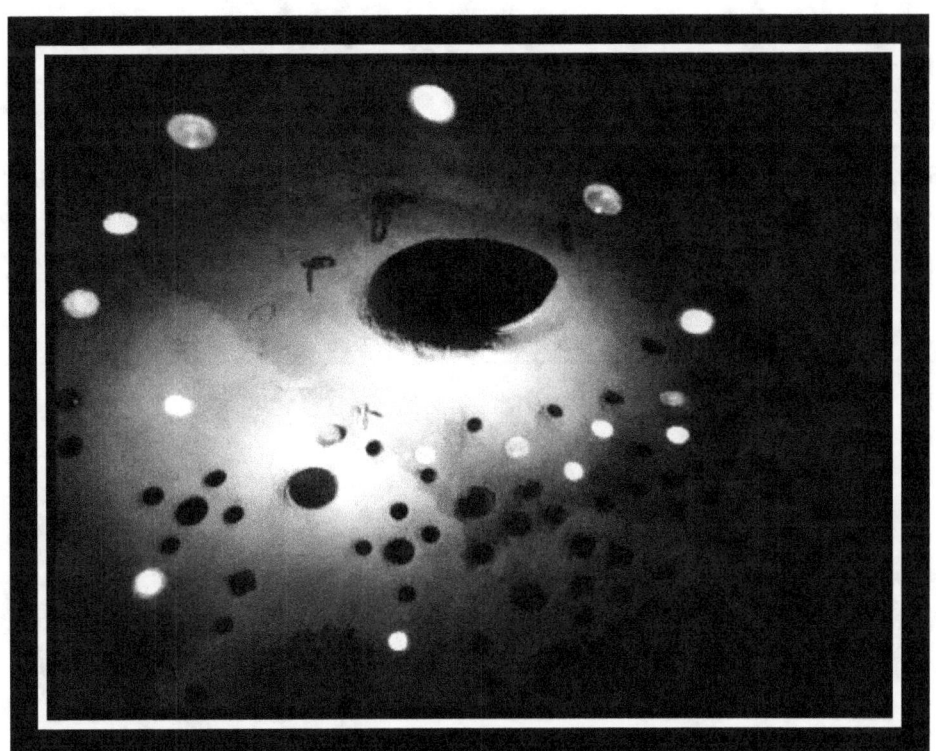

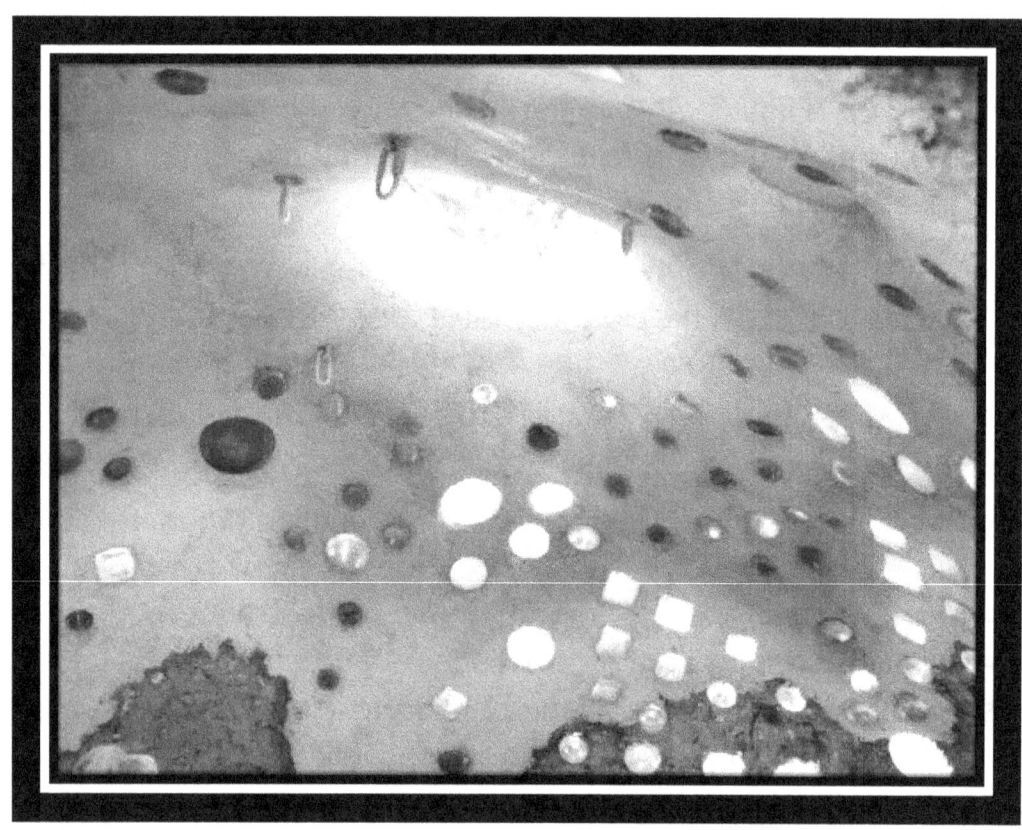

Day 3 plasterdome, working a little blind and pretty much in the dark by the end; as evidenced by my solar LEDs all clicked on. 7 31 14.

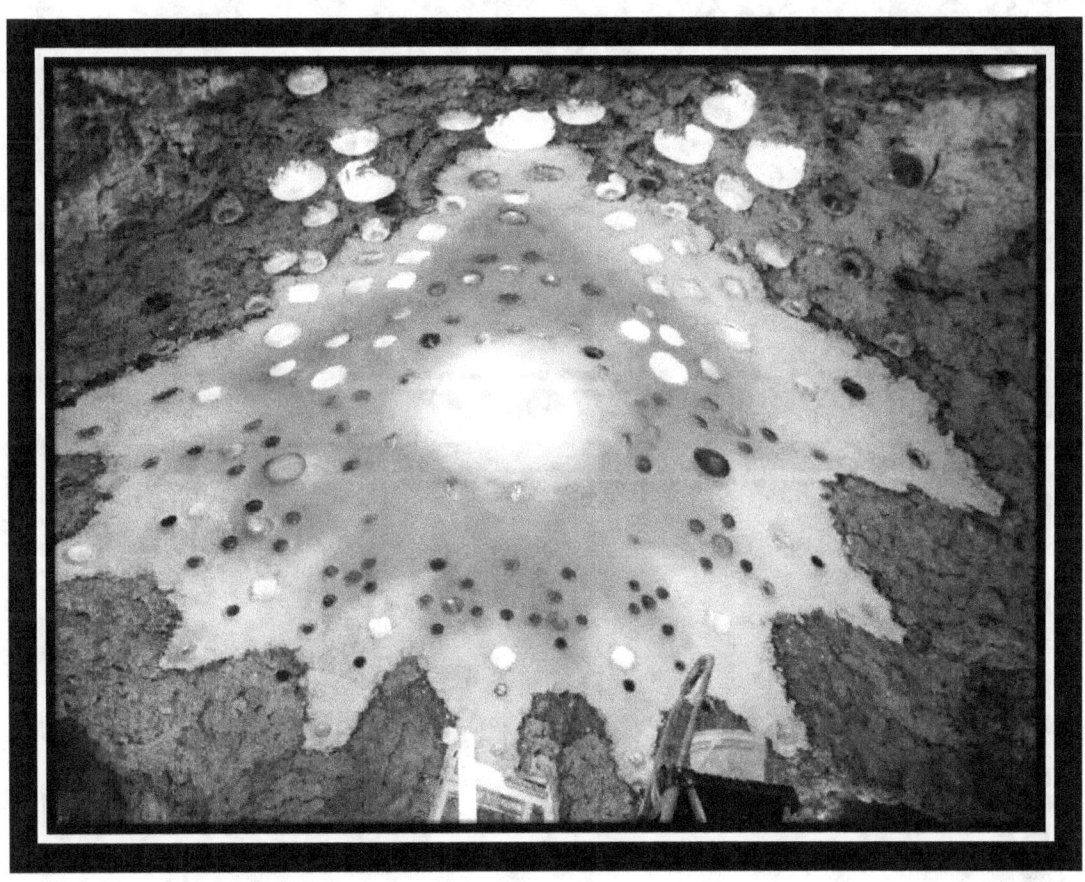

Day 4, 8 1 14. I think I was successful at hiding my cold joint under the yellow oxide.

The Head Hutt Picture Book

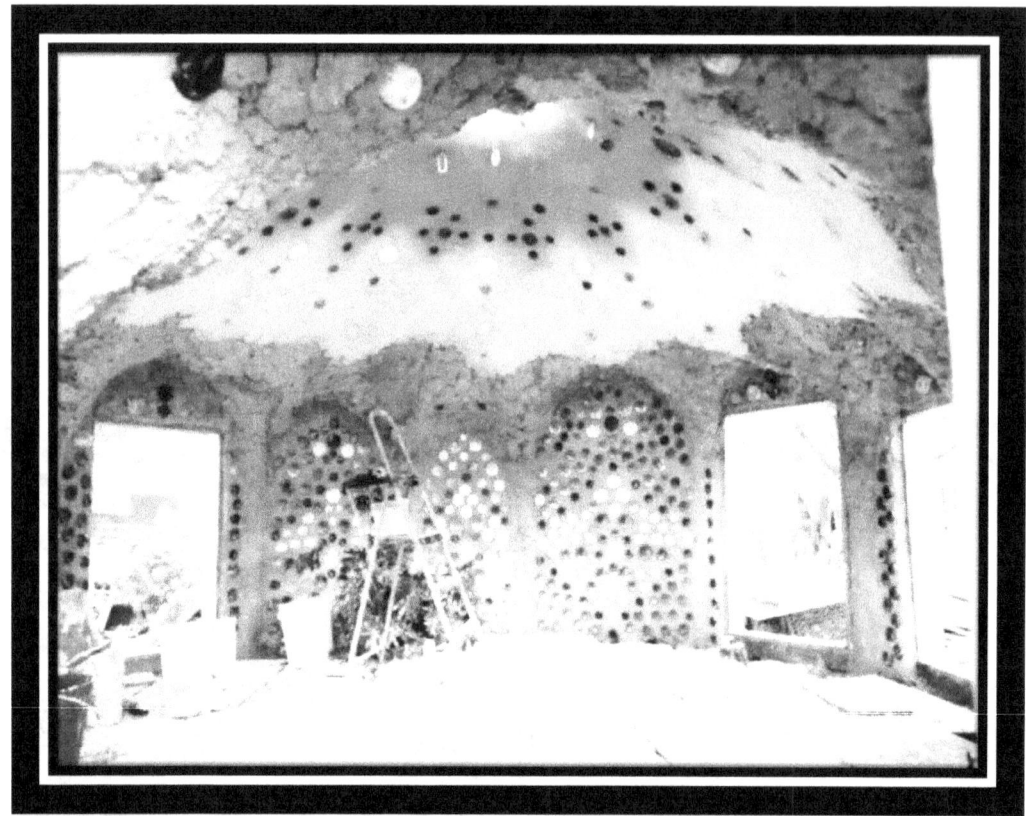

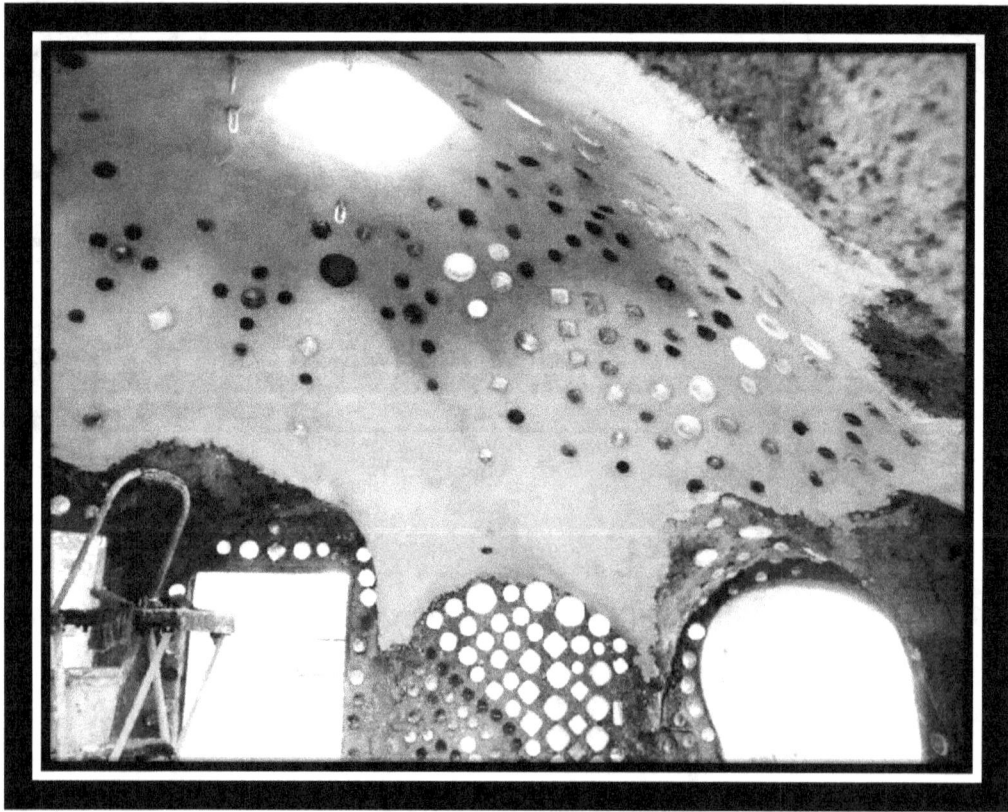

Lime, paper-mash, and pumice (and little borax for good measure) is the mix I have settled in on for my plaster. It is rough, and dries very slowly, which makes it fairly forgiving.

Trying to cover this entire dome without cold seams/joints as best as I can. So far, I give myself a solid B grade. :) Next time I think I can ace it. 8 2 14.

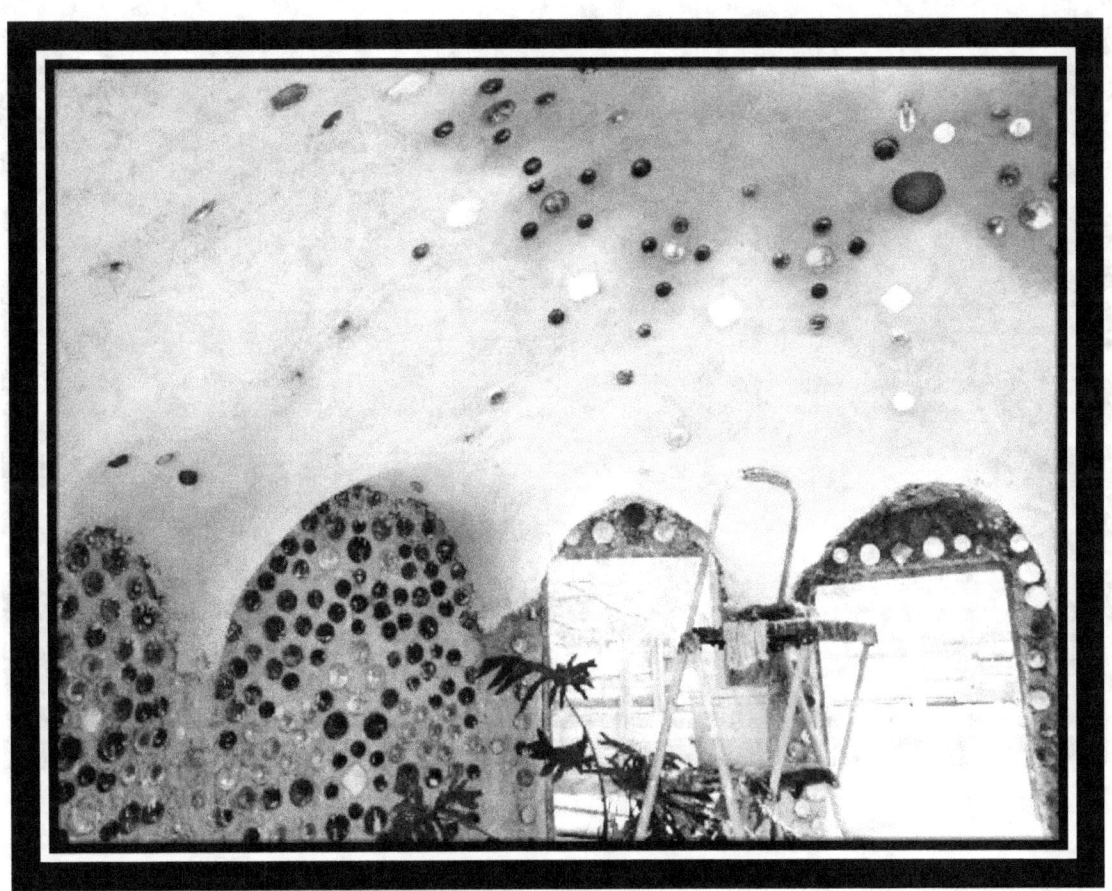

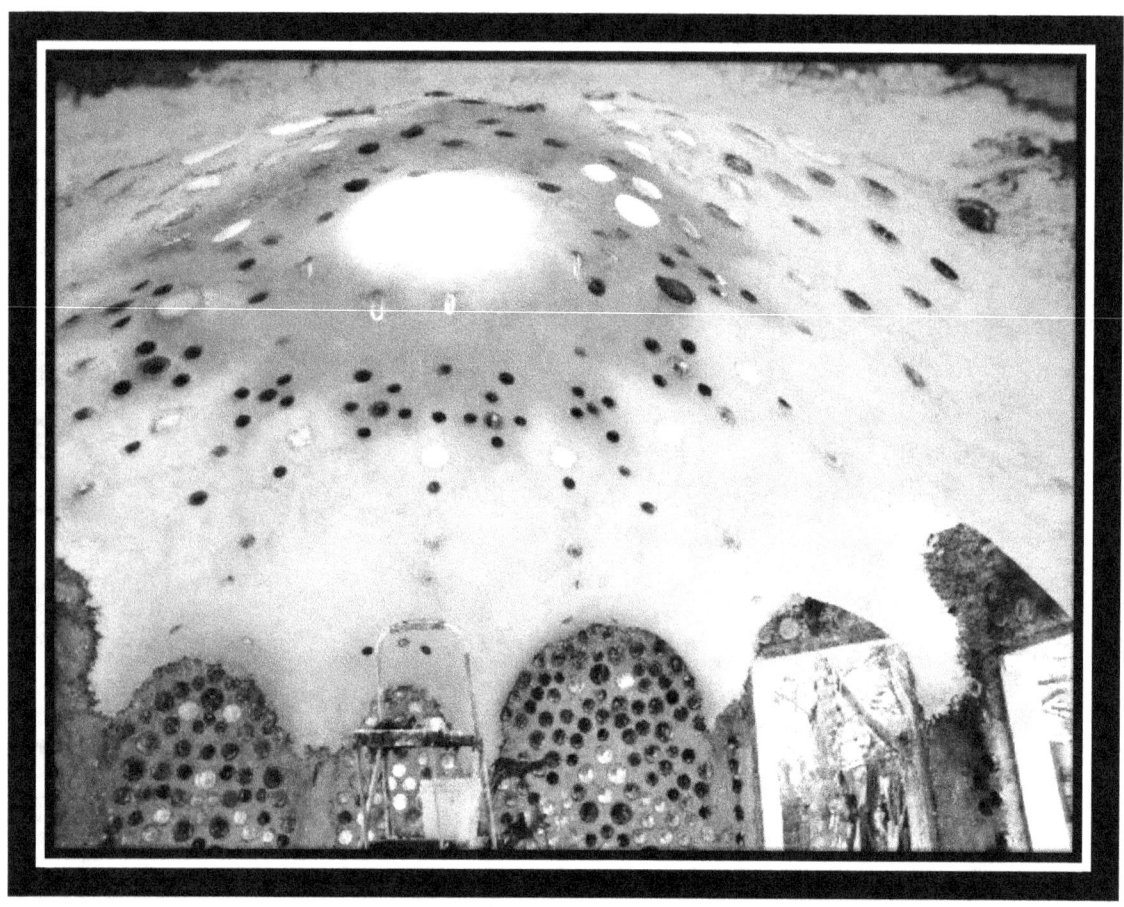

8 3 14. Getting closer. Closer.

Closer. 8 2 14. Here you can see my cold joints more than I wish, but, thankfully I put them into a pattern that I think works with the overall decor...like I meant to do that! =P

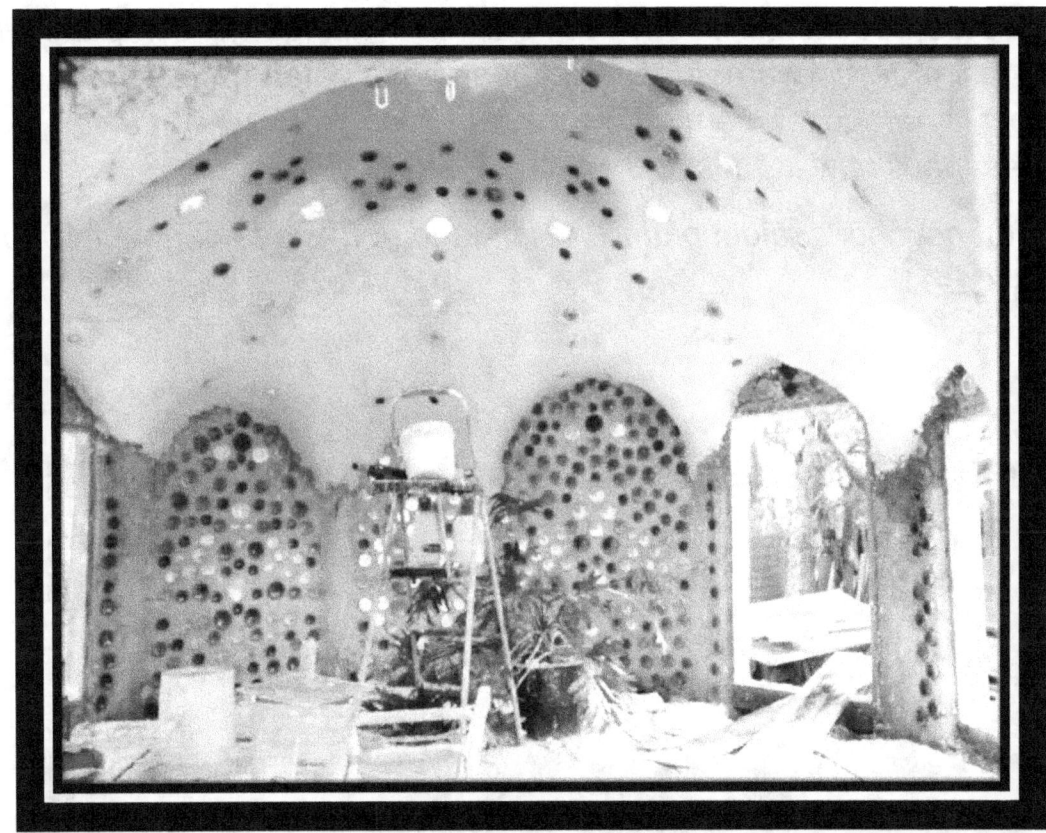

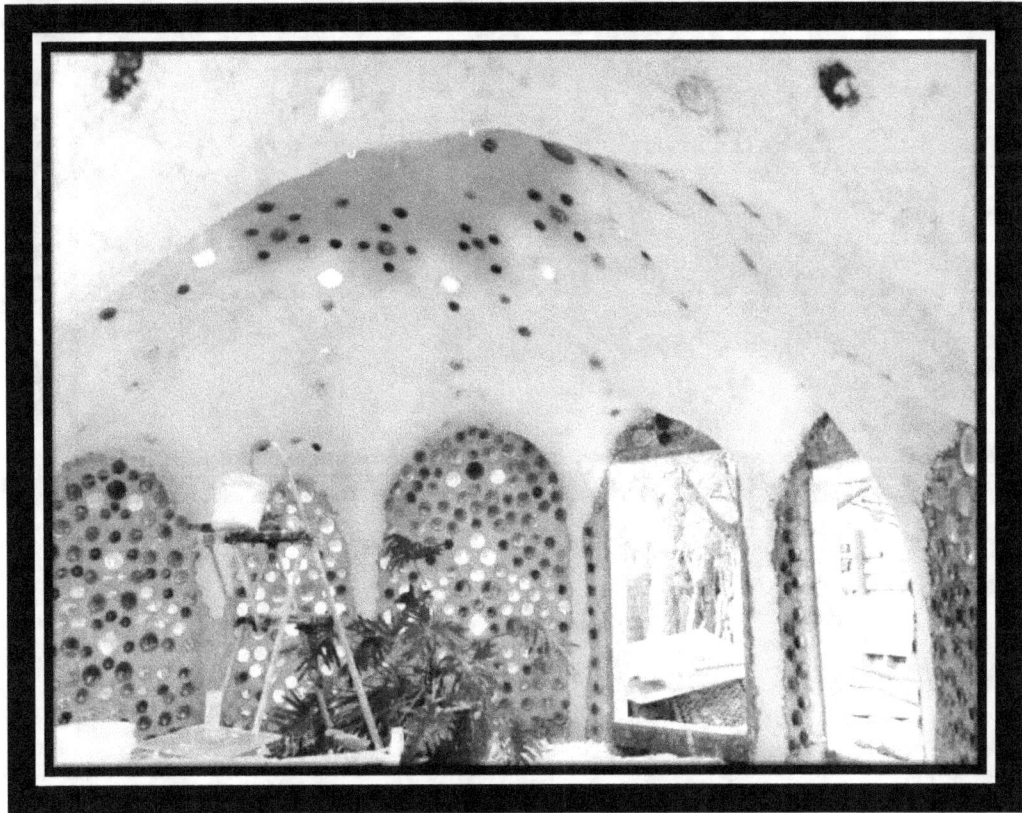

Day 6/7 Finally got the curved overhead parts mostly all done...now for the sides and bottom, and outsides. Then doors & windows. I keep contemplating *these sculpted tree motifs. Today I am back to thinking I will scrap the whole idea and just move forward. Ideas like those have eaten up hundreds of hours, so it is hard to let them go without anything 'to show' for it, yet, sometimes that's how it goes! 8 3 14.*

Nothing left now but straight plumb walls....and both sides of about 1000 bottle bricks. 8 7 14.

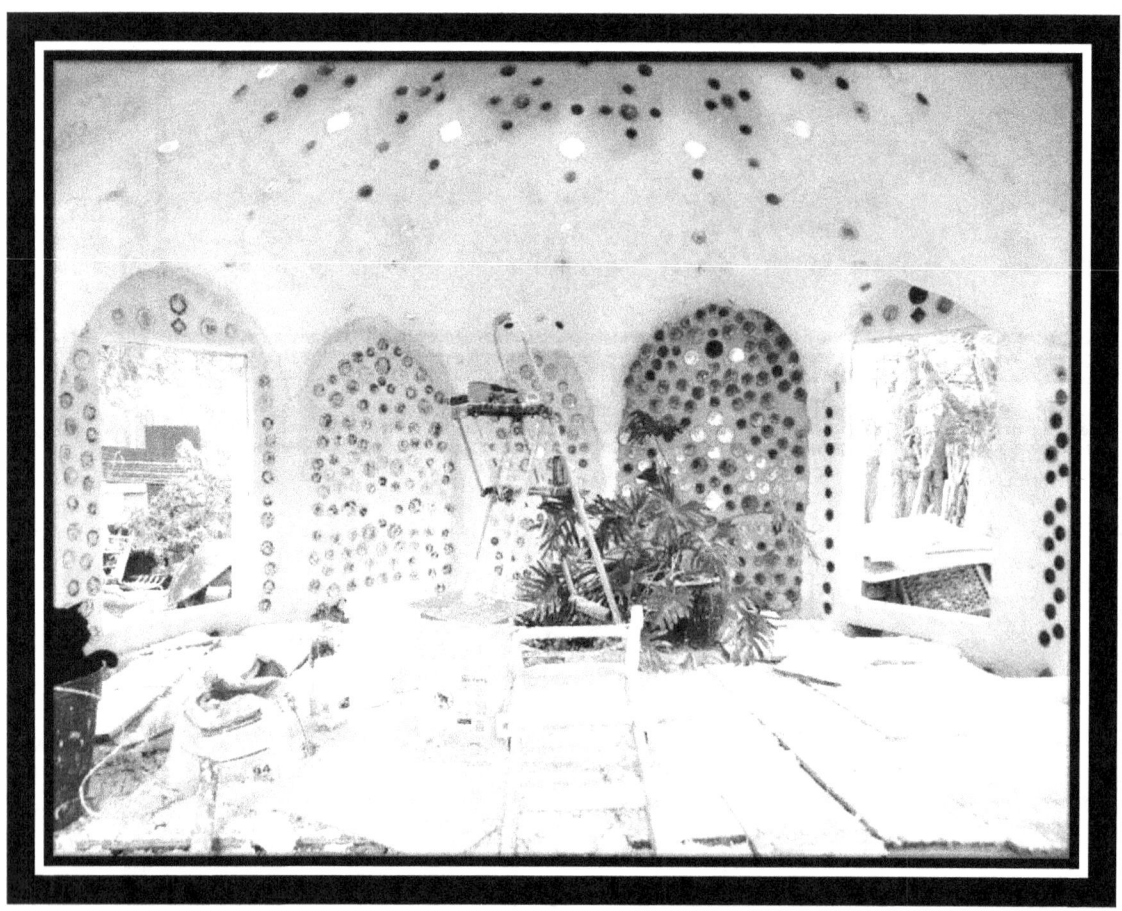

8 10 14. Before cleaning, as it got too dark for photos before I finished scrubbing all those bottle ends (several "what was I thinking?!?" moments today)...about 1/2 the way done with the inside sides. Still have the outside and bottom to finish plastering. Not sure if I will add color to the sides or not, though I am leaning towards yes. Wooo!

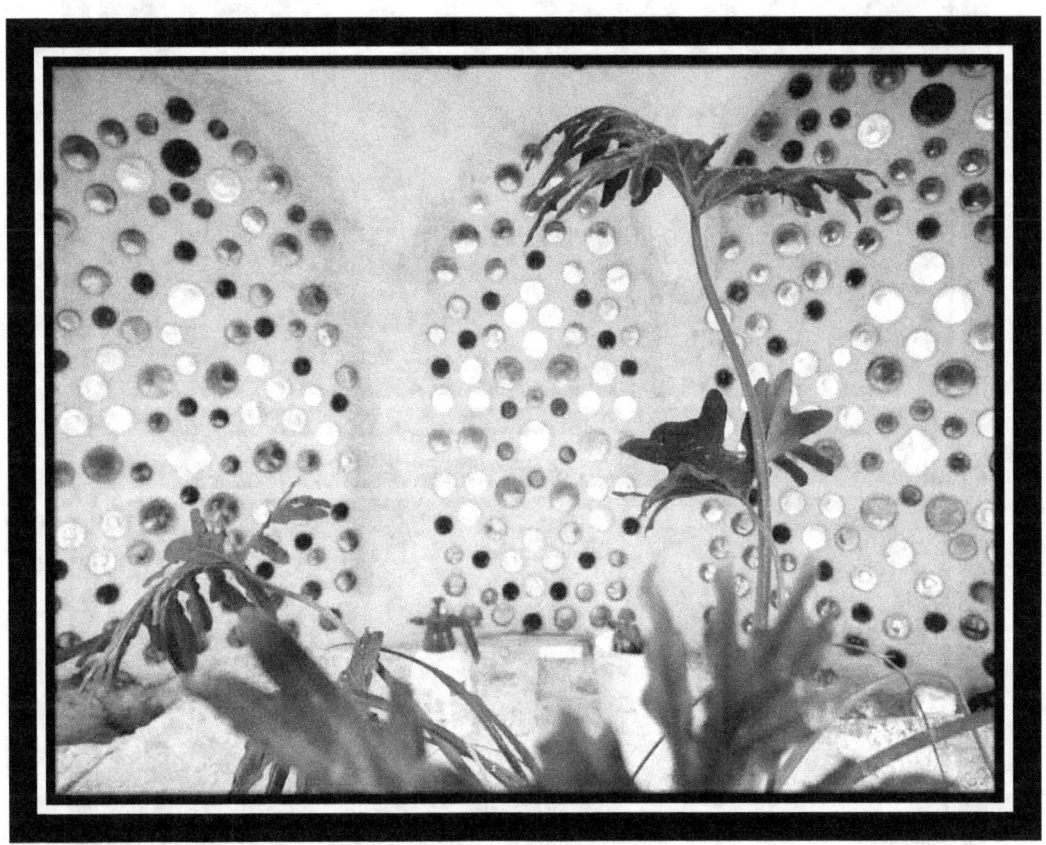

8 11 14. Pointing Purgatory. Pointing is pressing the fibrous plaster down around the edges of each bottle end with a spoon to decrease the odds of cracking and make it look nicer. Still not sure if I will add color to the sides, or if I will build in tree motifs on the pillars yet. For now I just need to get it plastered!

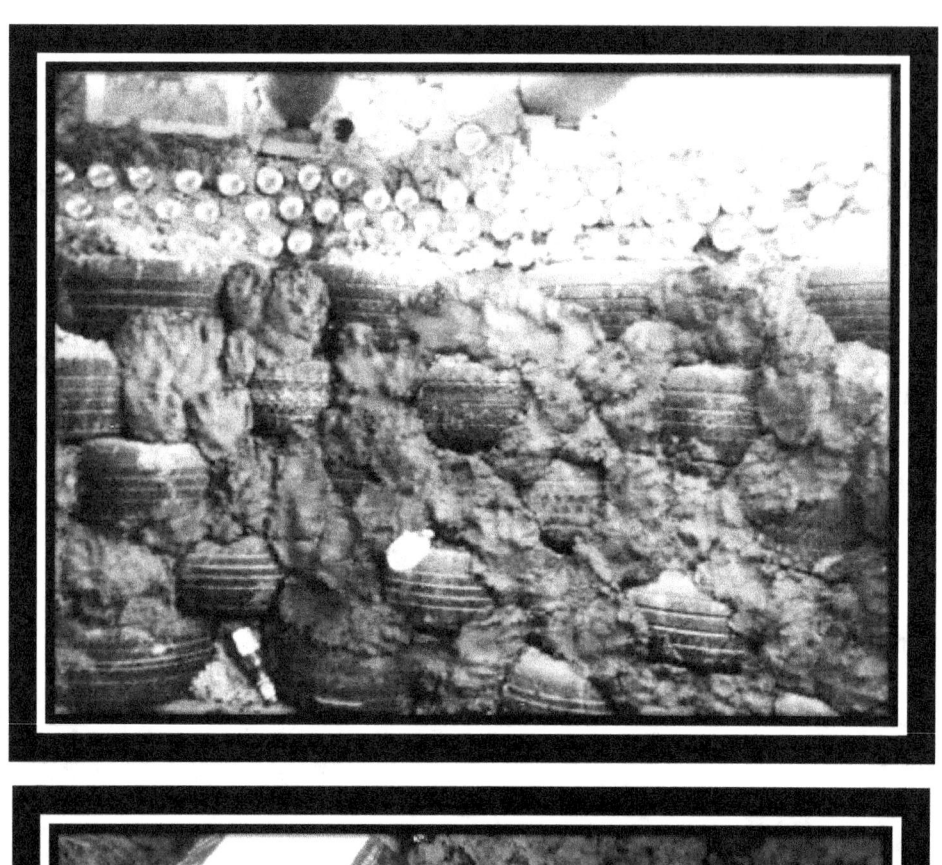

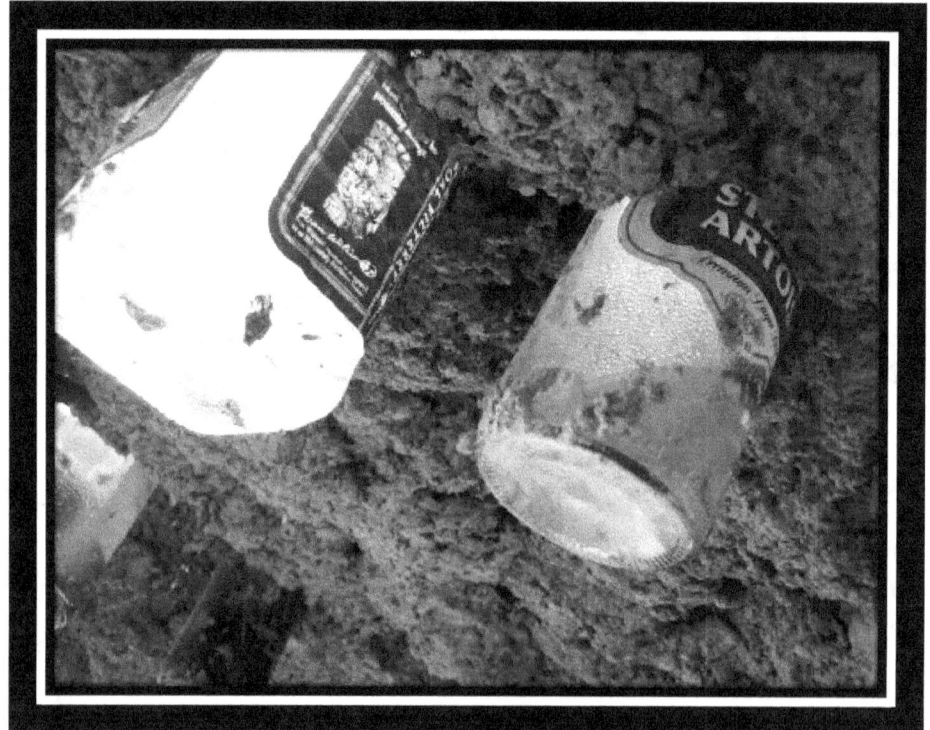

We got rain! And it went in all my sloped bottle bricks. (Sigh)

The Head Hutt Picture Book

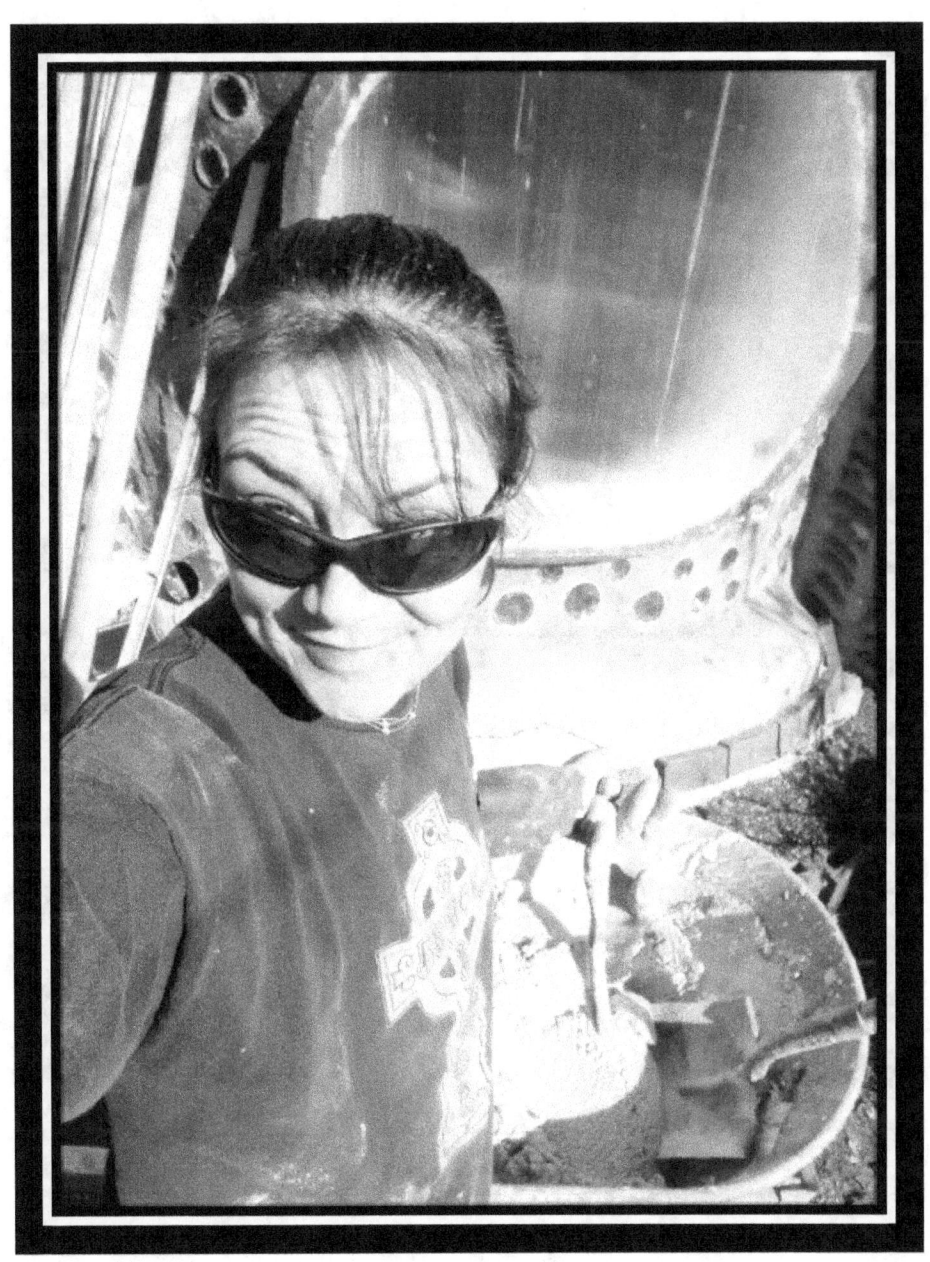

The Head Hutt Picture Book

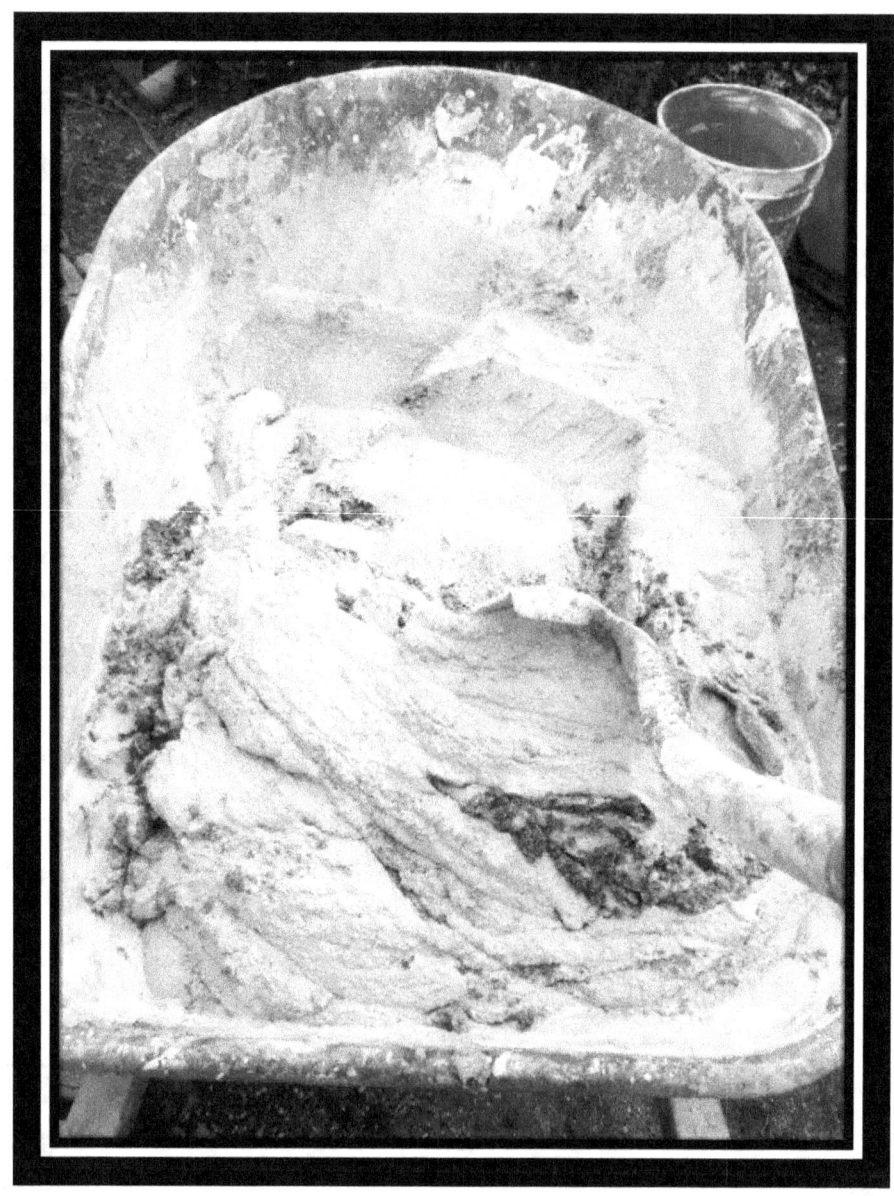

Mixer is dead. No matter, lime plaster shouldn't be mixed in a mixer anyhow, now I remember. 1 18 16.

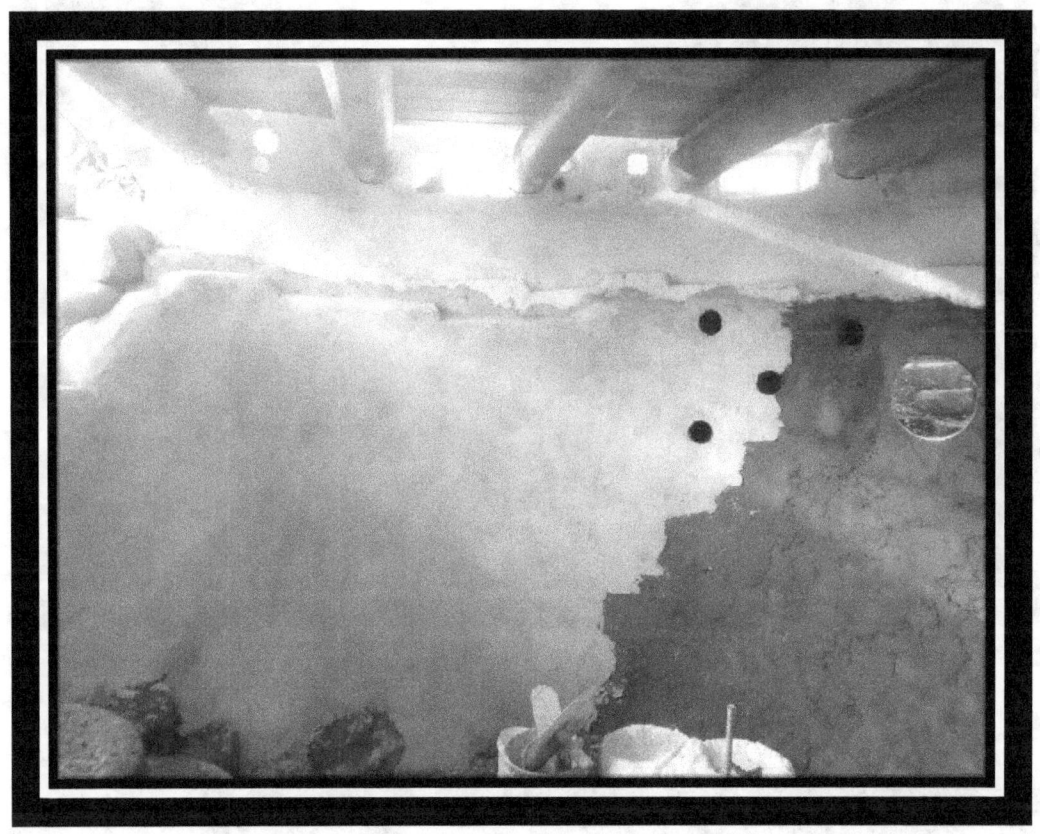

Pretty good progress on the first batch. My plastering skills are improving, though there is still much room for improvement. Not too hard to mix by hand-- only takes 10-15 minutes, which isn't much longer than in a mixer. Though it does take more woman power. 1 18 16.

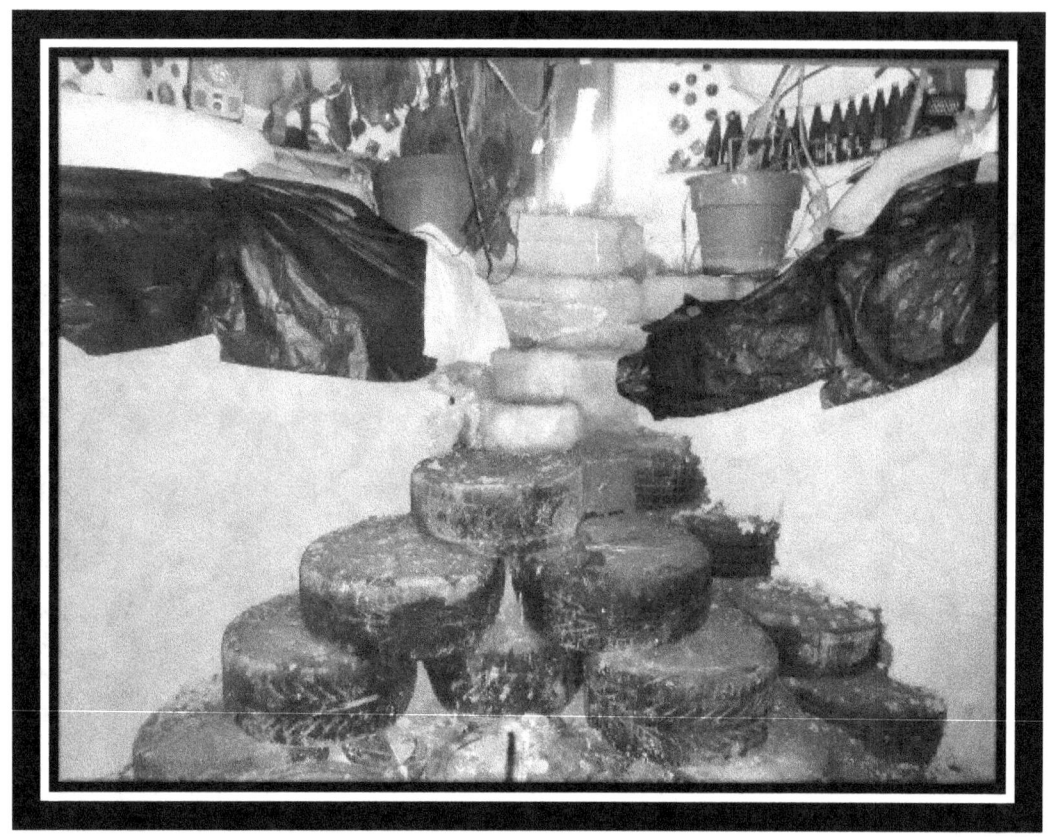

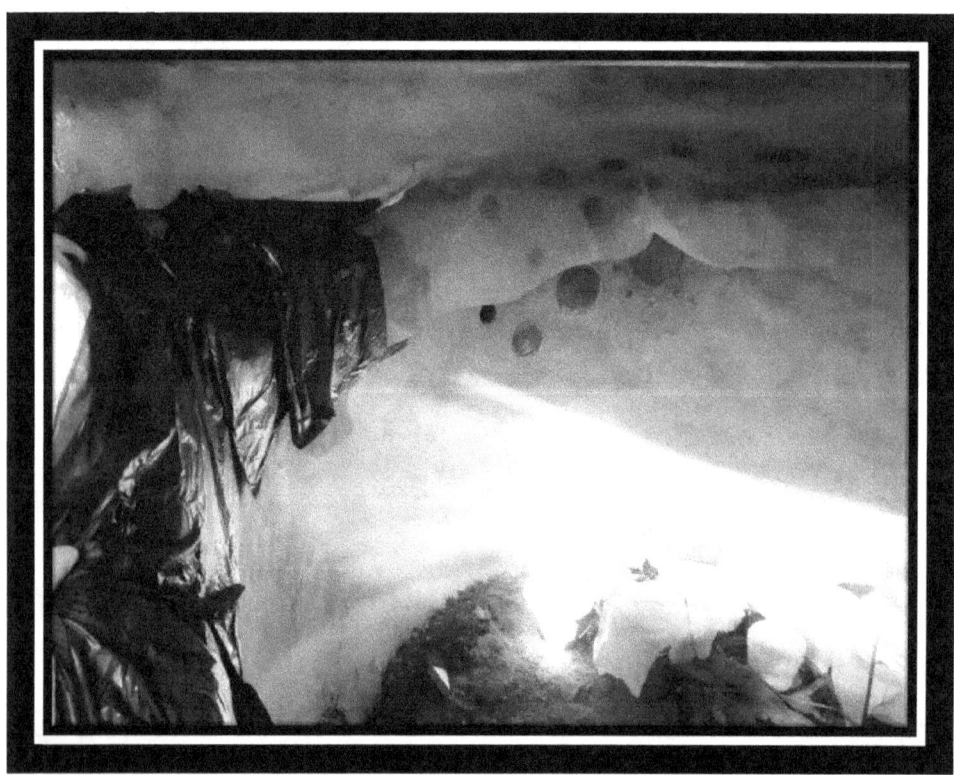

I should have the entire wall covered for at least a few days, but, I am just keeping the edges covered, and wetting it down daily until I am done working on it, later this week. 1 19 16.

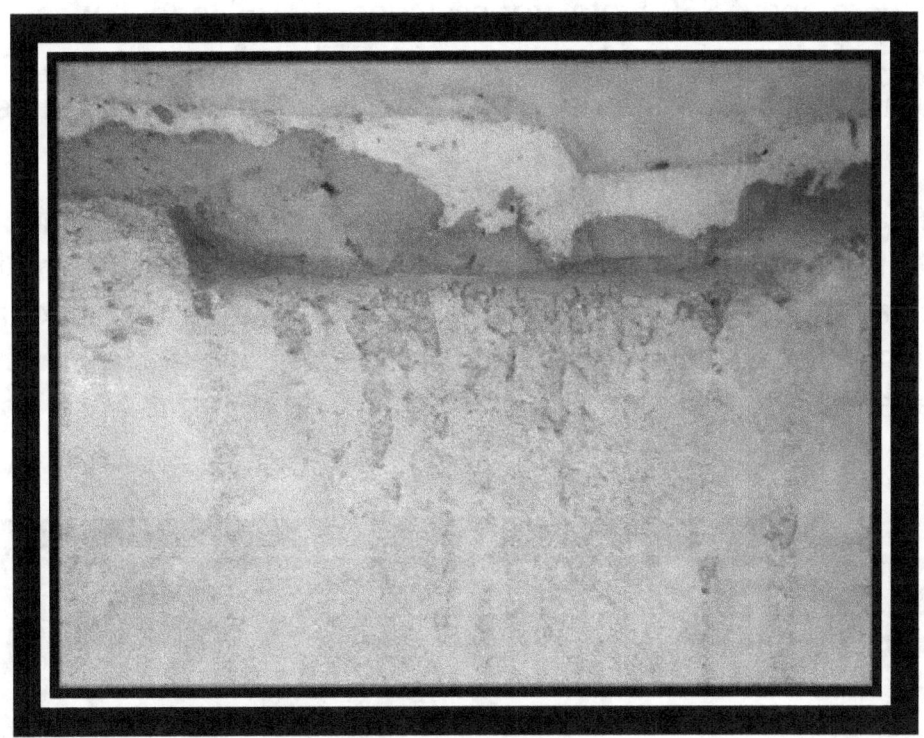

Opps! A little too much rewetting! Lucky for me, lime plaster is very forgiving, and I haven't finished the edges yet anyhow, so this will get fixed up tomorrow. I am enjoying the workability of the lime plaster! Hoping it cures well, and that I can put a nice finish on it tomorrow. 1 19 16.

Vigas and Floors

I thought a lot about the vigas, like pretty much every other part. I decided to splurge and order some freshly cut, straight, skinned, and topped vigas from a nearby supplier. I paid a bit extra for 'beetle cut' which is forest deemed infected, often dead standing wood, which needs to be removed. I thought it might have some extra character and be already partially cured, hence, much lighter.

I think they were about $500 total, for six vigas, 12-16' long. It was one of the larger chunks of money I spent on this project. The other being concrete for the bond beam, flooring, and of course, tools and cement, sand, lime powder and more.

I also spend a couple hundred dollars on these prefab hopper windows, which I have yet to use, though initially i thought it would be important. In hindsight, I could have saved myself some trouble and expense by eliminating those. They do let in a nice amount of light downstairs, and I imagine I might want to use them at some point, depending on how the temperatures and use evolve.

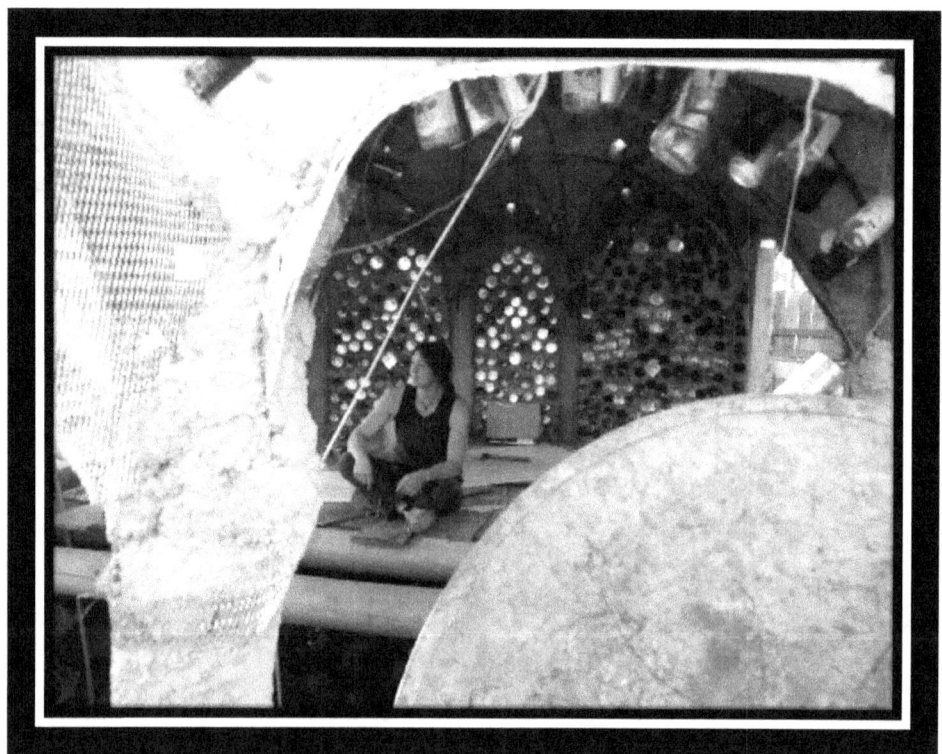

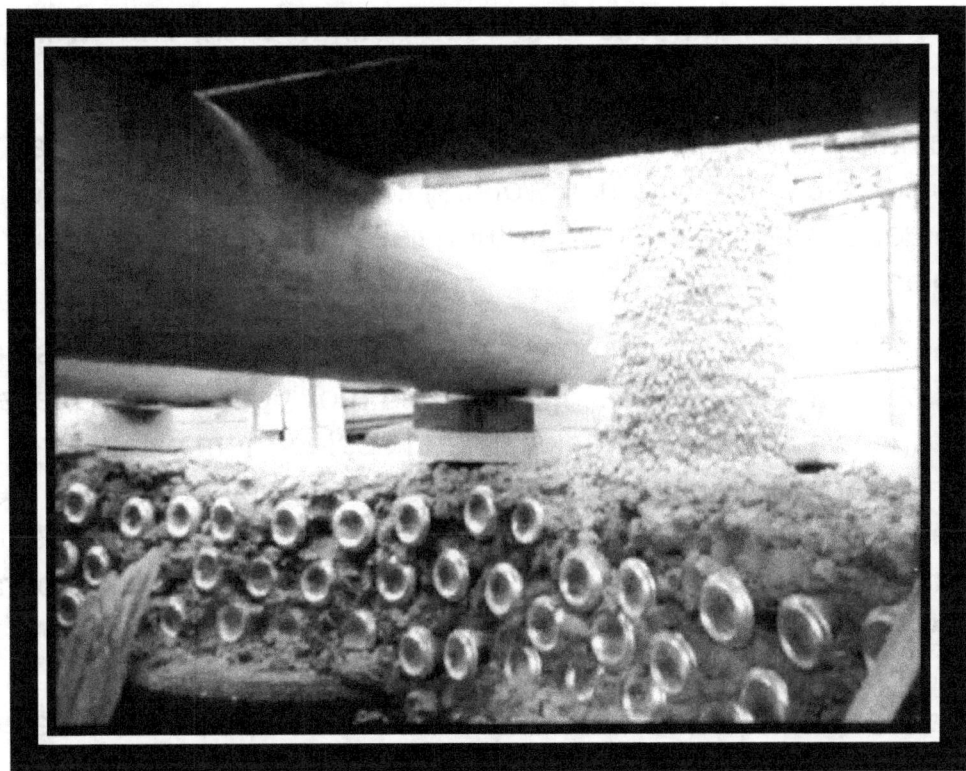

I was excited about the vigas and I needed them to move forward with the dome building. So, when they arrived, even though I had an injured foot and it was raining and I didn't have any help lined up, I went directly to the supplier. Rio Grande Supply is just outside the city.

When I arrived and went in the office to pay, the guy asked me how I was getting them home. I told him I would take them in my van, hanging out with the back door tied shut.

He smirked and said,

"No way you are getting those vigas in that van by your self. And I think they might be too heavy for one load. They are pretty heavy."

I smiled back.

"I understand why you might think that, but, you don't know me. I will get them in the van and home. Watch me."

I paid him and went out to the yard. Lucky for me, my vigas were tied in a tight bundle, and on a lift. Two men in the yard helped lift the bundle onto the back of my van and partially into the van, so I did not even have to lift them. Good thing, because they turned out to be 3-4 times heavier than I had calculated!

They probably weighed a thousand to 1500 pounds each! They were totally green, fresh cut, and had been sitting in the rain for two days.

Sliding them into the van with the metal guides did work though I was very grateful for the help of the two men working in the yard. I don't know how I would have gotten them into the van otherwise, though I know I could have devised a plan.

The greenness of them caused more delay in the dome building, as I needed them to dry out some before sealing them and moving them into place. I dried them in my driveway for a few weeks. Then I sealed them with some expensive eco-friendly sealant, which seems to be holding up fairly well. I used the same stuff on the flooring, which I am also happy with. The flooring did not go in until after I built the main dome. Before that I had temporary flooring down, which did get quit messy, so I was glad I waiting to put in my main flooring. When I did, I went with the less expensive, 6 x 2 inch lumber, sealed it, spaced it well, and screwed it down over strips on the leveled vigas. The whole thing is quite functional.

I managed to make most of the textbook mistakes on my bond beam on my vigas, making this an awesome learning experience, and me well practiced in fixing or rationalizing the sufficiency of mistakes along the way...so far, so good. I put all the vigas the same direction, so I had to block up one side twice as much as the other, but in the end I got them all relatively level--It did take days longer than I thought it would, like so many parts of this project. 9 2012.

Looking at the viga blocking from underneath. You can see Sapphy in one of her favorite odd sleeping spots on my backwall. 10 6 12.

The Head Hutt Picture Book

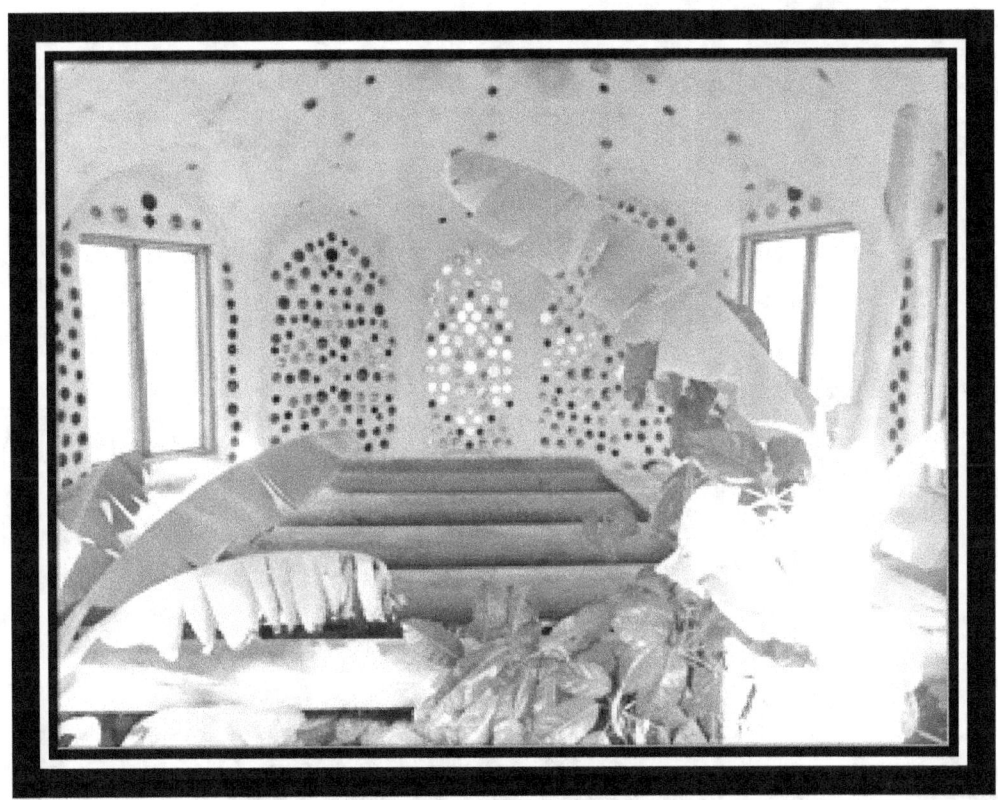

For a while my houseplants were thriving in the HH. Then, one fateful stormy night the roof-plug blew off, and a set of shutter doors came loose, and it dropped below freezing. I lost the plant you see in the middle here, which I had kept alive for about 25 years before that. The bananas were moved to my mom's greenhouse successfully before that. They are still thriving, though not producing yet.

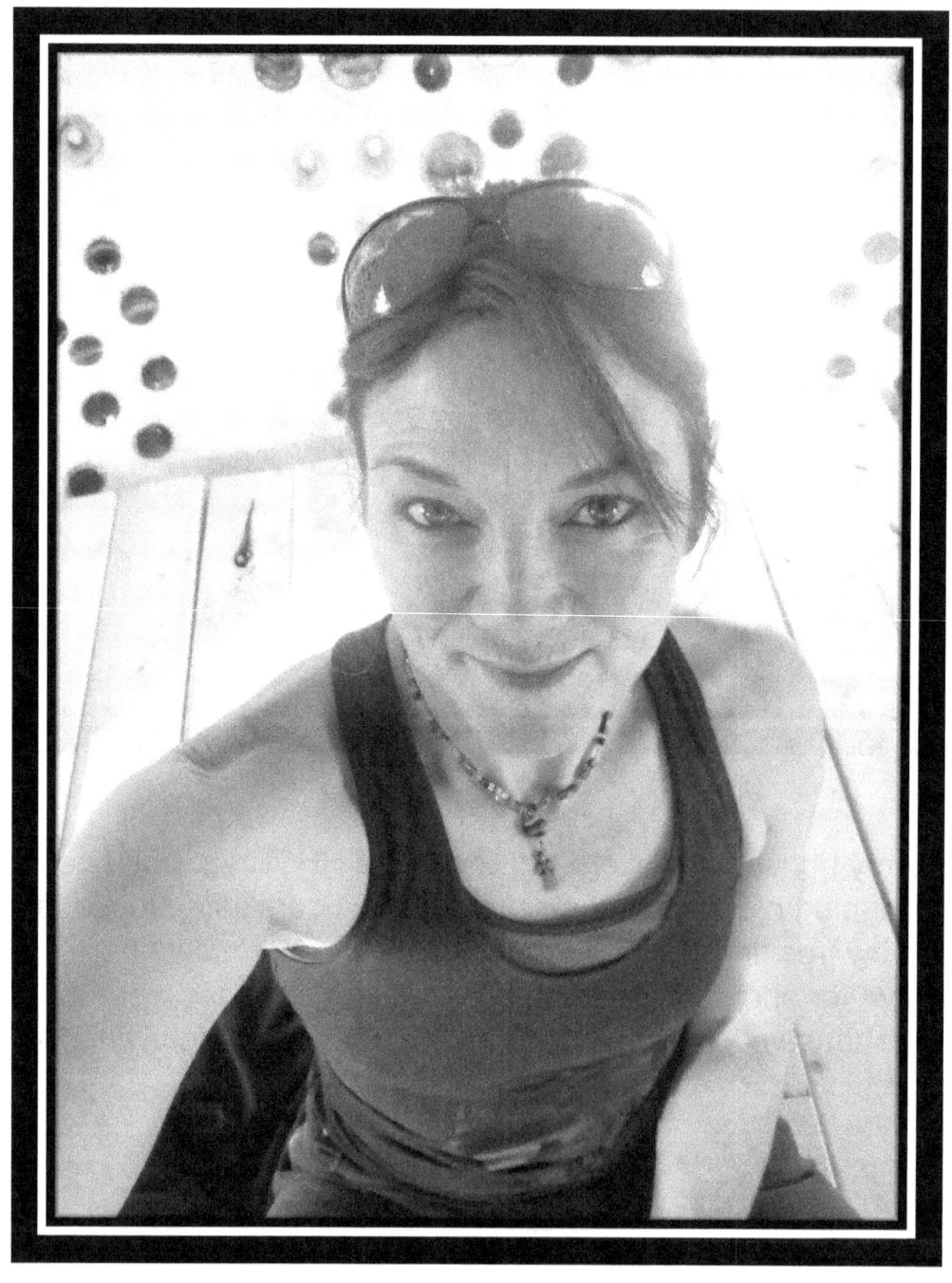

Almost ready for sealing and then "finishing" the deck/floor! It has taken me months to do just a few hours of work, plus a few hours of mistakes. 2 20 15.

I waited quite a while to put the flooring in, and I am glad I did. I made a HUGE mess doing the infill. Even though it might have been nice to have a more solid feeling base to stand my ladder on, it would have been a lot of extra work to keep it clean or to clean it up after each session of infill and plaster.

I ended up going with some simple kiln dried 6"x2" lumber. I thought through a system that seemed logical and went for it. I cut them, spaced them, and then painted them with sealant on both sides. Then I screwed them into running boards (2"x 4"'s) I had screwed into my vigas. This just cuts back on drilling into the vigas and assures a flat surface to secure to, though I did have the vigas flat topped and I leveled them. The flooring lumber and sealant cost around a hundred dollars, I think. It took me some days to measure and cut and seal and screw it all down. I am happy with it.

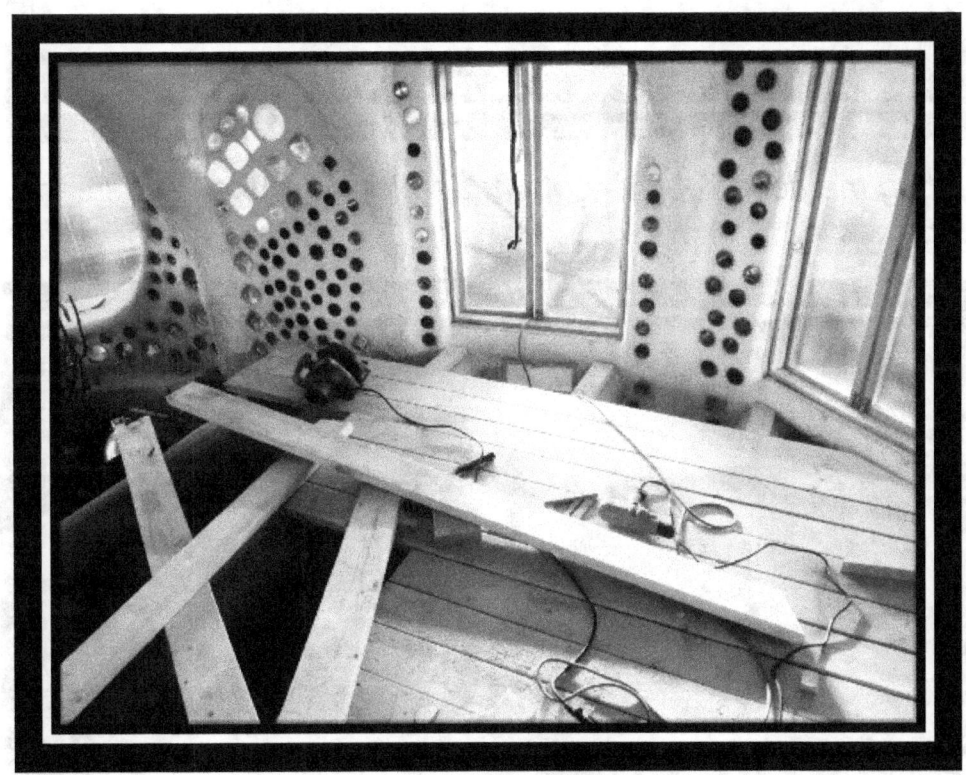

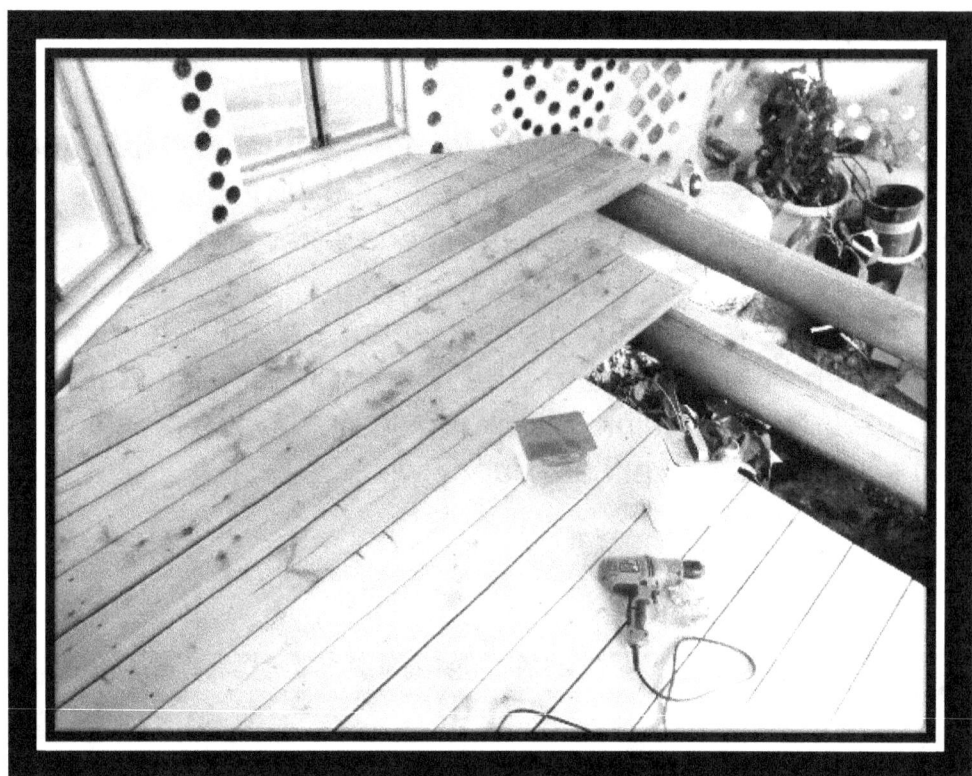

3 6 15. Getting the deck sealed--bottom and top in one step instead of three like I thought.

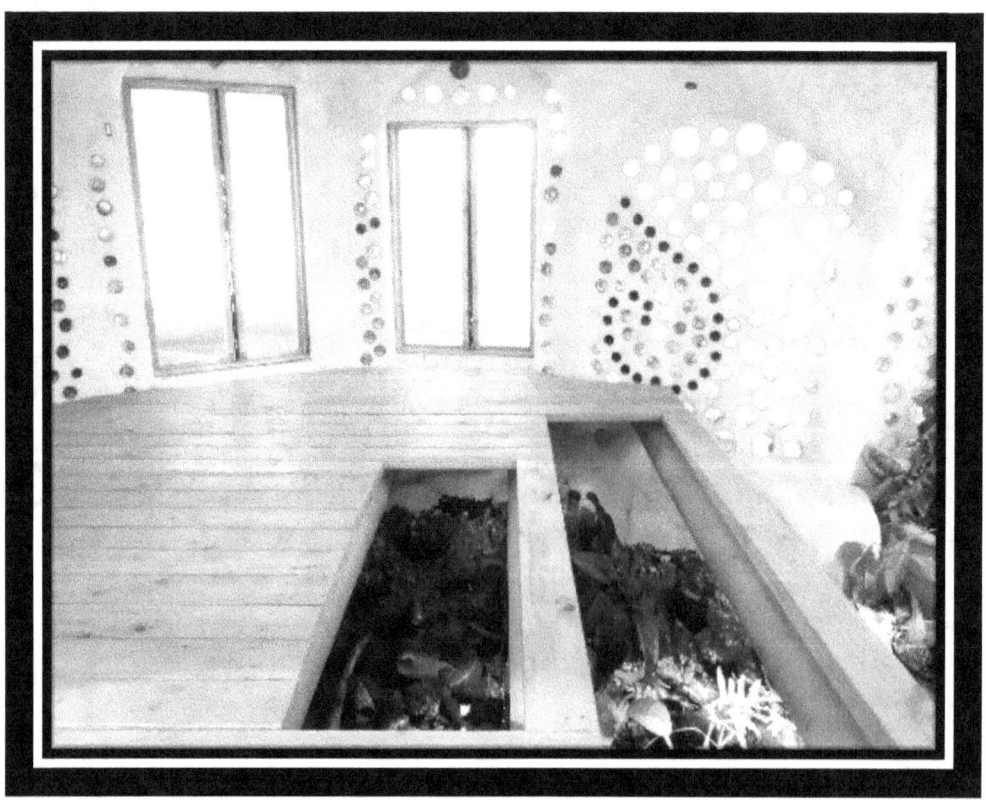

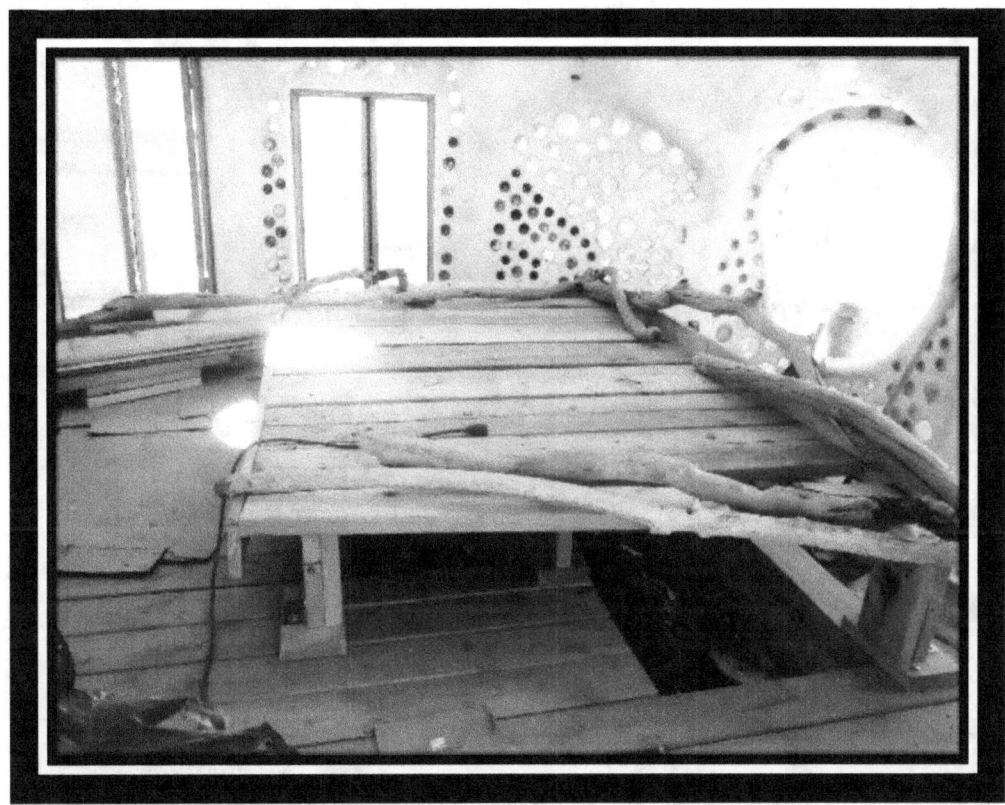

Got a tiny bit more done to the floor. Soon I will cover it (for protection) and continue! 3 10 15.

These openings were initially part of my plan to let more light into the lower section, though at the time of publishing, I am not sure if I would keep them or put in more flooring. I may take the bedframe out eventually, at which point we will see, we will see...

Yay for free pallet wood! Getting closer to functional in here... July 12, 2015.

This is a temporary (isn't everything temporary?), bedframe I made completely from free pallet wood, most of which came from a machine shop near my house. They import engines, and so I was able to salvage some great kiln dried 2 x 12" lumber for this project.

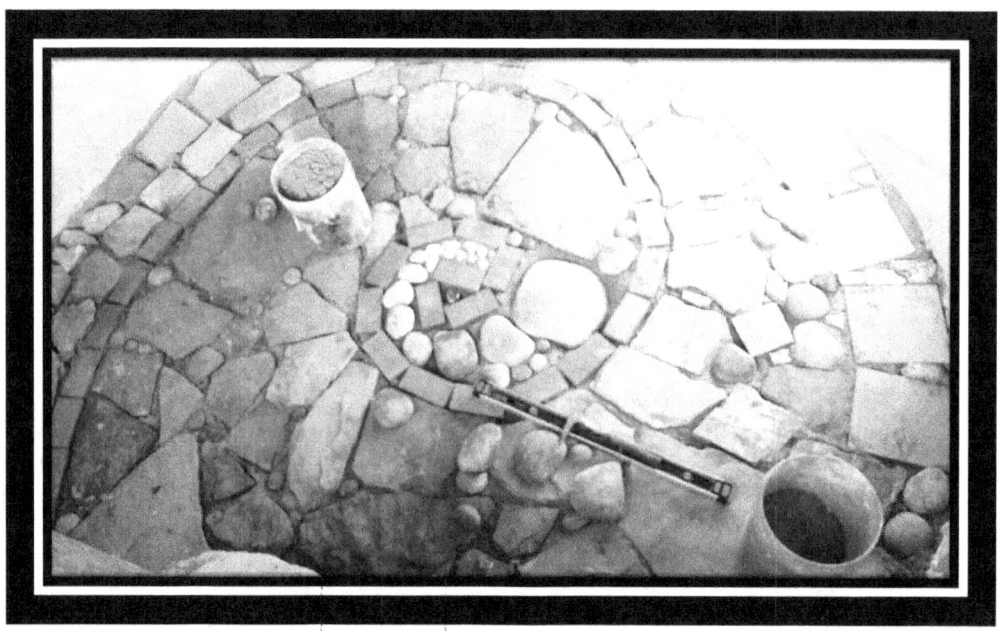

Feb 11, 2018. It took a while to get to the lower floor.

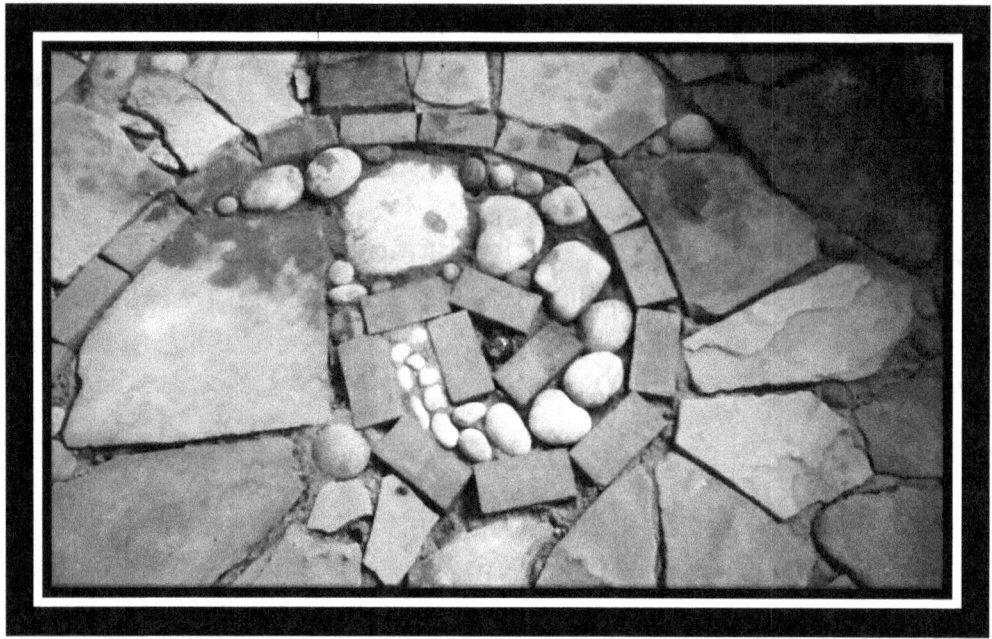

Openings Are Eyes

Giant round windows are a feature I have always found appealing, so I knew I wanted to incorporate two of them in the Head Hutt from early on. I made head sculptures and busts for the majority of my art studio assignments in my undergrad years, and so this was a natural evolution of my work.

I used a large watering tank that a friend gave me as a form to measure my lathe supports. One of them ended up a bit out of round in order to fit into the opening.

The entire structure is asymmetrical, in what is to me a playful way. I suppose it is probably aesthetically problematic for some.

7 14 13. Using Quikrete on the bottom half of the front eyes, because I want them to be very sturdy so I can sit in them.

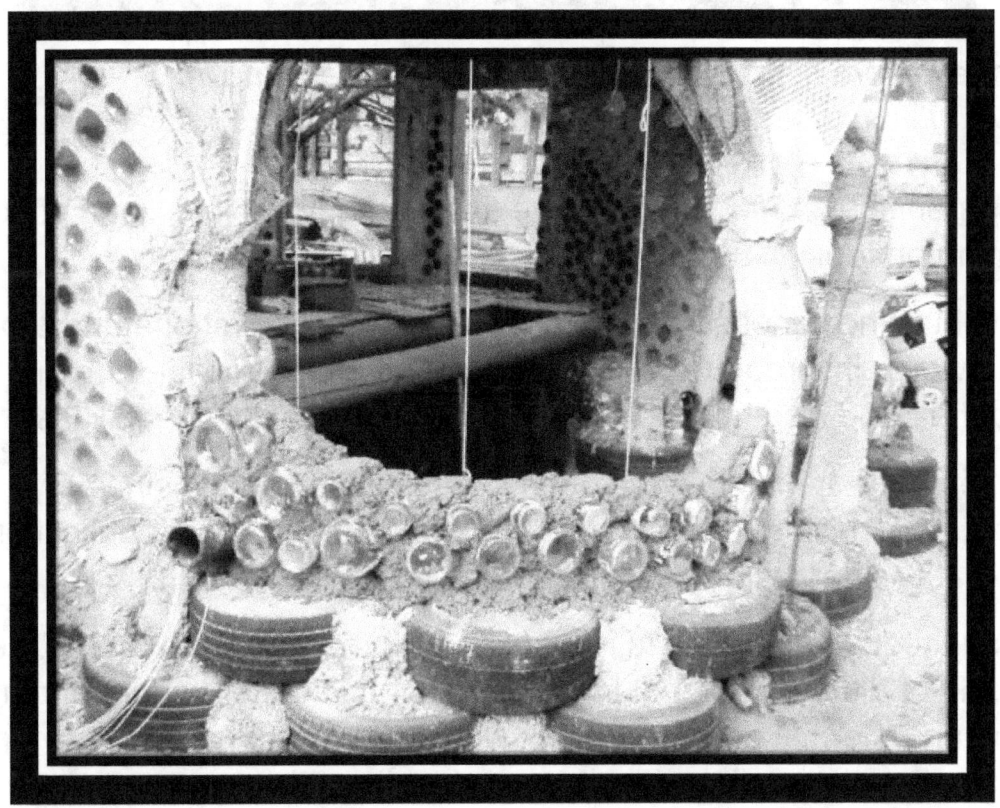

The Head Hutt Picture Book

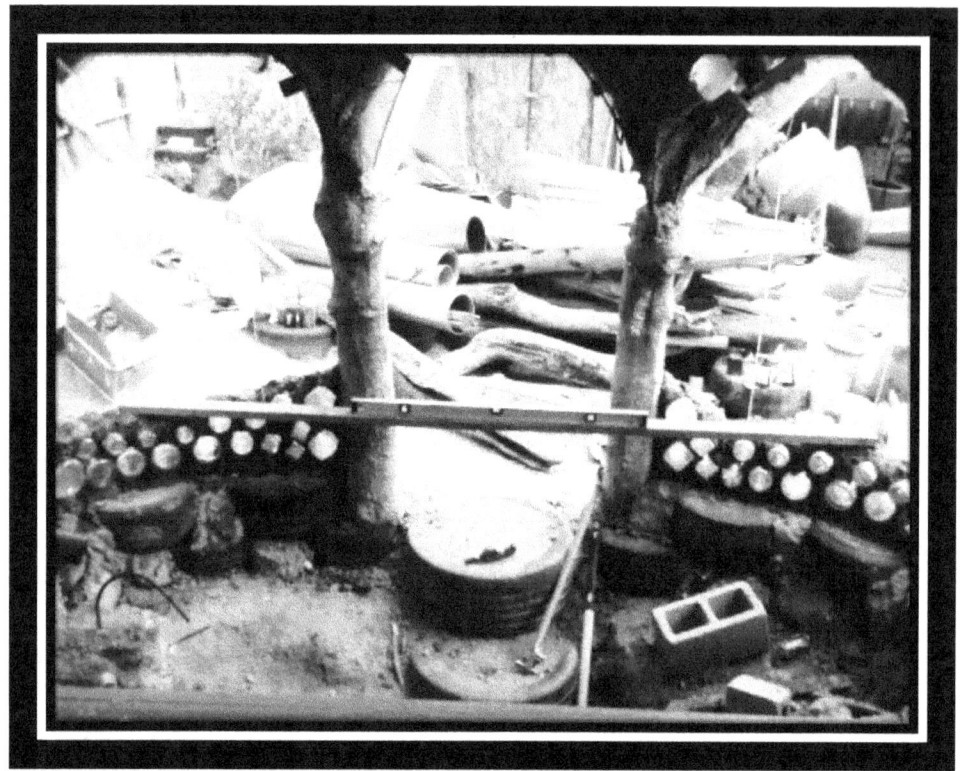

The front eyes are started! 7 13 13. Front eyes are going in! 7 13 13.

The five openings on the top level give airflow many choices...and of course, the opening on top.

I envision building various hats for the Head Hutt. The first one and probably main one would incorporate some reeds or something similar to mimic the effects of hair and also help add temperature moderation capabilities.

Passive temperature control has been a fascination of mine since my childhood, and these structures were explorations of real-life application of thermal mass, solar gain, and insulation.

In building these structures and in working with the Earthship Biotecture crews on a couple of different homes, I now have a much better understanding of insulation and thermal mass storage. I would have put in an insulative ring outside my retaining wall, I think, if I were building this structure to maximize passive temperature control potential.

The glass bottle walls, loose fitting shutters on openings, and sometimes open top sort of make this a moot point.

The Head Hutt Picture Book

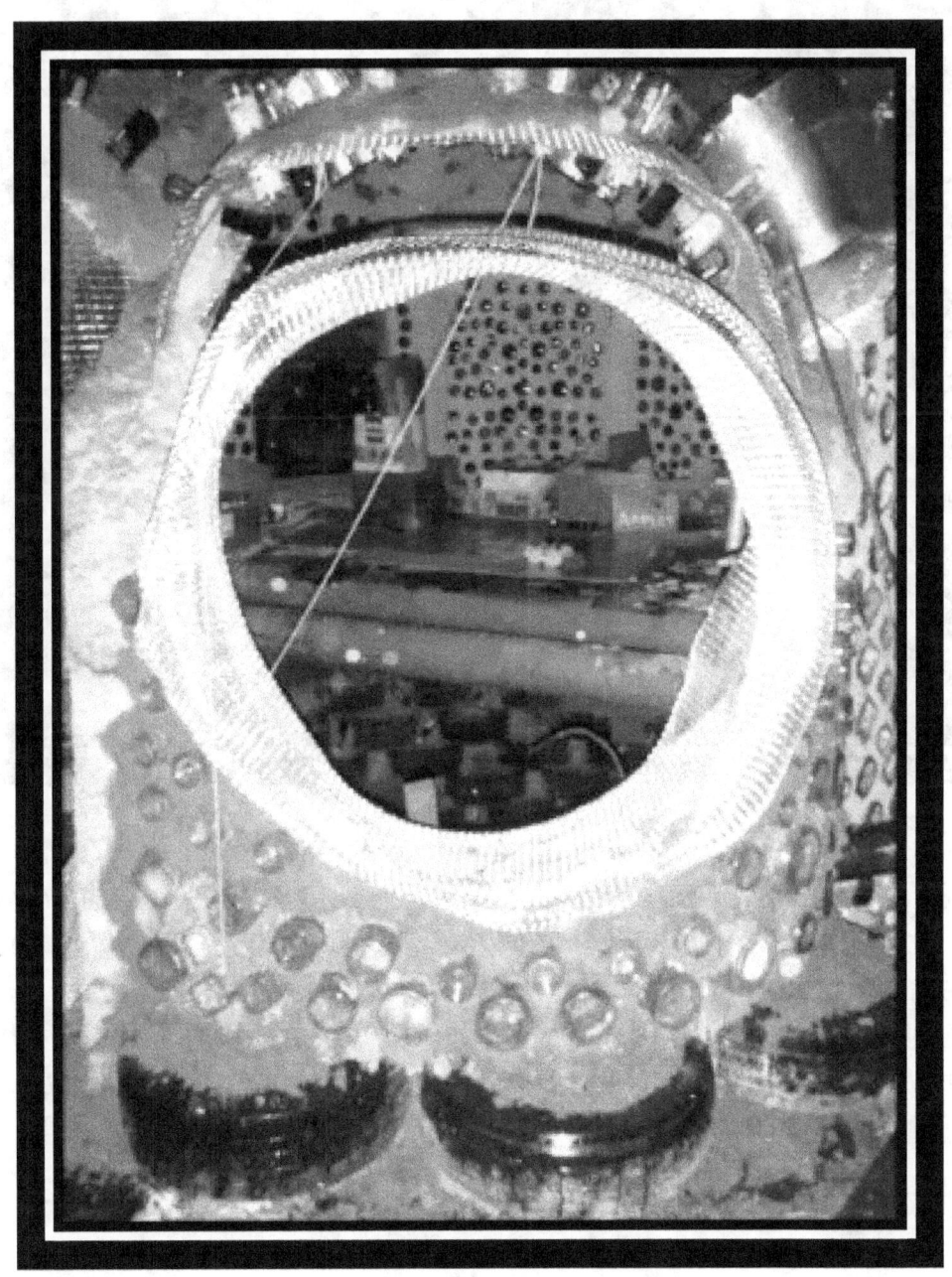

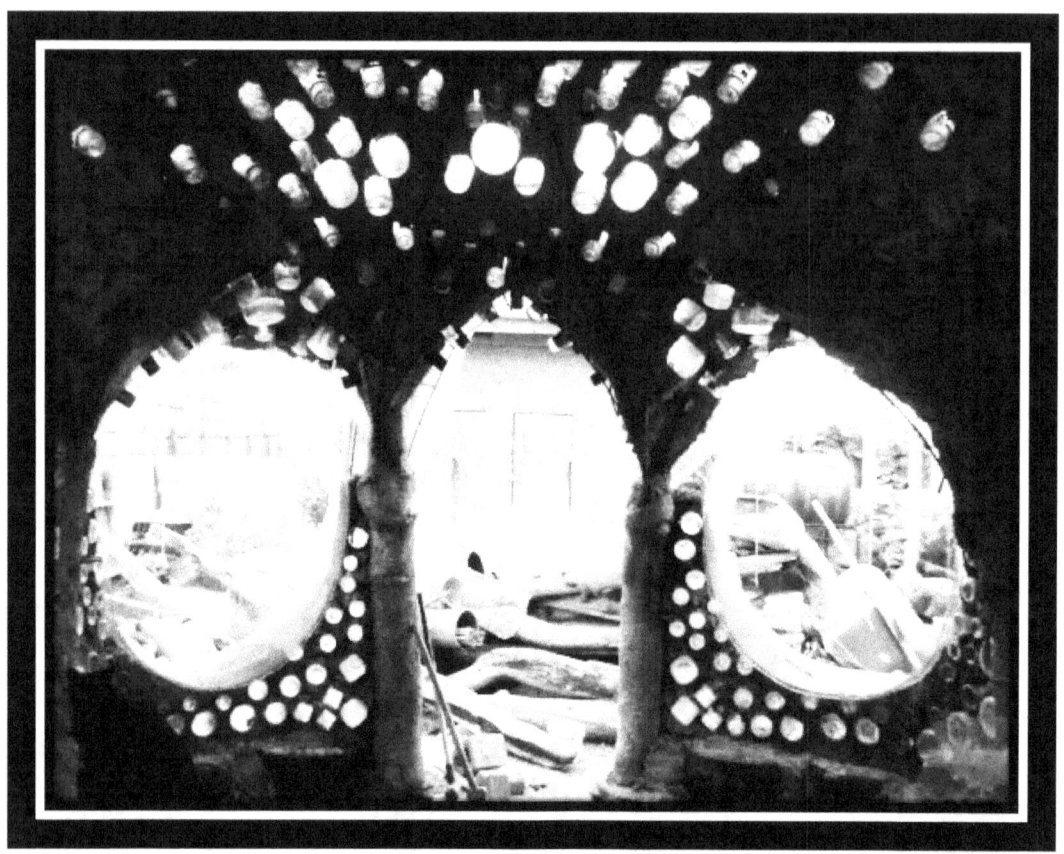

Yes, I have a water problem! Who'd a thunk? Luckily, it is 'just a sculpture' and not a home, so I think I will just live with it, though I am hoping that I can at least get them to dry themselves out before I seal them up better. I went through a lot of trouble to clean and seal them before installing, but the slanted angle makes them very prone to taking in water. Live and Learn!

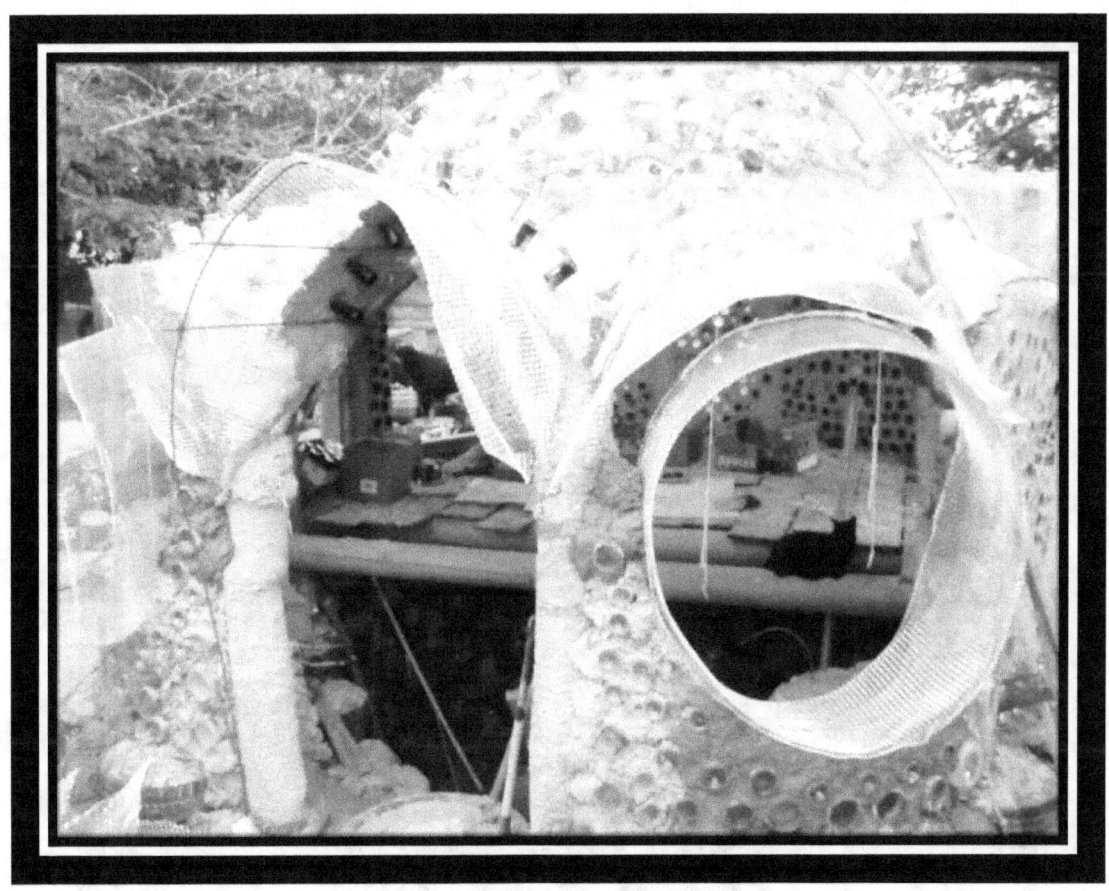

The Head Hutt Picture Book

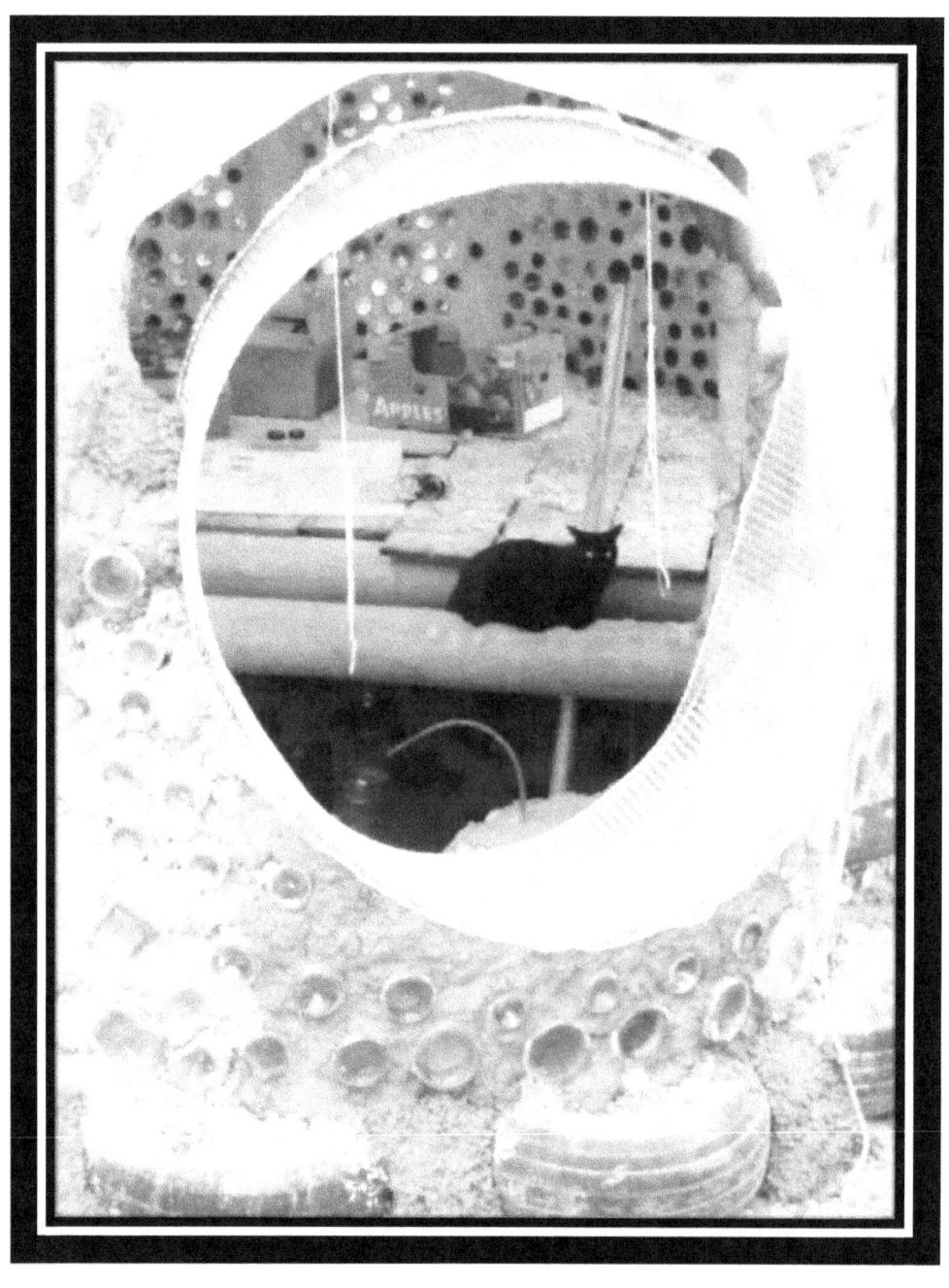

7 15 13. Coming along! Building a curved bottle wall is a bit tricky, then add the big round flat-plane opening and it just got a bit trickier than that. I plan to plaster over the top and bottom arches before filling in the top bottle-bricks (like I did in the Foo Dog). I ran out of sand, once again though, so, more sand tomorrow!

7 15 13. These front panels are even more curved than the others, and the flat-plane giant round openings are adding to the challenge--but nothing me and some concrete, plaster, and pumicrete can't handle!

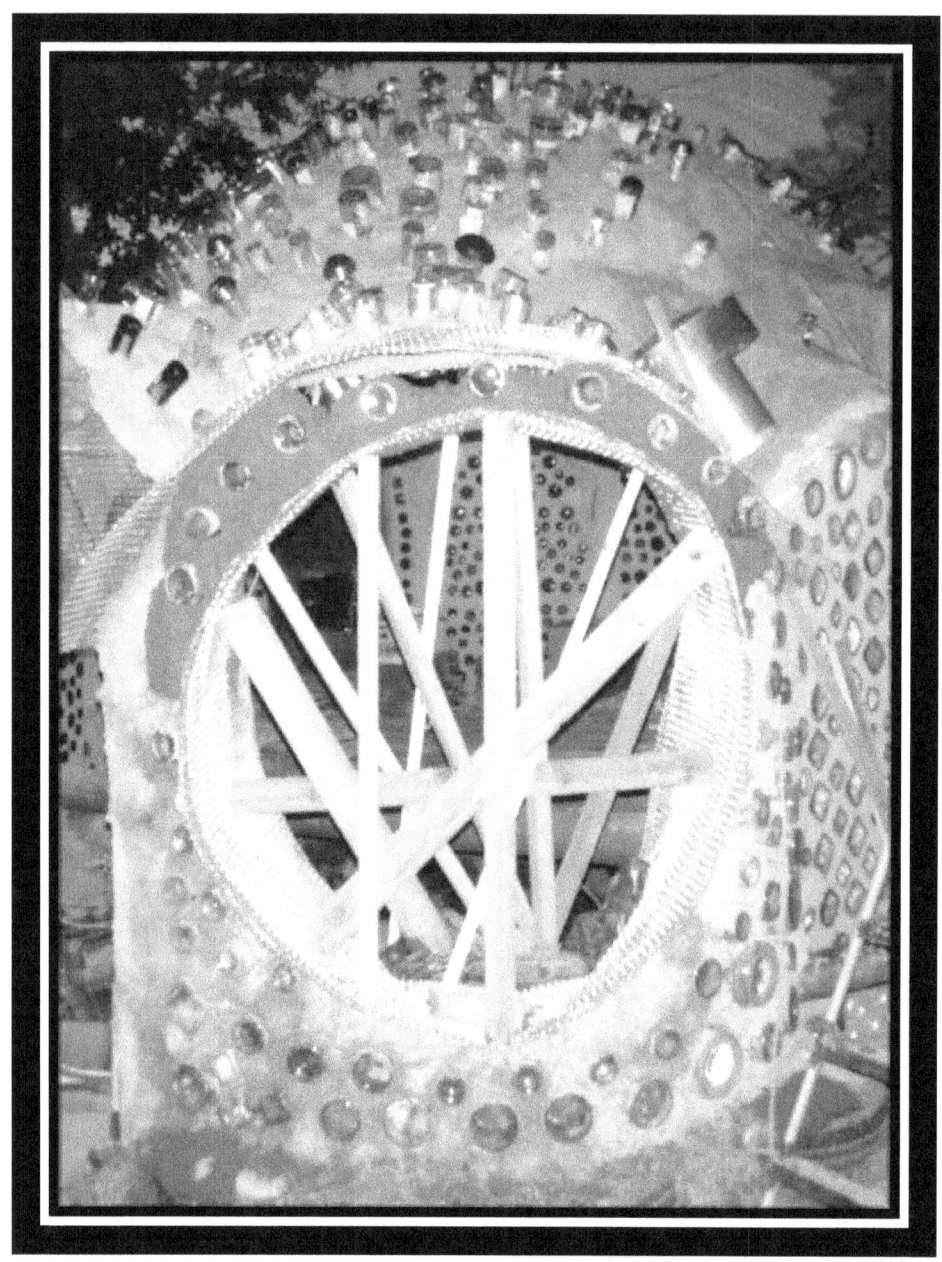

7 17 13. Left eye; going in rough.

The Head Hutt Picture Book

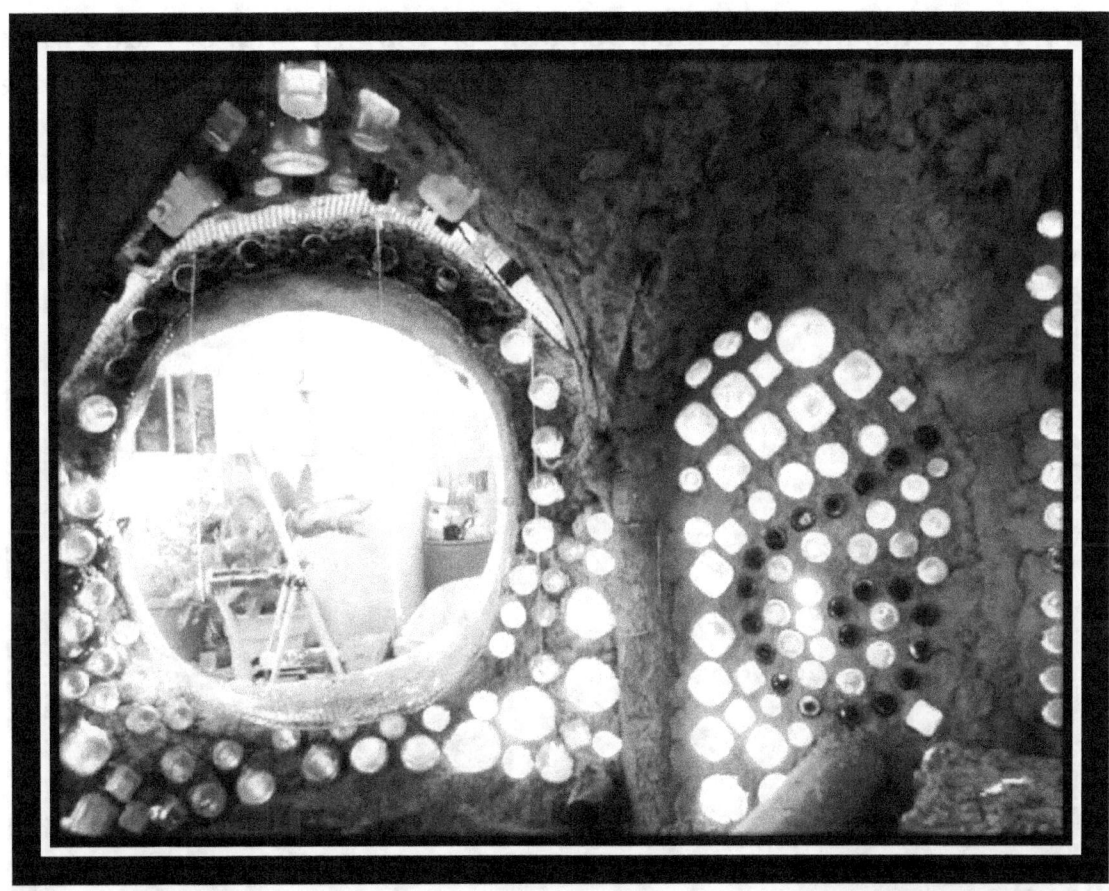

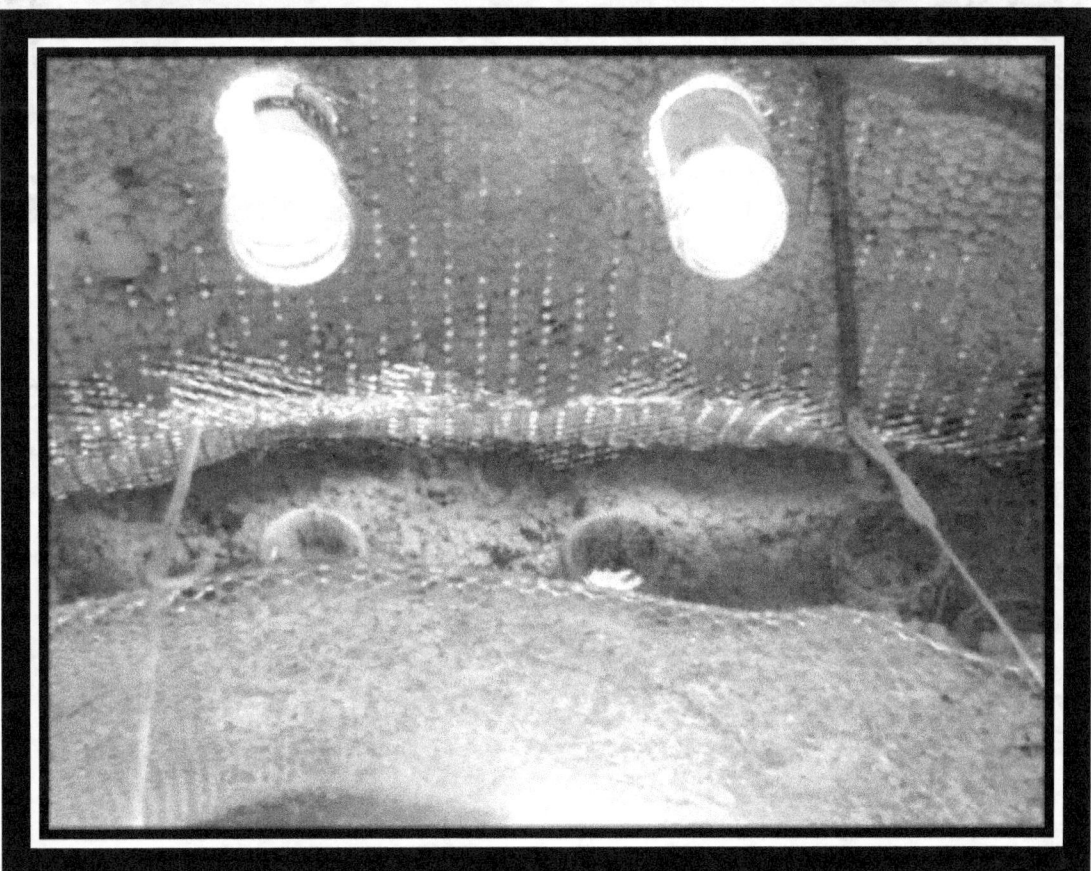

I should have brought those ends back to flush with my ring, or made the ring smaller. I tried to shoot for my lower plumb line, but realized afterwards that was silly, and less pleasing. Live and learn! 7 18 13.

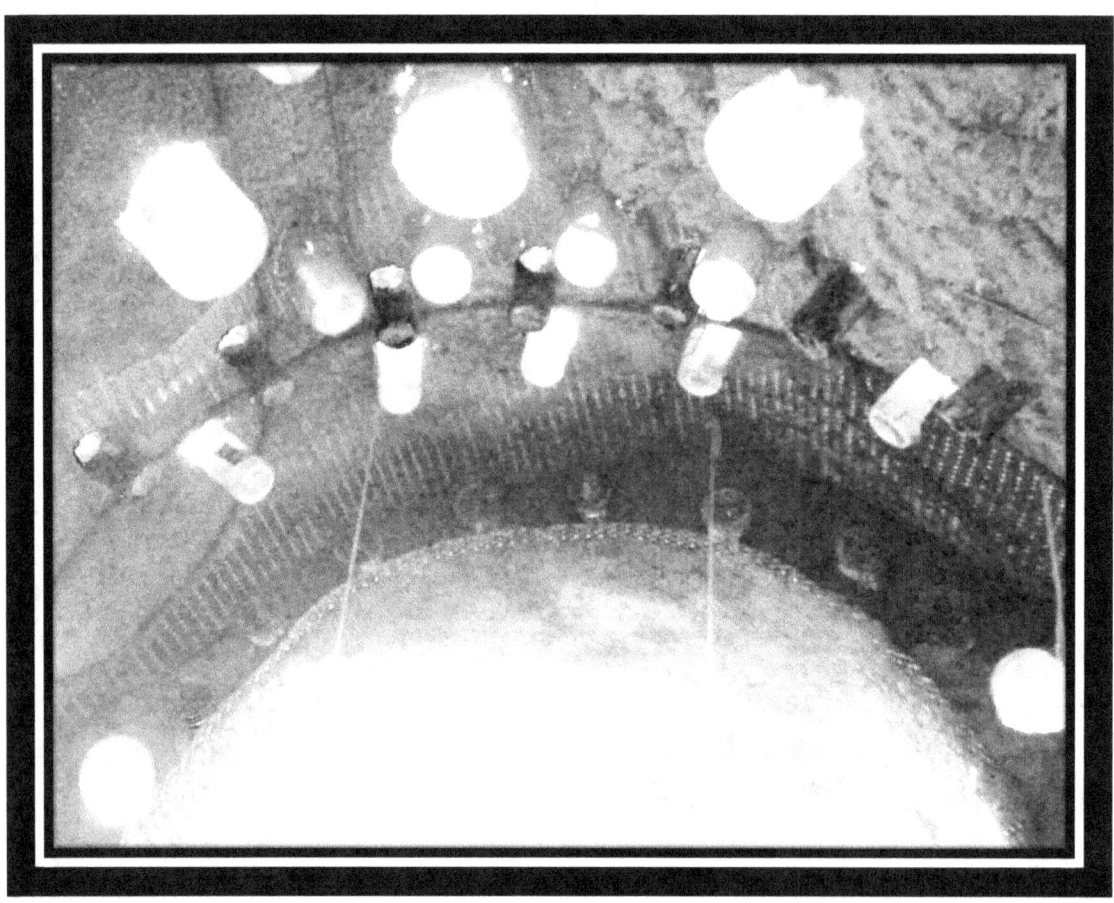

Right eye roughed in. Still infill and plaster and more details to go in. I know this level of imperfection/roughness would/probably makes many people cringe, but I love it!

7 18 13.

The Head Hutt Picture Book

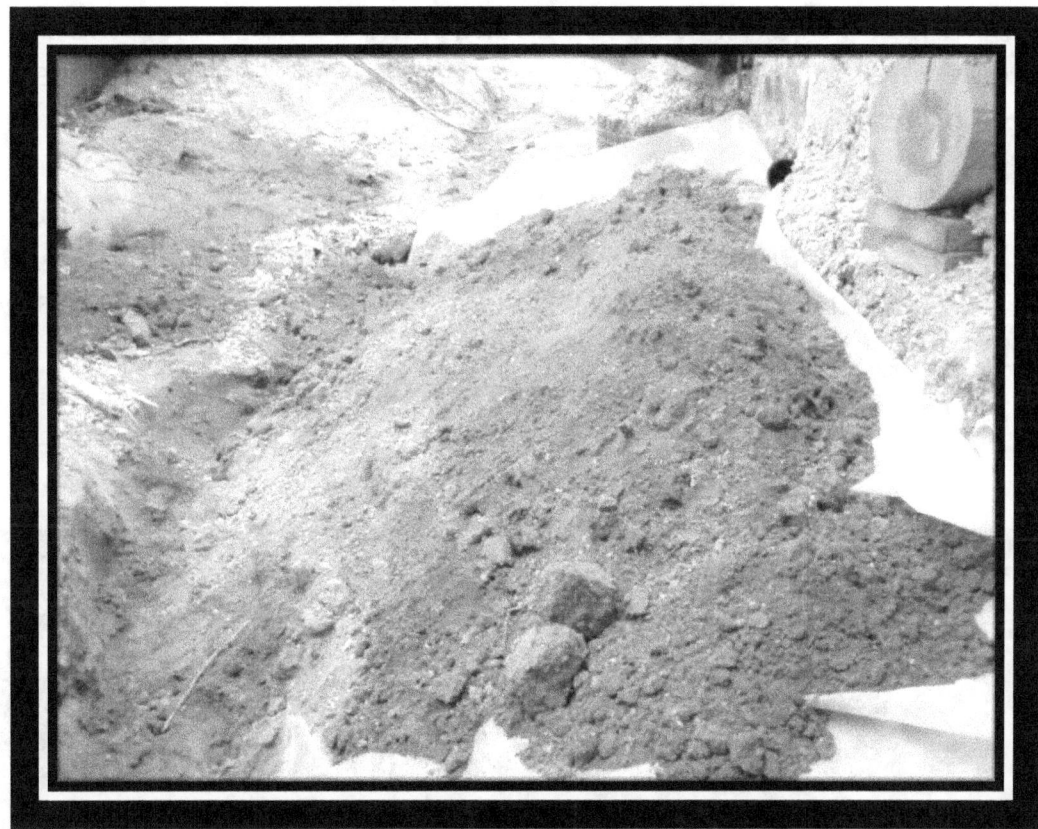

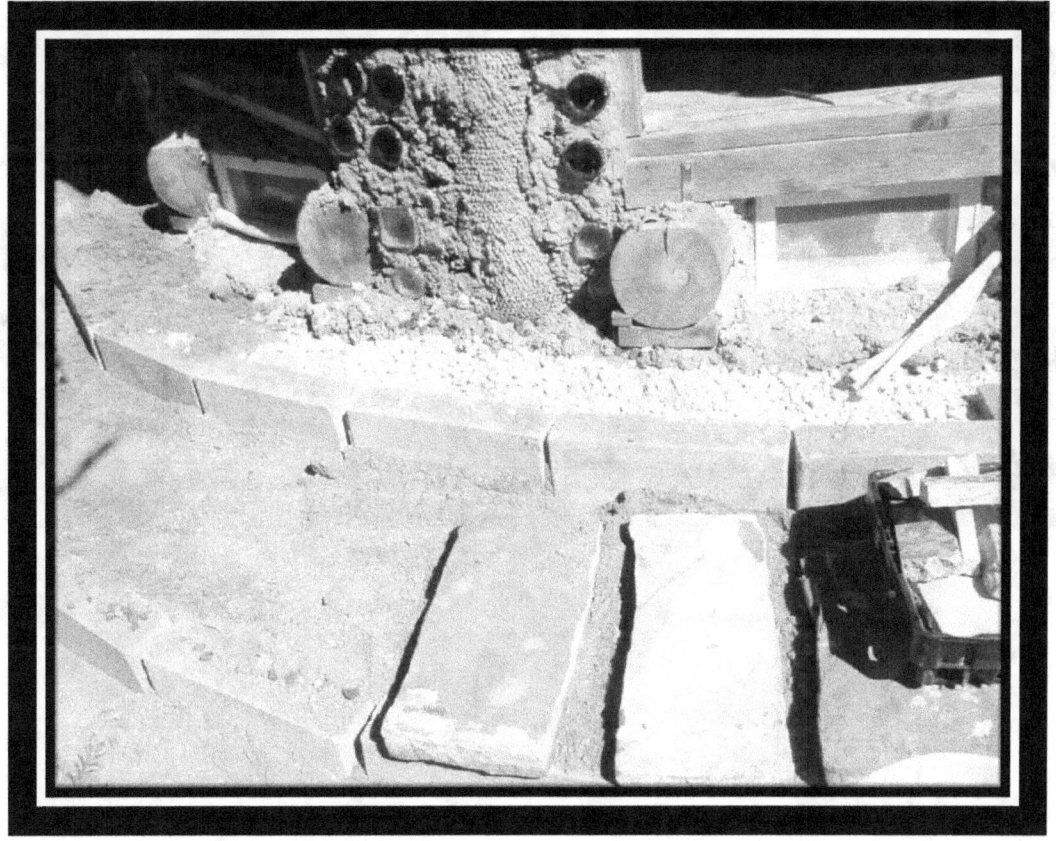

After scoria and dirt against the bond beam, I dug down so there was a slope to lay down a layer of plastic and covered with more sandy dirt (to keep the scoria from puncturing the plastic). 9 28 13.

Perimeter--insulating layer of scoria first. 9 28 13.

10 5 13. Sloped perimeter over plastic, scoria and pumice. This layer has functioned fine so far, with no moisture seeping into the lower level as of the publishing of this book.

Working my way down the inside. 10 6 15.

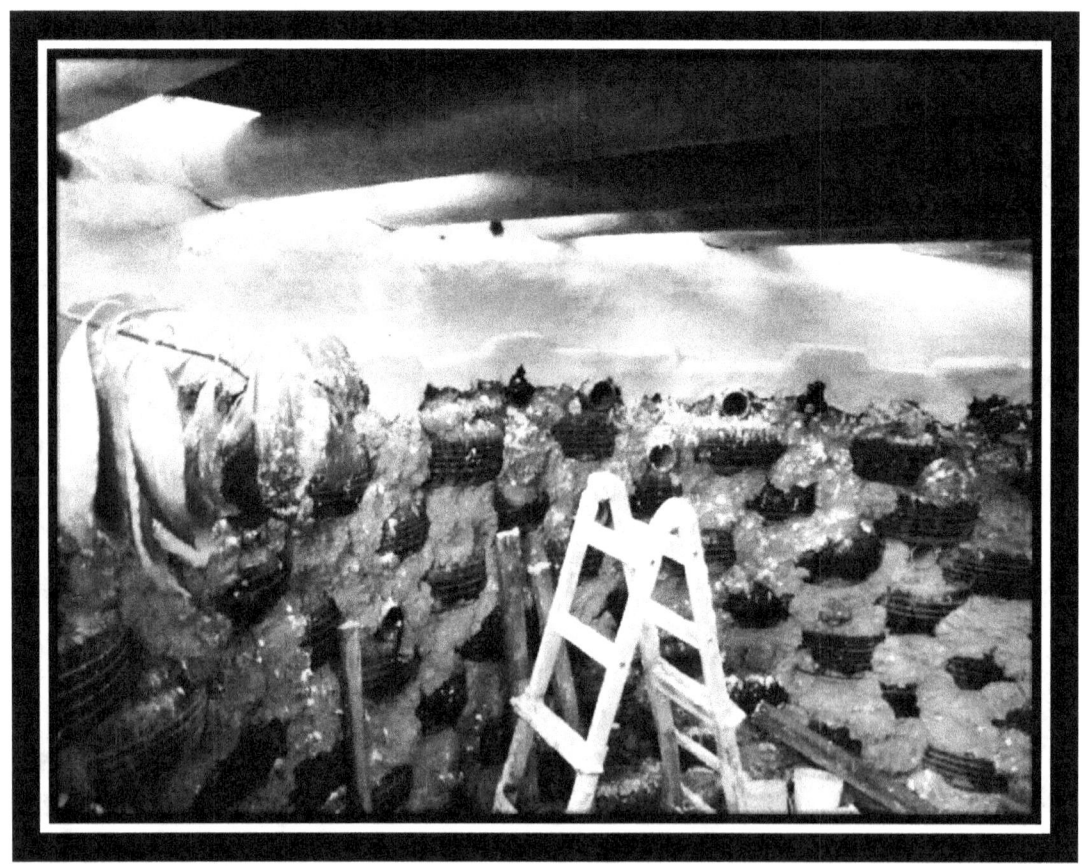

Cob Infill, Lime Plasters, & Steps

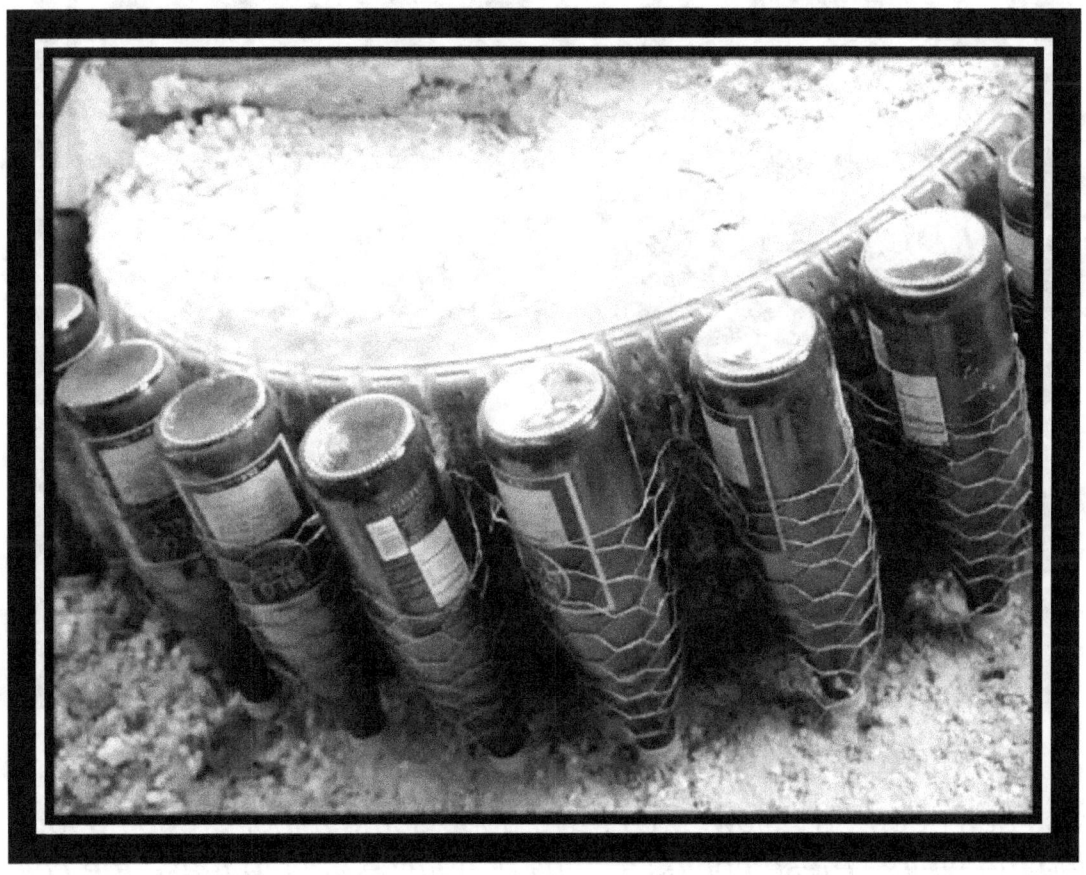

The Head Hutt Picture Book

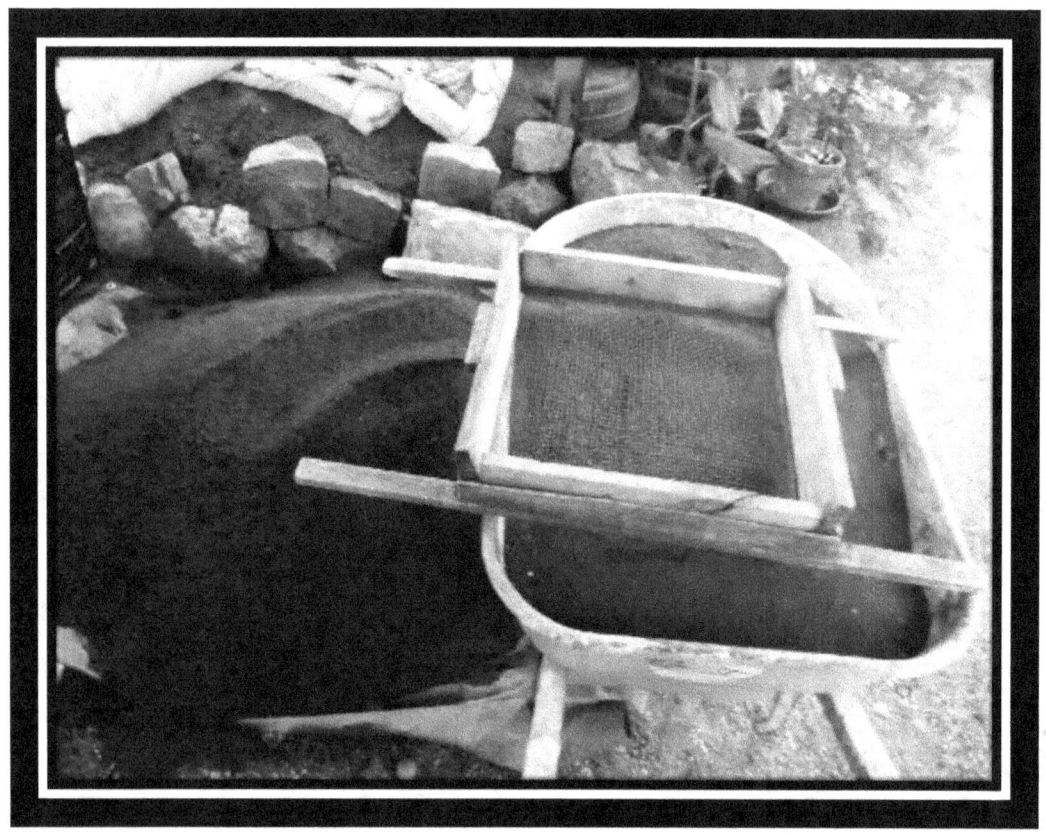

Progress has been very slow, but I have done some minor prepping for finishing the stairs. These bottles are full of pumice dust to make the color pop a bit more. They will get set in concrete, I think. March/April 2015.

Lovely adobe makin earth! All screened and ready for making mud. I found a special deposit of clay rich earth in the mountains outside of town, just a bit off the freeway. It took some doing to drive there, dig a yard or so, bring it home, screen it, and have usable cob making clay mud. It feels very good to use materials from the earth which will also go right back to the earth when the lifespan of the Head Hutt has come to its end. I cannot say the same for cement based products, which is why I have come to prefer using less and less of it.

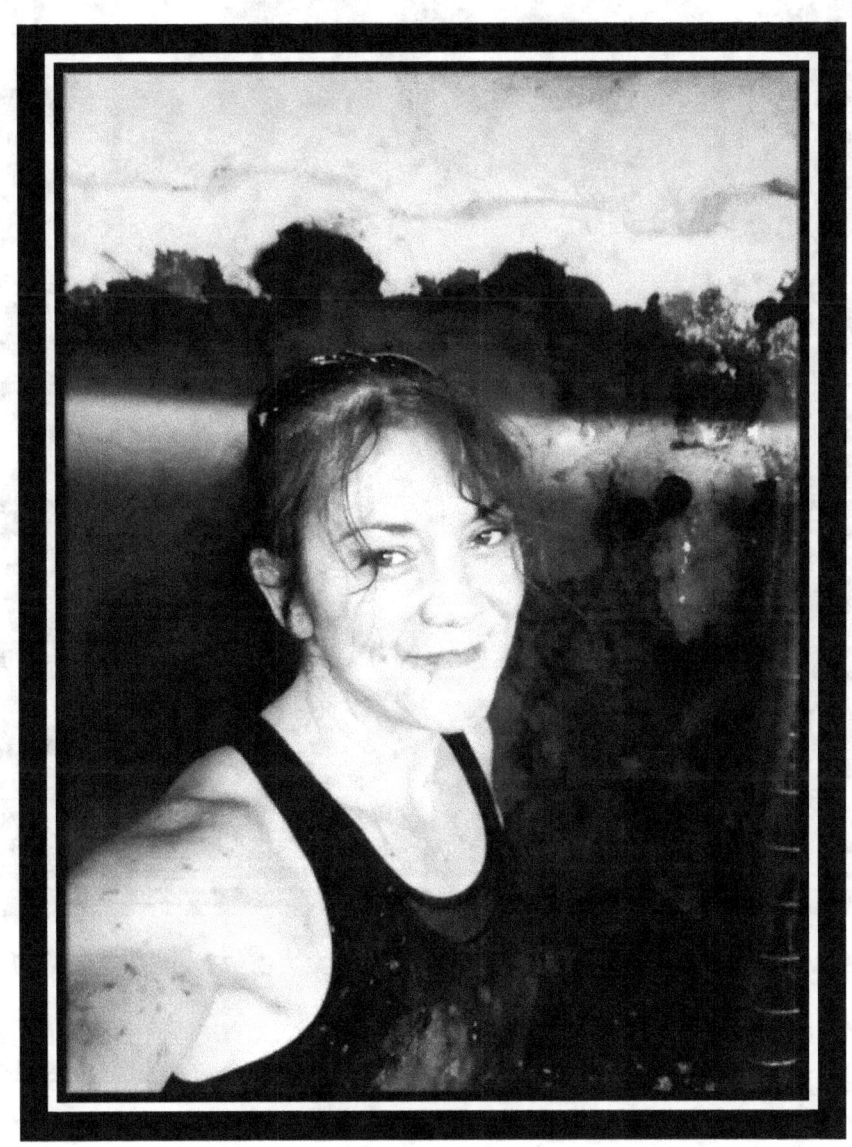

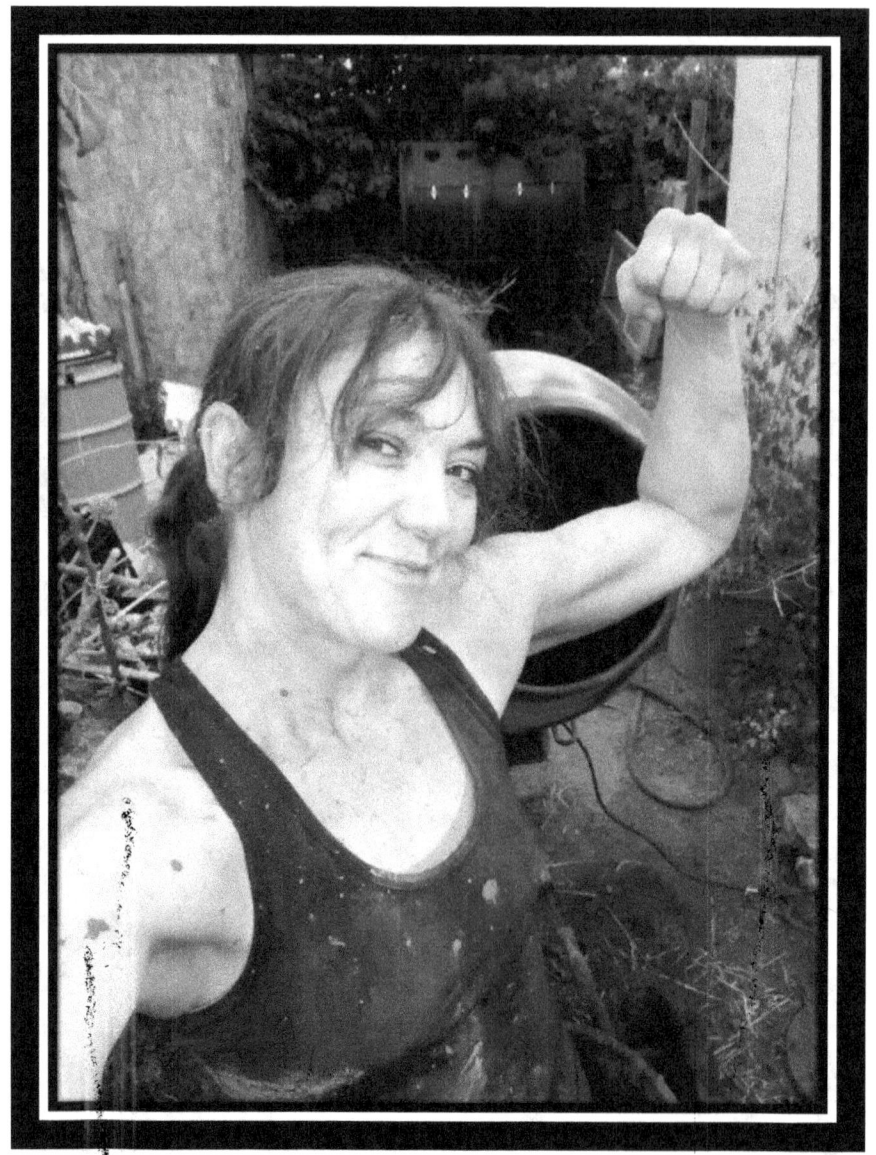

About 2/3 the way around the final infill around the lower floor. 8 17 15.

In case you were wondering, I haven't forgot about the Head Hutt and RCDC/Foo Dog. Part of the reason I decided to start the outline of the Ra Temple/Eye of Horus out on the windy flats this week is that I had to take the van a third of the way there for clay-soil anyway. On the agenda: More of the same, and then some!

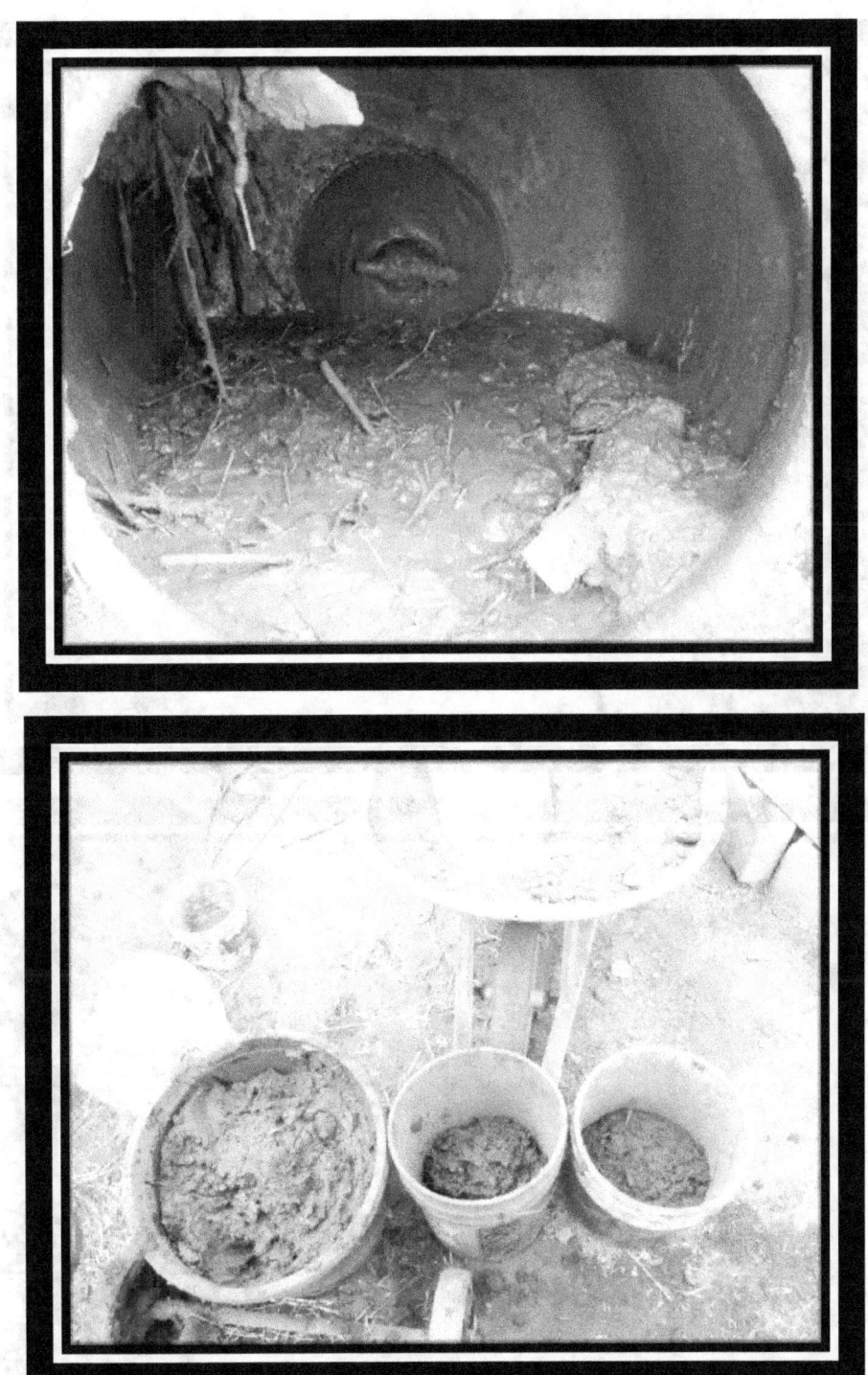

8 23 15. Mud infill. Little bit, by little bit I shlep it down the hole, then up onto the walls. 8 23 15. Last load of infill for the HH!

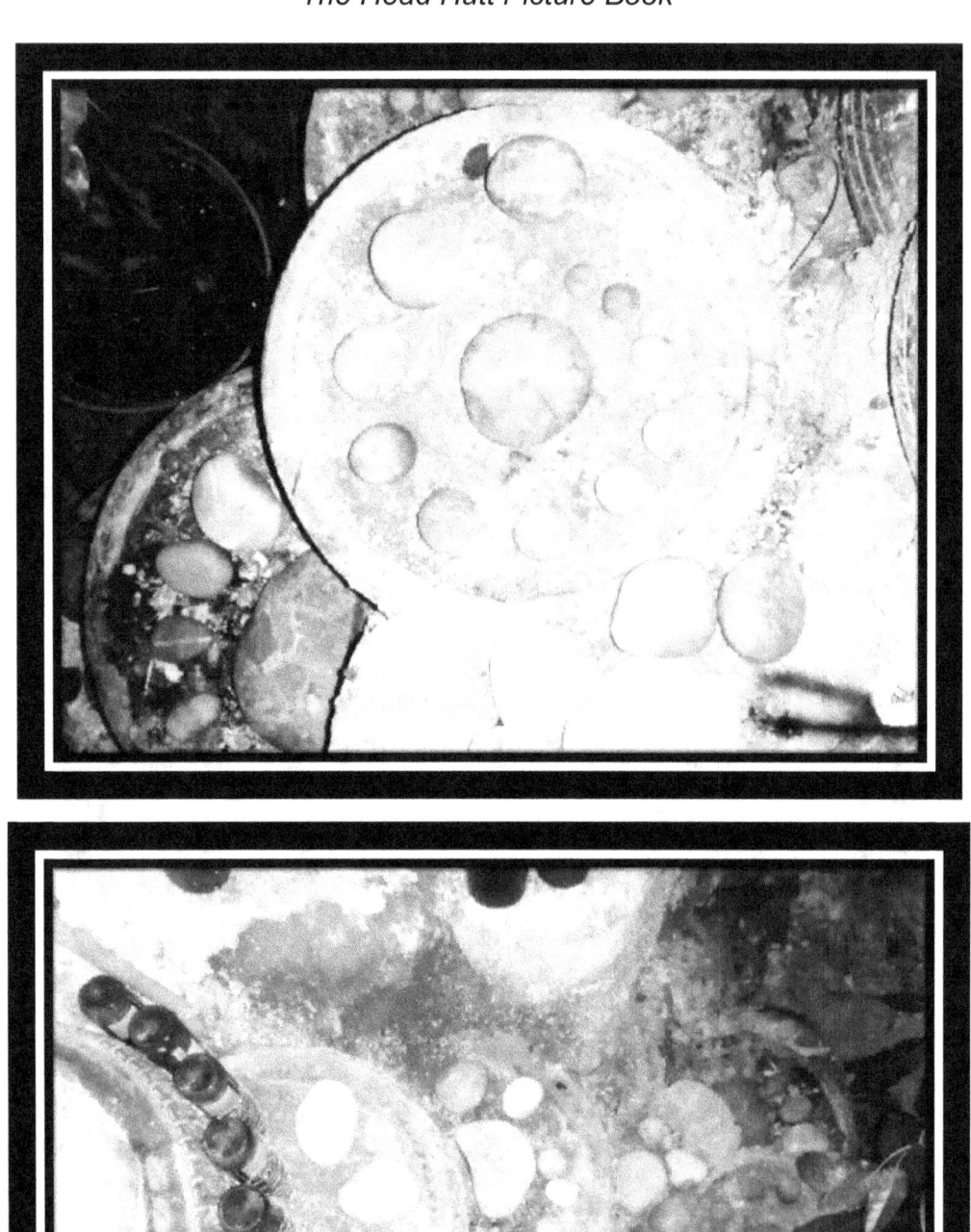

Prepping stones for the stairs. 5 28 15.

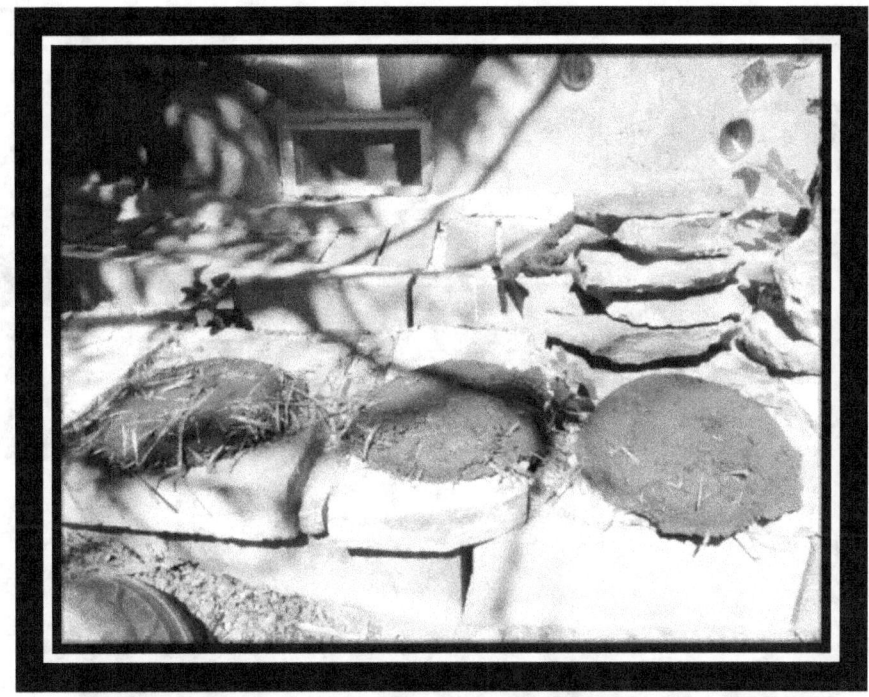

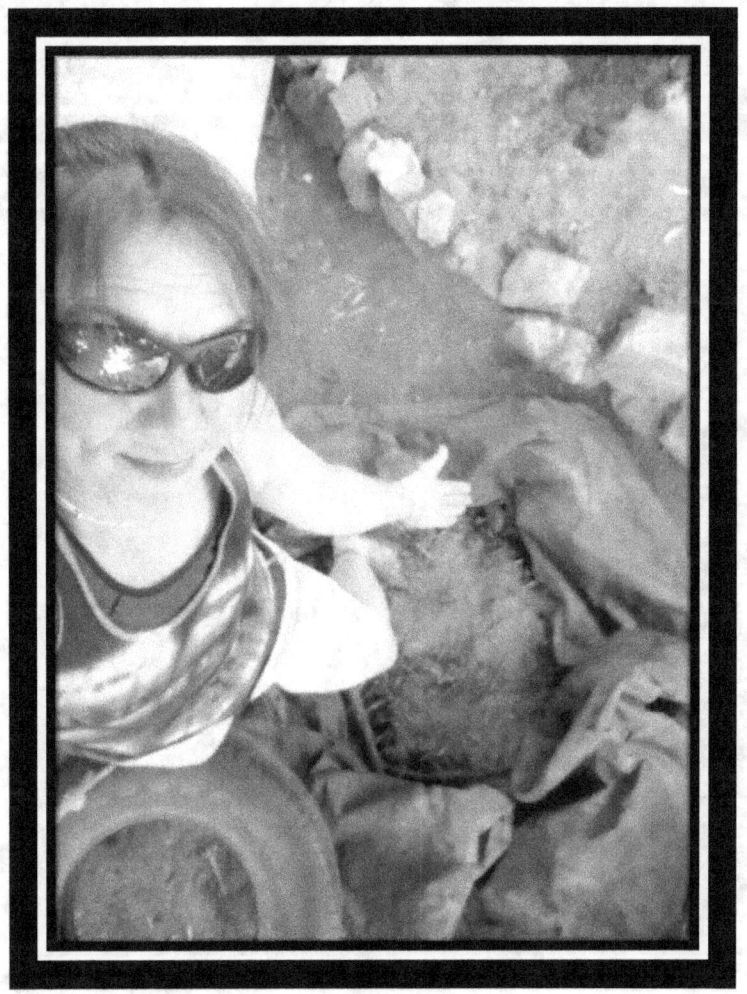

Cob trials.

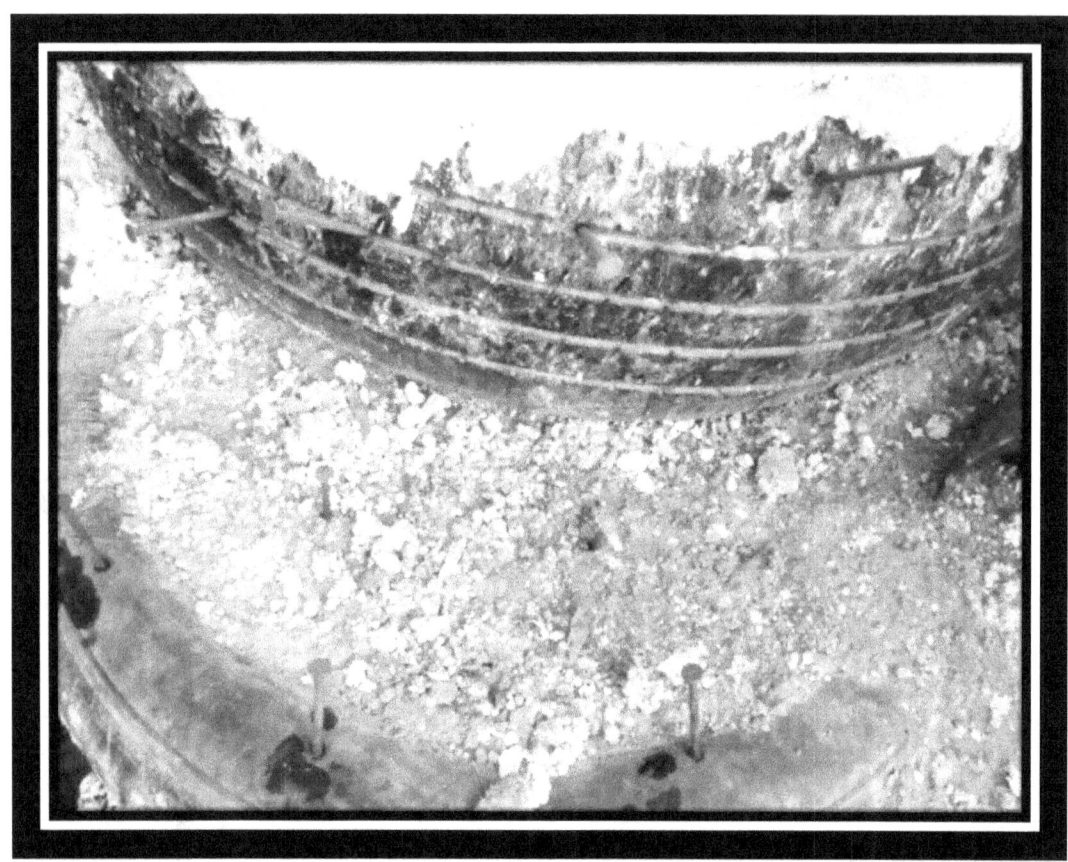

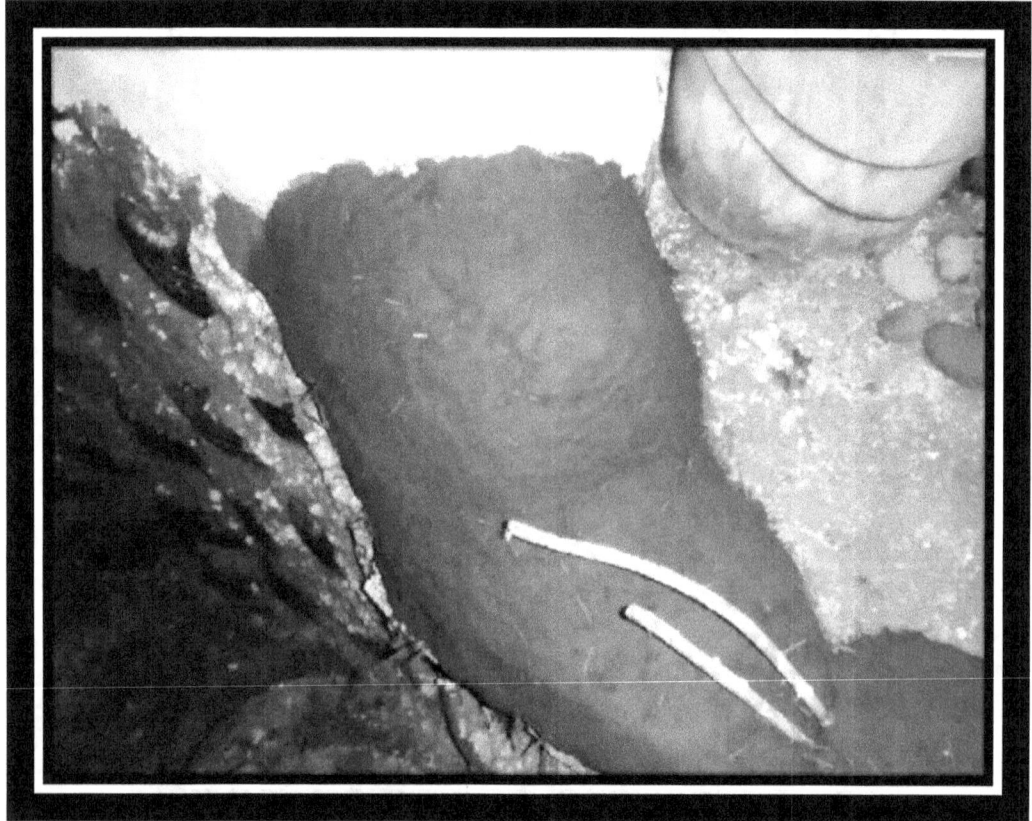

Prepping for infill, I am putting in some rusty nails to help hold the cob.

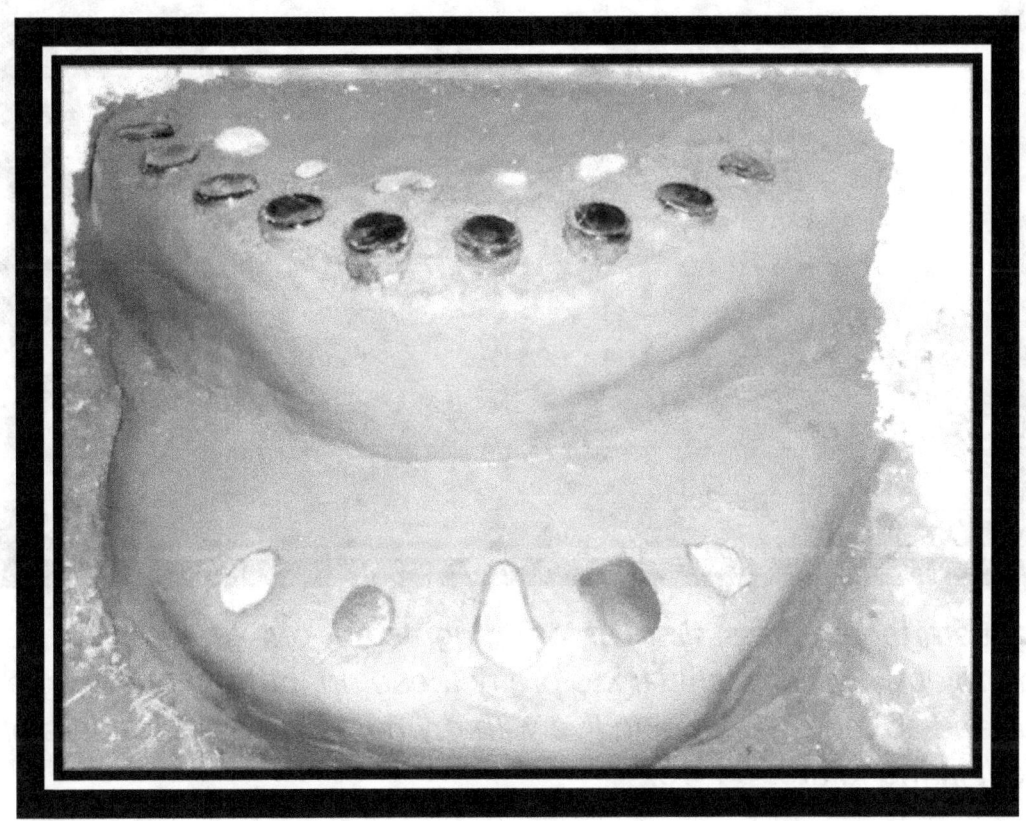

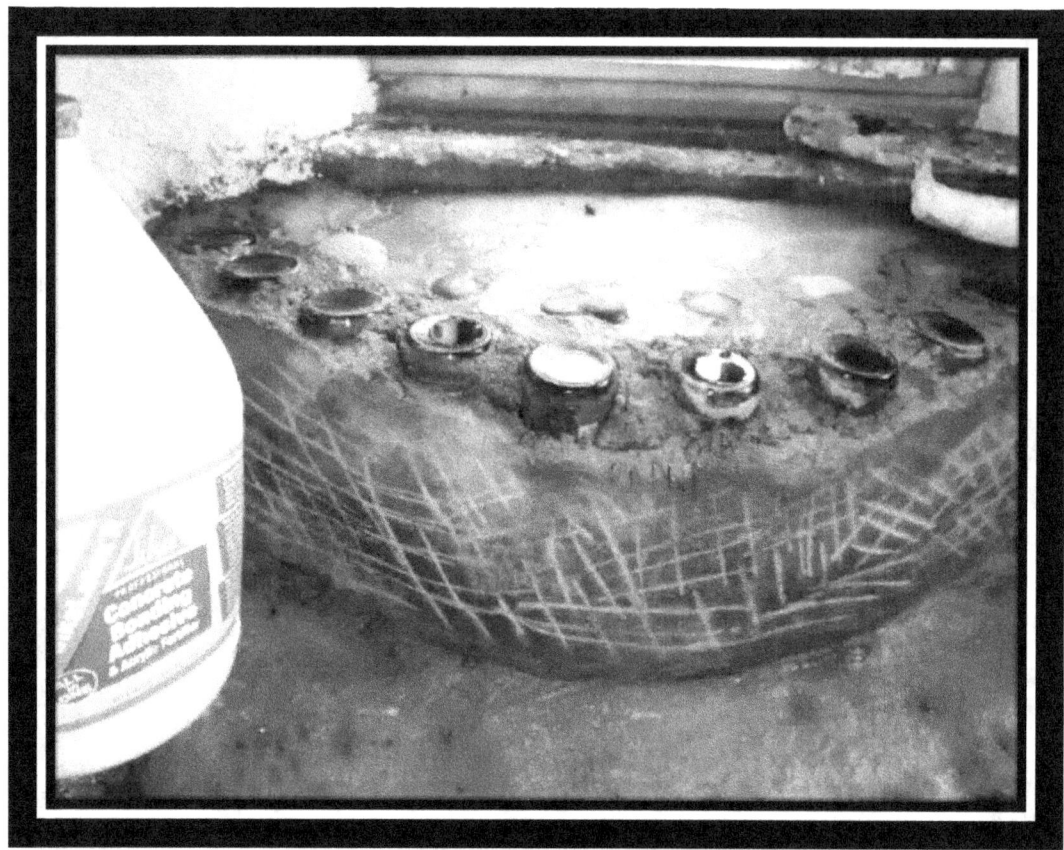

Finally got started on the stairs! Off to a rough start, but, that is why this is a learning project. I will probably try to pretty these up, but ran out of time to do it proper, and so may just have to live with my mistakes as reminders of how not to do it in the future. 6 7 15.

I didn't end up using the adhesive, as it froze and got grainy.

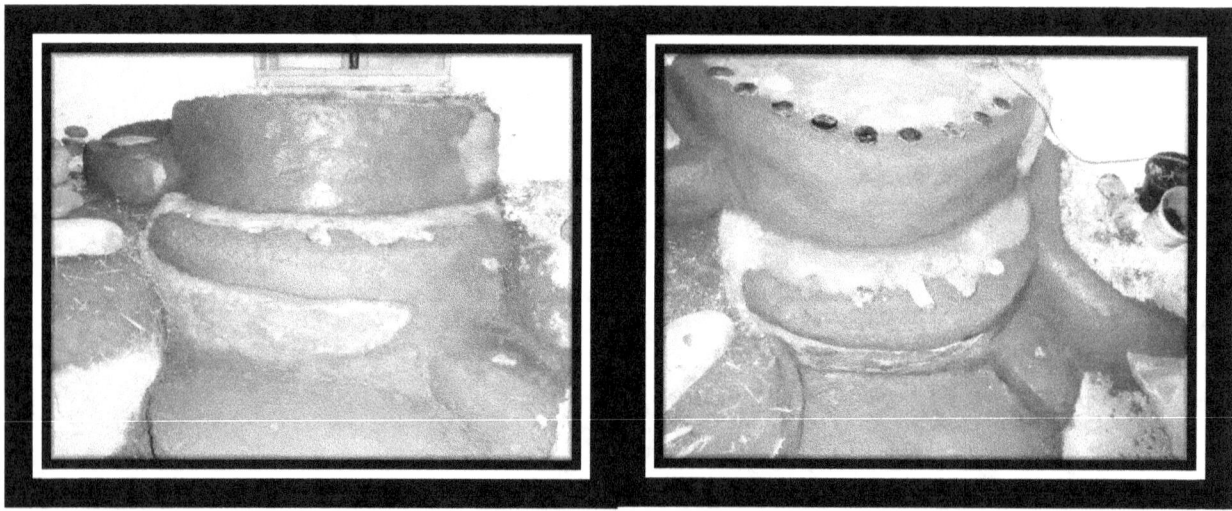

I did decide to score and redo while still curing. It may crumble, but since it was going to be less functional without the addition, I decided it must be done now. And, maybe it will last. 6 8 15.

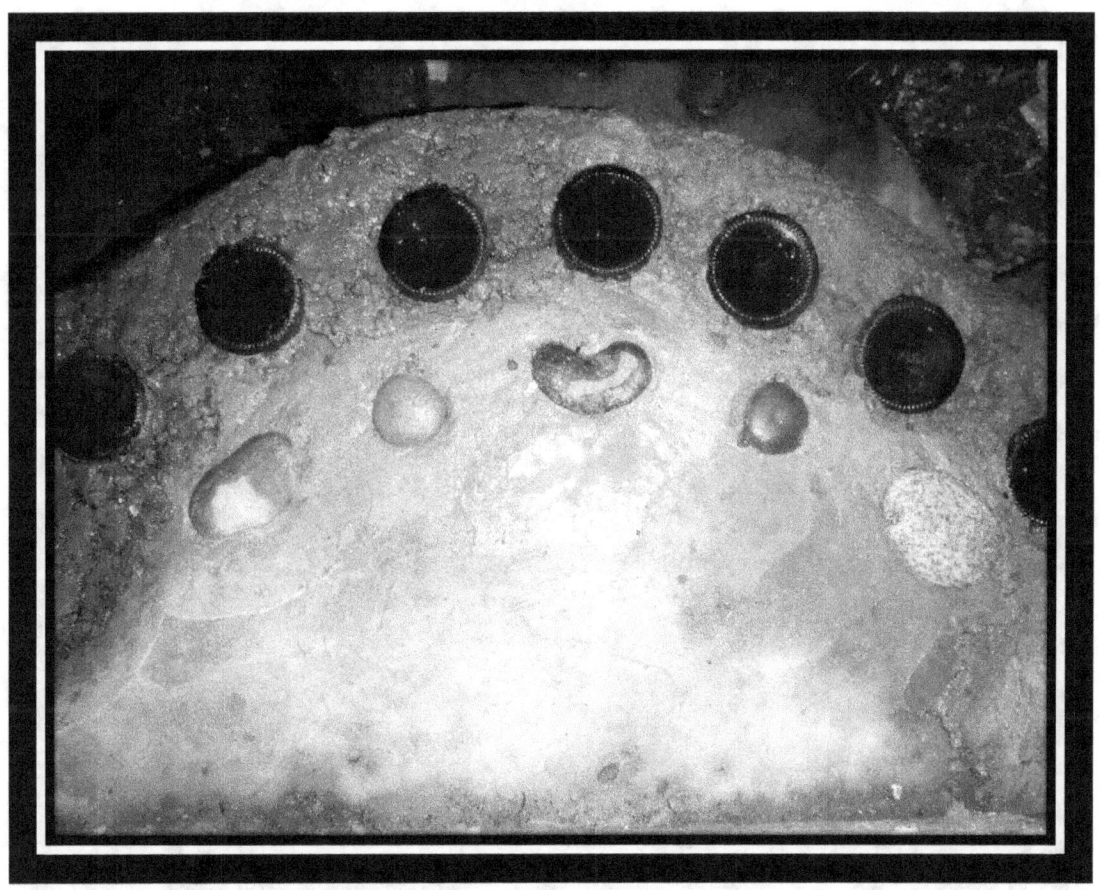

10 3 14. last of the top side and outside plastering on the HH! Now on to the bottom!

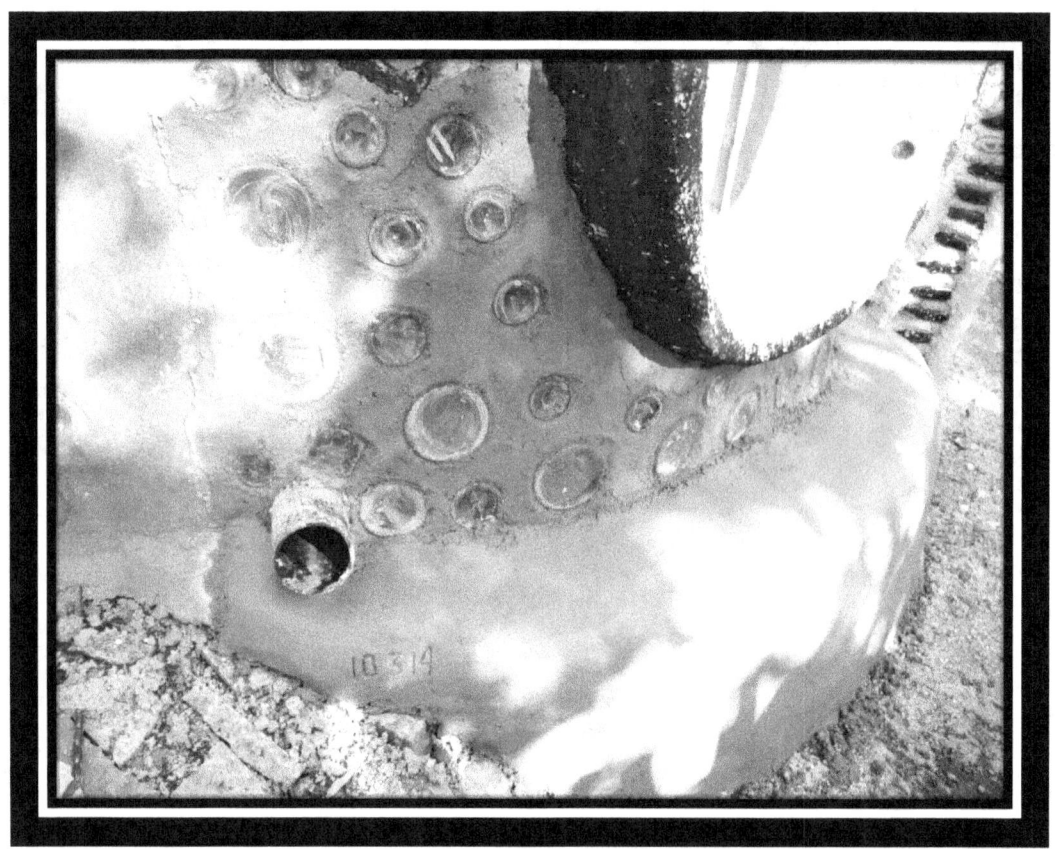

The Devil is in the Details

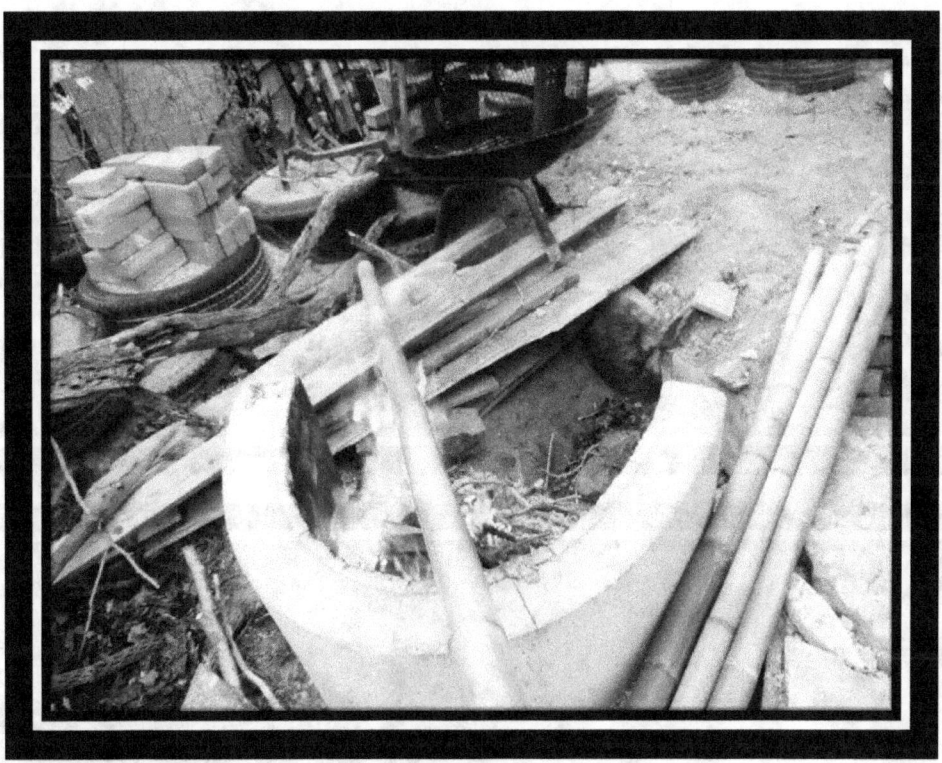

Just a few hours and minor burns to get the bamboo fire-cured. There probably is an easier way, and I think the bamboo could have used a few more months to dry, but the end result is beautiful, shiny, and strong! 3 12 15.

My friends Mike and Amy brought me some bamboo to try out. I had fun curing it and dreaming with it, though I did not end up using it yet. There were a whole lot of things like this that I spent a lot of time on only to abandon or set aside. That is part of the process. You must have a willingness to fail in order to succeed. To try what you don't understand and gain a better understanding.

The Head Hutt Picture Book

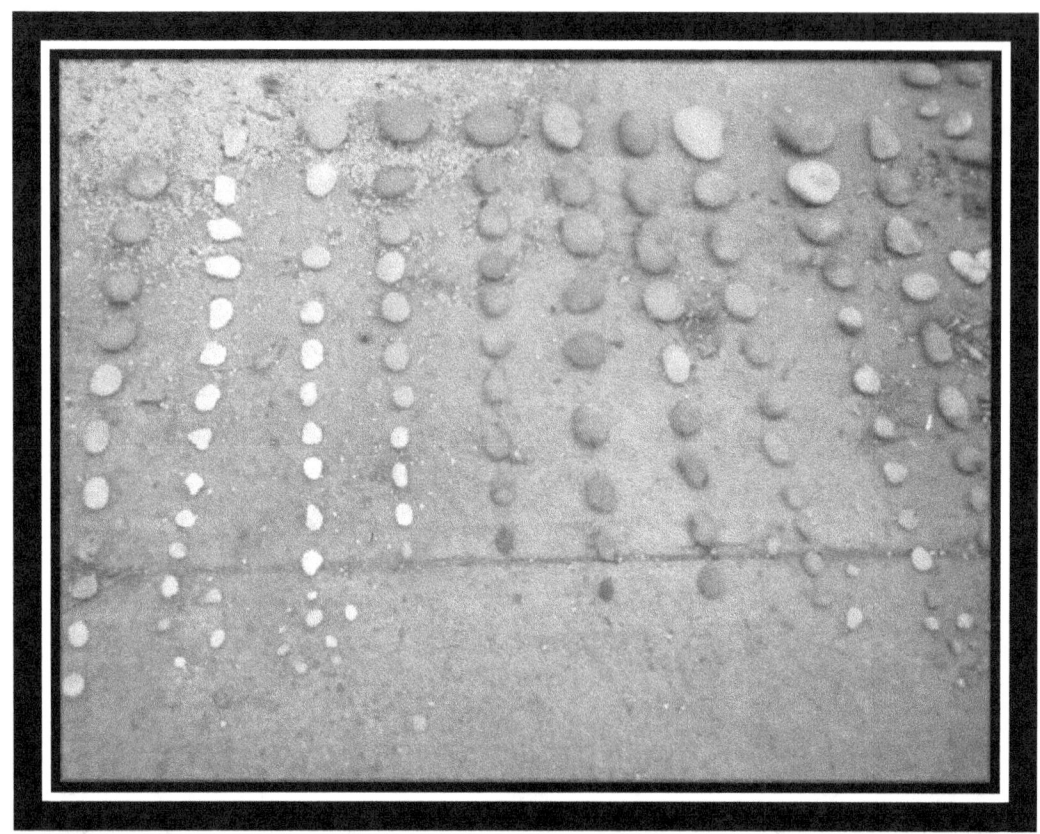

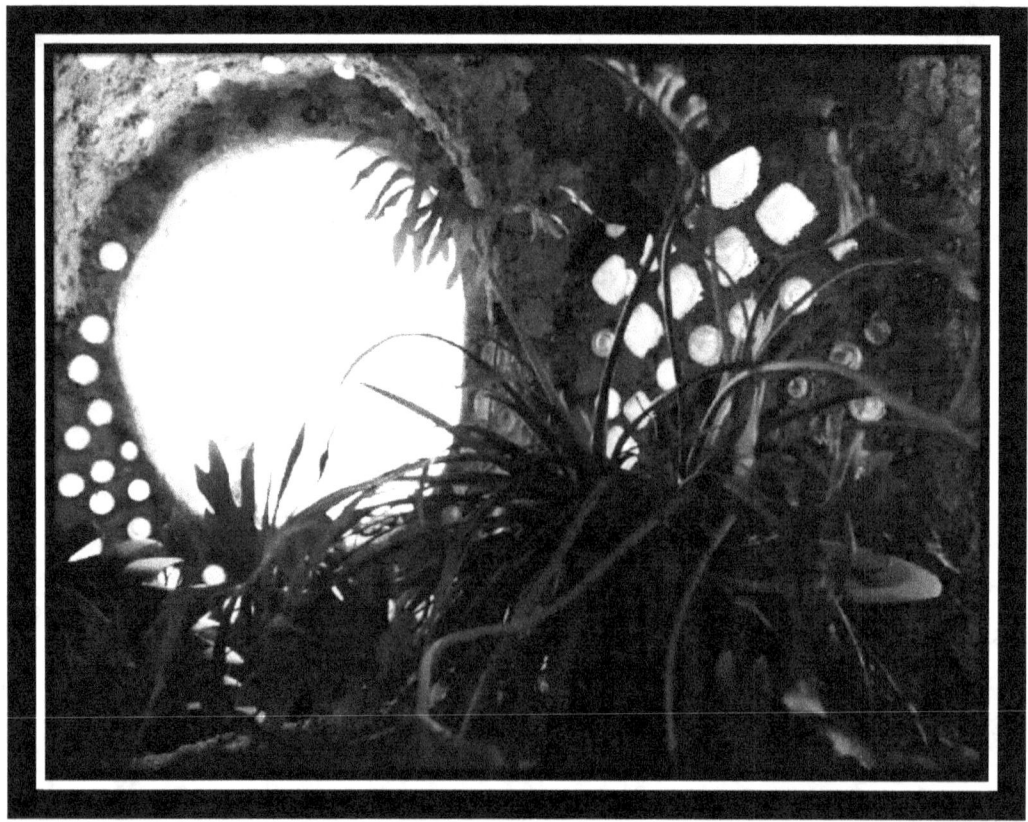

I collected and sorted stones into various matching sets. Still working on those tree motifs...from cholla to stones. I will find the right design/s. 5 27 14.

I moved a few houseplants in here for the summer. They seem pretty happy. 6 21 14.

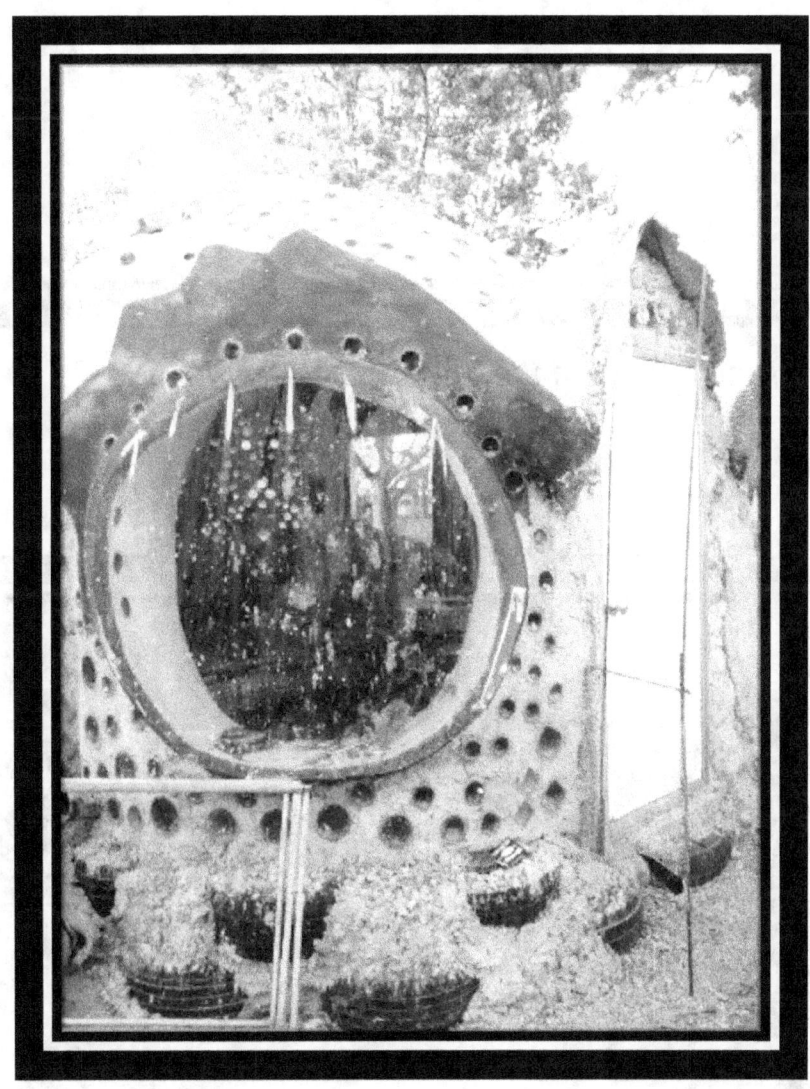

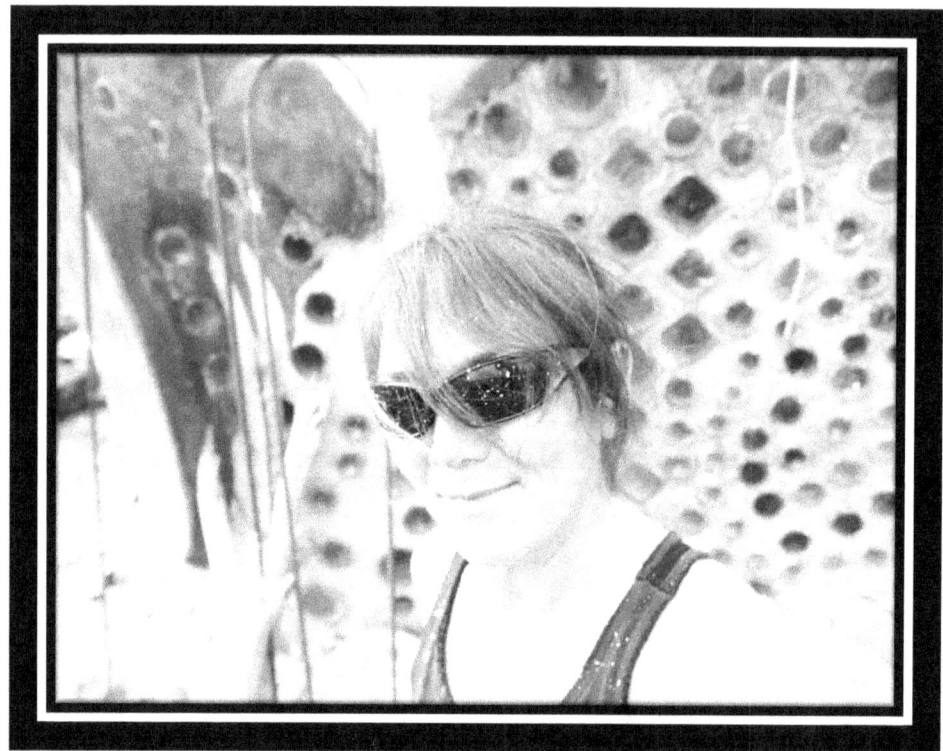

6 26 14. getting ready to put in the Beak/Front Entrance. Messy girl.

7 17 14. Before the rain.

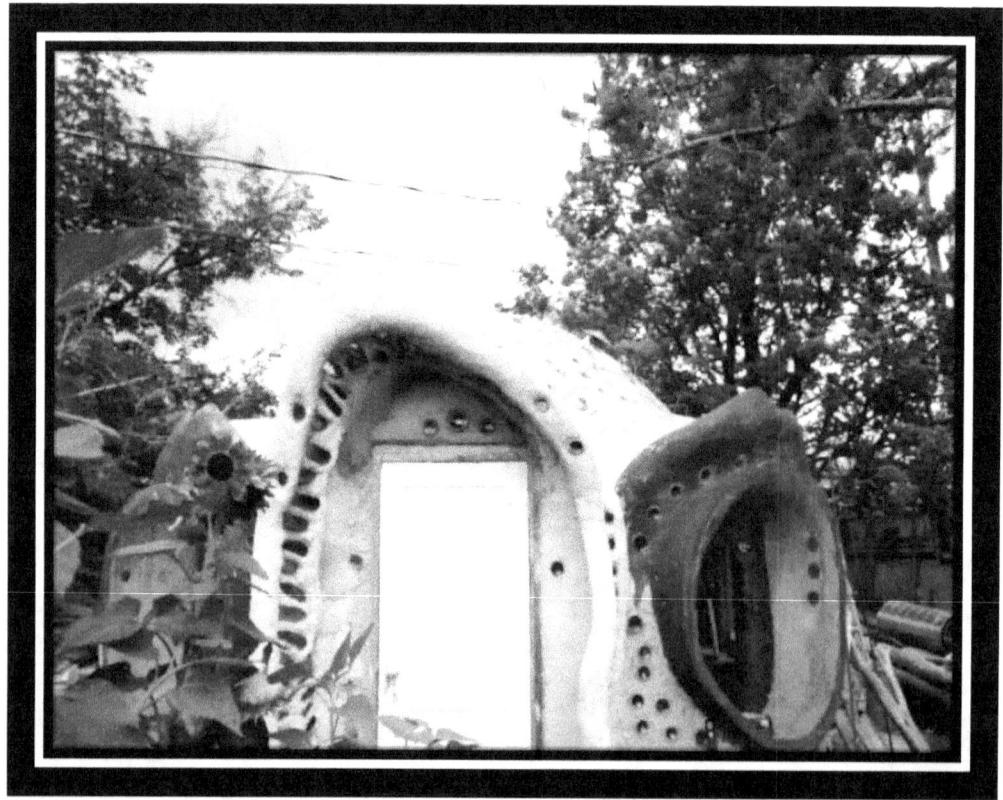

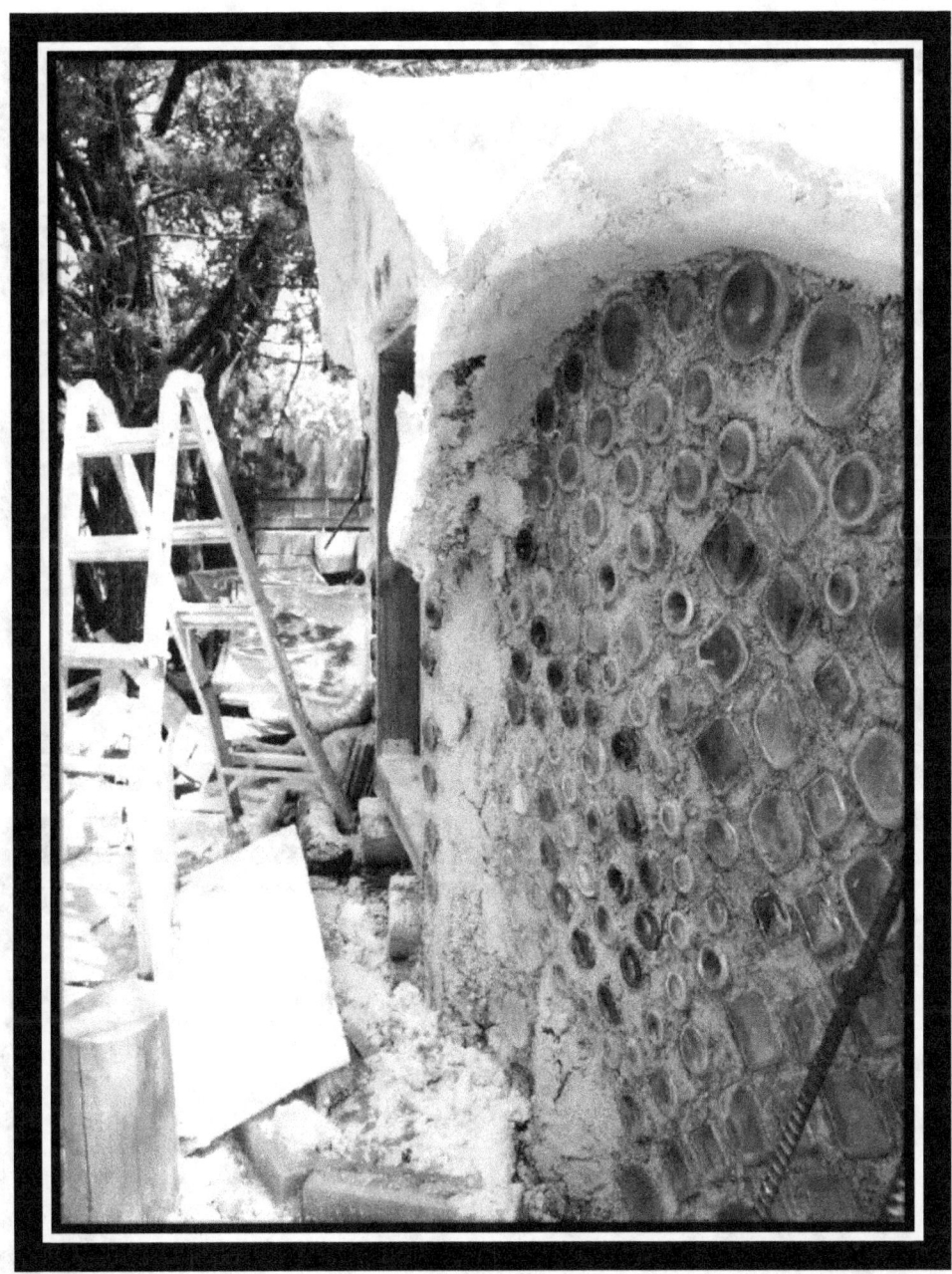

After rain, second collapse/fall of these overhangs. This was one of a few areas that I had to do and redo several times to get it right. My mix was too wet, or I over-worked it, or I put too much on the overhang, so during the rain it shlumped off and had to be built on twice more. 7 19 14.

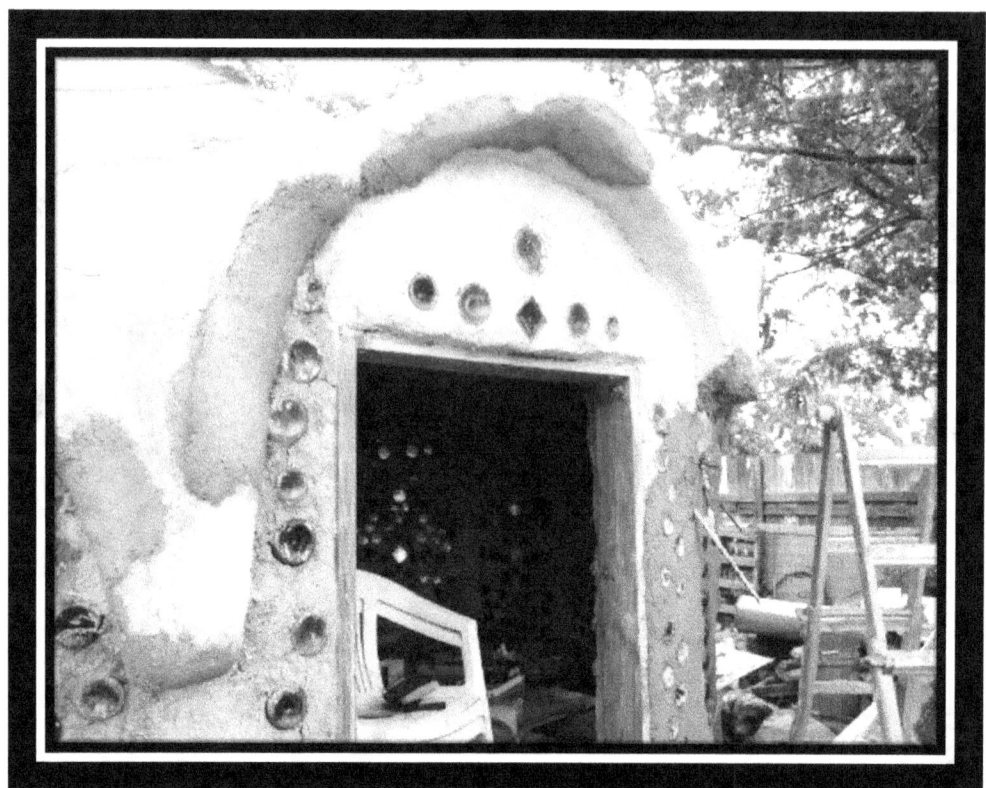

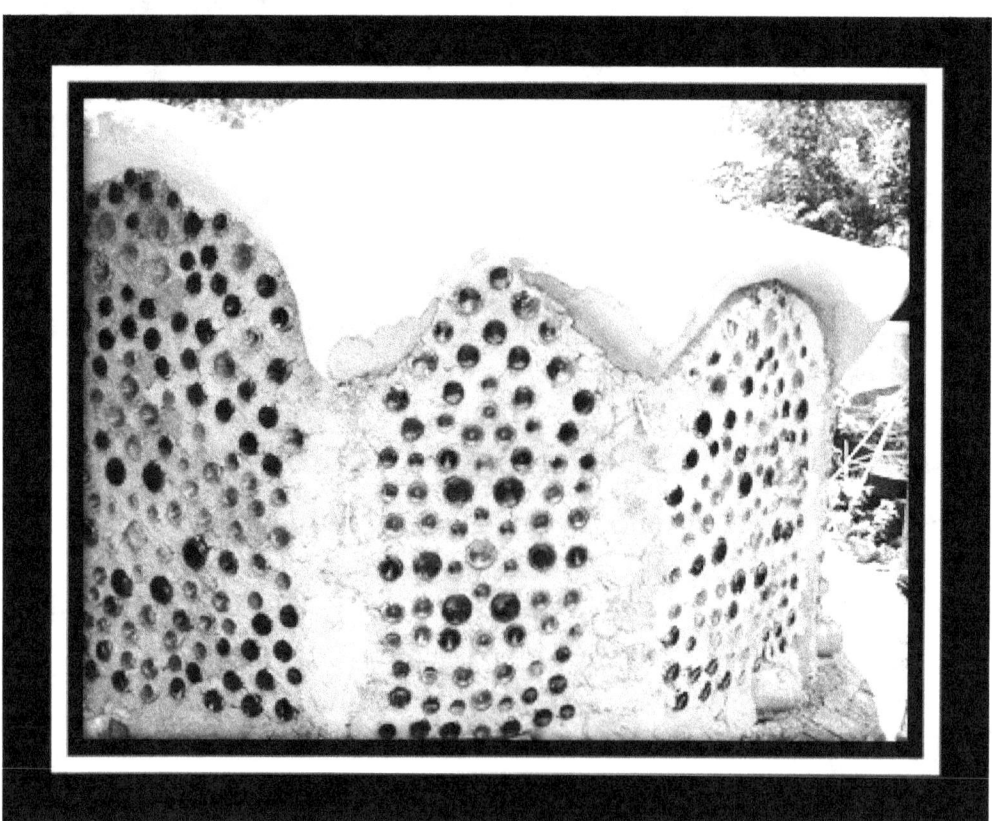

Third time is a charm! I finally got the mix and timing just right working with gravity to keep the overhangs in place long enough to cure fully. Onwards and upwards! 7 19 14.

Overhangs are redone. Still rough, but good enough for color I think. 7 29 14.

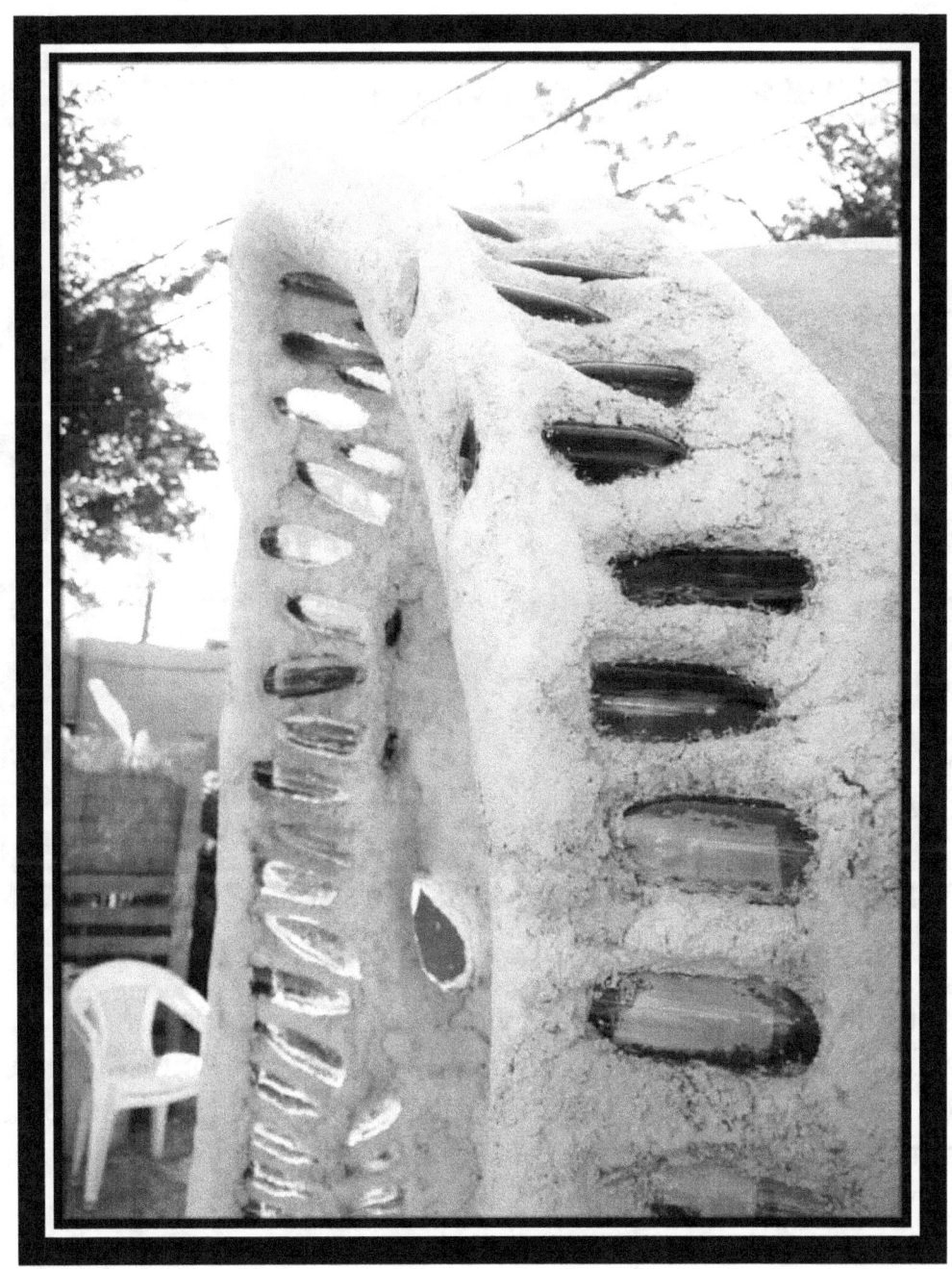

7 28 14. All dry and ready for final color. These bottles sure are pretty in the sun.

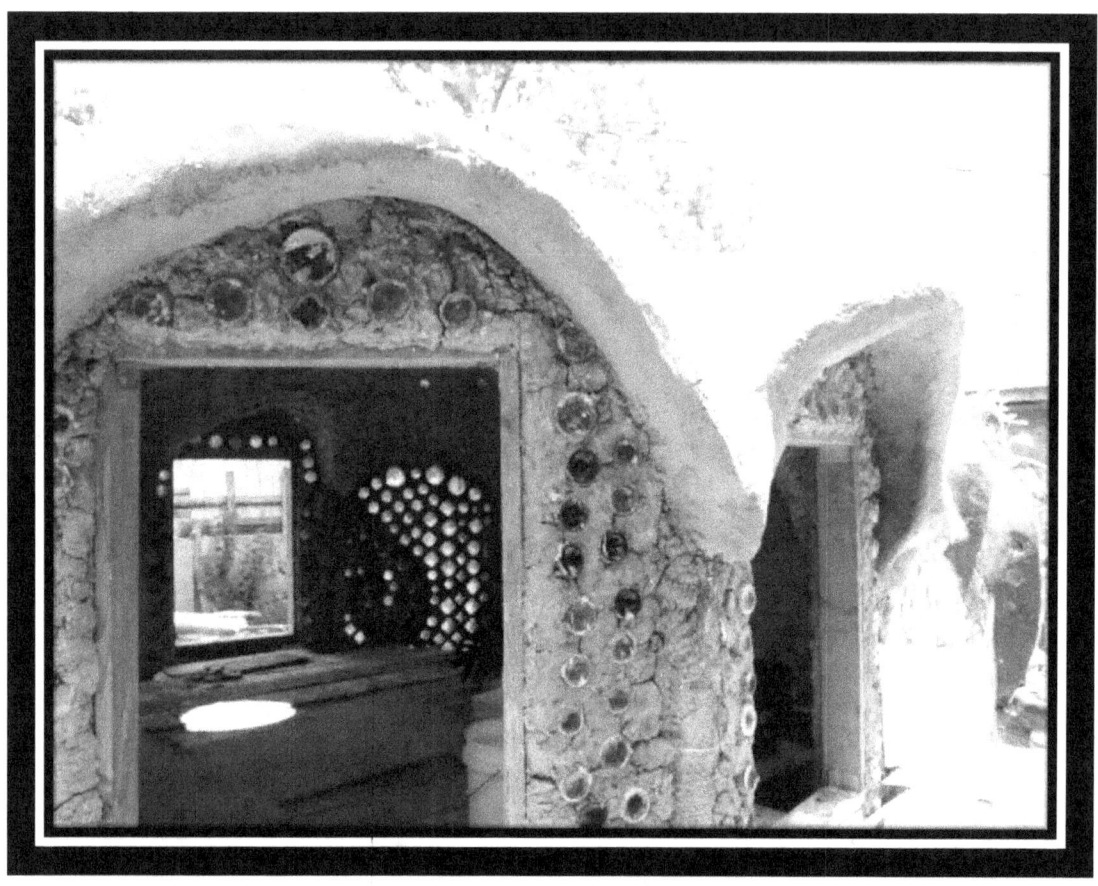

The HH sat without plaster for a long while. Just curing, cracking. It actually only cracked at first drying, due to shrinkage of course. For plaster I used more force (and a trowel, knife, or spoon, instead of just hands) to press the fibers together and got little to no cracking on the final finish. If there had been cracking, I would just go over it another time.

The Head Hutt Picture Book

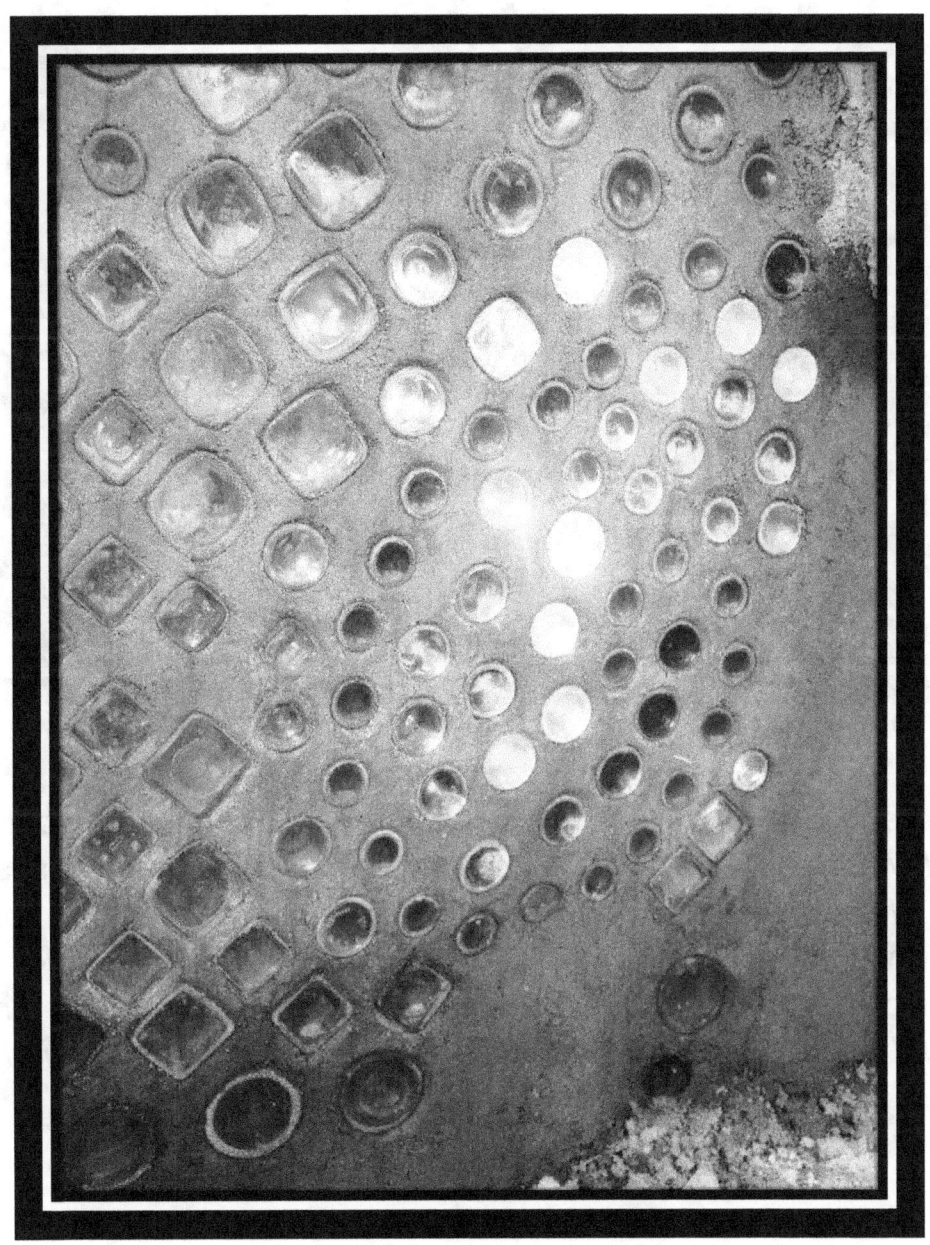

This is what the east outside looks like just before sunset. I'm going green! 8 16 14.

8 18 14. Working around bottle ends with a spoon is a bit difficult in the shadows of lamp, but not as difficult as in the dark! "I love lamp."

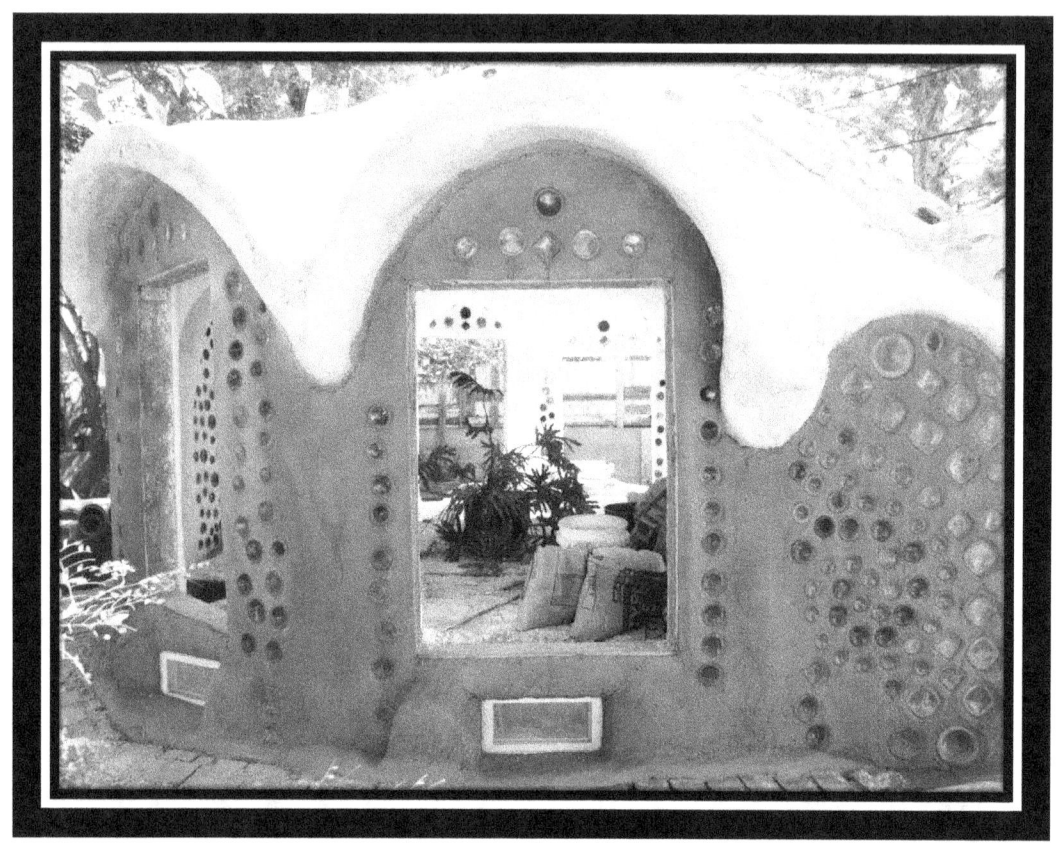

All the green is in! Excepting lots of touch ups. I used a spray bottle with watered down green oxide for most of the green, and in many cases sprayed in on wet. It seems to have cured in place, though now and then some does come off on hand, especially where I sprayed it on dry. I think adding lime to the water would help it bind better, or perhaps spraying it on over it now…in a few years I will probably touch up or redo the color on most of the HH. 8 21 14.

Here's one of the bottle ends I plastered over and had to dig out. Amazing how many times I did this, even double checking myself! 8 21 14.

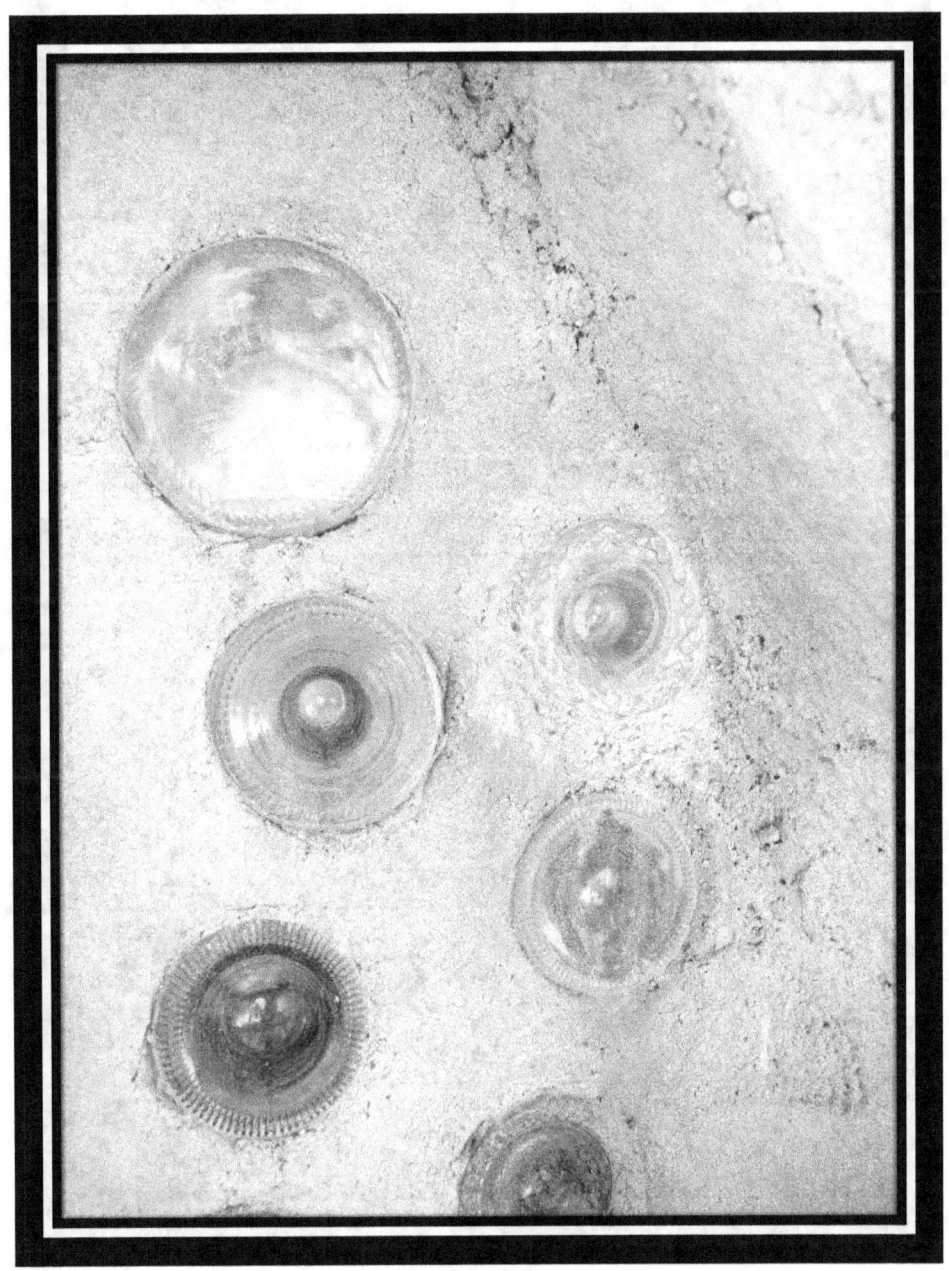

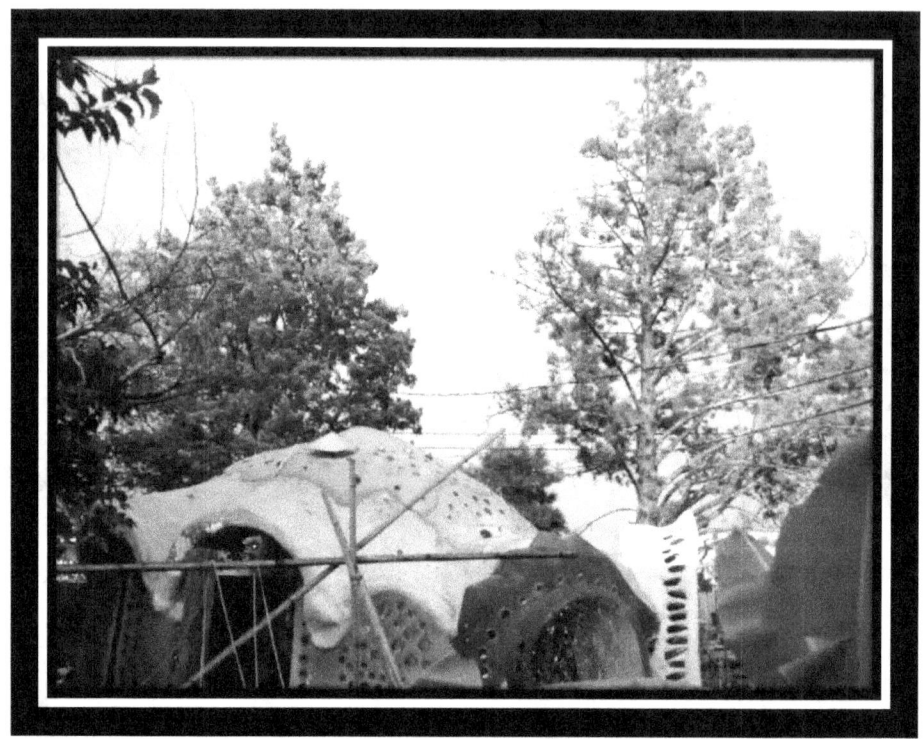

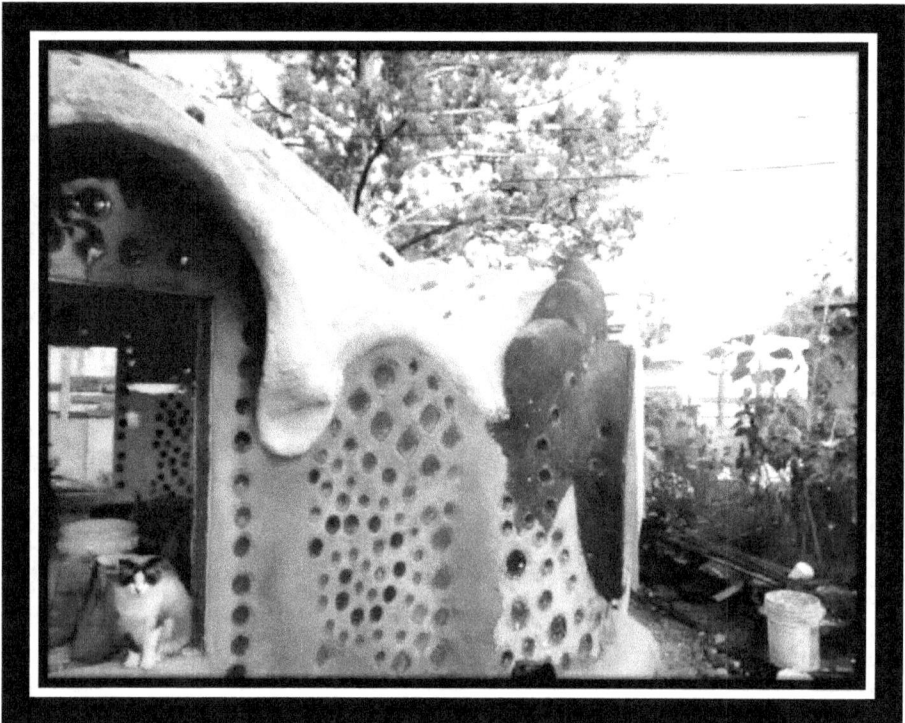

My life is full of rainbows lately! 8 22 14.

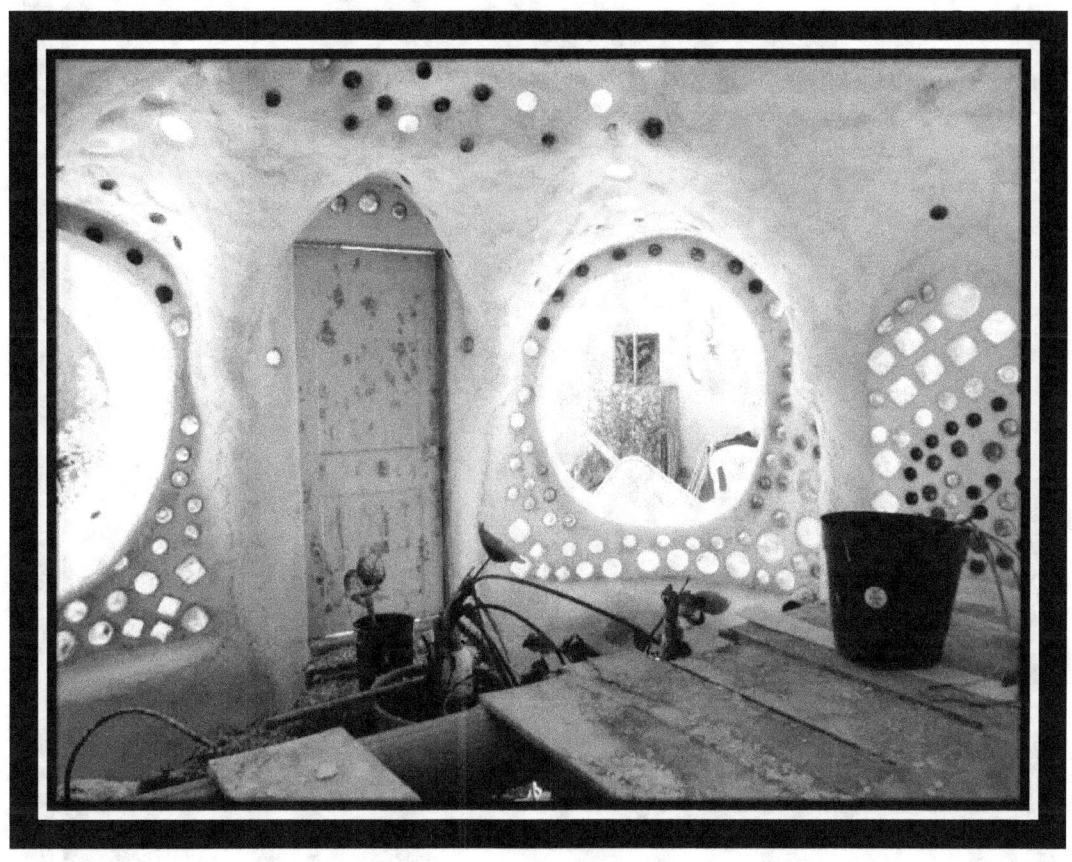

Right eye plastered inside. Just the outside, color, and bottom to go! 9 19 14.

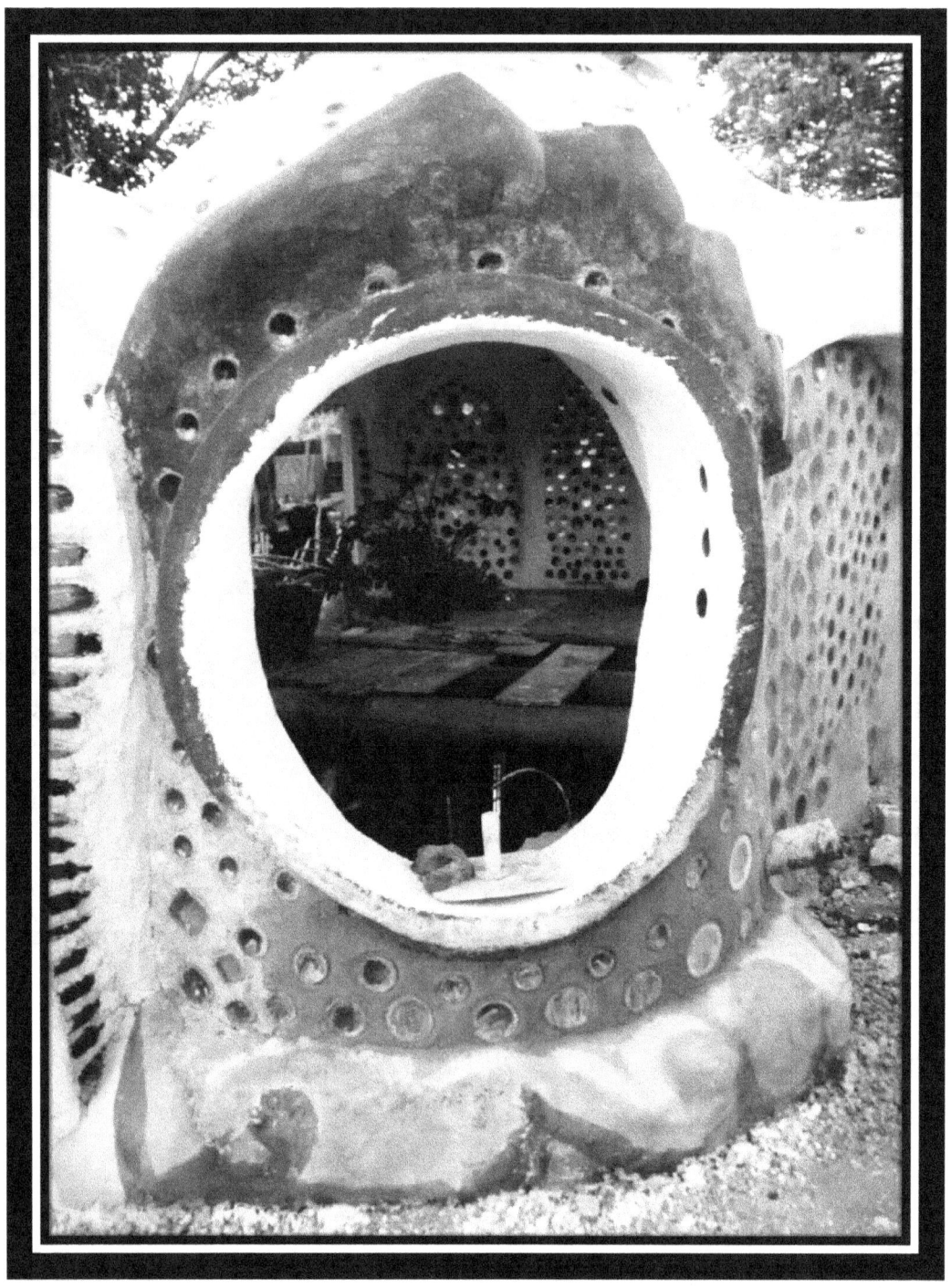

About halfway done with the front eye color. Still lots to do but it is exciting to get to play with more colors! This is what my natural pigments look like at half strength on the already dry side. 10 3 14.

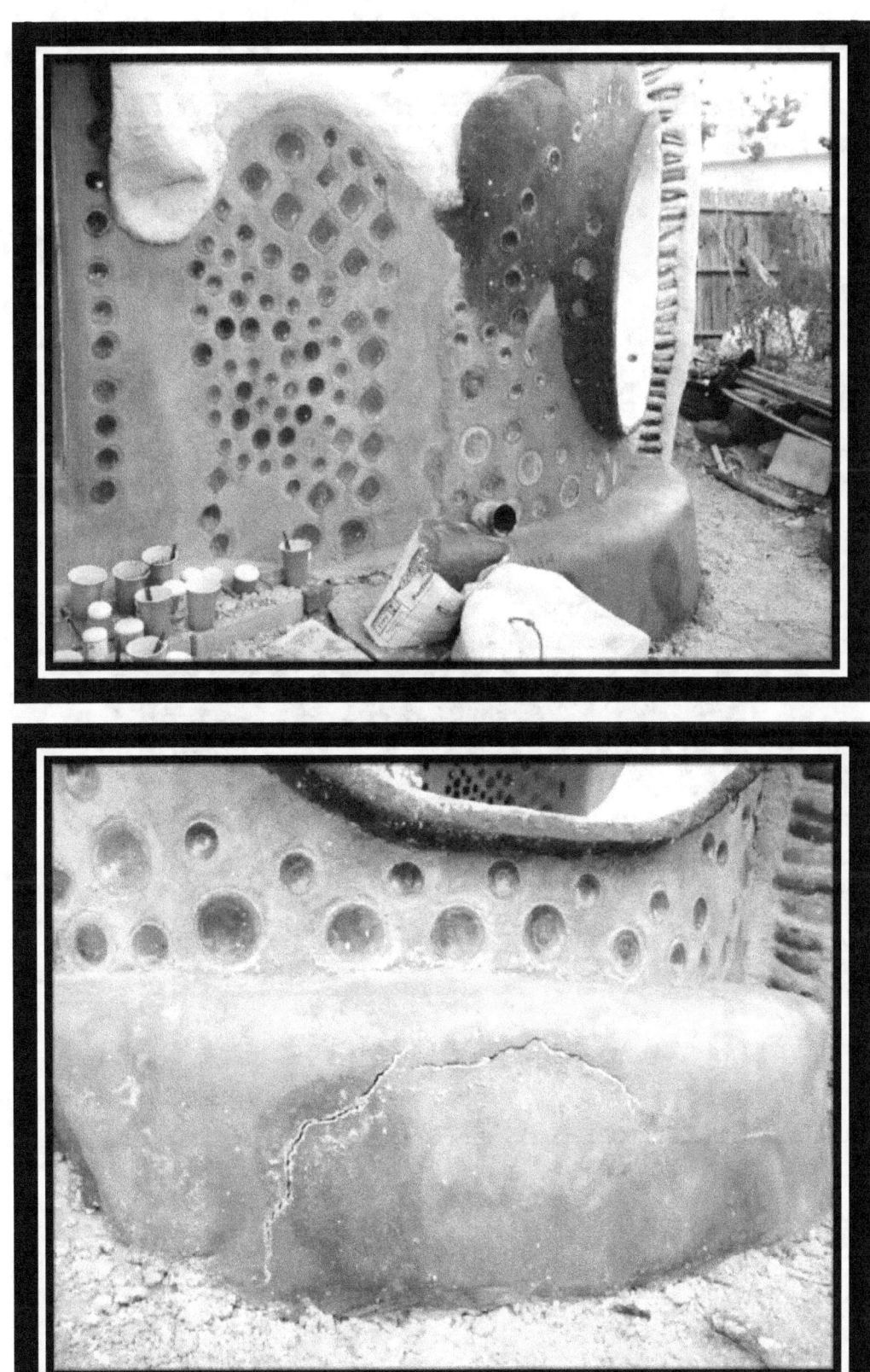

10 6 14. Big crack I knew I should have put some screws in. It may sit until next spring though. Update, still there in 2020.

Shutters!

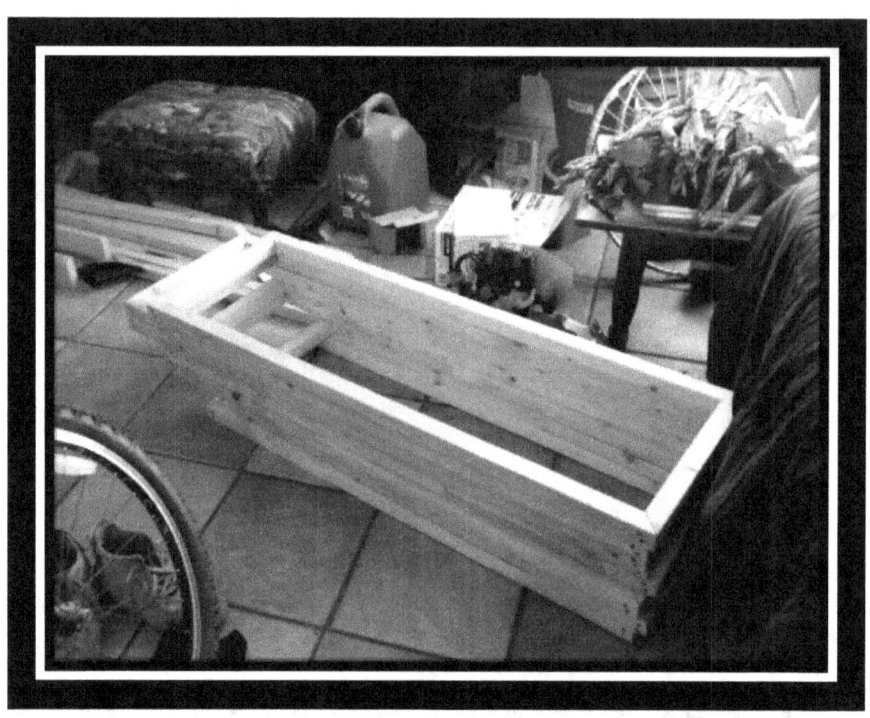

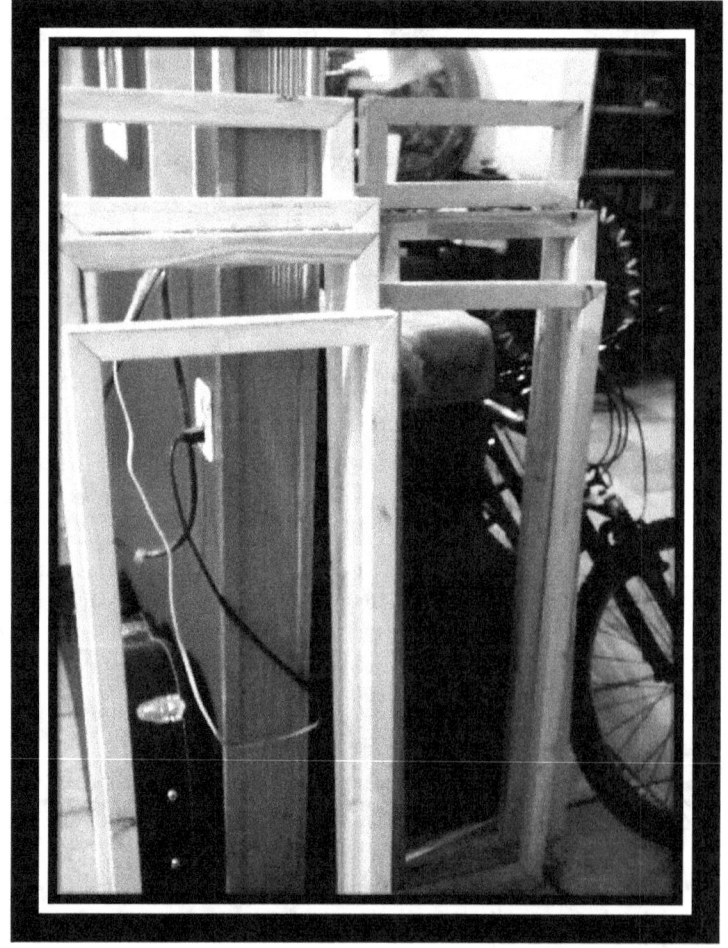

Shutters under construction. The second round was faster and easier. The third round should be even easier and faster, when I get to it. 10 2014.

Next time I WILL use a table, clamps, and probably even a square! All 8 of these are different sizes (by design), and not one of them is quite perfect, but they will all work. 10 2014.

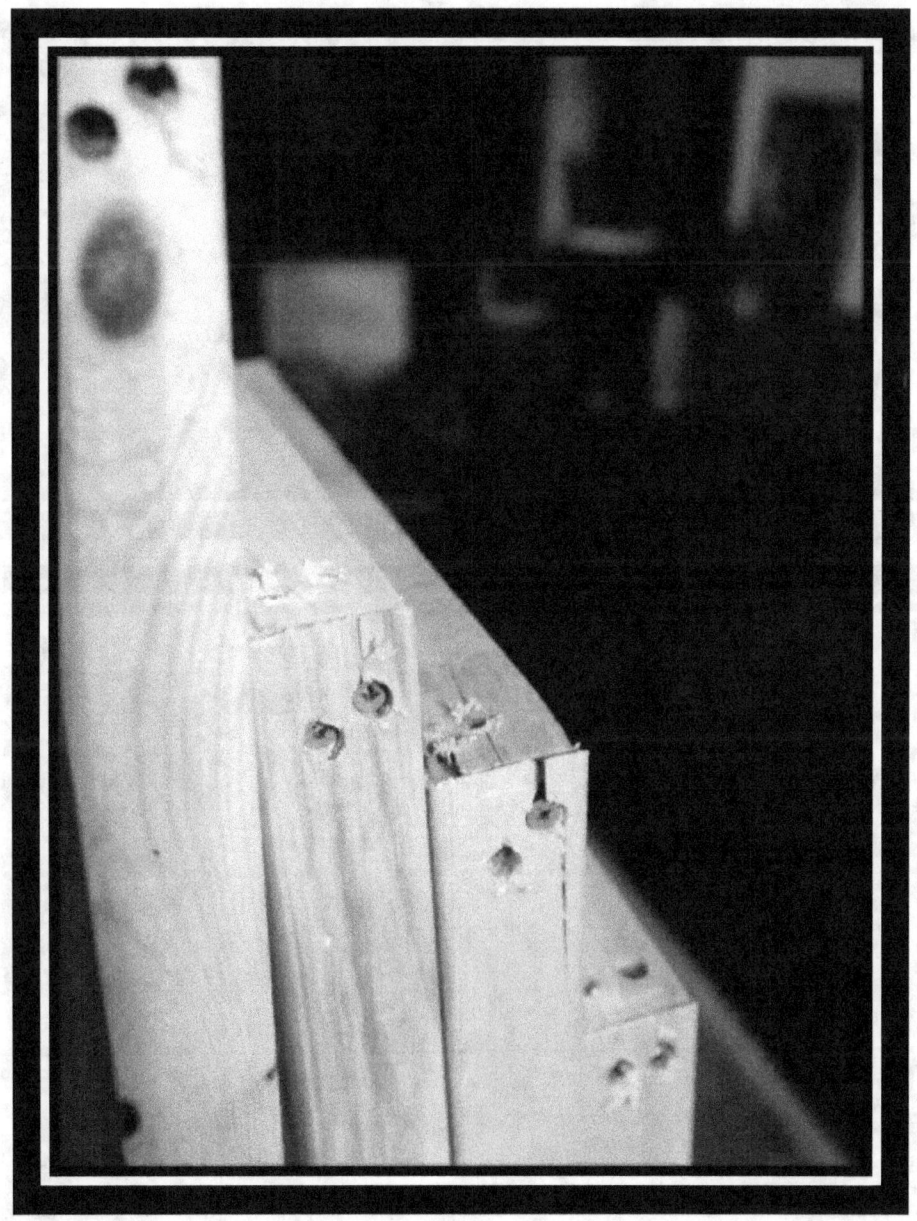

It got this bad. First try at shutters. Next round will be much better, but for now, these will have to do, as I am out of time and money for a redo before next year. Lots of putty and some caulk and they'll work. 10 2014.

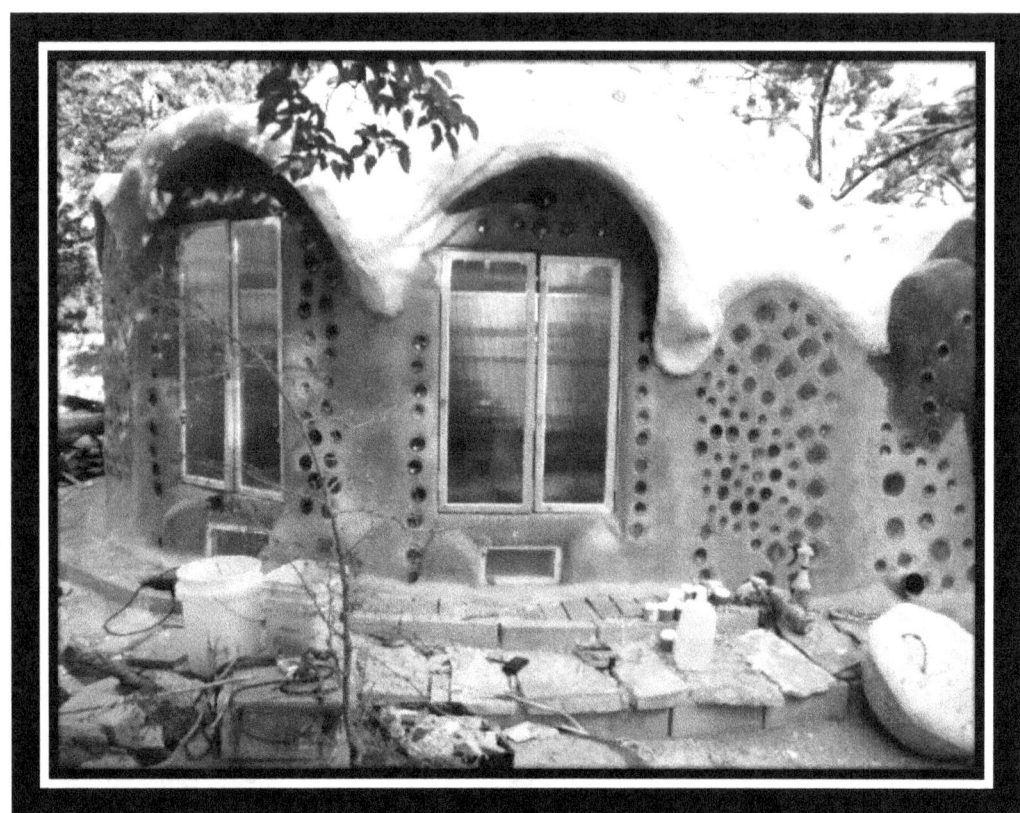

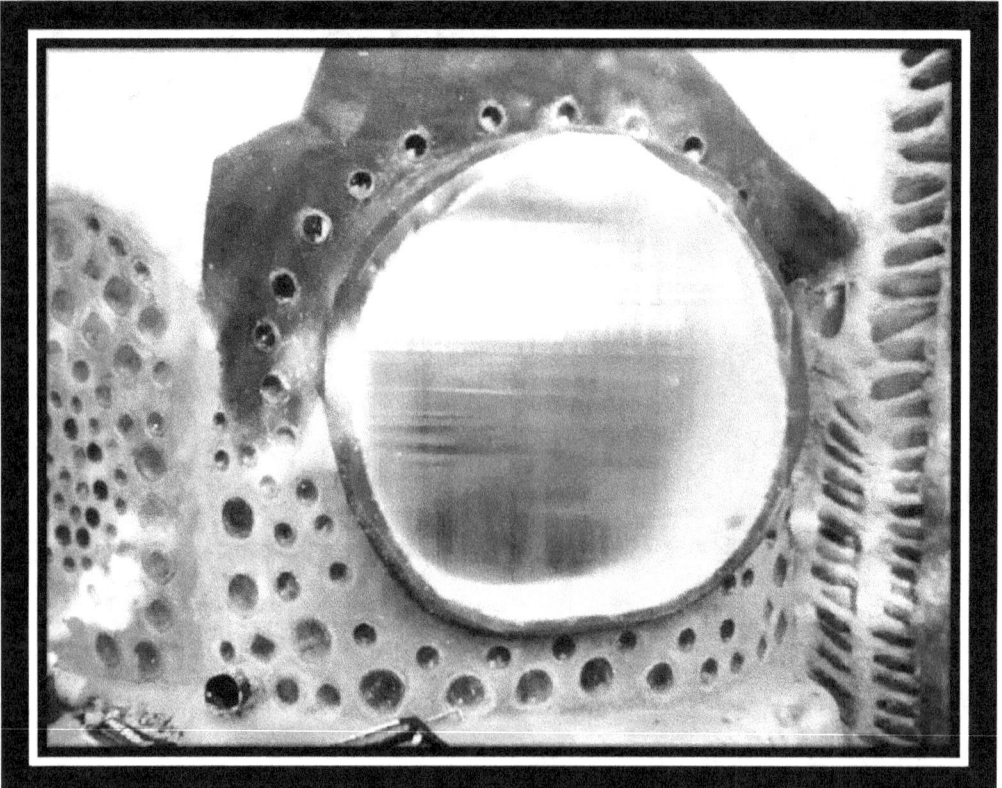

Fixed up with putty and caulk, crooked as they are, these shutters are in! 10 15 14. 2002 Update, they are still in right where I put them, have not changed much. They are super light, the Lexan is very easy to work with, and I plan on

using more of it in future projects. The 2" lumber was very cheap and sufficient for this job.

I FINALLY got my front-round-eye polycarbonate in. Trim is yet to come, but they will function for the winter. I went with double walled stuff that is not completely clear, but cheaper and more insulating. This stuff is VERY easy to work with, though also quite easy to punch through. Later comes decorative trim to hide the edges. 10 16 14.

I went with double walled stuff that is not completely clear, but cheaper and more insulating. This stuff is VERY easy to work with, though also quite easy to punch through.10 16 14.

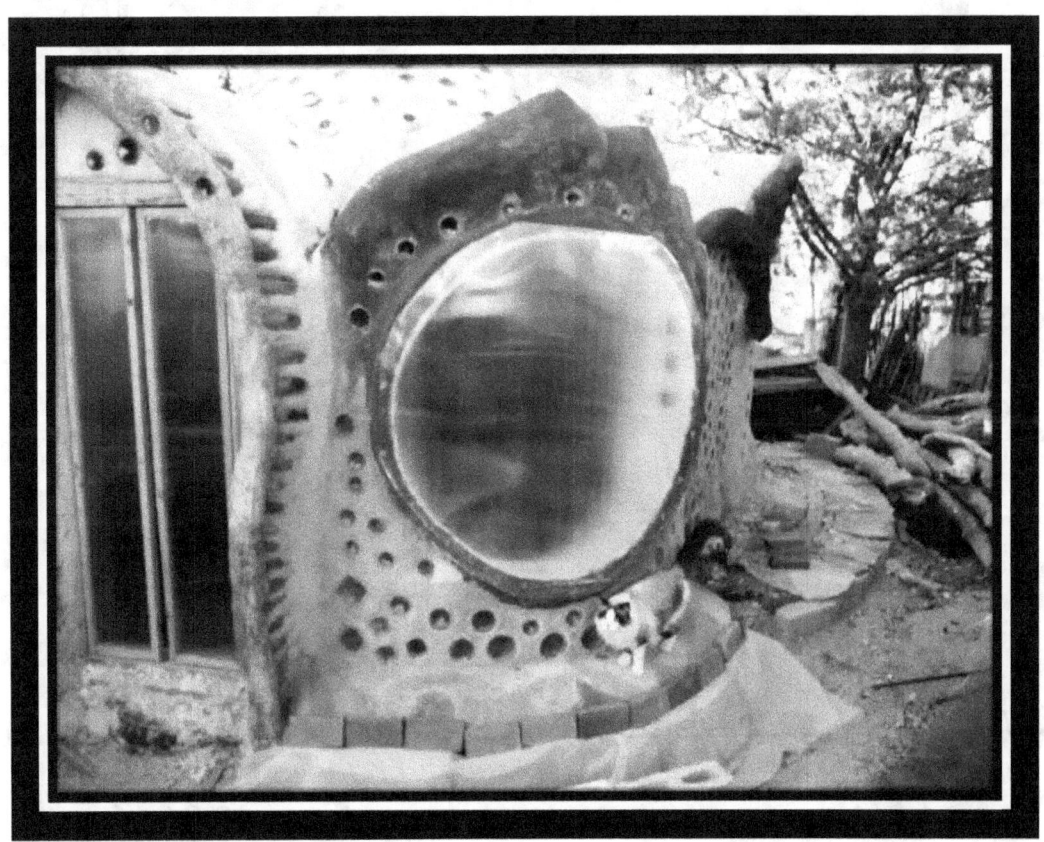

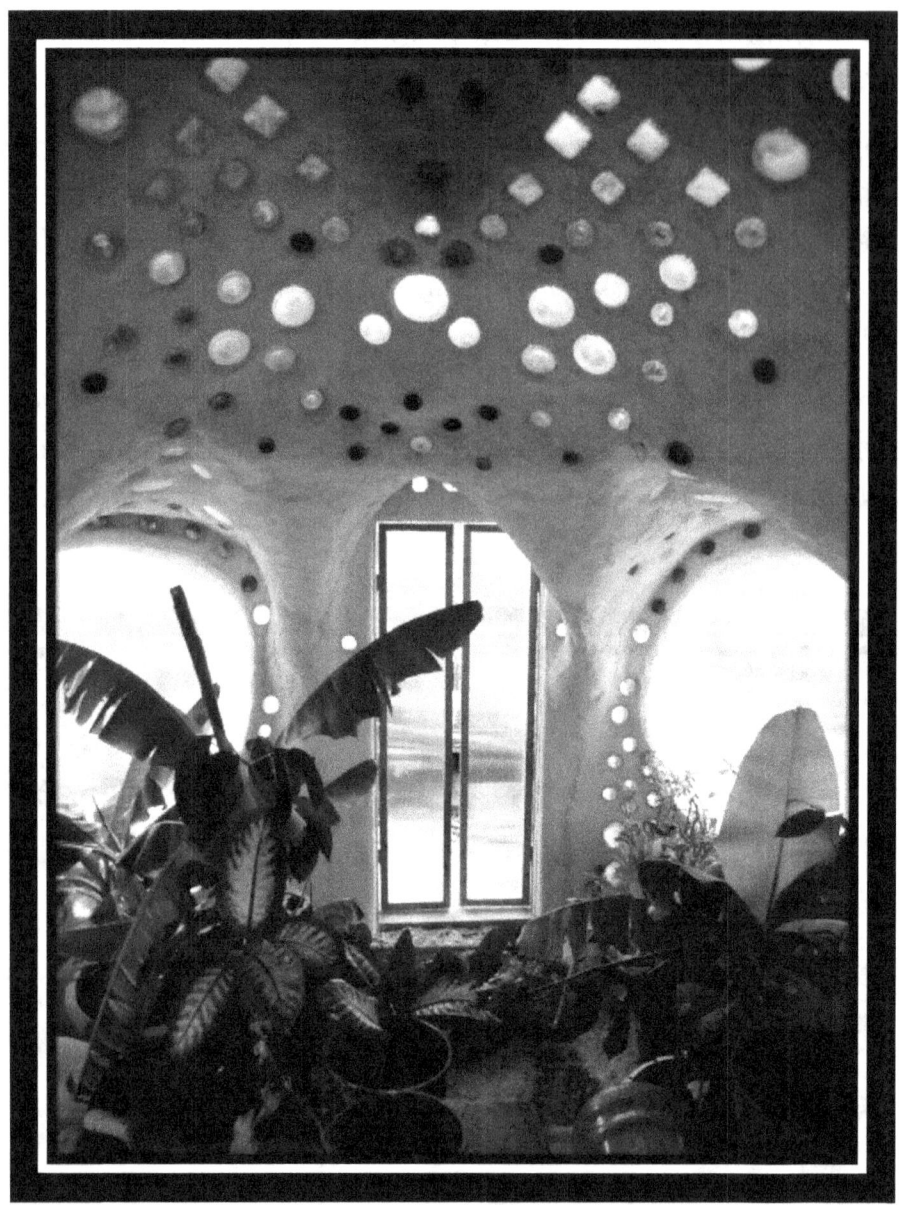

I realized the front eye tire walls are not buried/backfilled deeply enough, even for our mild climate, so I am putting in insulated beds in front of them to reduce the risk of heaving and then cracking over time. 10 31 14.

The Head Hutt Picture Book

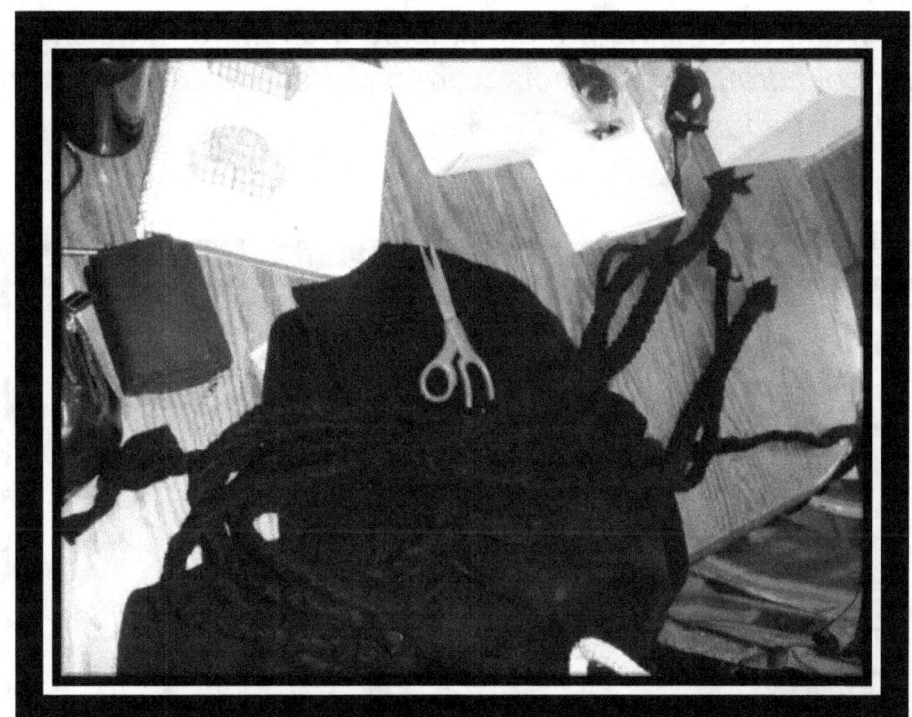

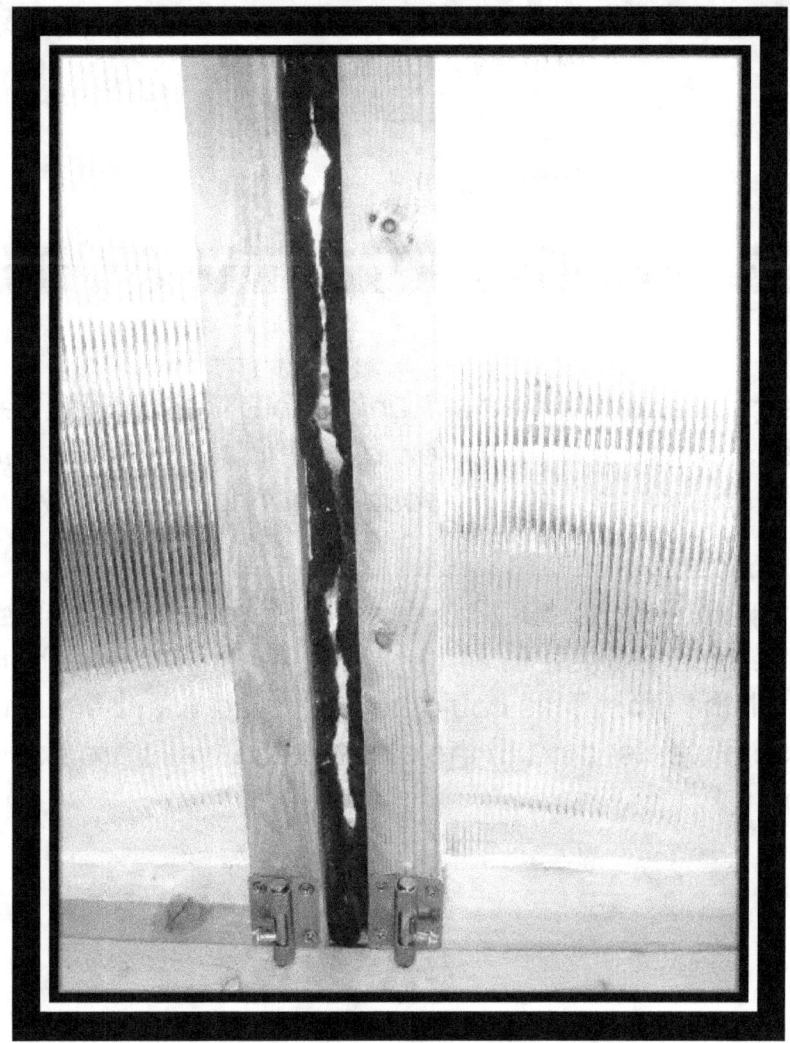

I made some weatherstripping braids, stapled them in for a quick partial fix to the oncoming cold draft. Some spots were more successful than others, but after trim it will all be functional. "The Bad, and the Ugly." 11 23 14.

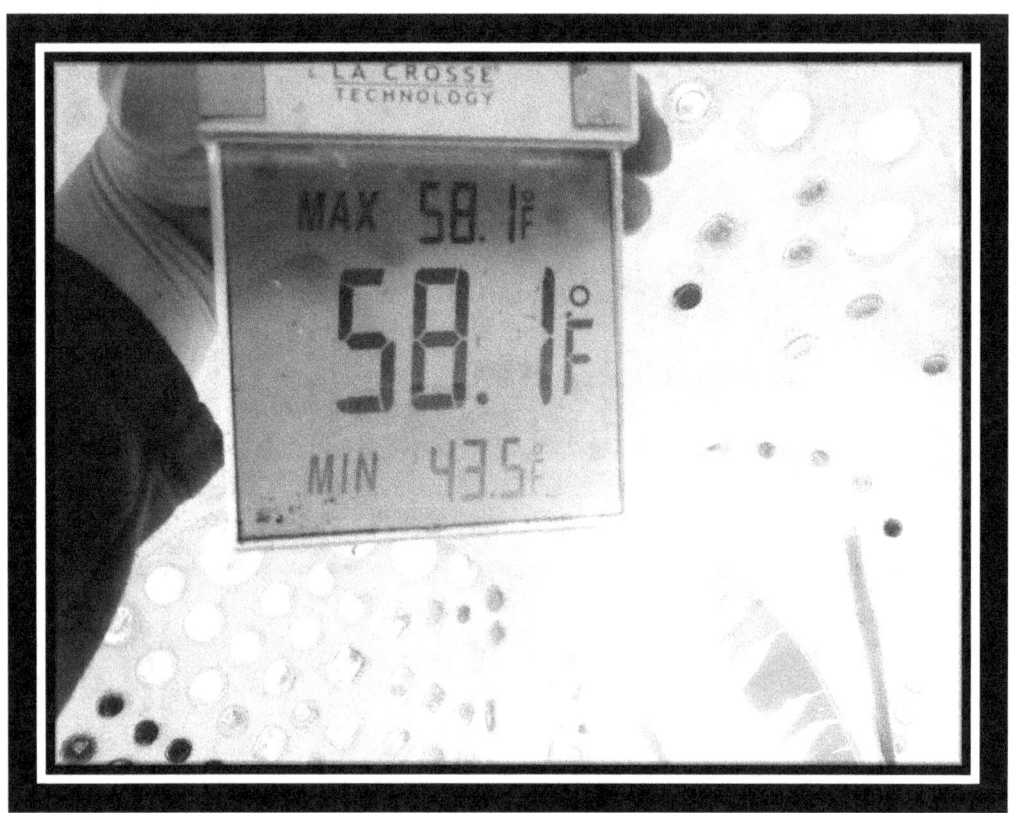

Even with large gaps and the front still unlatched, the HH has held mostly above 40 degrees even through the few dips into the 20's we had. The bananas are still upright and green, though I am not sure they are happy. 11 23 14.

In general, the HH maintains 10-20 degrees difference from outside temps (cooler in summer and warmer in winter), with the lower floor being close to 10 degrees cooler all the time. This could be improved with better weather stripping and use of vents, though the glass bottle walls are not ideal for temperature control.

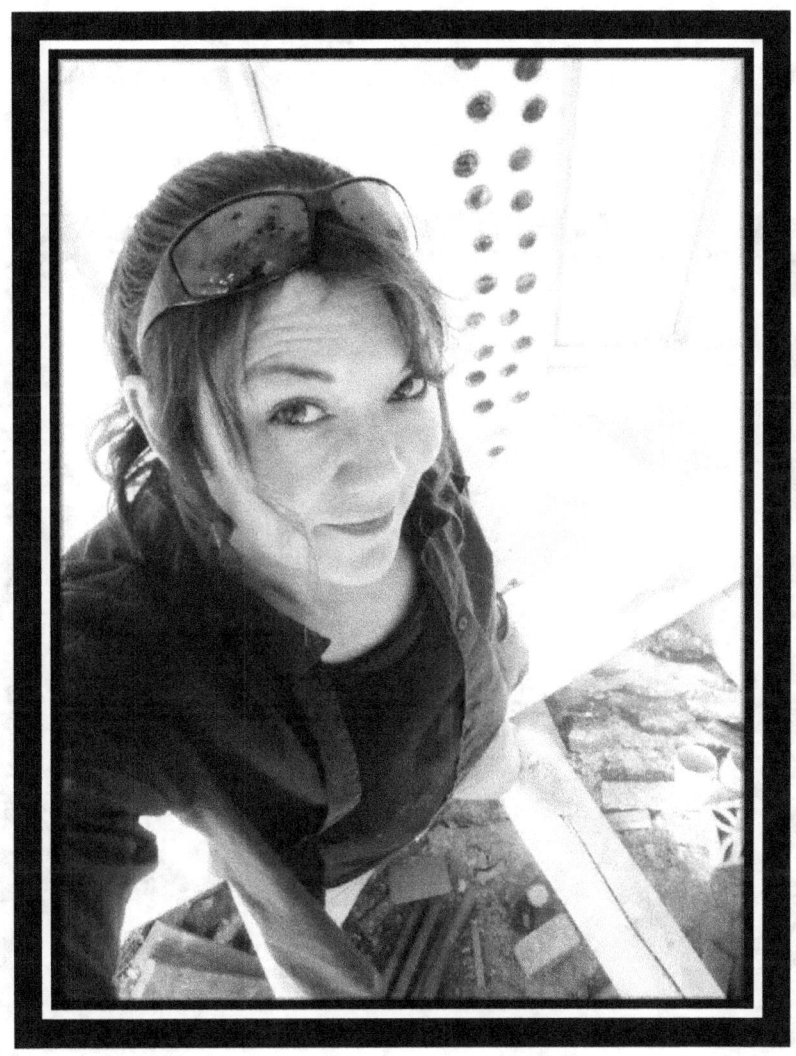

It might have been a bit easier to do some of the infill with a floor. It was kind of a long way down and balancing on vigas while throwing handfuls of infill overhead did prove challenging at times.

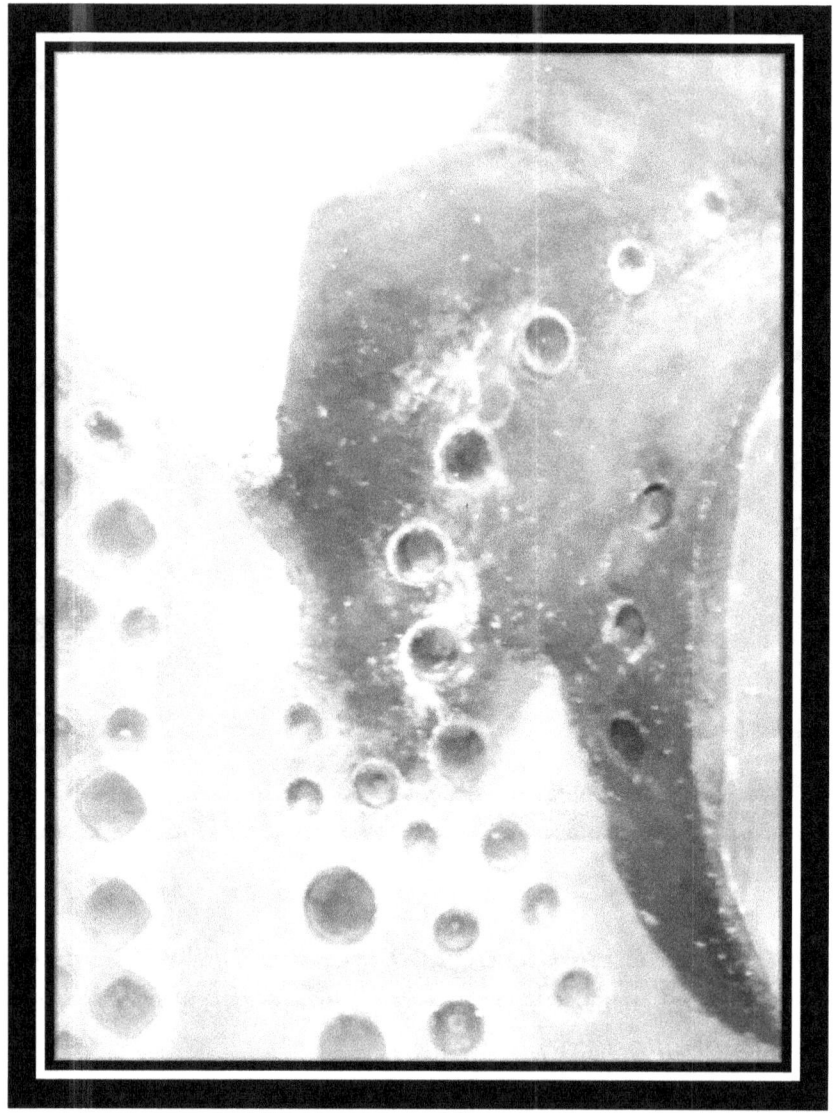

Getting some efflorescence, as I expected, where-ever water is running onto color. I don't mind it so much, but I will be doing a few things to cover and lessen that affect in the future. 2 20 15.

Snow Day! 2 28 15.

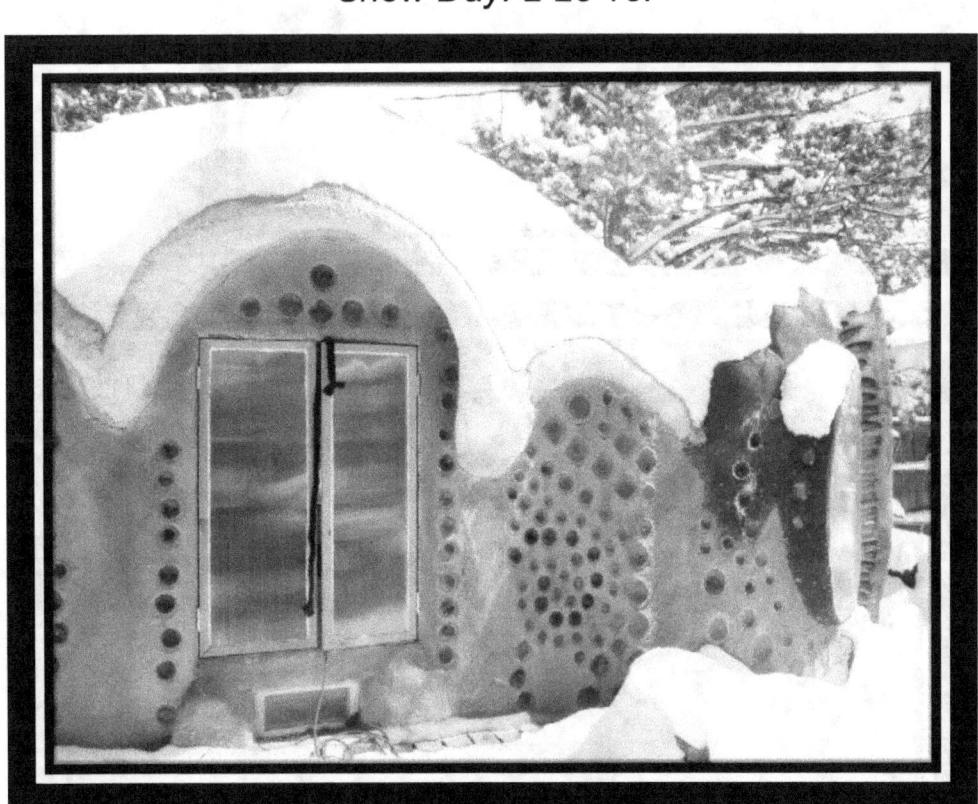

The HH holds up just fine to snow days, and I love how pretty it is in the snow. Of course, the glass bottles do get covered and darker and sometimes moisture gets in and around them, however, it has not been a major problem, though I have gone up on the roof several times to put caulk and silicone in cracks and around bottle ends.

3 6 15. Getting the deck sealed--bottom and top in one step instead of three like I thought.

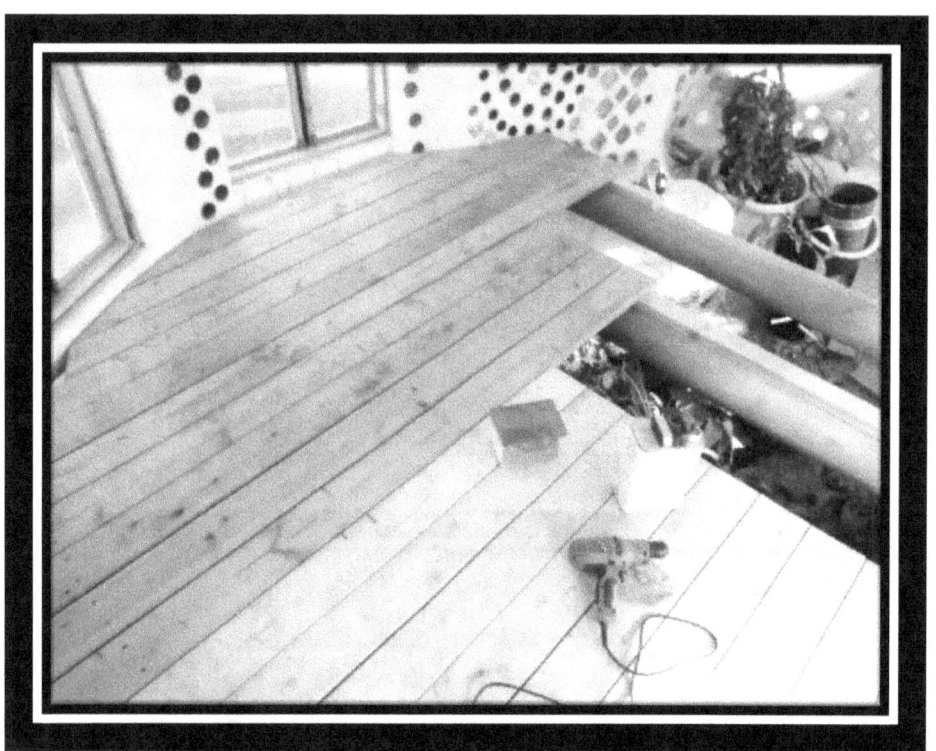

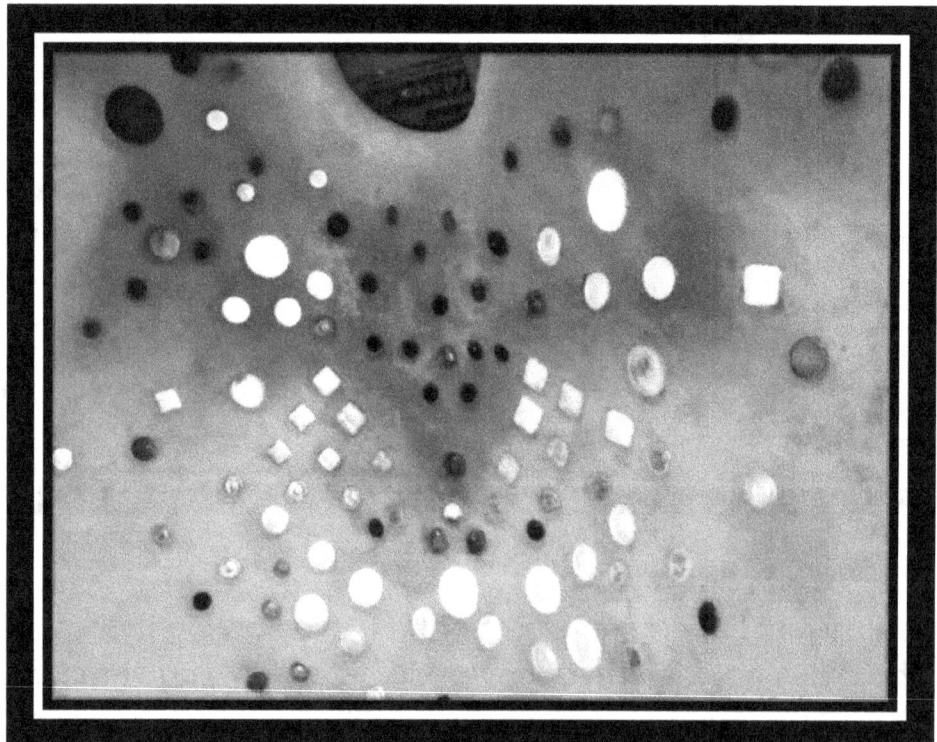

Some water is seeping into the infill and plaster. Discoloration in spots but no structural worries. I will do some more sealing to the roof this summer,

especially around the bottle bricks, and that should be reduced or eliminated. 3 6 15.

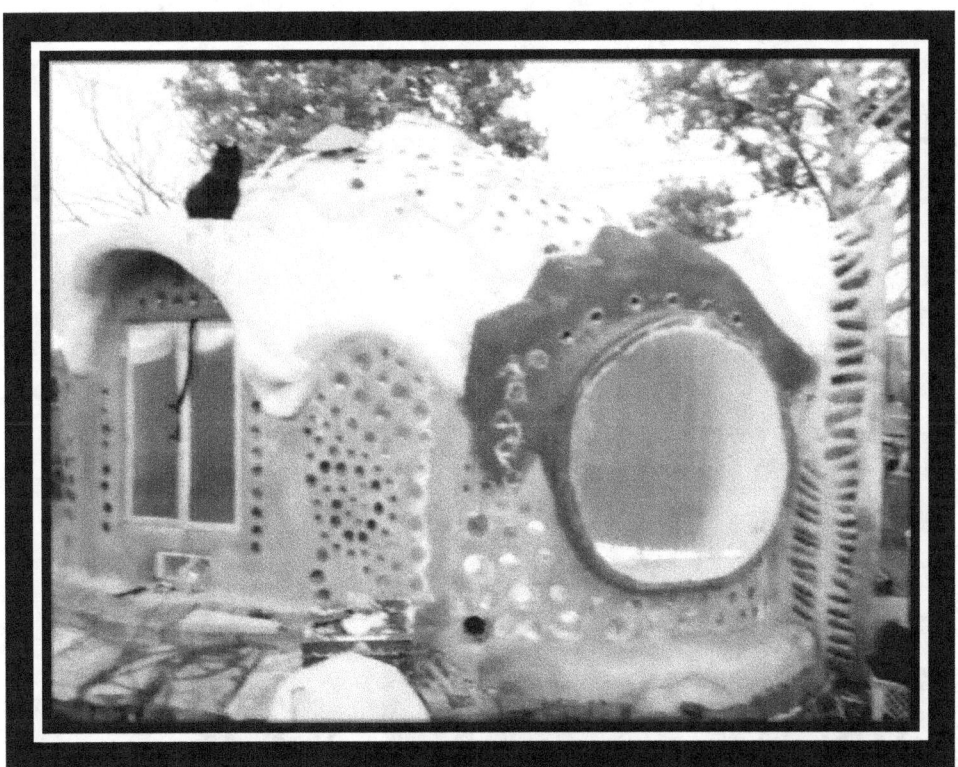

A neighborhood kid told me 'they say Chucky lives there'.

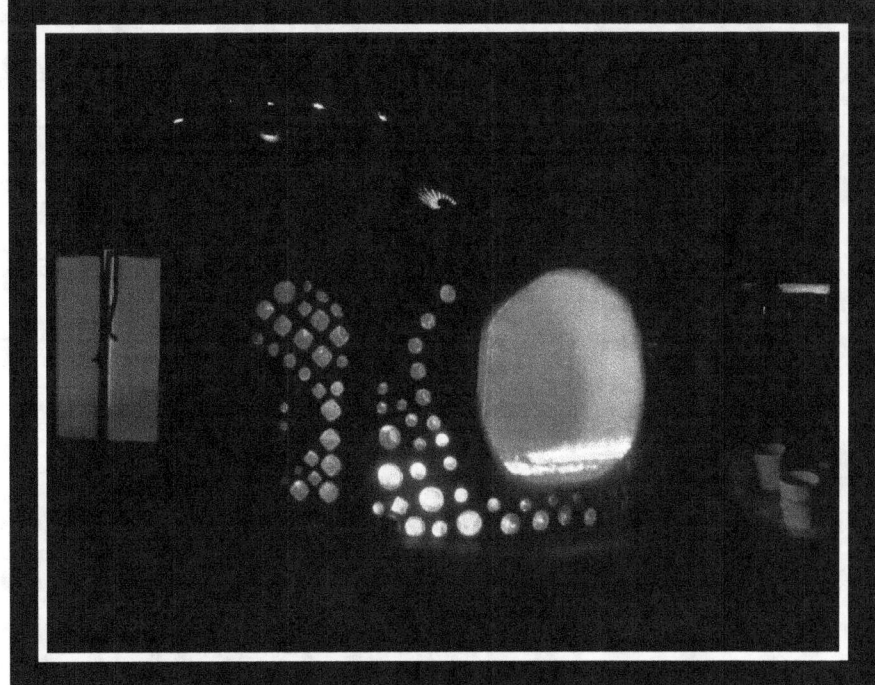

The heat lamp was glowing red at night.

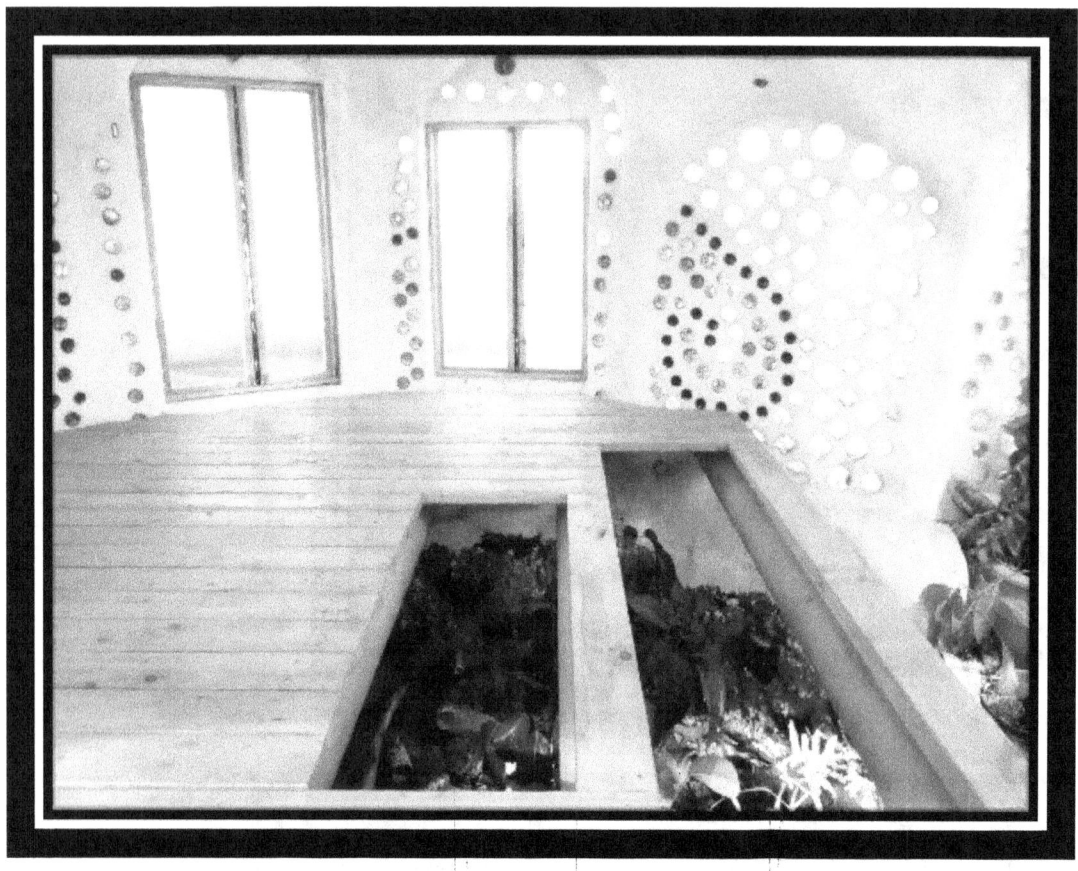

Got a tiny bit more done to the floor. Soon I will cover it (for protection) and continue! 3 10 15.

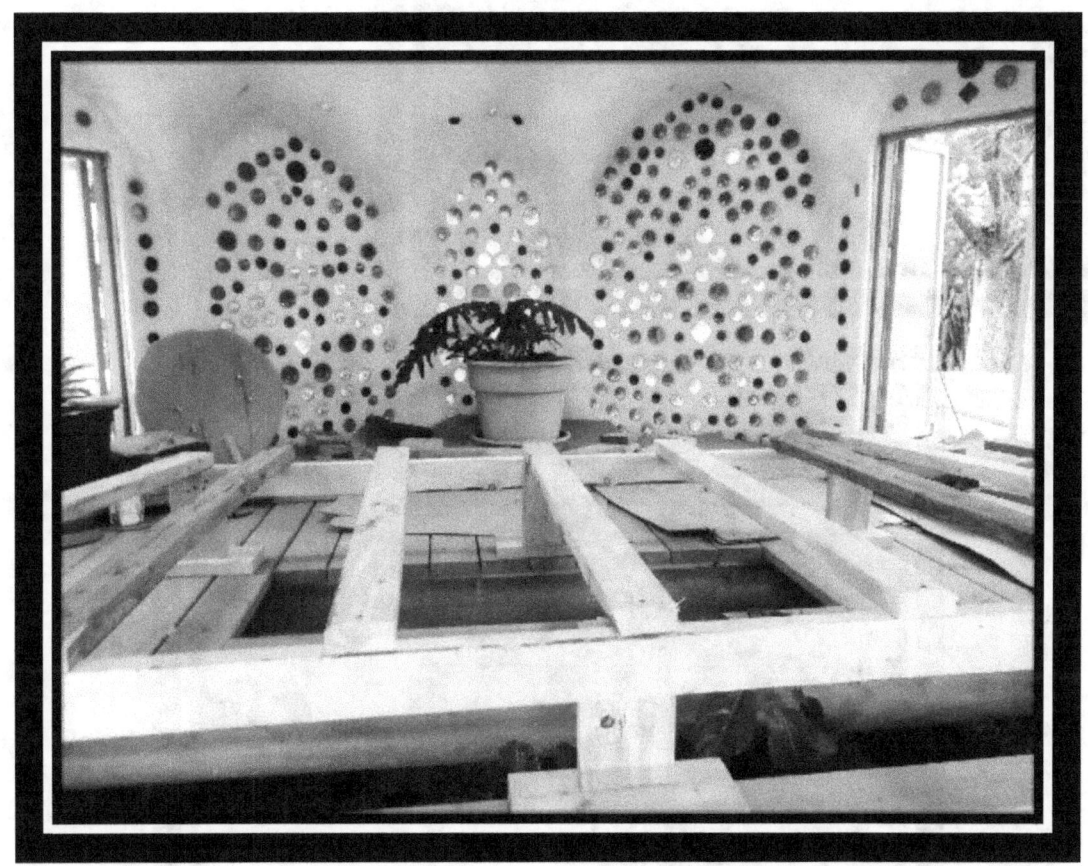

I am still not completely happy with the usability of the space, though it is functional, with two queen sized bed in it now, a nice yoga space and some plants. I would like to make it even more functional in the future, and so this flooring may get changed. For now, it is sturdy and looks nice enough, so I am happy with my choice.

After deciding it was too high, I took off the legs and replaced them with shorter ones. Now I think it could have been about 4" higher, between the two, but, it is going to stay as it is for probably a long time. Early July 2015.

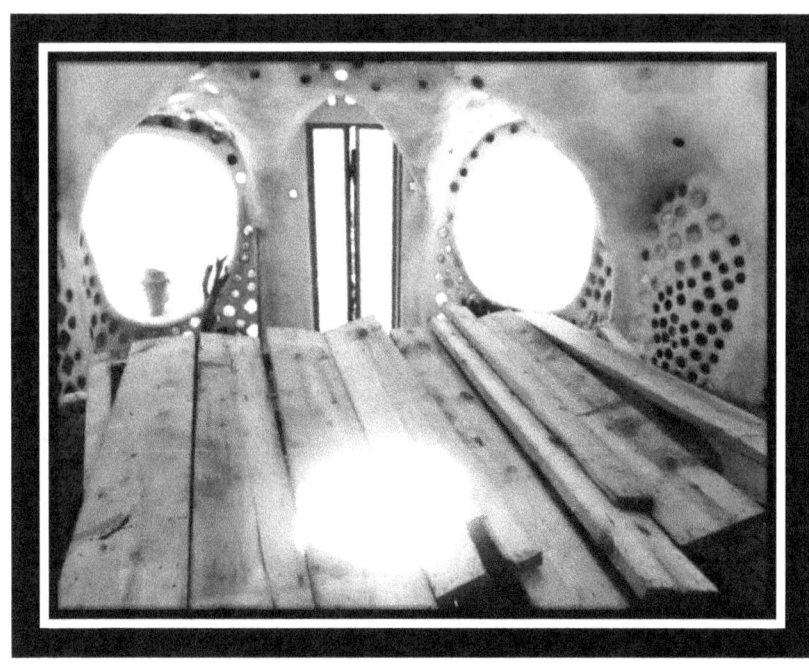

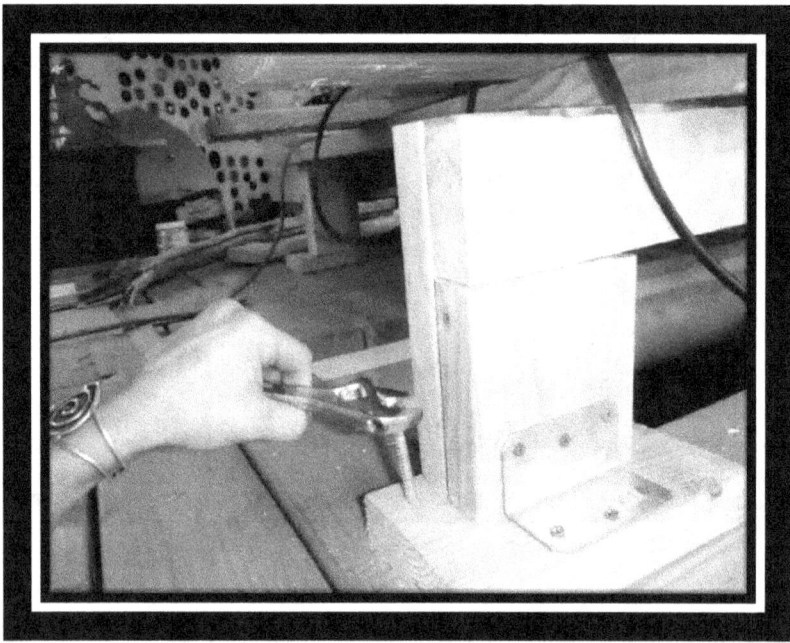

I salvaged all this wood from pallets I got for free less than a mile from my home. July, 2015.

In the spirit of making things harder than they have to be, I screwed and bolted the bottom down AFTER screwing on the top, making it extra difficult to get a drill or sometimes even a wrench in there. July, 2015.

The Head Hutt Picture Book

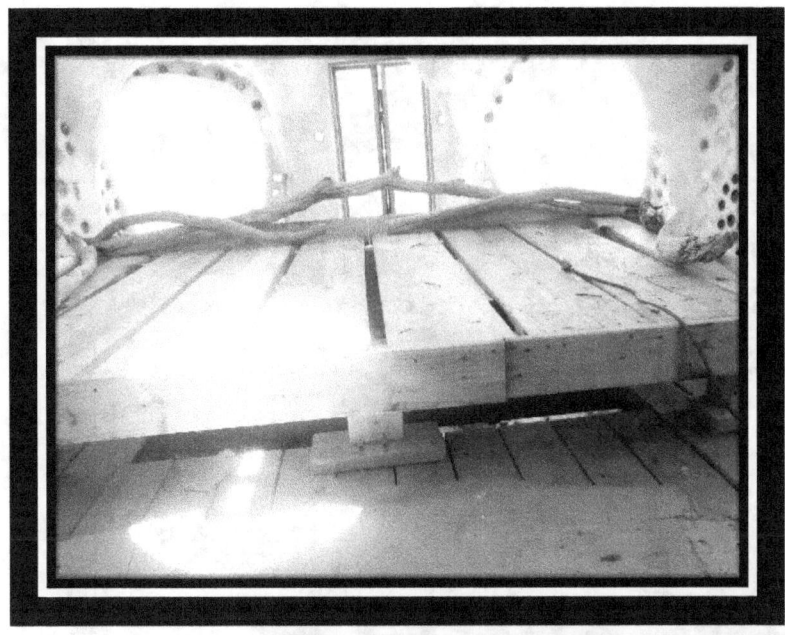

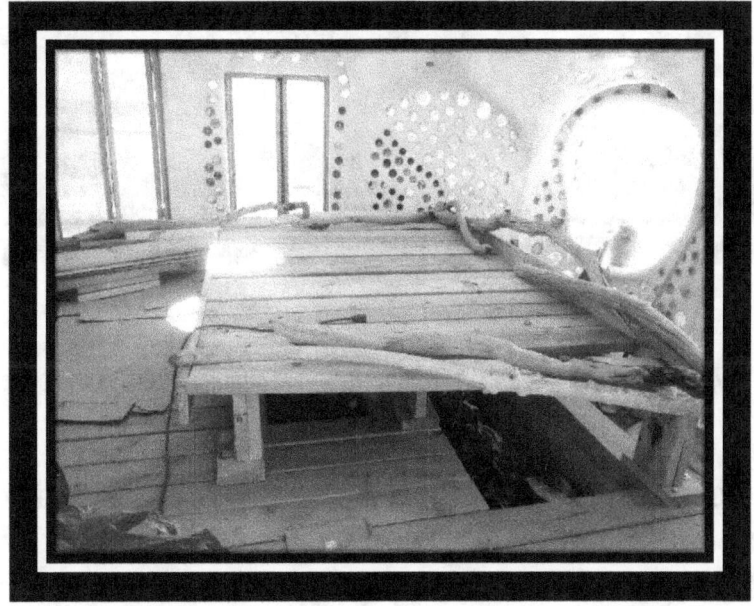

With trim on the edges (back and sides are still not in--still looking for the right wood), it seems a tad lower than I planned, but, I can and will live with it! It is nice and sturdy, and I will be adding a few more braces, bolts, and screws, as soon as I get them. July 12, 2015. July 20, 2015.

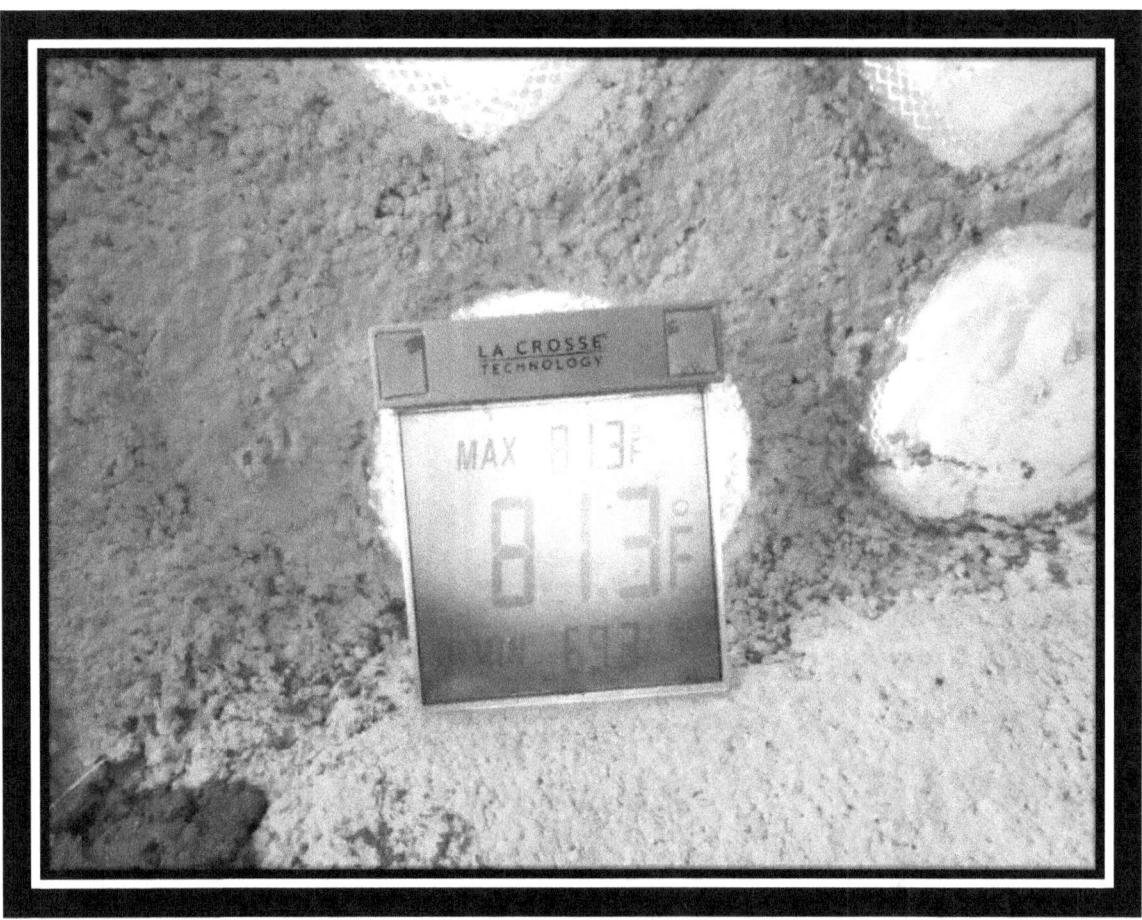

Temps in the HH run 10-20 degrees cooler or warmer than outside. This day it hit 100 degrees outside. 8 4 15.

Passive temperature control (as in, without using utilities/additional power) is another passion of mine. The HH is lacking in many areas. The glass is terrible for moderating temperature, and the solar potential is mostly lost on wrong angles and less than ideal materials. Also, I did not add any insulation outside the tire wall, which might have had a significant effect, though also, might not have made a lot of difference. As it is, it does a very nice job of mitigating the summer heat, especially in the underground floor, and a fair job of keeping out the brutal cold in winter.

I am making little time capsules for the wall openings in the HH before I plaster over them. I had a lot of fun thinking about what to put in them, and who, if anyone, might discover them one day, and how… 8 3 15.

The Head Hutt Picture Book

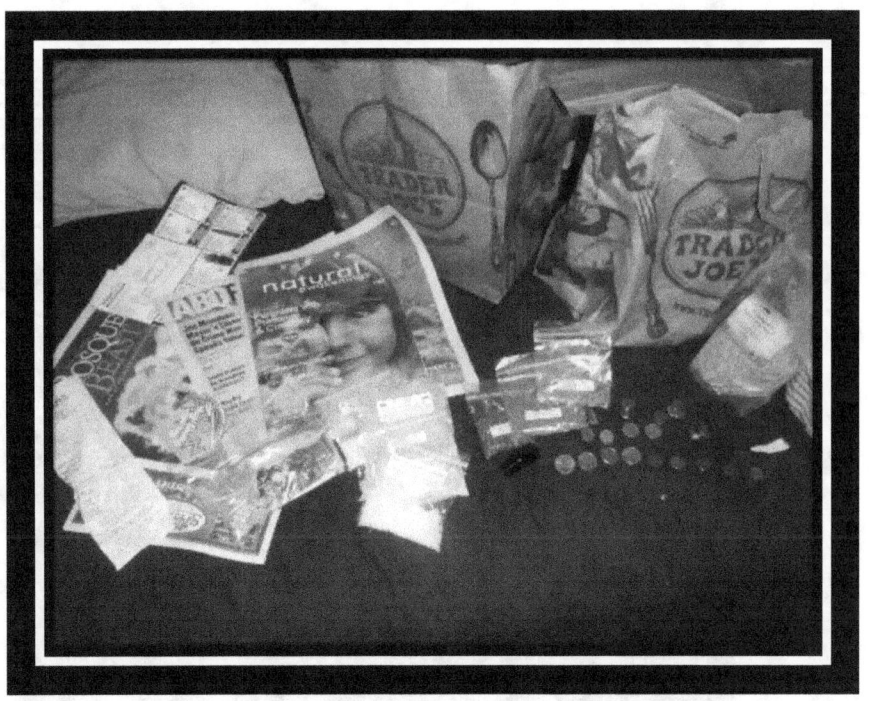

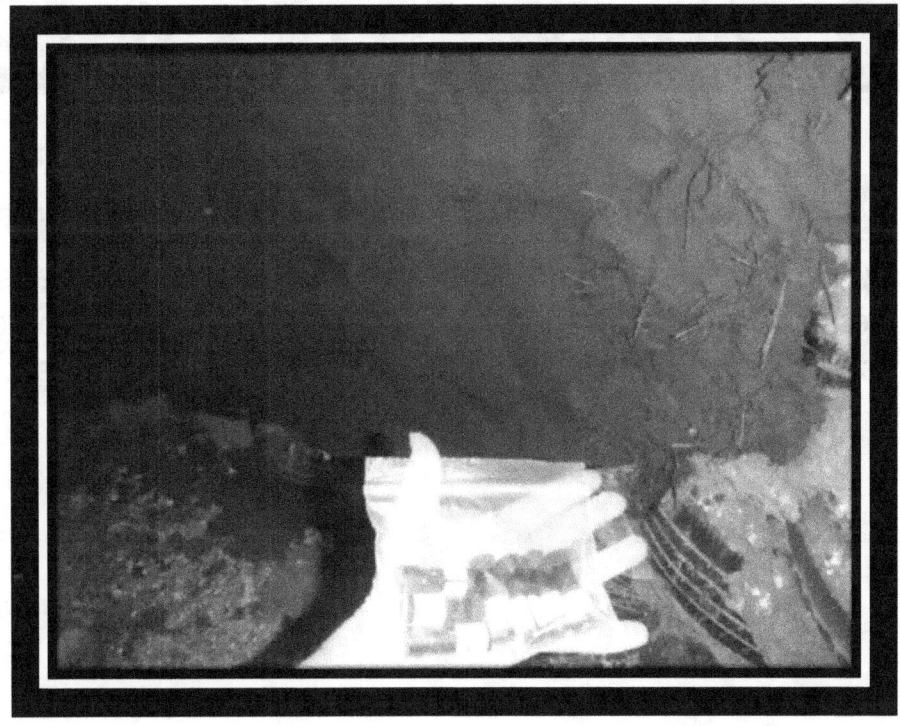

Another random-stuff-bag I put in one of the wall cubbies before plastering over. Makes me think about the reasons people stash things in walls. And the amazing stories we can make up from things found later in time. 8 7 15.

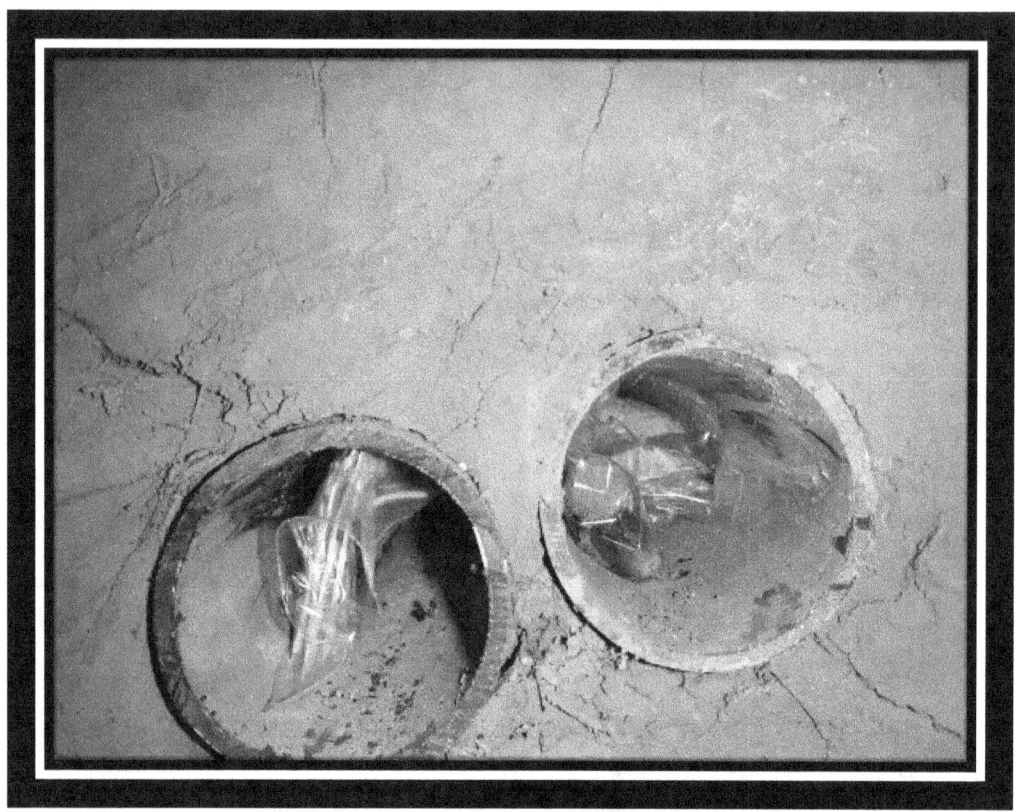

9 8 15. More seeds in cubbies--to keep future aliens guessing, if nothing else.

What would you put in your secret cubbies or time capsules? Seeds? Money from your time and place? Newspapers? I put in some of my favorite seeds, some coins, some essential oils, some magazines and newspapers, and a couple notes.

The Head Hutt Picture Book

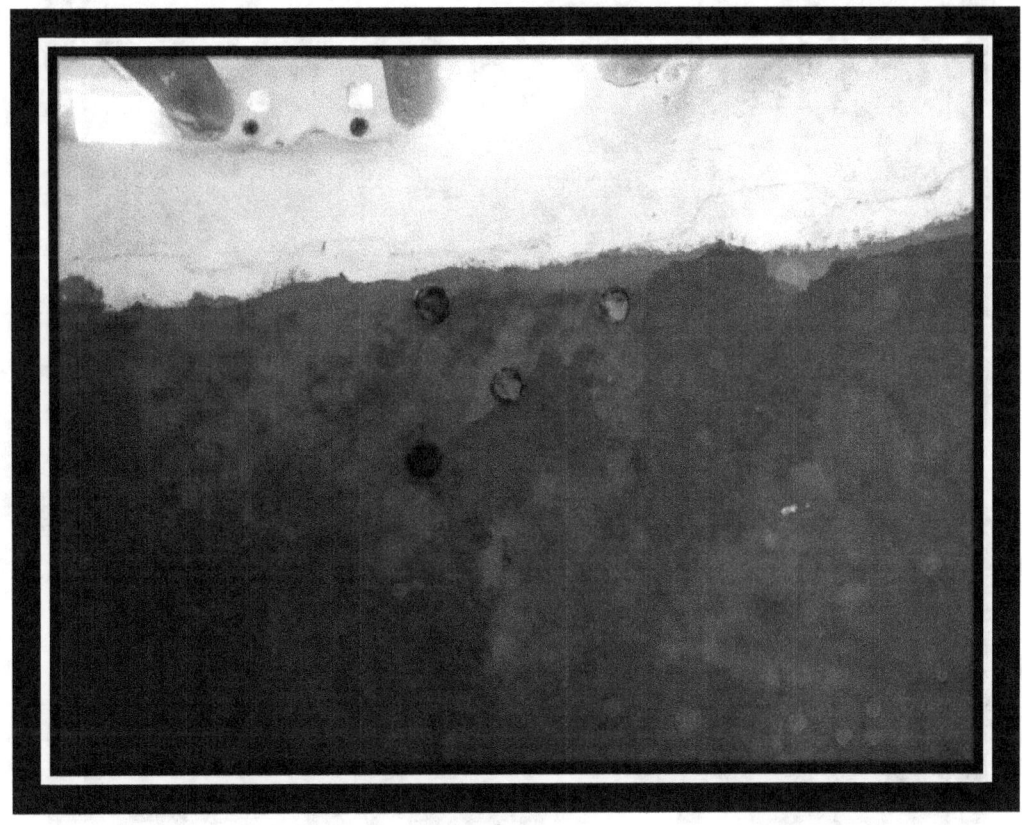

Yes, I thought I was finished in-filling the bottom, but as it turned out, I needed another half a van load to smooth things over. 9 8 15.

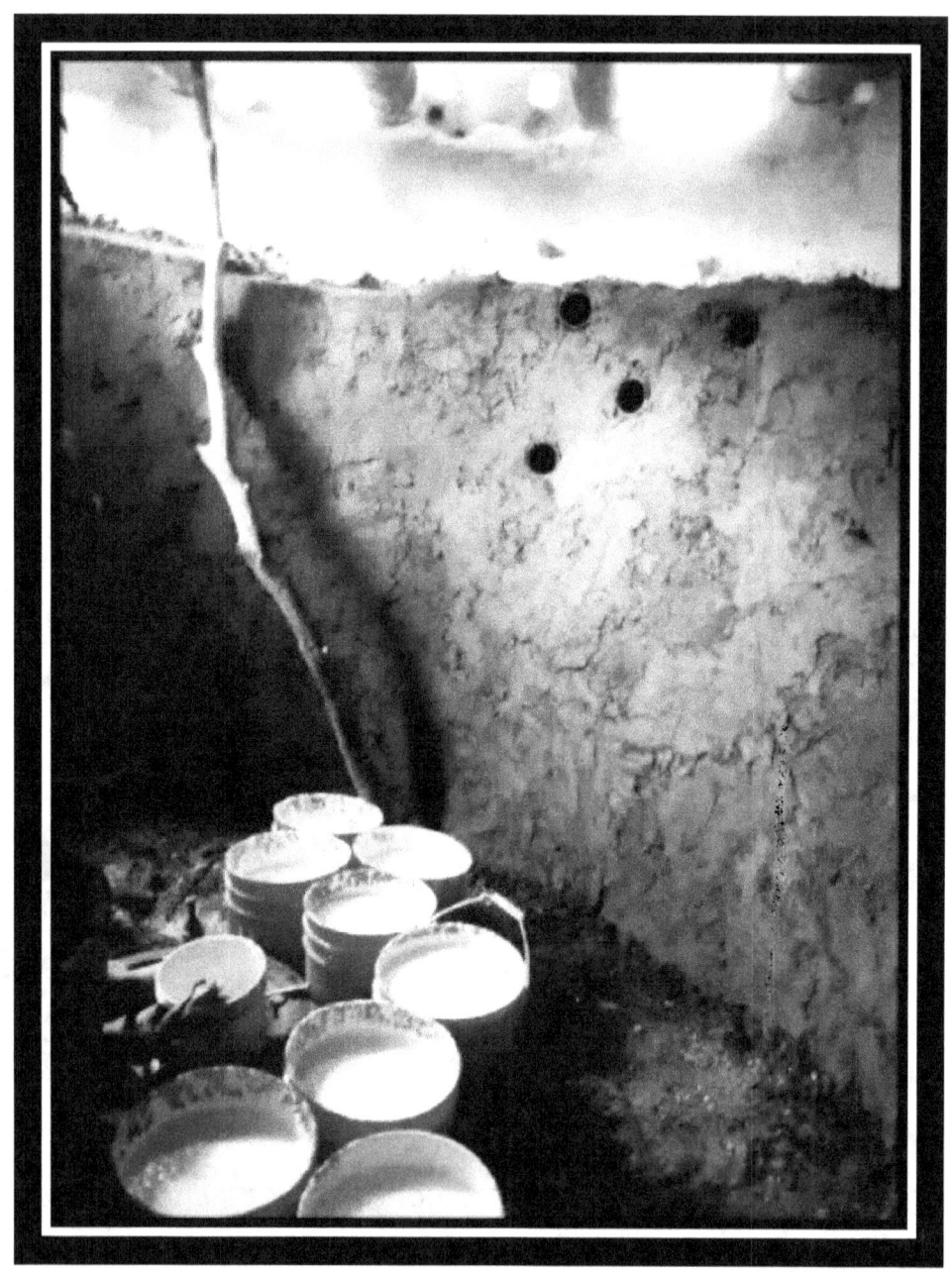

Lime putty mixed and ready to sit for 6 weeks or more.
10 24 15.

The Head Hutt Picture Book

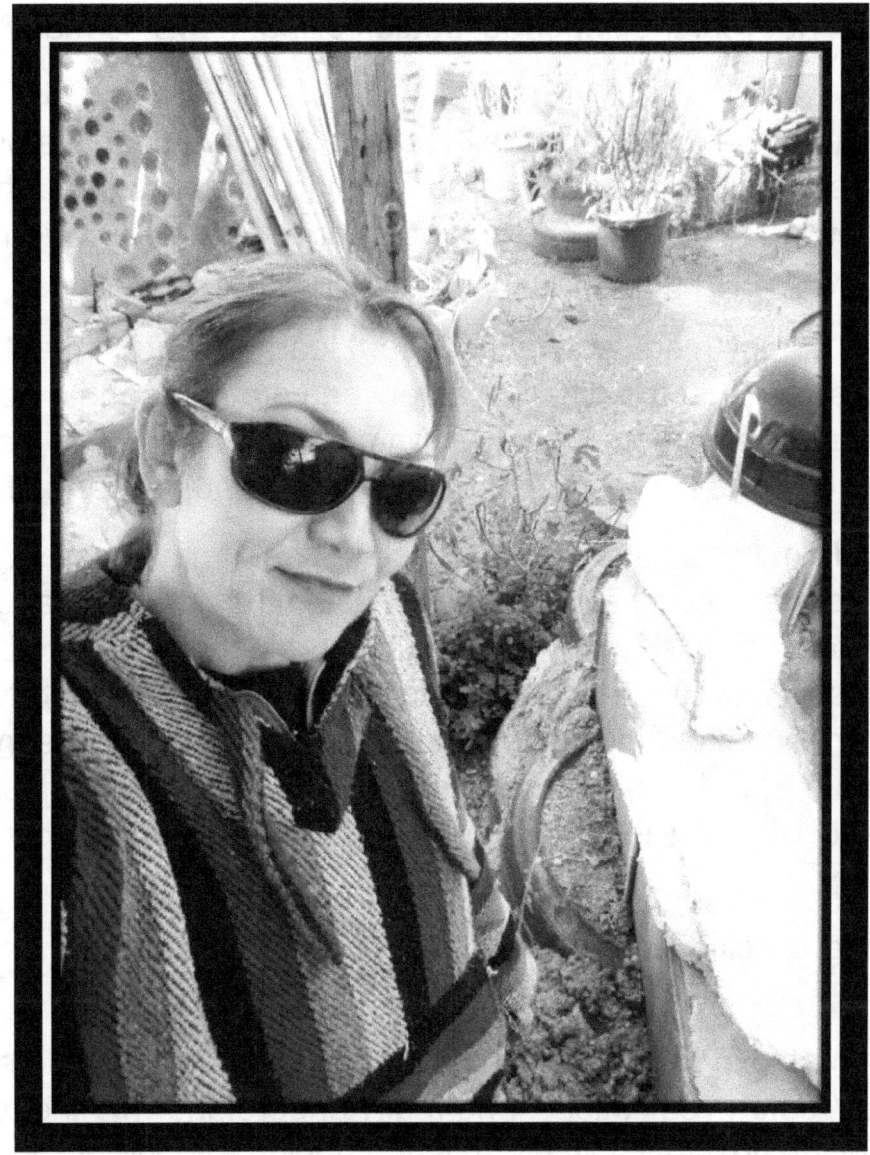

Making feather leaves for the eyelash trim. 11 9 15.

Problems are in the details. I mean, opportunities. Opportunities are in the details.

Some of my favorite details have also been the most problematic. Funny how things work out that way, isn't it? The feather leaf lashes, the polycarbonate shutters and front eyes, the imperfect bottle ceiling. I love so many things about it.

I did have some of the feather-leaf-lashes break off in a couple storms. They will be repaired soon. And I have had some minor cracking through the dome, around and between the bottles. A good demonstration of why you should never run glass at an angle through concrete like that.

I learned I can do anything I set my mind to. I learned that I am apt to make many mistakes, and that the difference between a master and a novice is the master has made many more mistakes, and learned from them. You can't be afraid to make mistakes. They are often the most beautiful parts of everything.

I also learned I am not a carpenter, at least, not yet. I have a great deal of respect for all sorts of builders. The physical stamina, fortitude, and persistence it took to do so many steps in this project would have been a bit less if I had more knowledge and better tools. As it was, I wanted to build something by hand, exploring what it might take for a single person or a couple to build a livable dome structure. It could be done for far less time, money and effort if one was building for livability and not to make a sculpture.

My background in art studio, specifically in ceramics and in building ceramic heads, and site-specific art made this the perfect project for me, on my specific path.

If you are interested in building a sculptural building, I urge you to study up on building codes, safety regulations, and really understand why the rules exist before you decide how to follow them. If you decide to bend or break the rules, which, by the way, I want to state for the record, I do not recommend, please be sure you are safe and considerately kind to the environment and all creatures that might be affected by your building.

A special note on 'playing the artist card'. This may or may not help with regulations/permits/permission. It will probably give you more freedom and more expense, time and money-wise.

Speaking of time and money, everyone wants to know how long it took, and interestingly (to me), hardly anyone asks about the cost.

I am going to estimate both here, as best I can. Be assured, I am probably underestimating on both counts, and of course, in the ten years since I started this project, inflation dictates that most things cost more.

I took lots of pictures, though I did not save up my receipts or anything that official, so again, these are just estimates.

Estimates:

Let's start with materials, and then talk about time.

The tires were free, but they did take a lot of time and effort and dealing with dirty tires to gather, sort, stack, fill and pound them. I was fitting like 35-50 in my van, filled to the ceiling with the seat out. After I found a regular supply, which happens to be very near my house, it was easy to get a van load. Before that, I did some running around and asking various tire shops with mixed results.

It takes a skilled pro with a good back and strong arms 20-30 minutes to pack one tire, if there is good dirt/packing material on hand, or being bucketed or shoveled in for her/him. Most of us can't really pack a tire well, in my experience. It takes a lot of 'umph', from the core of the earth, through your core, and into the core of the tire with an 8lb sledgehammer. If you have to dig/move earth, that also takes time. I would do 2-4 tires at a time, and that was usually enough to use up the little time and energy I had to spare.

Keep in mind, I was raising my son, running a successful business, and learning about building while I was doing this project. There were many delays, long periods I did not work on it at all.

I estimate that if you wanted to pay me enough to build one for you, say, $100,000 or so, I could get it done in one summer. Especially if it was not too customized, or if we knew exactly how you wanted it. Depending on where it was to be built, of course. So…three to twelve months, with help. It has been ten years since I started this project. I know I mentioned that already. It is still somewhat remarkable to me, the way time just flies by, faster and faster.

I recall feeling old for the first time when I had just turned 39 and was working with the mostly much younger Earthship crew that spring. I chopped off my braid and donated my hair to charity, gave up on intimate partnerships, just worked and worked. I worked for play, and I played for work. I also took up snowboarding around the same time. I suppose that means I had my last "real" break up a year or so before all this started too. Though I have had some other endings in that time, and cried my fair share of tears into beers.

Earth was free for me too, because I dug it, though on other projects it might need to be imported. If you hired me today, dirt could be one of the most costly parts, again, depending on where and what resources are at hand.

I think I spent a few hundred dollars on rebar and lathe, nails, wire, screws.

Probably more than a thousand on cement, concrete, and lime.

A couple hundred on hopper windows, and a couple hundred more on Polycarbonate.

A couple hundred on lumber.

About five hundred for the vigas.

At least a thousand on tools, including two mixers, wheelbarrow, shovels, buckets, tarps, drills, trowels, wet saw and diamond blade (for cutting bottles).

I probably spent another thousand on things I didn't actually need or ruined before I used.

Maybe three hundred on pumice and gas to get it.

A couple hundred on gas to get red earth and tires.

A couple hundred on pigments, sprayers, brushes, rags.

So, around $5,000 total, which was my estimate. Let's round that up to $7,000 to account for gas and wear on the van. Ten years, which was two or three times longer than I expected, or needed. This was really about a three-year project, even in spare time for one person with occasional help from friends. Again though, I had several long breaks, most winters, and at least two summers that I was injured…and then a super slow-down, due to business transitions, health issues, and financial hardship.

While I am on the topic of getting over and above financial hardships, let me say thank you.

Thank you for buying this book, and for reading it all the way to the end. Unless you are one of those people who starts at the end, in which case, still;

thank you.

I love sharing what I learned, answering questions, and talking about my vision for the future, so please feel free to contact me. I sometimes give private or small group tours of the Head Hutt and Foo Dog Mega-Sculptures at my home in Albuquerque, New Mexico. Please let me know if you would like to arrange one.

I also love helping others design, or designing and building special projects for people (read that I may be for hire), when the pay and timing are right, and when it sparks my imagination.

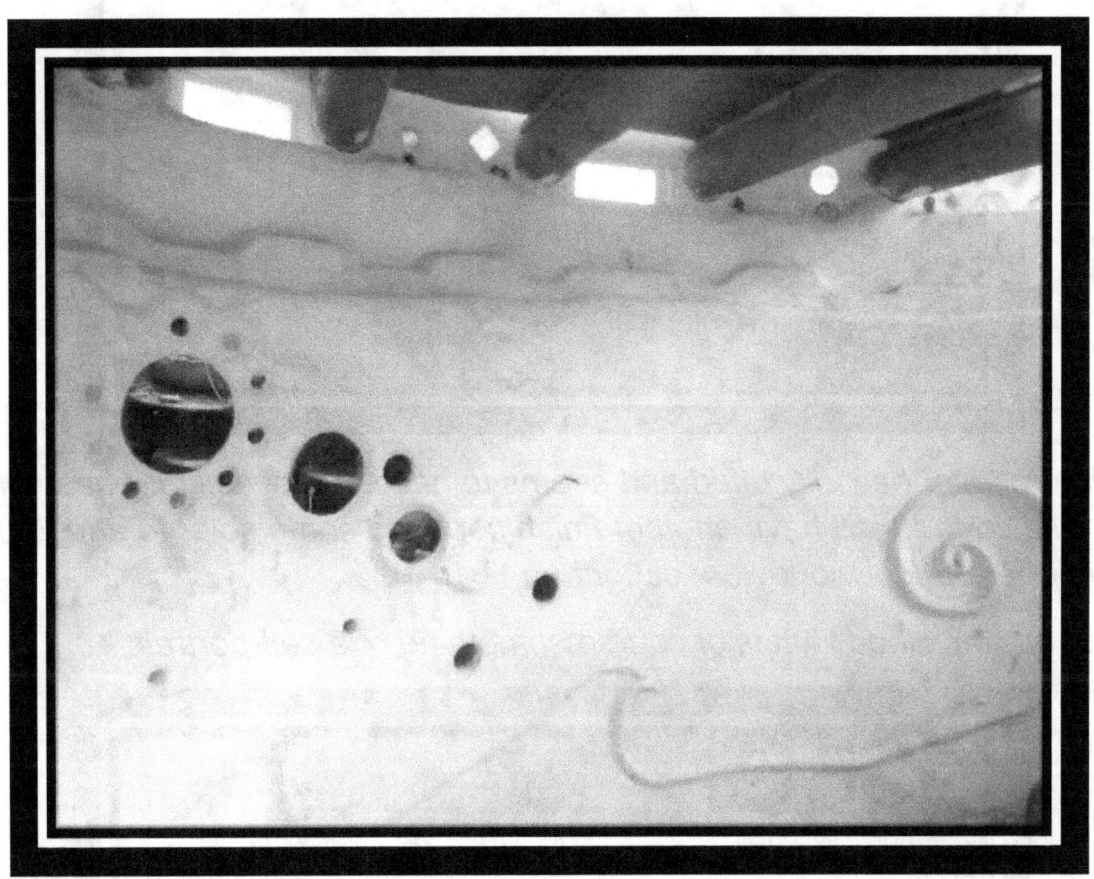

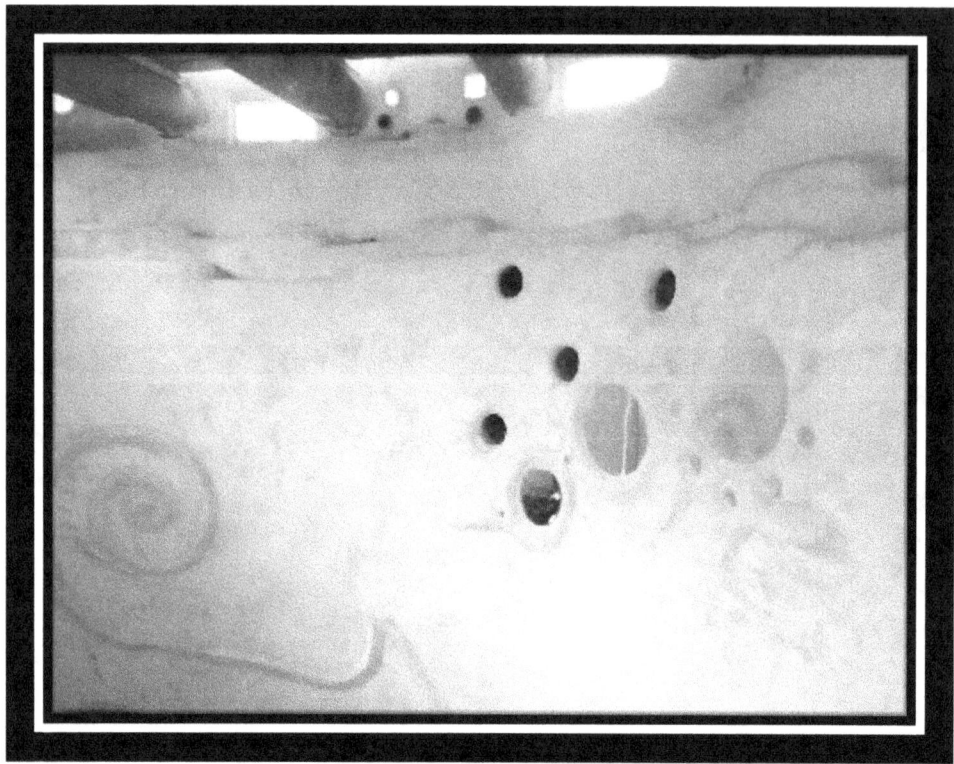

The lime plaster has fully dried and seems to have cured well for phase one-- no cracks so far! I still have another finish coat and some color to add, but had to break here to get work-work caught up. 2 14 16.

Like all art, the Head Hutt is of course something of a self-portrait.

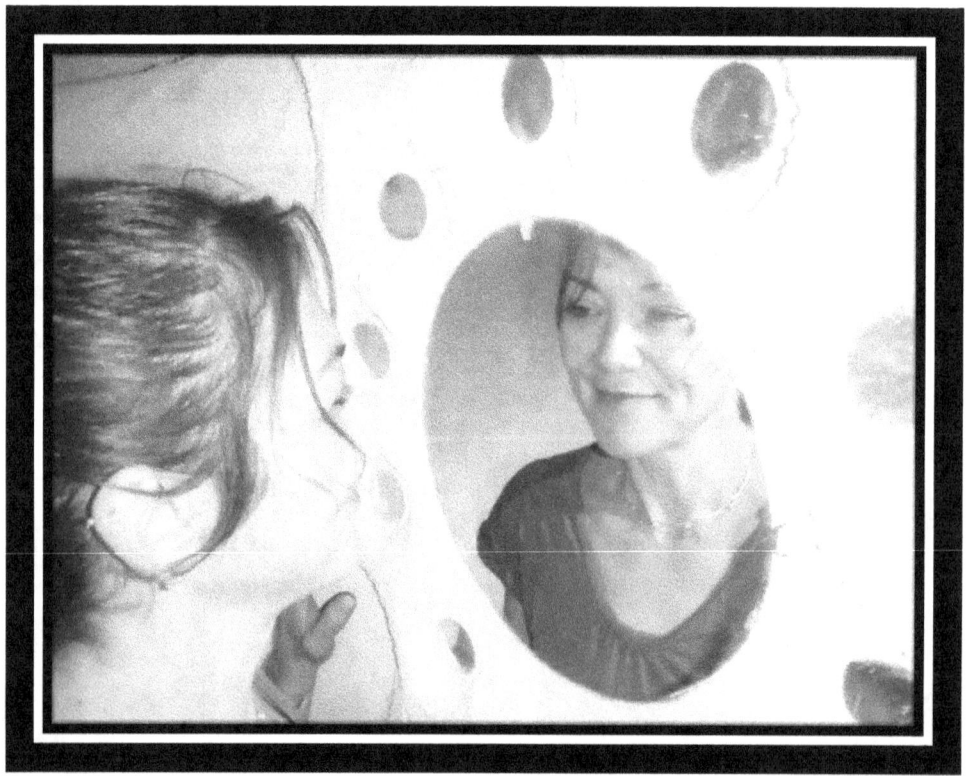

The Head Hutt Picture Book

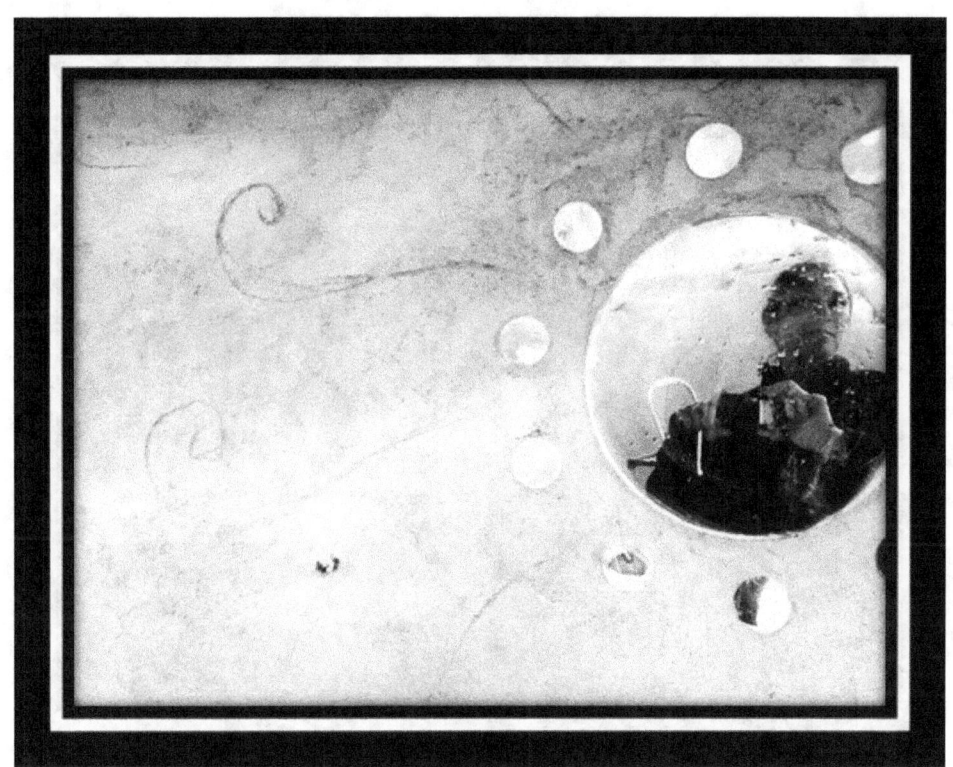

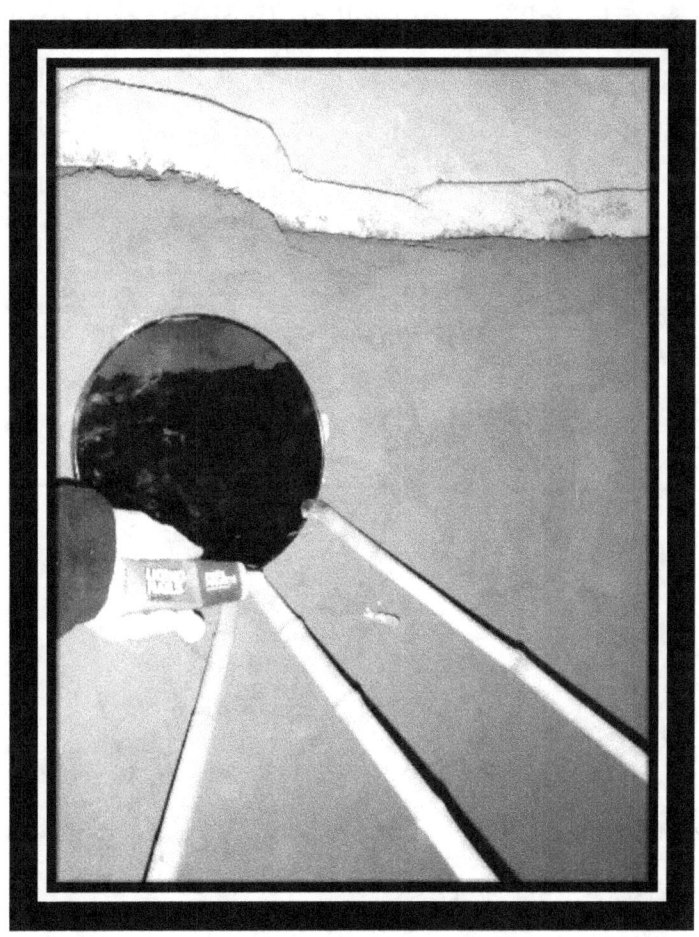

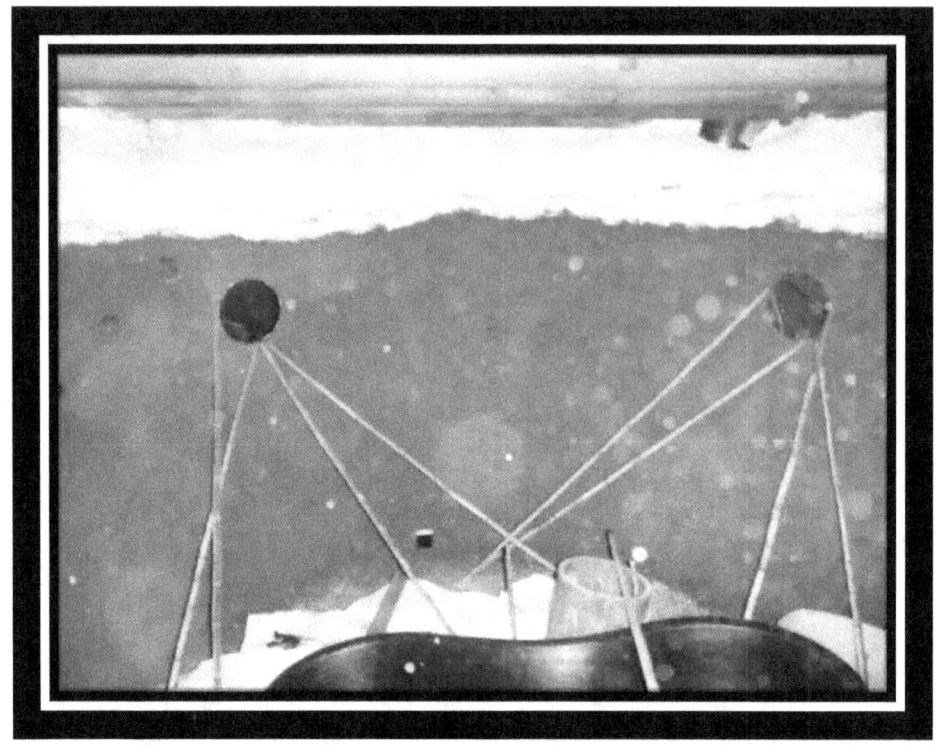

Getting these mirrors to stick on the wall so I can plaster around them. 1 16 16.

The Head Hutt Picture Book

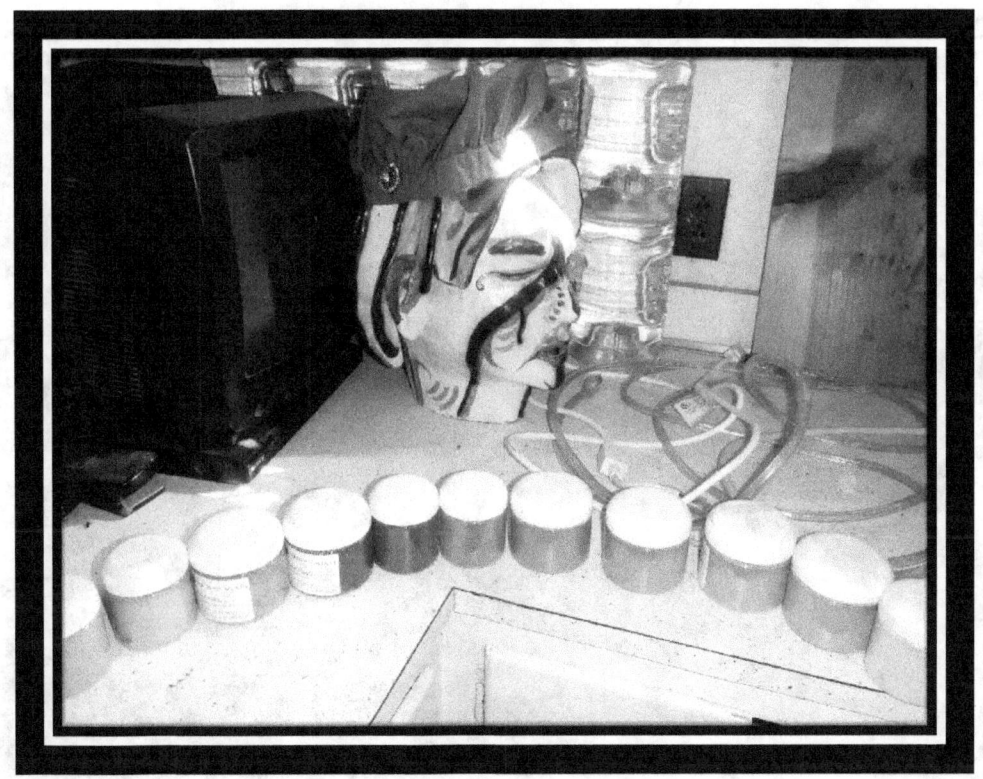

I was hopeful that I might get to some color today, but, I didn't. Not yet. 1 20 16.

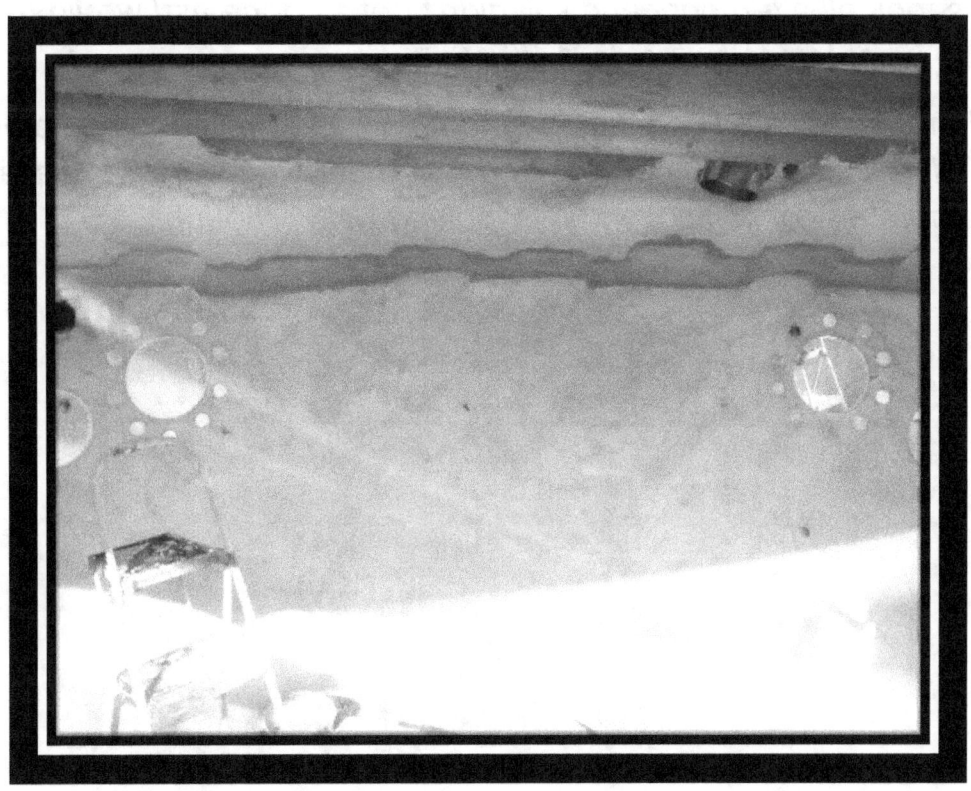

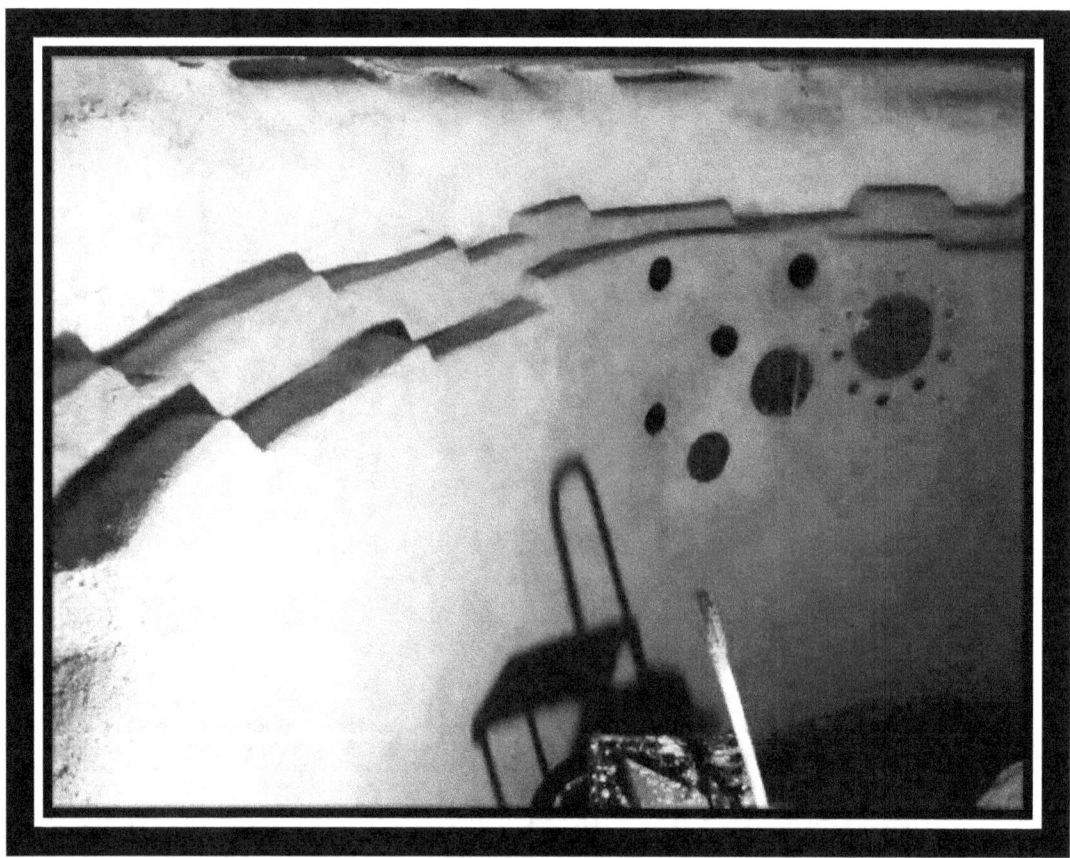

Top edges took all afternoon, and still didn't get as done as I would have liked. We will see what tomorrow holds. 1 20 16.

I had high hopes to finish edges and smoothing and maybe even color today, but nightfall, a cold wind, my aching body, and pending workload called for at least one more day of finish work. It is looking better though!

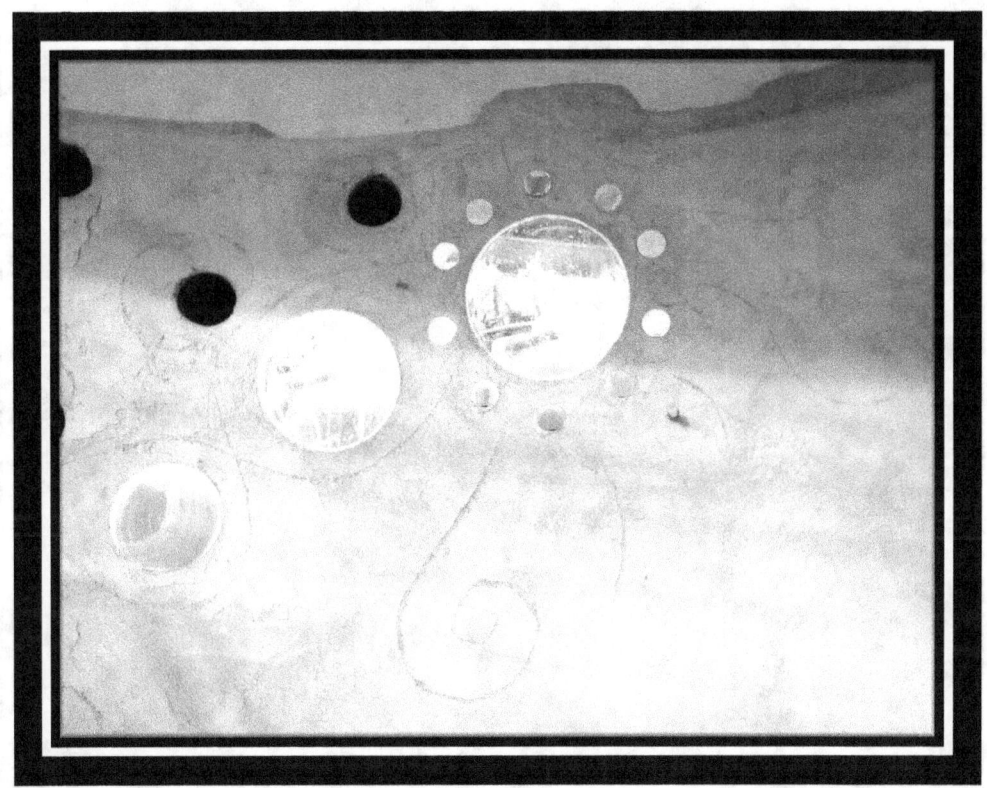

See the little spider? I played around with some rough sketches for design before I began plastering again--third coat, but, first layer with fibers. 1 24 16.

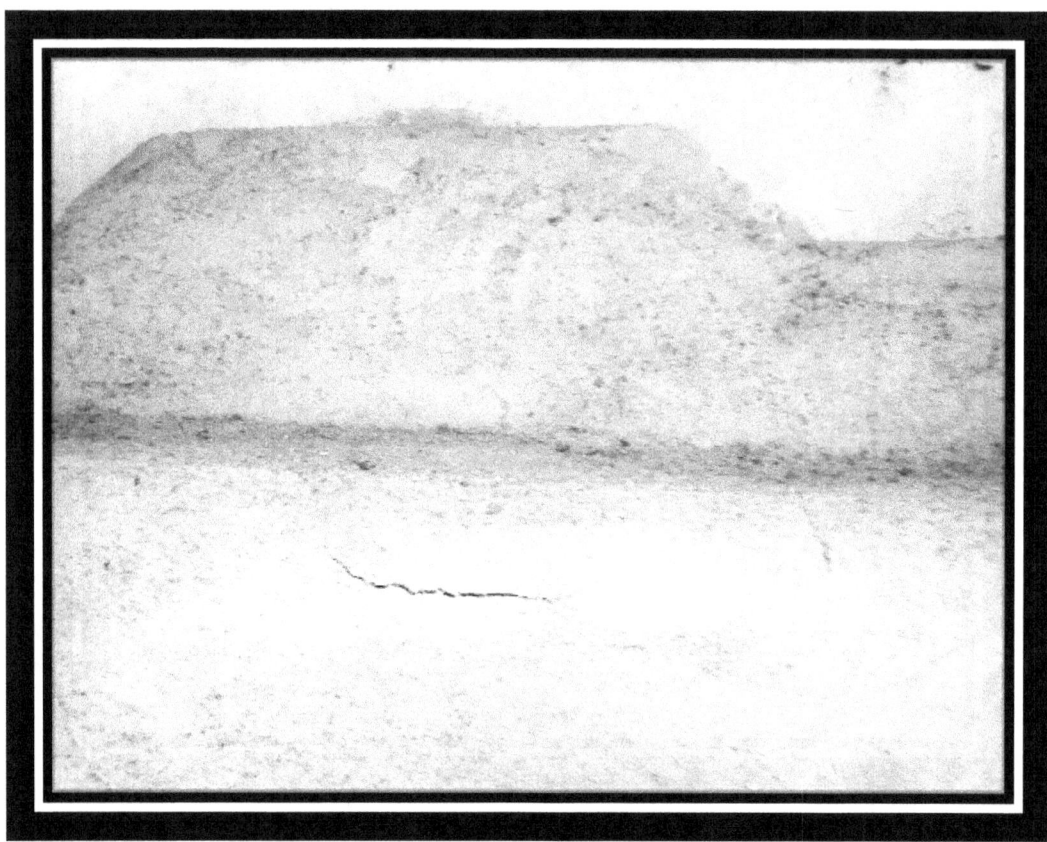

Had a little cracking already starting less than halfway through curing. Good thing I had already resolved to redo the base layer with engineering fibers, as I should have done in the first place--though in the long run, it is working out perfect, or course, as I needed the extra practice and extra layers are getting me closer to a smoother, better looking surface. 1 24 16.

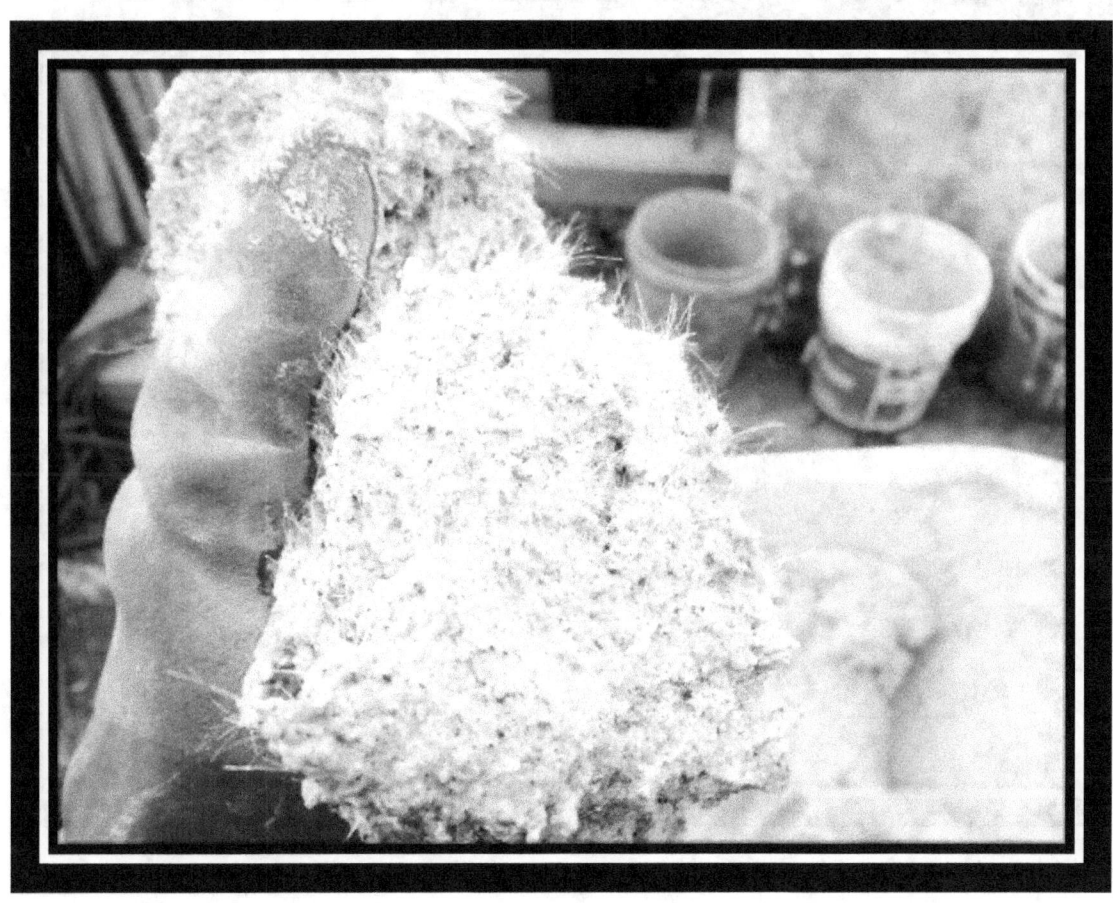

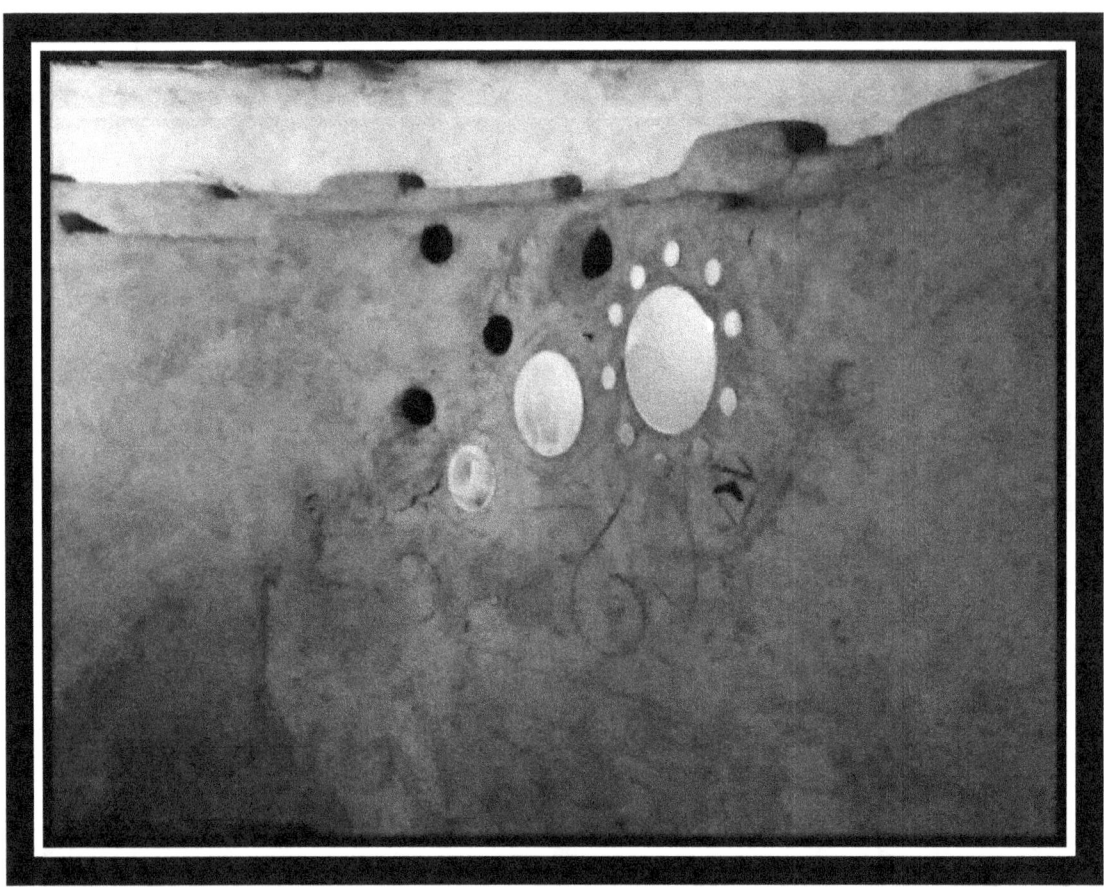

Decided to plaster again now with a layer of fibrous plaster before moving on to the finish layer/s. Mixing these in by 'hand' (shovel) was trickier than an electric mixer would have been. I could use more fiber-fluffing skills for future projects. 1 24 16.

You can barely see it, but this third layer is going on much thinner and smoother than previous layers. Next I will do some raised detail and go over the edges again, this time with fibrous plaster, and THEN I can get to the finishing layer and color coat. 1Today I tried pre-fluffing the fibers, but I think it just ended up tangling them up in more balls, which slowed me down considerably, and may lead to problems during/after curing. We will see.

I only made half a batch of progress today--slow going today, but, I did learn a couple things that don't work so well (pre-fluffing the fibers by hand, and trying to build with spreadable plaster. Nope. 1 25 16. Hey! It's my birthday.

The Head Hutt Picture Book

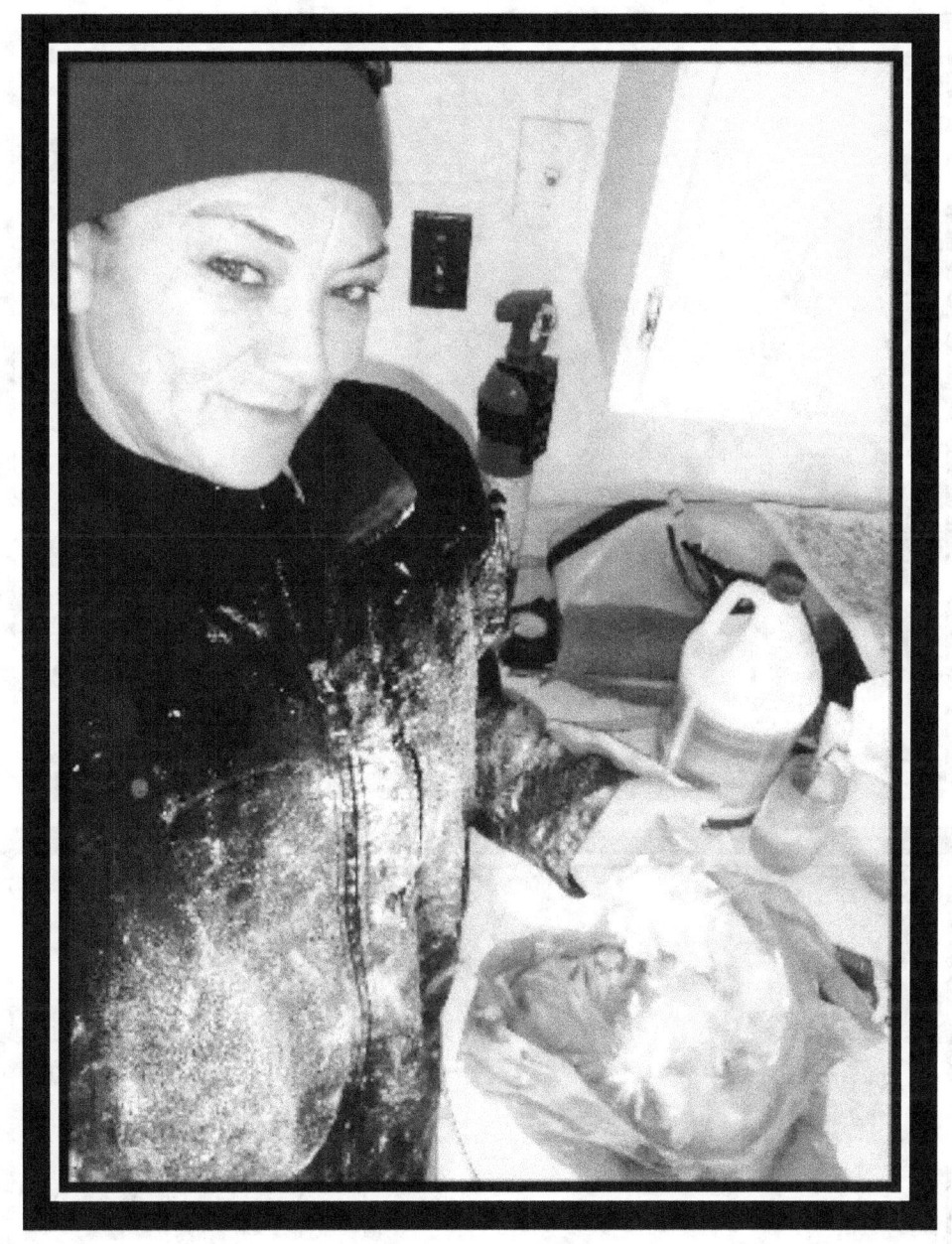

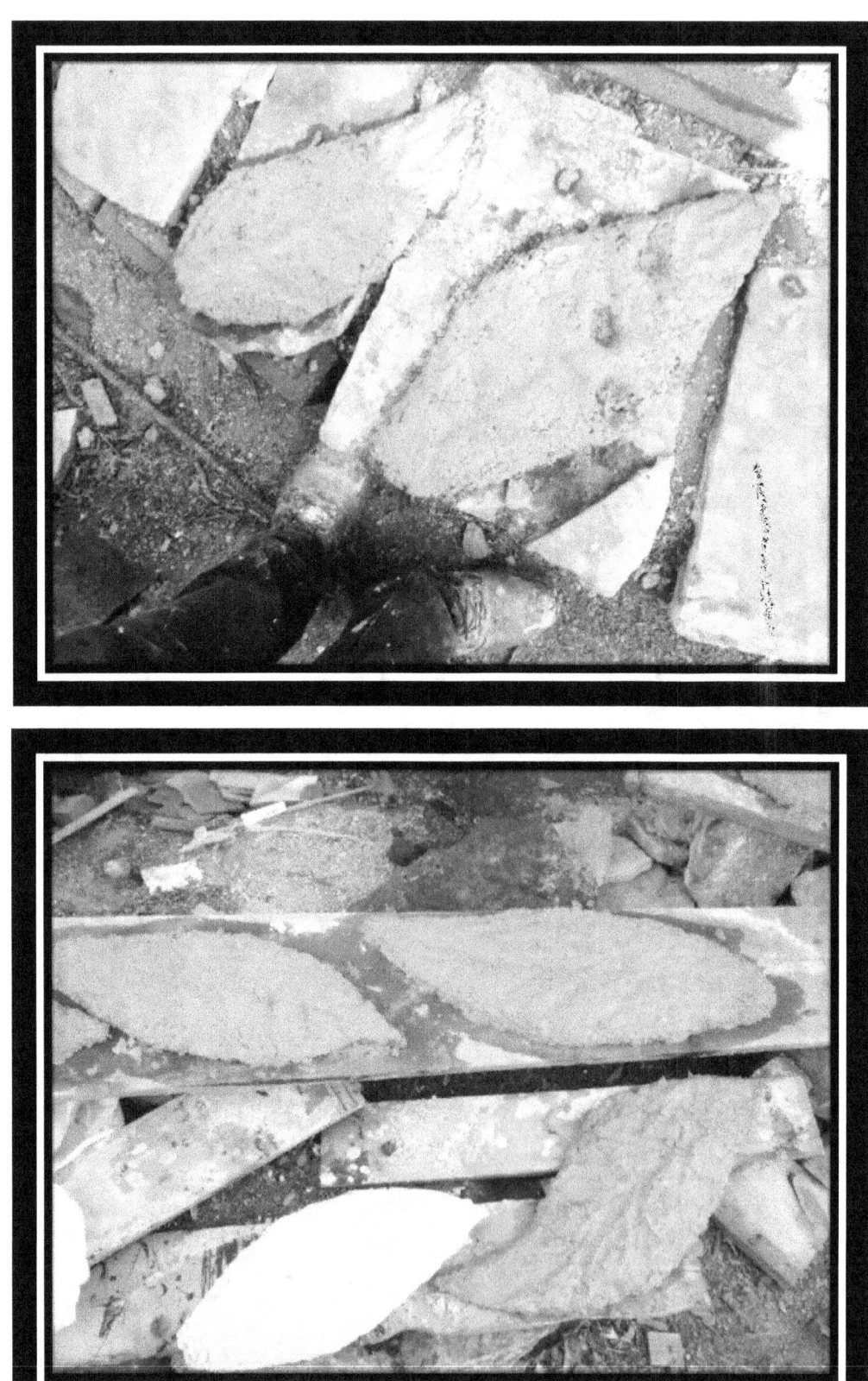

Making feather leaves for the eyelash trim. A papercrete job would hardly be complete without at least a couple cat footprints. 11 9 15.

The Head Hutt Picture Book

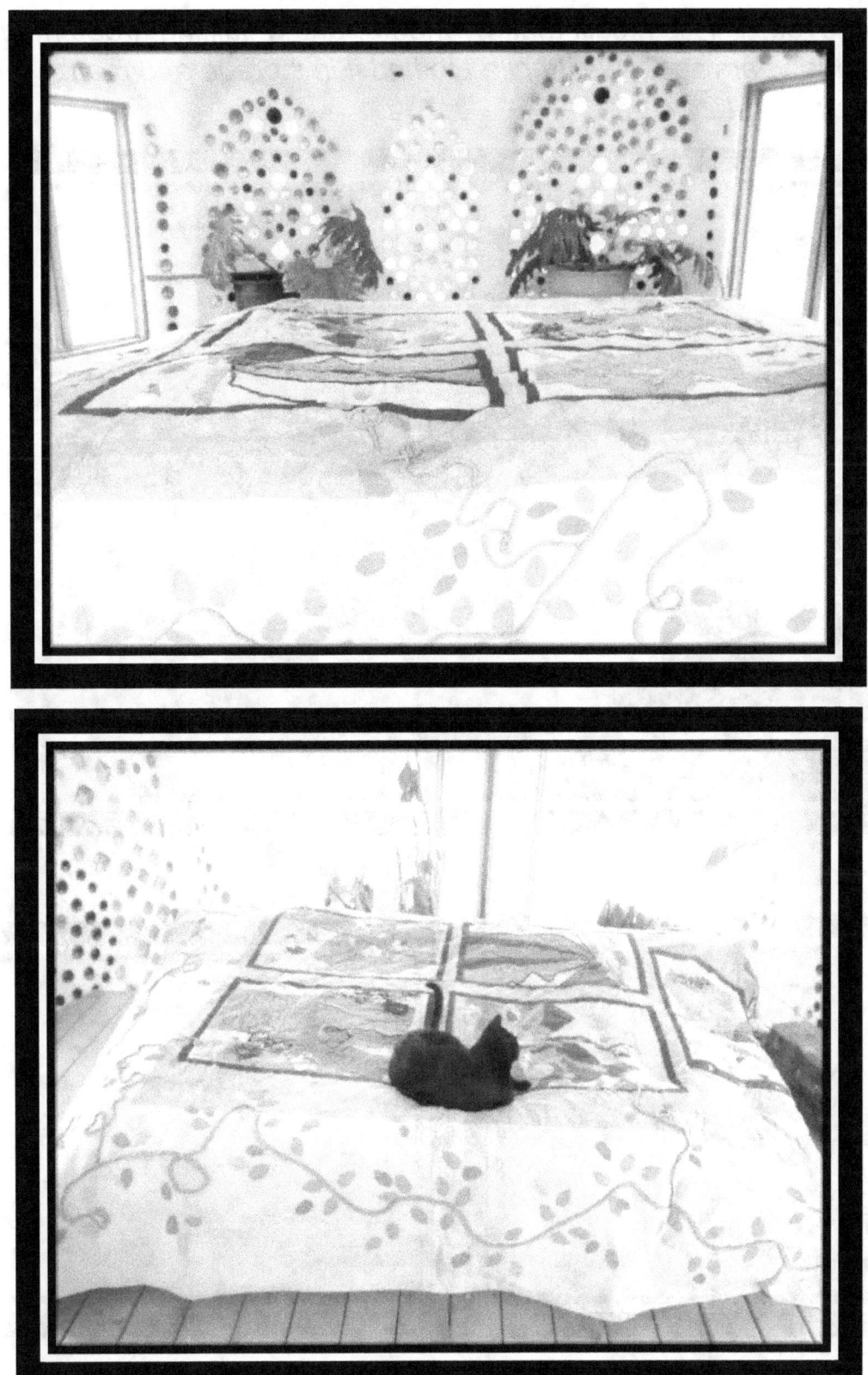

Finally got the bed made, though the frame is still not totally finished. 2 14 16.

Taco Approved. This is a quilt that my mother and a quilting group made for the fair some years ago. I was thrilled to find it in storage and realize it is perfect for in here! 2 14 16.

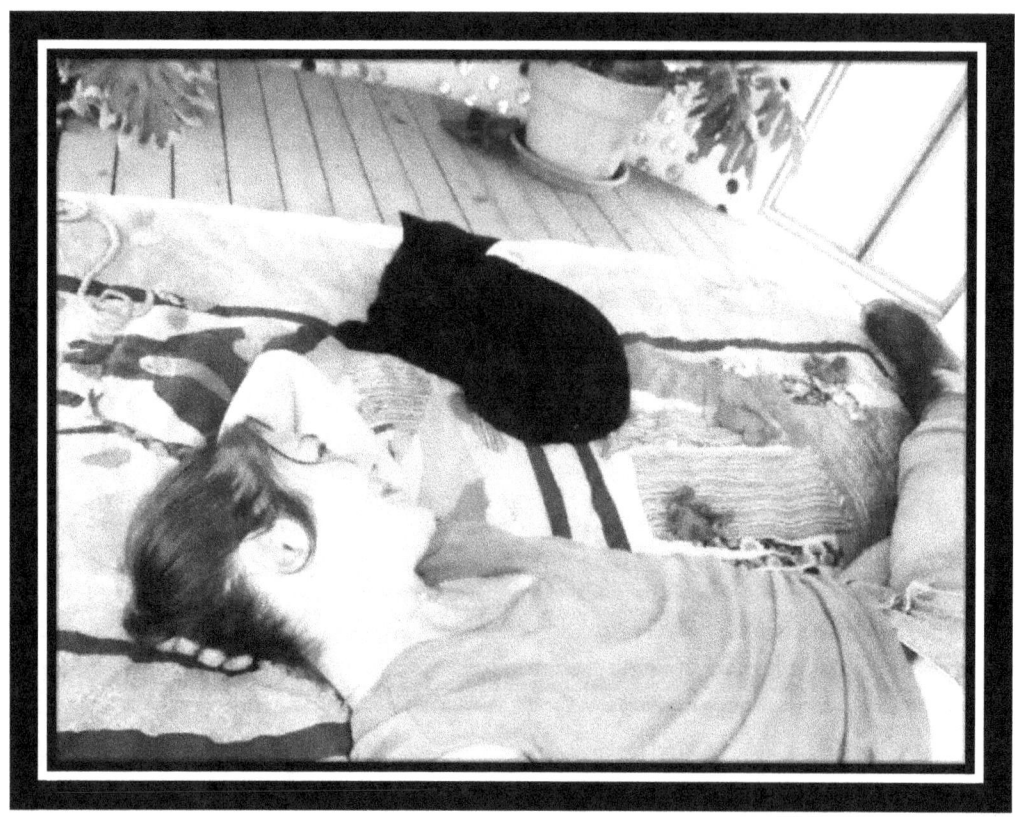

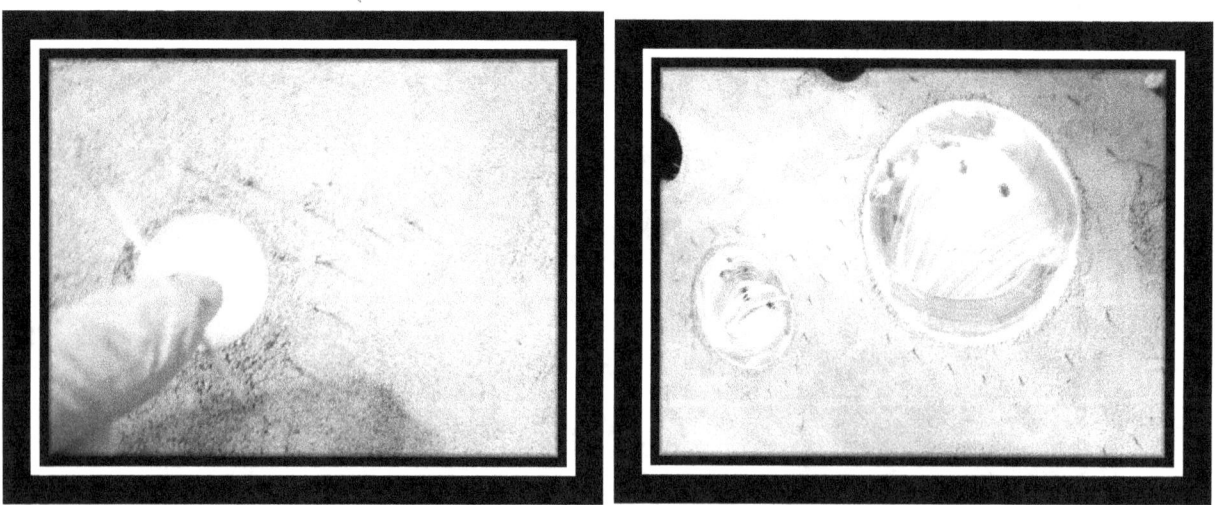

Decided to try toothpicks to give me enough 'tooth' to use the mix I have, since I am running lowish on lime putty now. 1 26 16.

Using toothpicks to hold on the lime plaster details, worked very well. Several years into curing, no signs of cracking on this wall.

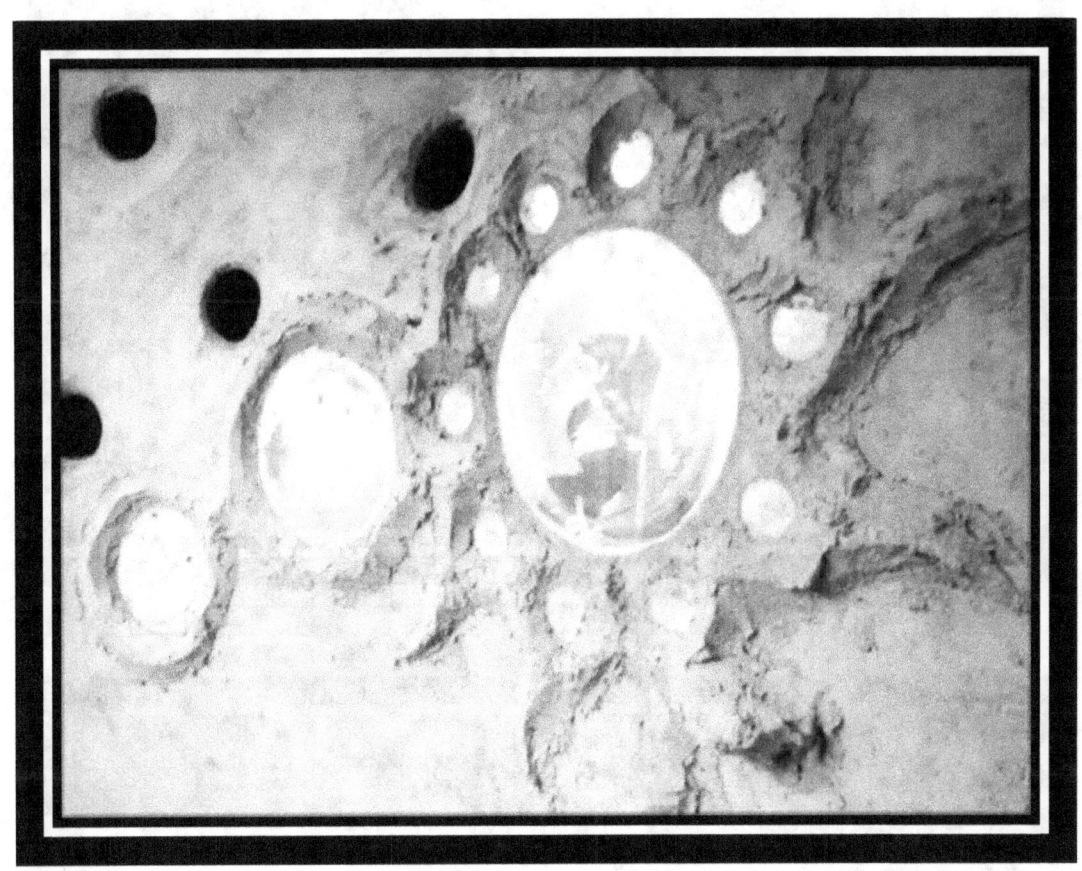

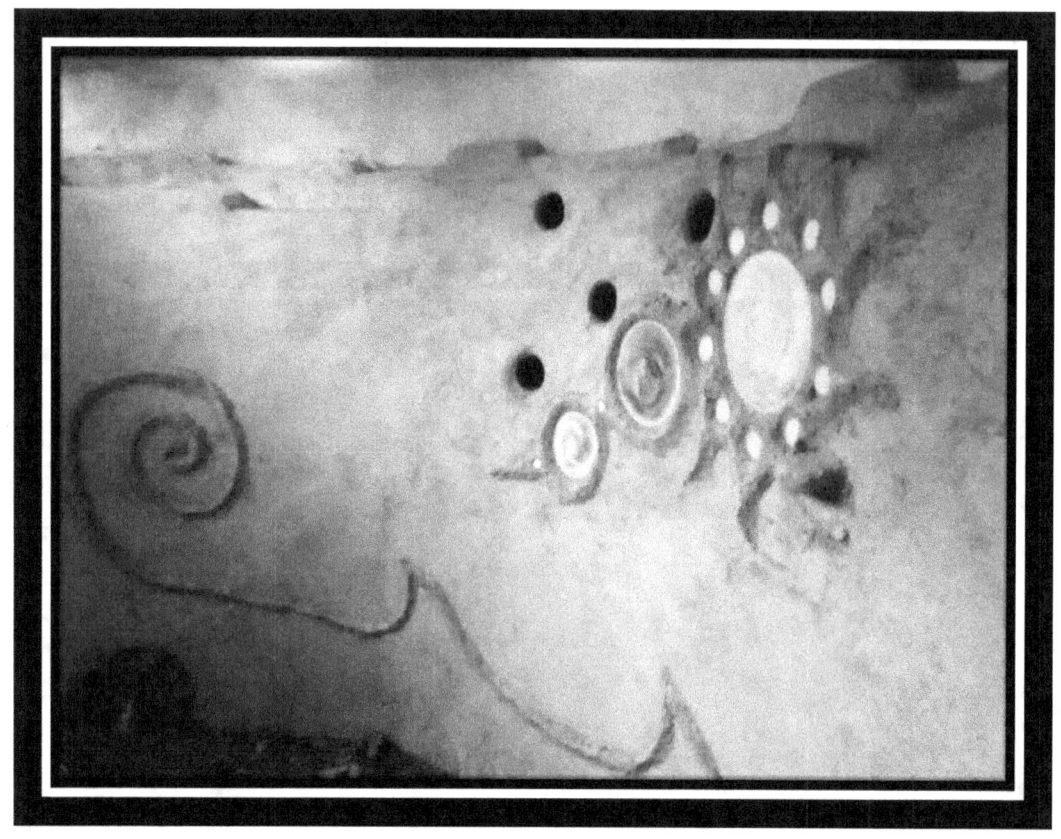

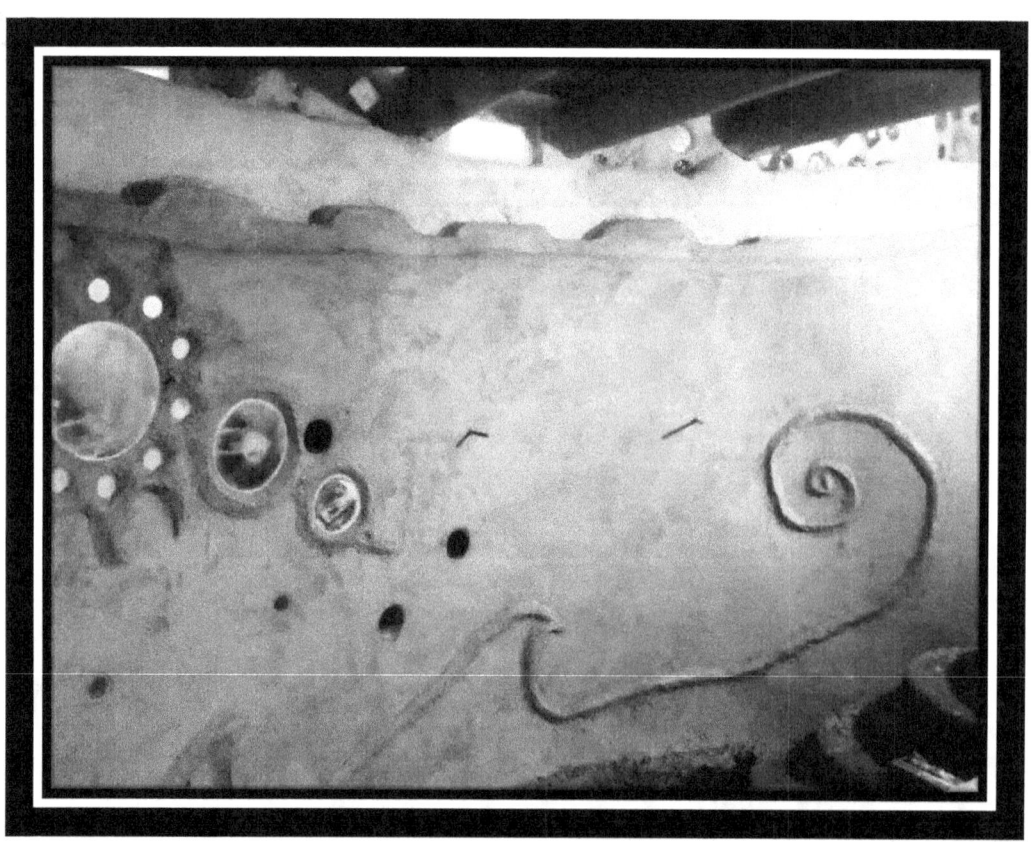

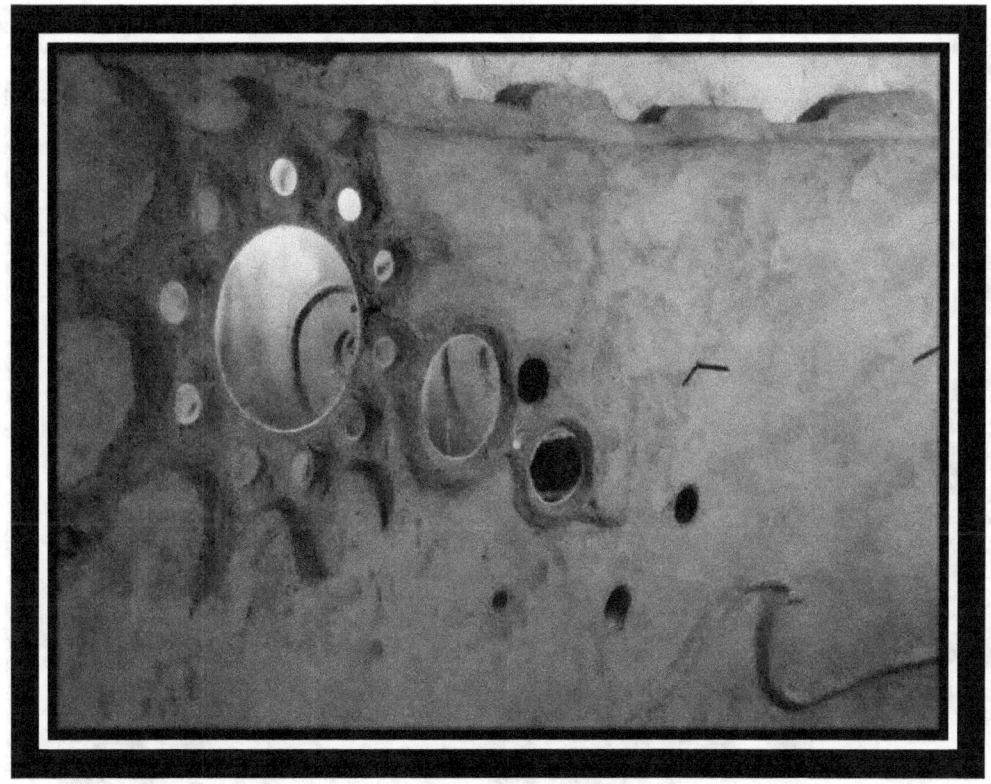

Getting smoother--ran out of time again today, so, almost ready for final coat!

About ready for the finishing coat and color, soon as I can make some more time! 1 27 16.

The Head Hutt Picture Book

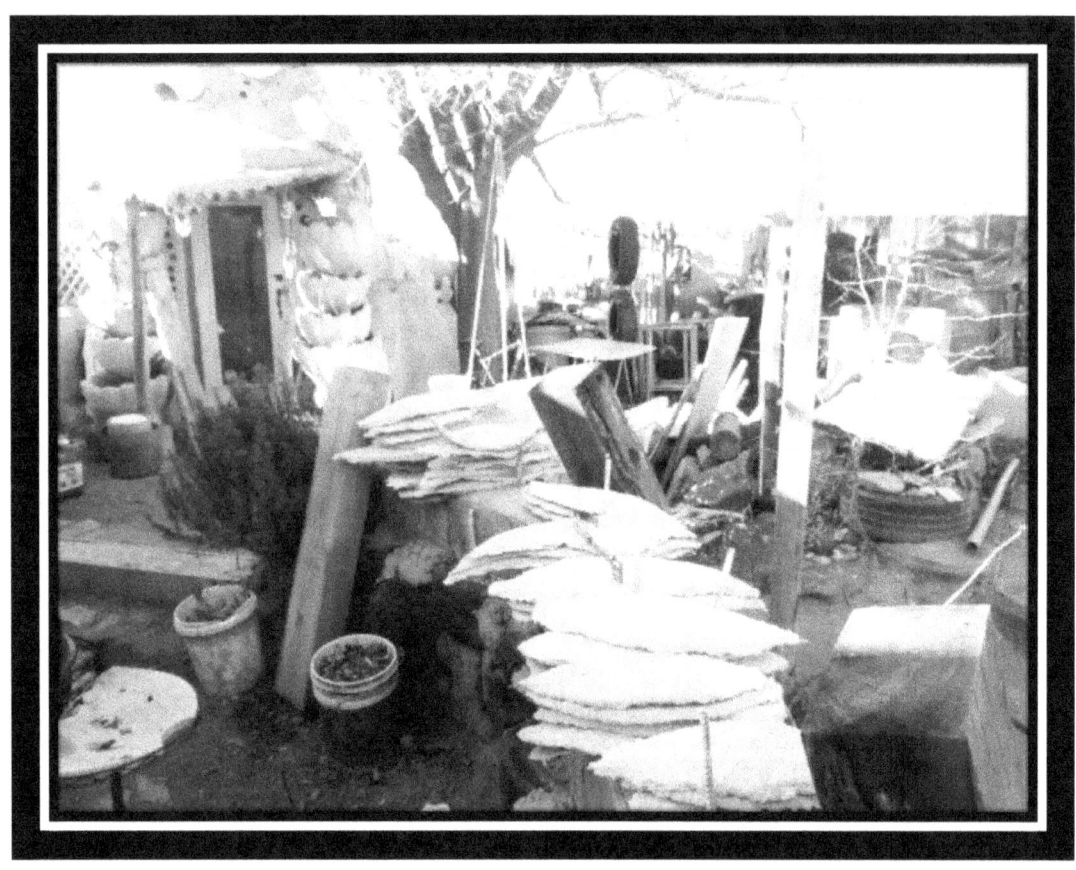

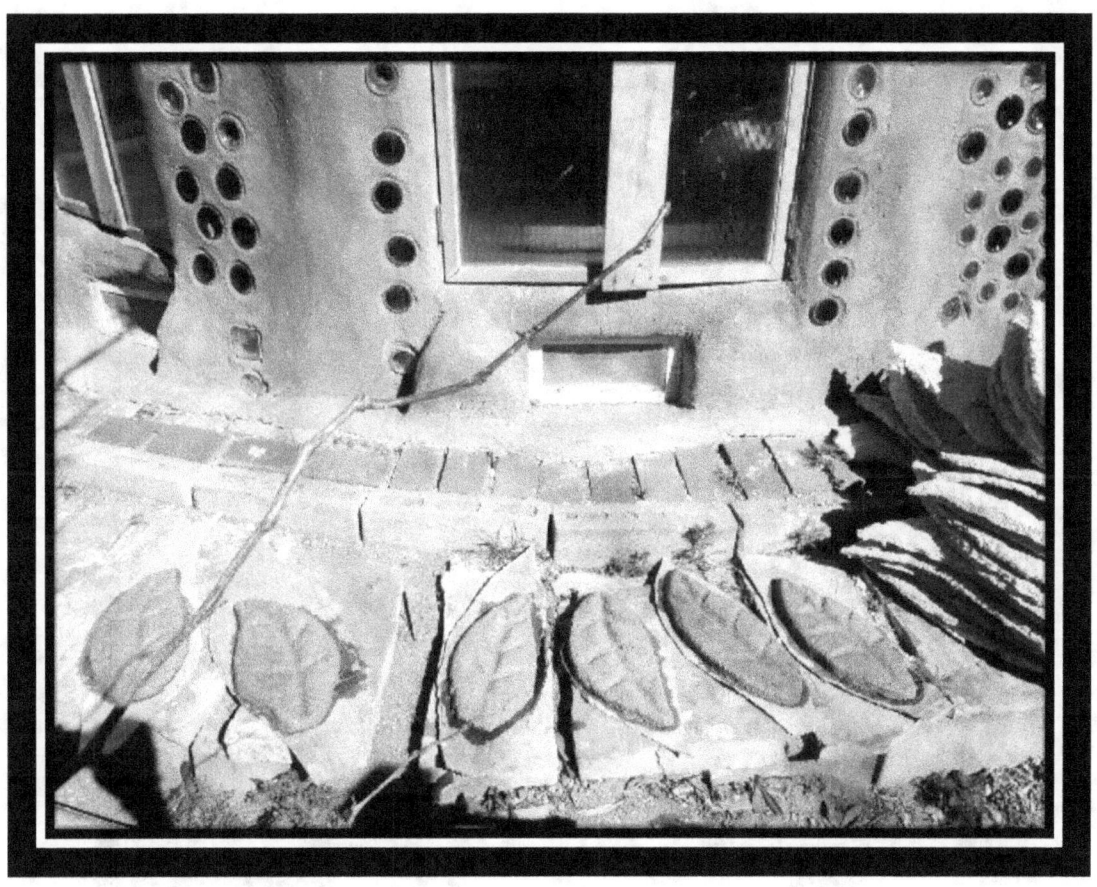

Prepping to finish the eyelash-leaf-feathers for the HH. This was the first batch--mostly too big, but, I may use some of them. 2 26 16.

The Head Hutt Picture Book

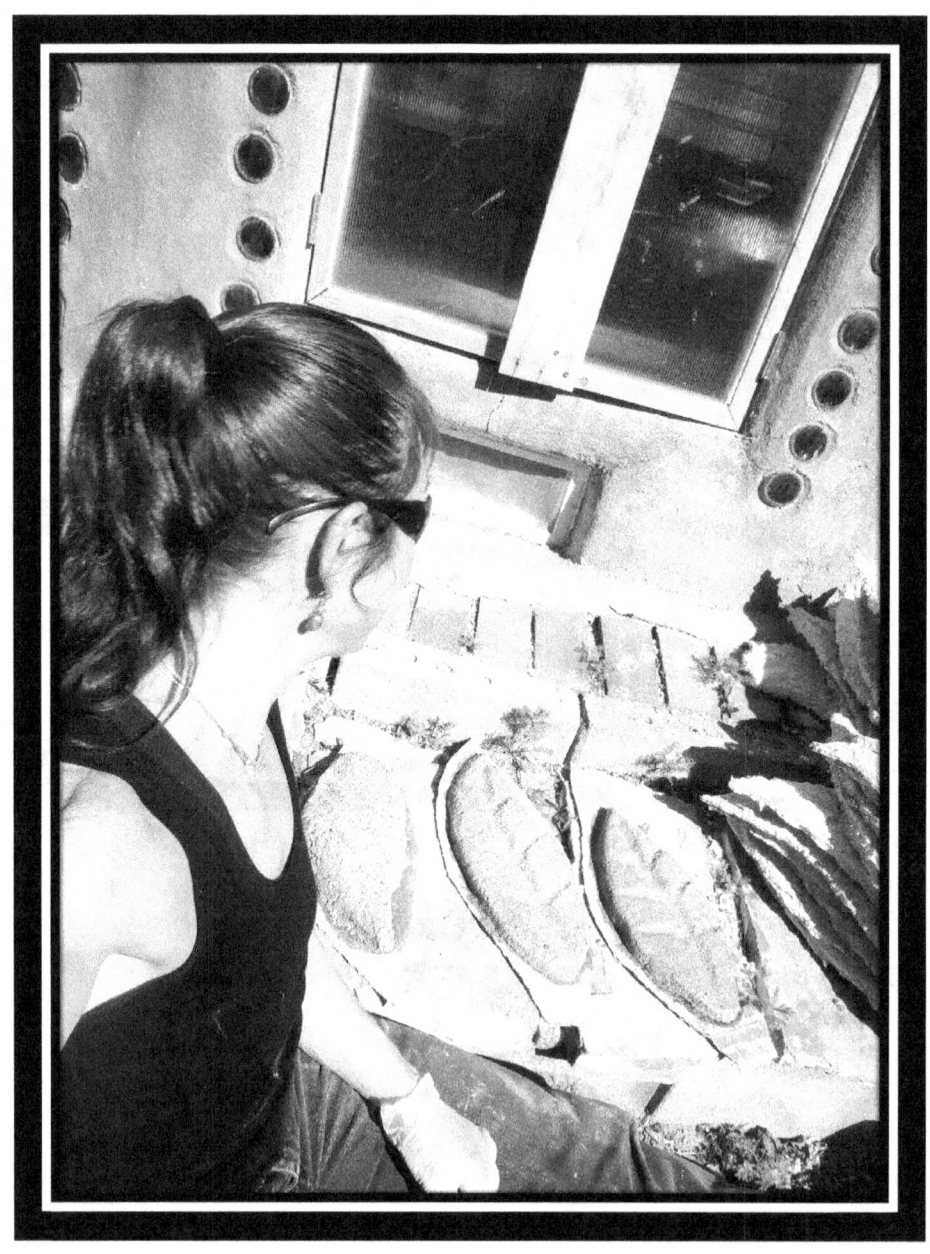

Progress was slow, but there is Making Progress. I am re-making the leaf-feather-eyelashes, and playing. Outside. In the sun. 3 9 16.

Leaf feather lashes drying in the sun. These are now a brilliant blue color.

The Head Hutt Picture Book
Mashin mo' paper. 3 10 16.

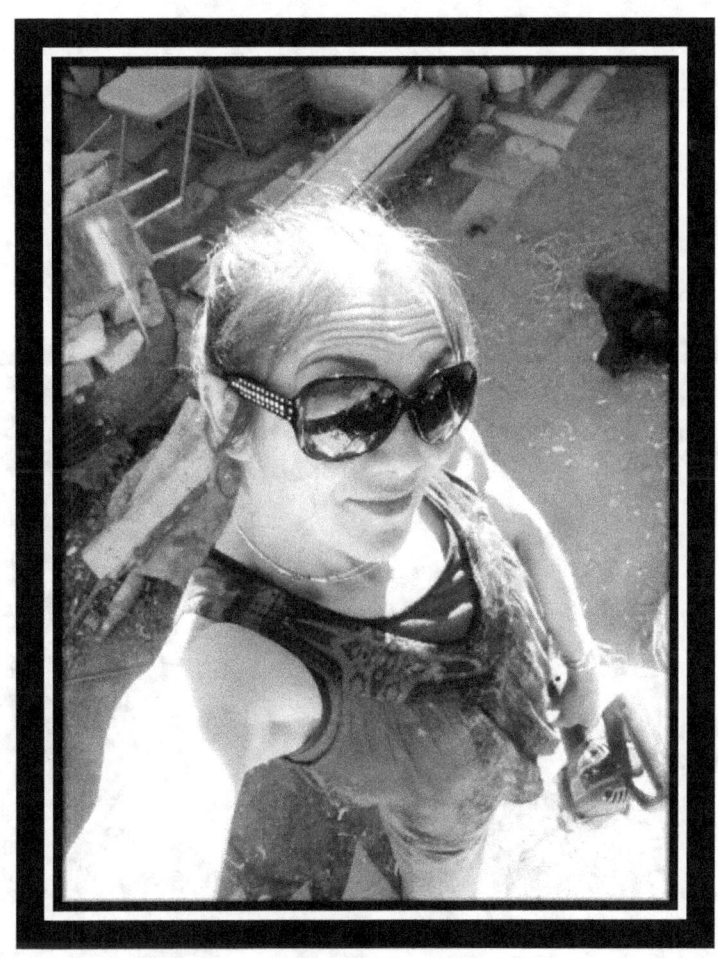

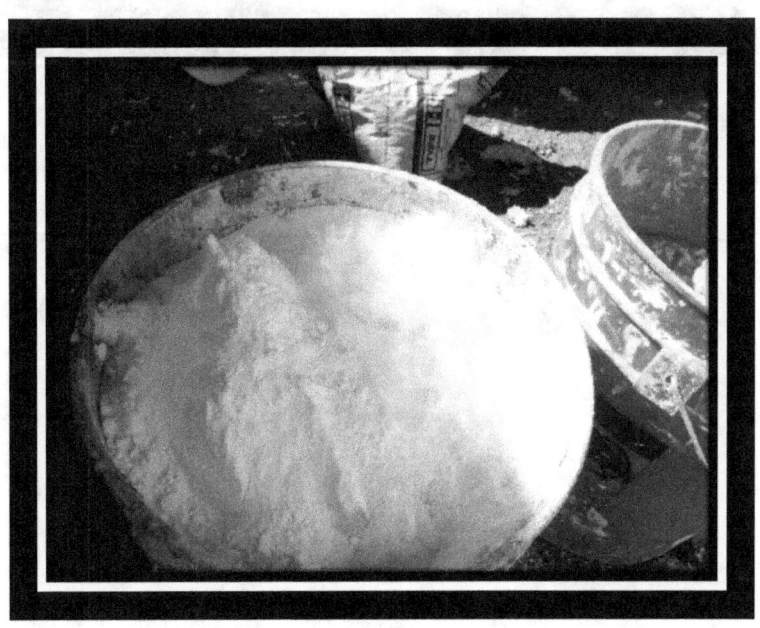

Mixin small batches of papercrete with fibers for more leaf-feather-eyelashes. 3 11 16.

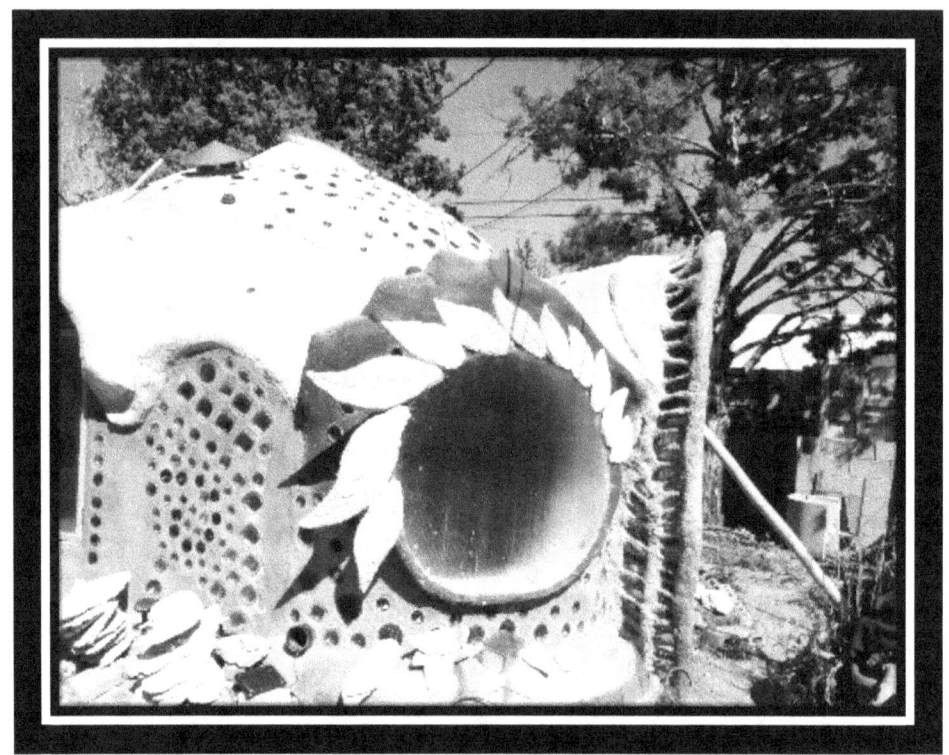

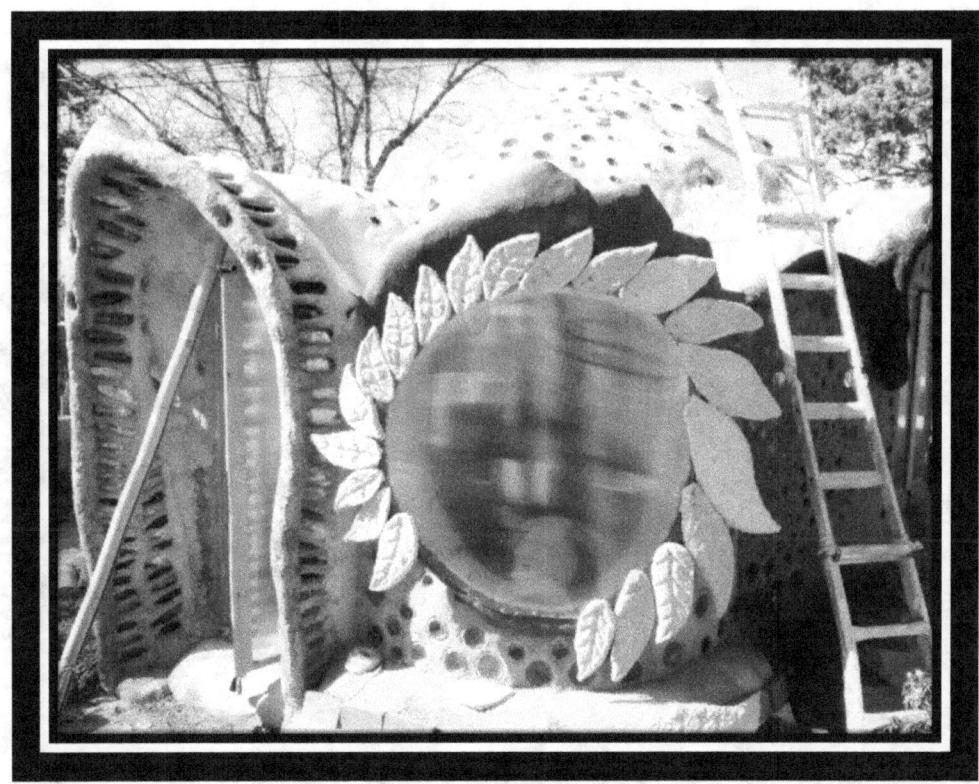

Finally getting the lash-leaf-feathers on...only wouldn't you know, I still gotta make one more batch to finish, then color! 3 16 16.

The Head Hutt Picture Book

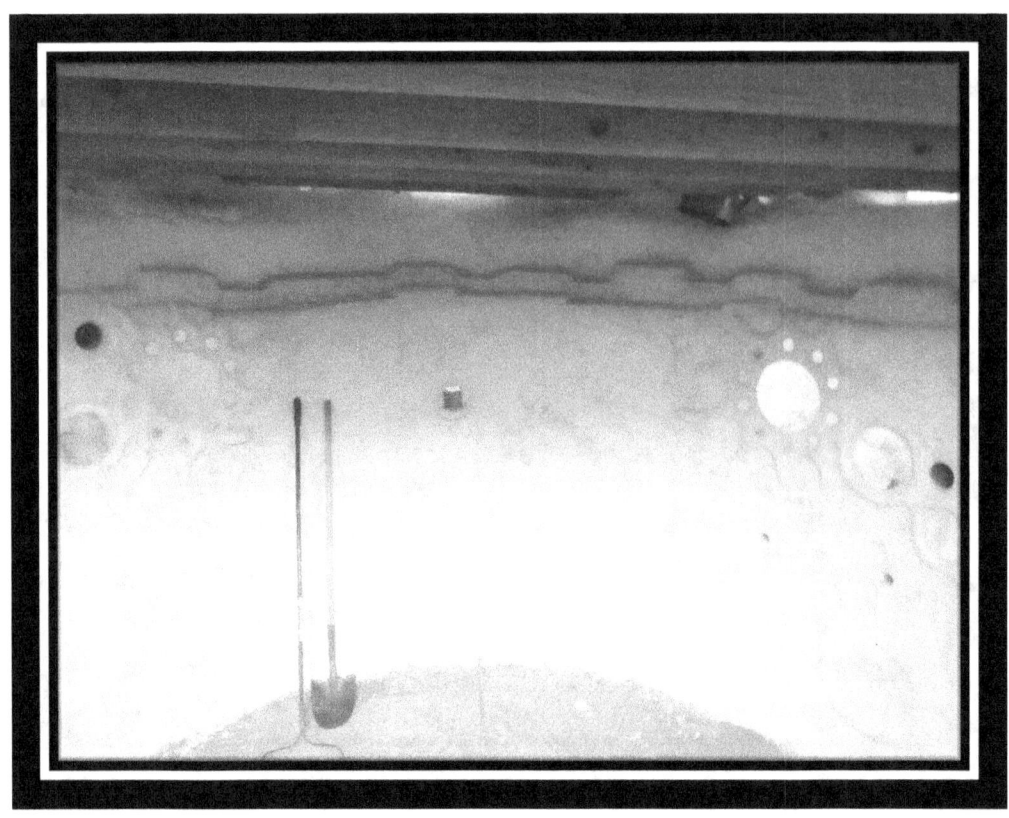

The Head Hutt Picture Book

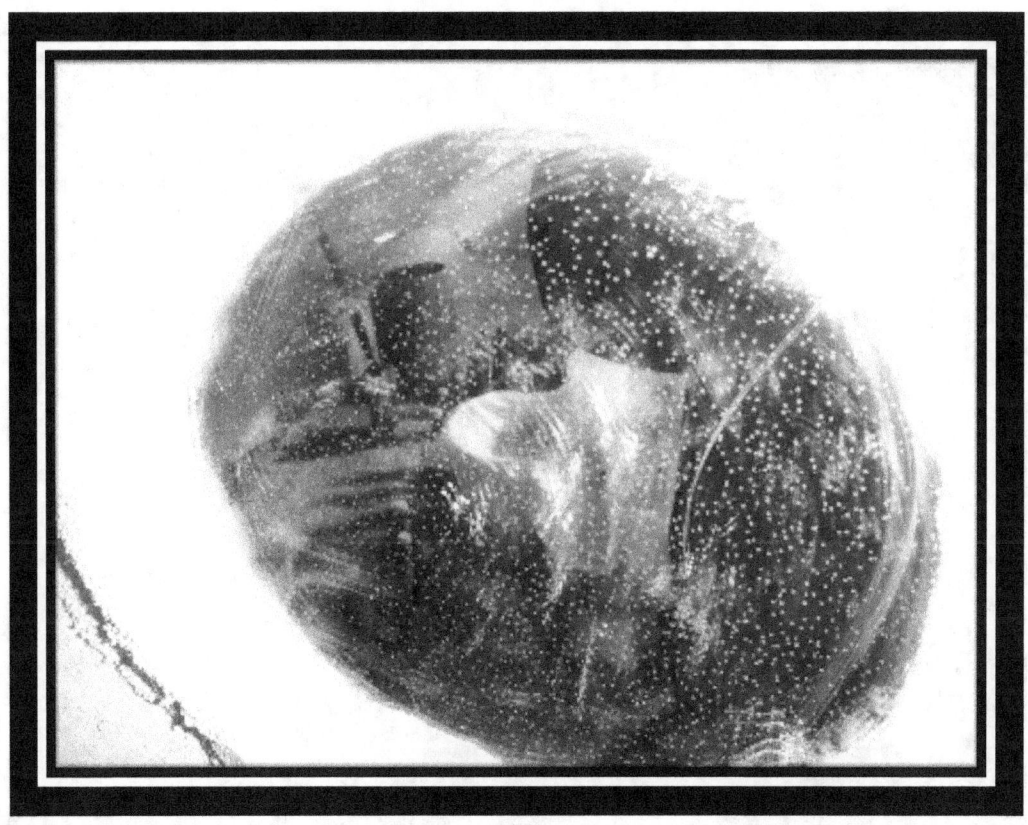

Here's something I didn't expect. The back of the cheaper mirrors is already being eaten away by the cob behind. 3 27 16.

The Head Hutt Picture Book

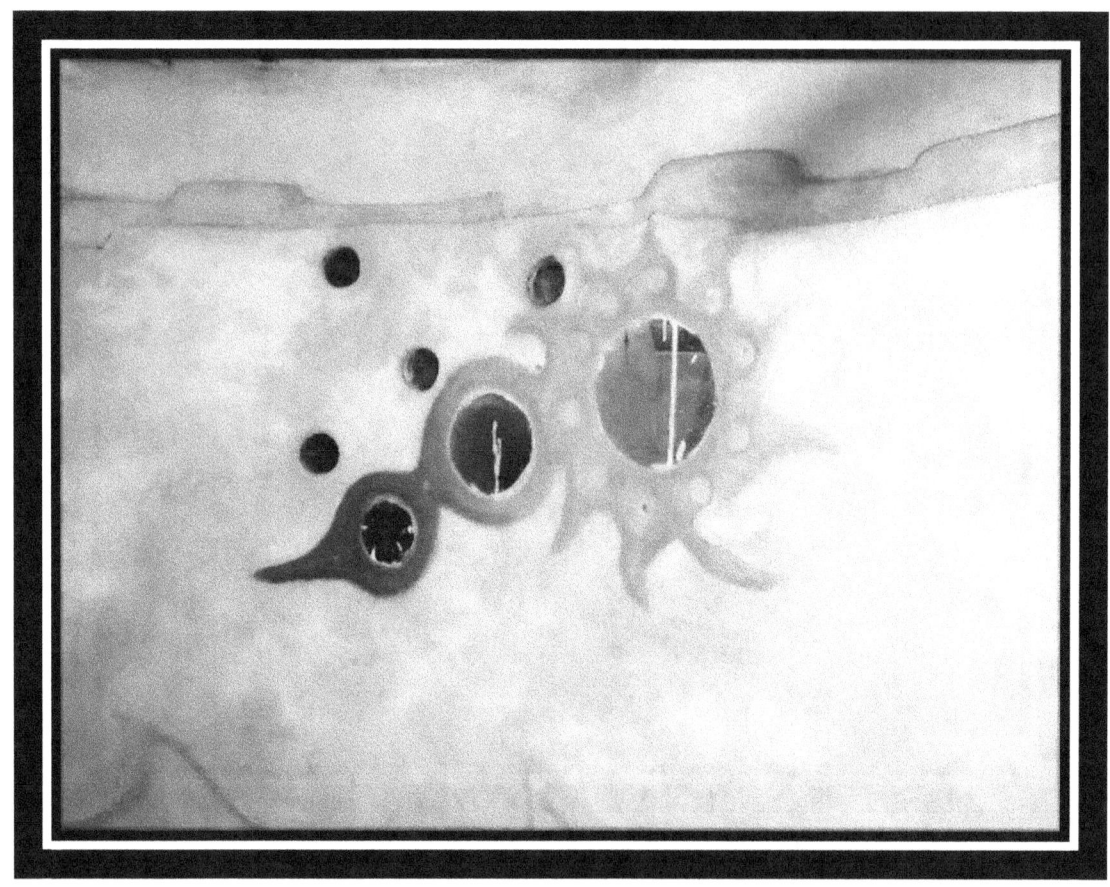

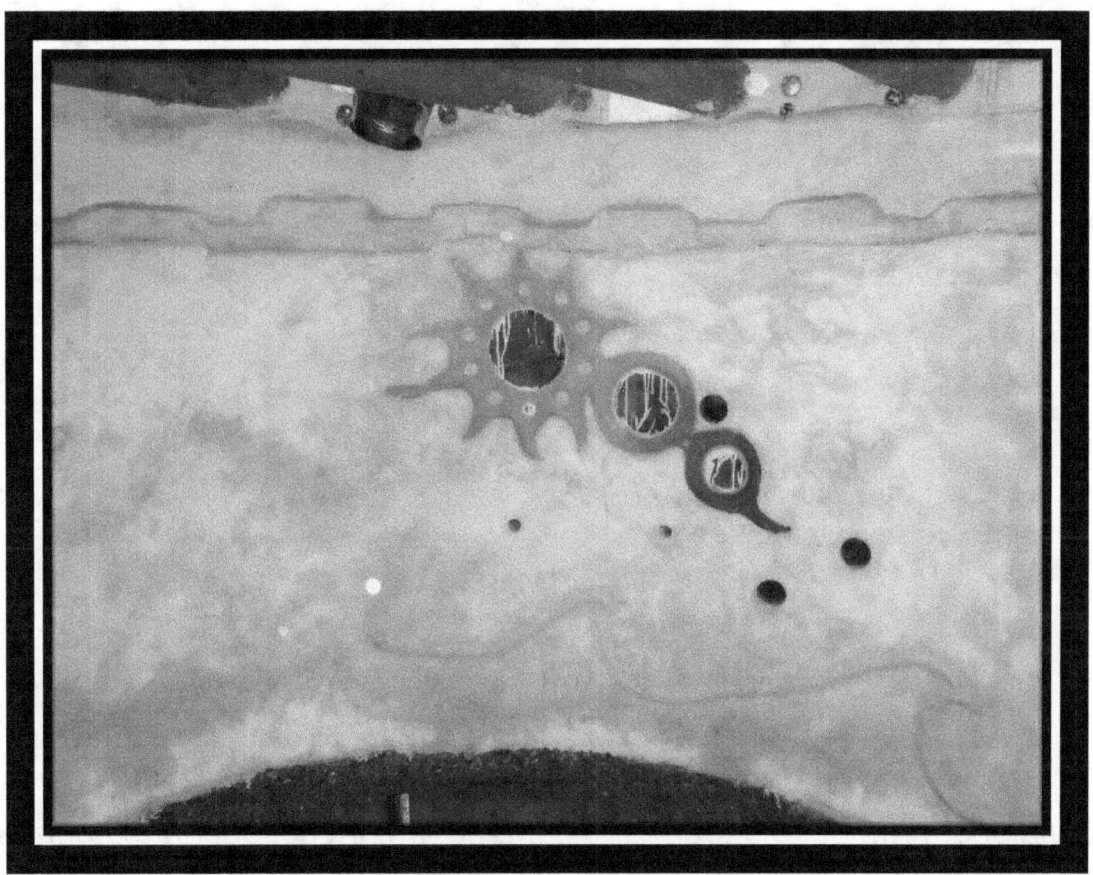

FINALLY getting back to some color! I am glad I thought about colors for a long time before I started, and glad this is a learning project, so there is no wrong! So far, so good. 5 4 16.

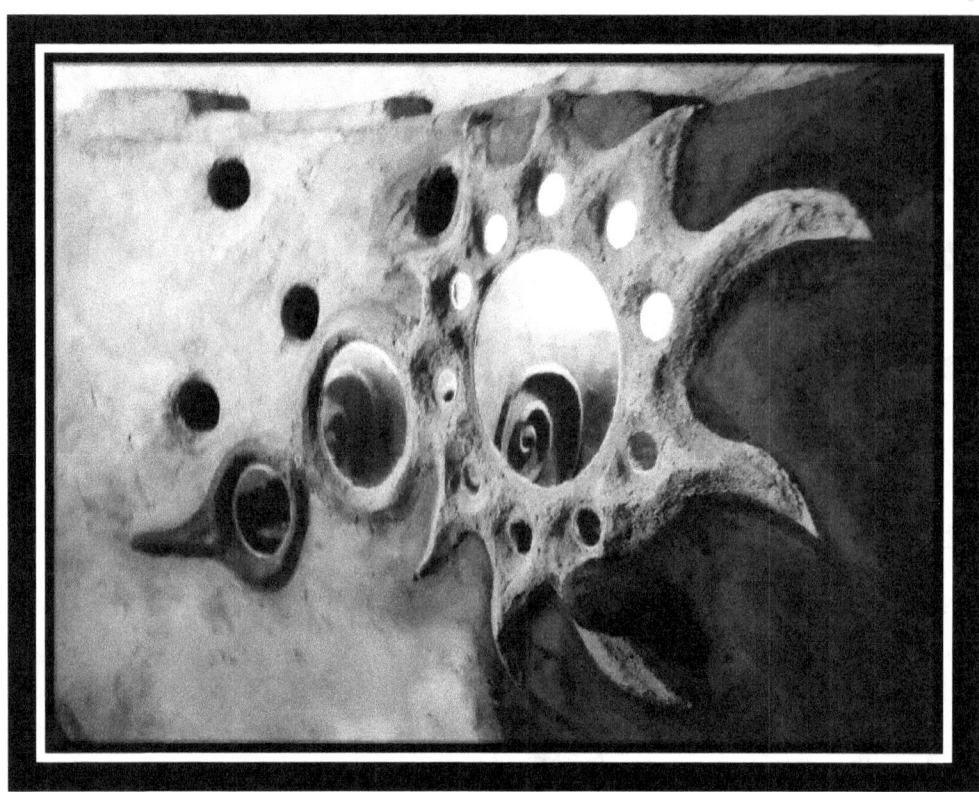

Coming along. I ran out of steam and light, so, the investigation/experiment resumes tomorrow. 5 4 16.

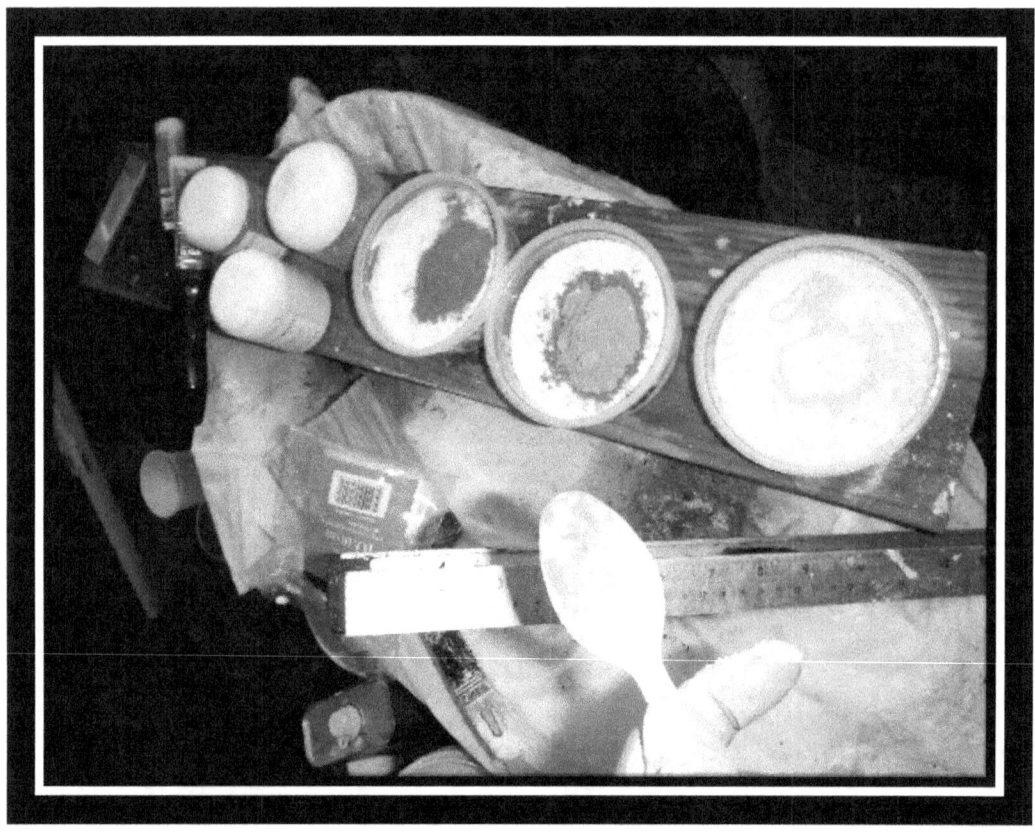

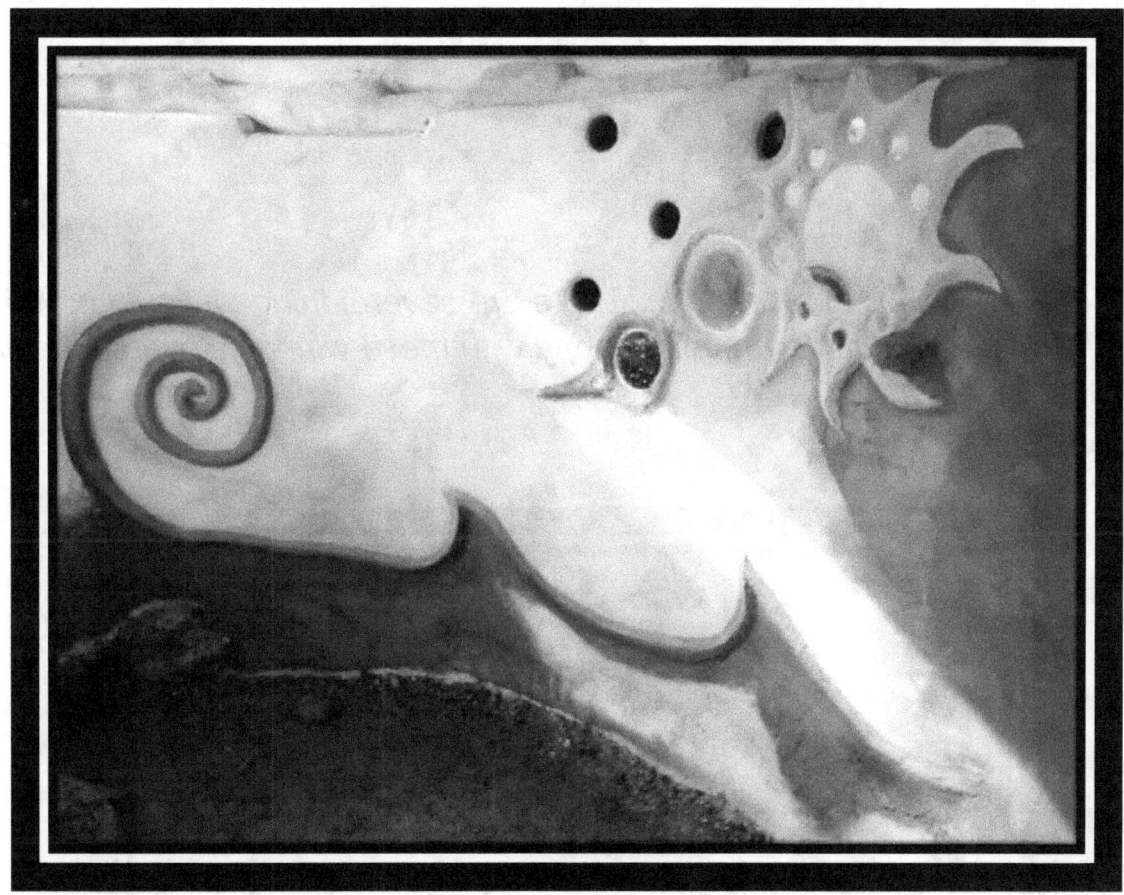

6 4 16. Mixing lime-based paint. I used about three cups lime putty, a couple cups water, and half a cup or so of boiled linseed oil for the base. Then I added pigments (mostly oxides).

The colors outside and downstairs in the Head Hutt went on and have remained vivid. I used natural oxide pigment powders, mostly mixed with lime and painted on, though in some cases sprayed on in a lime water. The pigments have bound to the lime plaster quite nicely and show no signs of washing off, even where I have frequent water running down the walls from watering plants on the upper level.

Leaf-Feather-Lashes are locked in. There are several things I would or will do differently next time, but I am quite happy with these windows overall. I have learned a lot! 9 7 16.

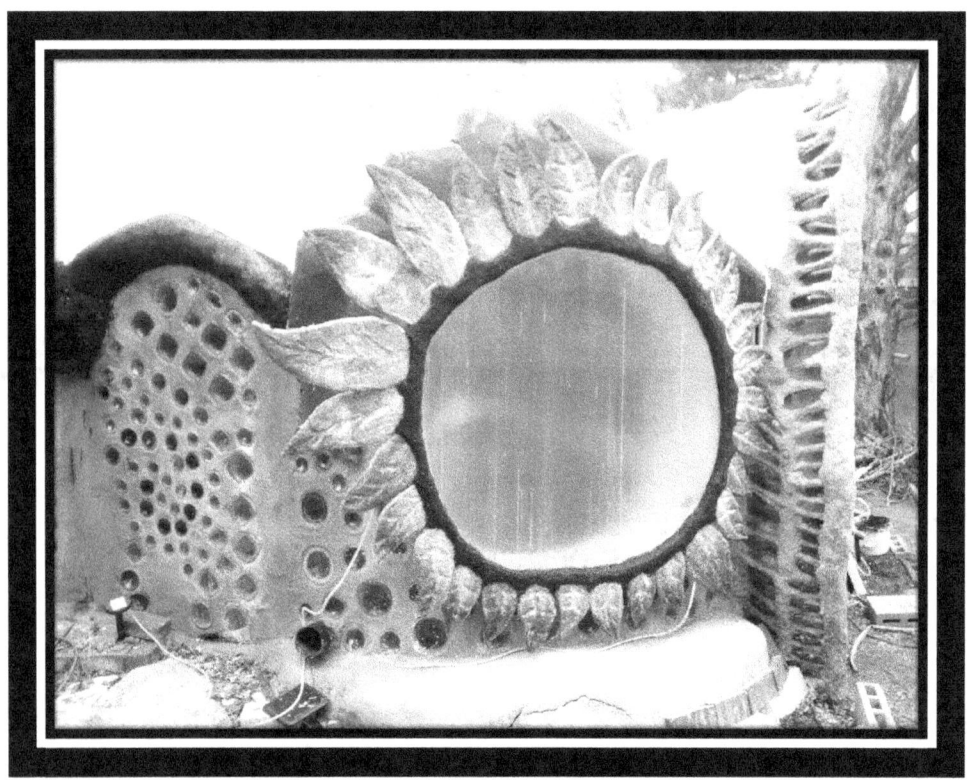

Closing Thoughts, Finishing the Future

What have I learned, what have I gained, what have I lost, or, at what cost?

I learned I am a little bit crazy. I already knew that, but, this project was further confirmation for me. Not the kind of crazy that I should or would be ashamed about. More the kind that makes me a bit different from most people.

People sometimes tell me that my building this inspires them to build what they dream of building, and that makes me happy. In reviewing the pictures and thinking about the process and delays and obstacles, I think, most people probably don't have it in them to build something like this.

I know that is not what some of you want to read, but I have to be honest, and it has come to mind more than once. If you are not sure, or not willing to fail, then maybe you should not try…or maybe you should. Maybe you should hire someone with some experience to build it for you. I am not sure. I just know that an incredible amount of work went into this. Like anything, the first time took so much longer than it would take me to repeat or modify a project based on what I learned by trying and often failing somewhat.

Also, I feel compelled to mention again, that I failed much, much, less than I might have in huge thanks to the Earthship crew, Mike Reynolds' books, his crew and the interns I worked with had a profound positive impact on my outlook and my ability to finish the Head Hutt. I don't know for sure that I would have been able to finish it if not for the valuable lessons I learned from the Earthship and other books, various videos, and most importantly, by working with the crew and other interns on two different jobs, as well as visiting the Biotecture school and touring several finished Earthships in Taos.

I gained so much insight. About construction, about concrete, and lime, and paper, and earth, about myself, about people, about learning, and teaching, and digging, and tires, and glass, and soils, and zoning departments. The insights have not ceased. I continue to learn about people now through sharing the Head Hutt. What questions, what stories they share…the insights continue to delight me.

The entire project took longer than I expected, and also, many parts were much more doable than I thought at the start. I had several injuries and some chronic inflammation issues flare up, as well as a general decline in my financial health which caused several 6-9 month periods of zero progress. Most of the time though, I was working on it, little by little by little. I spend a lot of time doodling and sketching and figuring. I spent a lot of time researching, figuring things out, thinking things through. And I made plenty of mistakes. So, even though I think it could have been done in a third of the time, I also think that ten years or so is a realistic time frame to get something like this done. I am proud of it. Happy to be moving forward from here with it feeling relatively complete and holding up to weather and time quite well.

You could sum it up with about $7000 and ten years of lots of extra time, space, and energy. I think I would charge about $100,000 to build you one this year, plus travel expenses of course. I still think the gains far outweigh the costs or losses, and so I don't see it as a loss to any degree. The monetary figure is just an estimation of money spent on materials. I think that is a pretty impressive deal even if my estimations are off by a lot, as the Head Hutt is truly priceless. It is a one of kind, unique Mega-Sculpture. I like to call it an Earthship Inspired Mega-Sculpture, because people often refer to it as an Earthship even though it is not and I make it a point to talk about why it is not (no water reclamation, garden/food production, or sewage, no insulation, and, well, the leaky glass dome…among other things.

The Head Hutt is Art. So is the Foo Dog, which I built alongside it, in much the same time frame, only slightly ahead. They are both site specific Mega-Sculptures. I hope they are first and second in a series of many. We will see.

The Head Hutt Picture Book

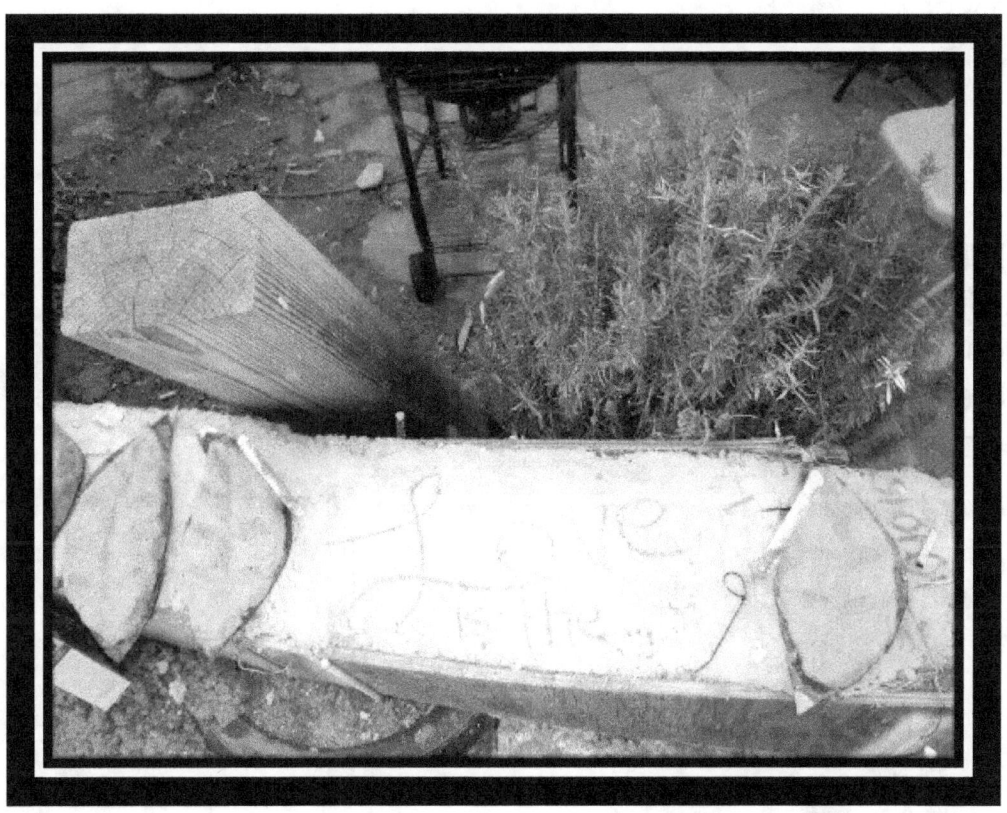

About the Author

Gabrielle Angel Lilly is a life-long learner, healer, practitioner of 'the arts' and a lover of science. She frequently finds herself writing about herself in the third person. Playfulness and positivity are at the heart of all she promotes, and you can learn more about her by inquiring within, as ultimately we are all one. Your name is her name too.

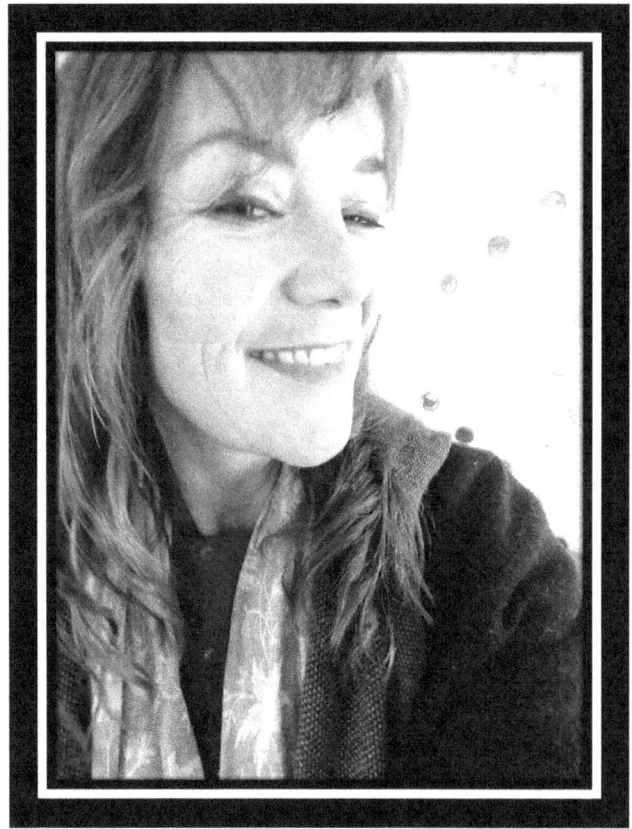

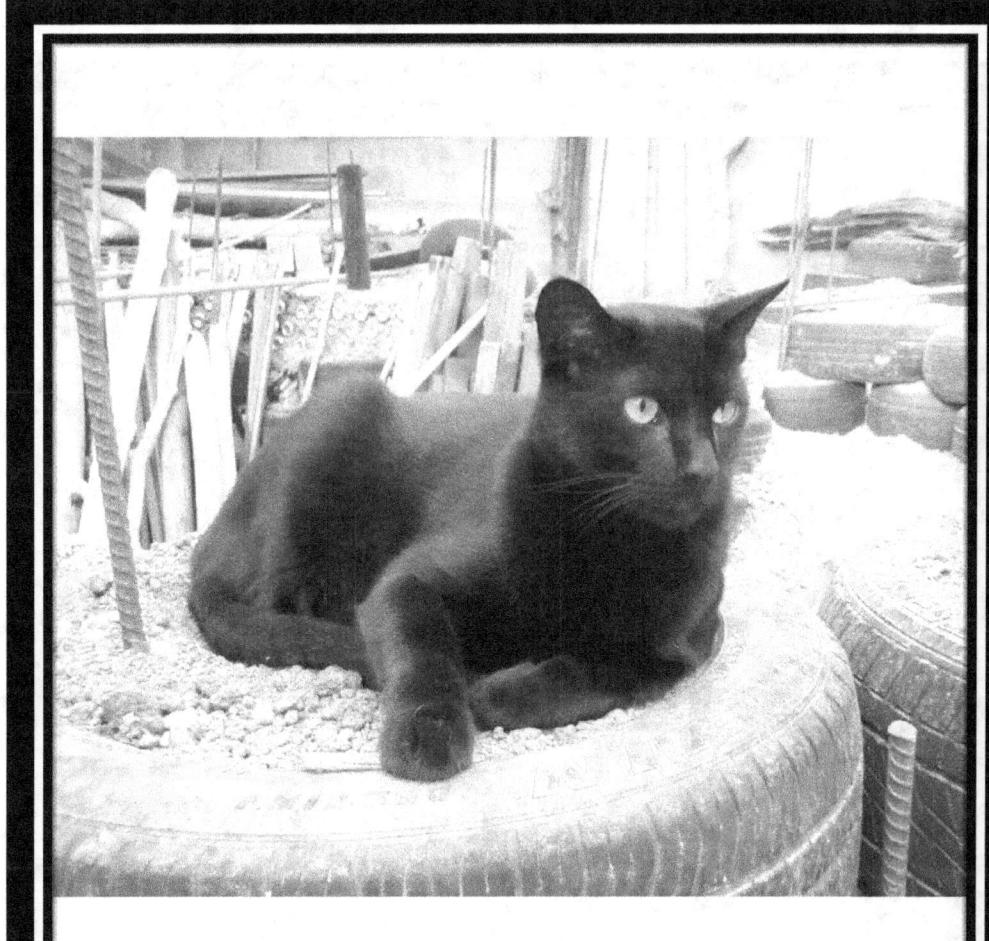

Thank you for reading this book, and allowing me to share my story and my vision with you. Don't forget to play every day! #UnityPlay

The Head Hutt Picture Book

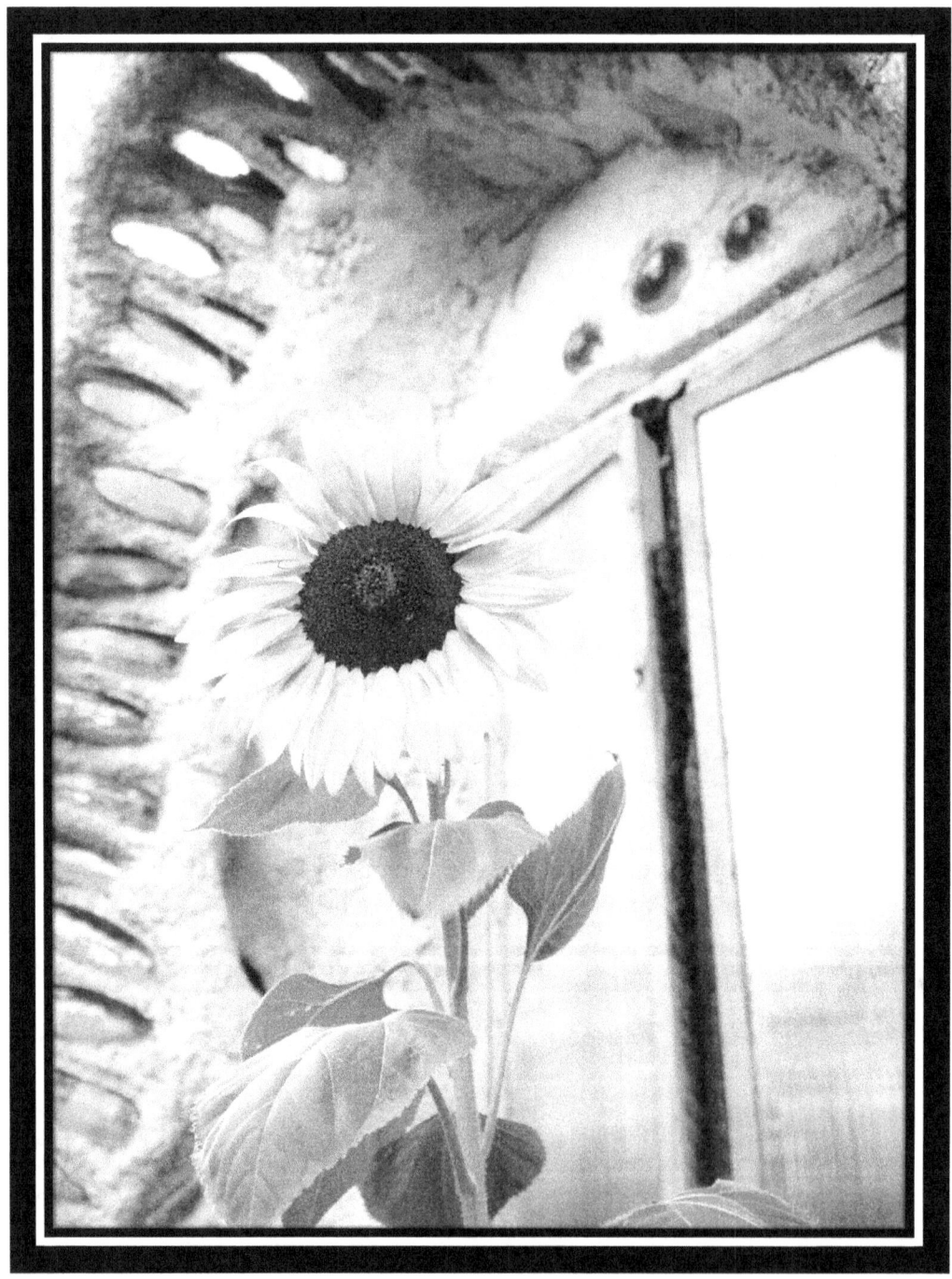

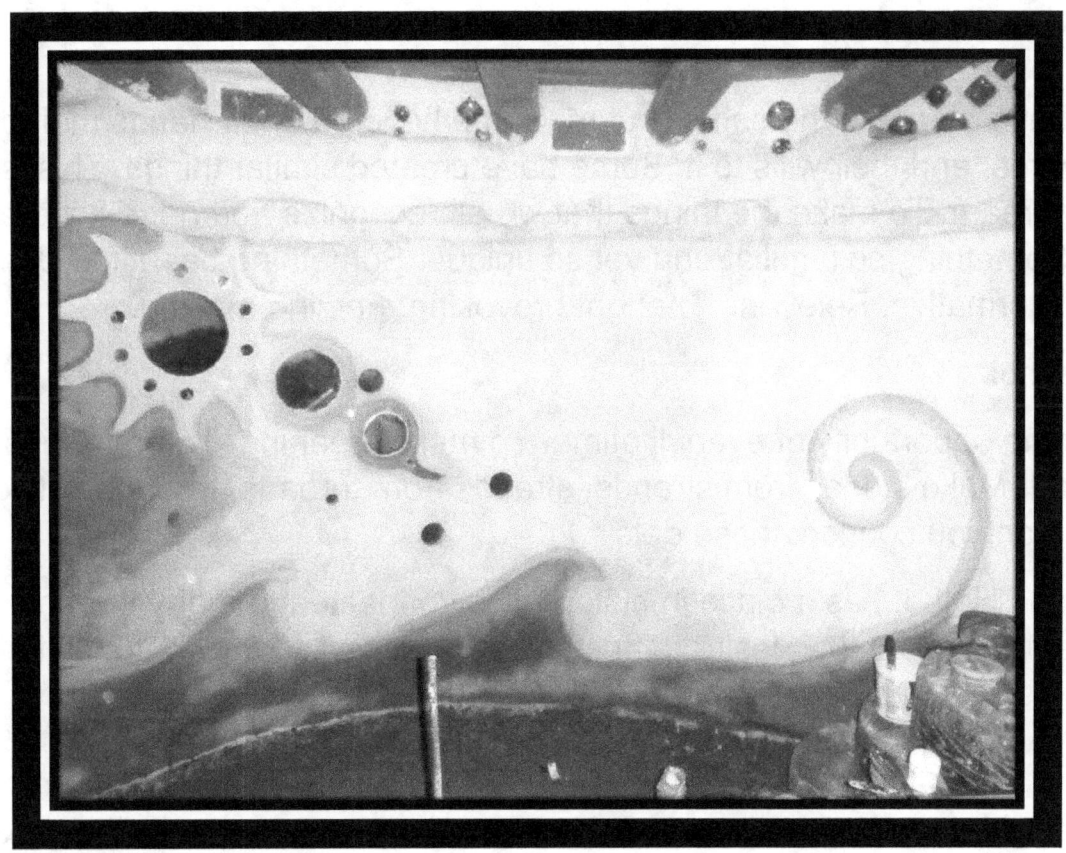

Still having a bit of trouble with blending and gradation, but learning lots and having a really fun time playing with pigments and lime! 5 5 16.

Epilogue

Many have dreamed the same dream. Some have put their hands their backs, their words, and their wills to it. Some have created similar things. This is an artist's dream. To make the things that we all recognize and none have ever seen. Something so familiar and yet so unique. Something beautiful. Useful. Novel. Normative. Relevant. Thought provoking. Feeling making.

Meaningful.

This is the opportunity of every lifetime. To make meaning. To draw lines in the sand. Make stories from strands, strands from threads, threads between dots… can you connect these dots?

The Head Hutt. It has a place in history. It is connected to many threads. Several to my past. My desire to build glass houses and throw stones in them. A stone skipping pond, perhaps.

I wanted this story to be about how I perfected my community building skills, and learned to rally people together around a common cause. I was hoping it would be about how I improved my communication and social skills enough to develop the partnerships that would help me develop and design this global system of unity play centers I keep dreaming about. I want to be able to tell you with great enthusiasm how the Authentic Action school is enrolling students and our first Unity Play center is well underway. I can say I still think these and many other great things will be happening soon.

Are rules are more important than those who make them up? I can see that society agrees the answer is yes. Another age-old questions. State vs Individual. We all know who wins, at least, on paper. Who wins in your heart? You decide.

If rules are all we care about, more than free thinking, more than health, more than evolution, then I am on the wrong side of the story. I might end up another bad example. If I am, then I will get my due in history. Kill me if you must. I won't stop living while I am alive. I suspect I will just get born again and continue this evolution even if you do kill me. Of course, I am not totally sure, which is part of the delightful mystery of it all.

The moral of the story is simple. Be true to you. To thine own self be true. Heal yourself and you heal us all. Be gentle and kind and playful with yourself. That is the best you can do for everything else.

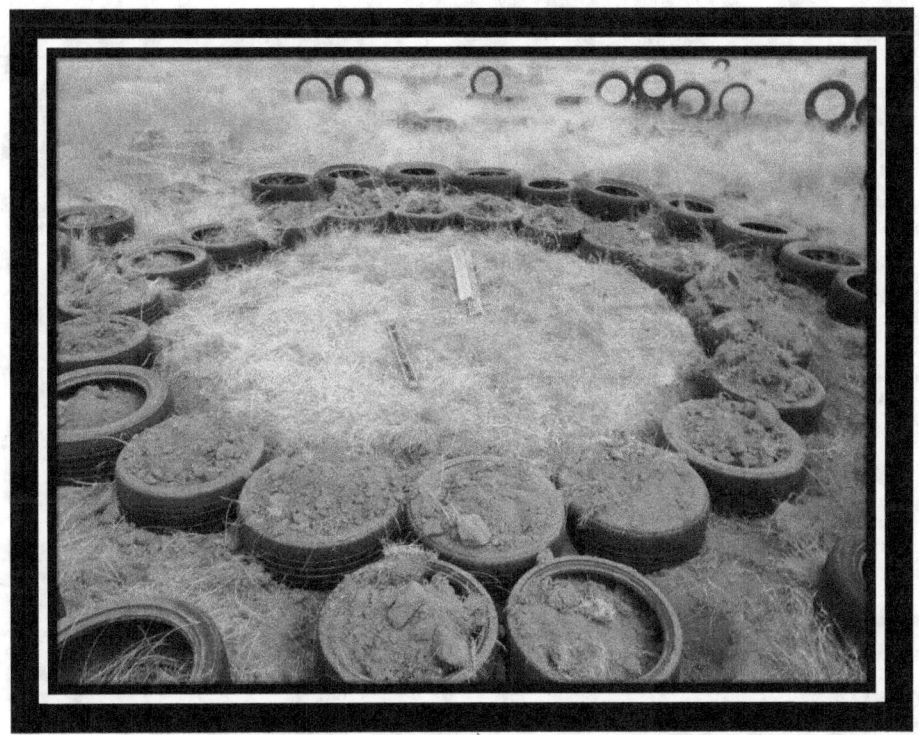

Eye of Horus, Temple of RAH Experimental Site, Story Hut, Sept 2015.

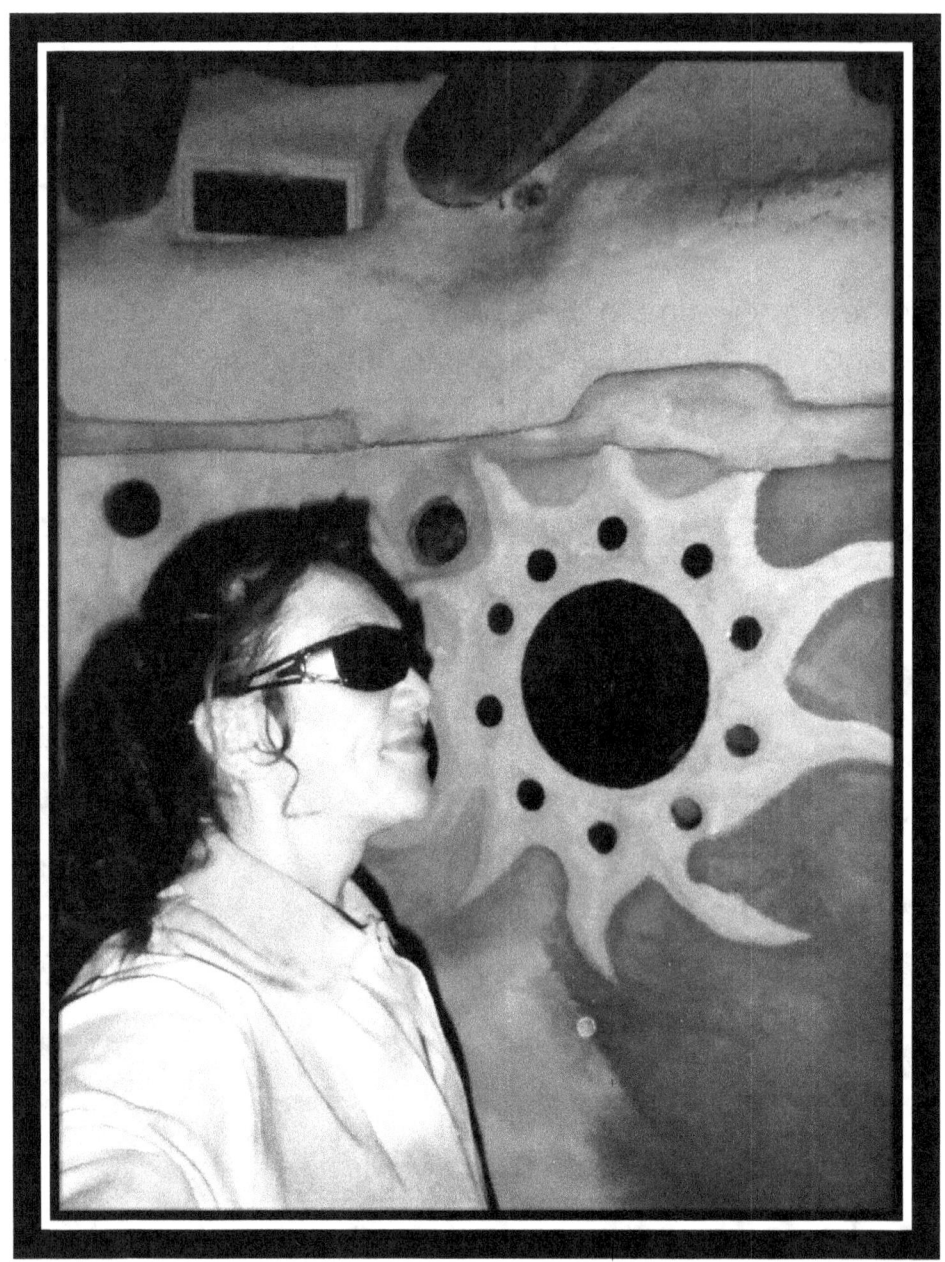

My future is so bright! 5 4 16.

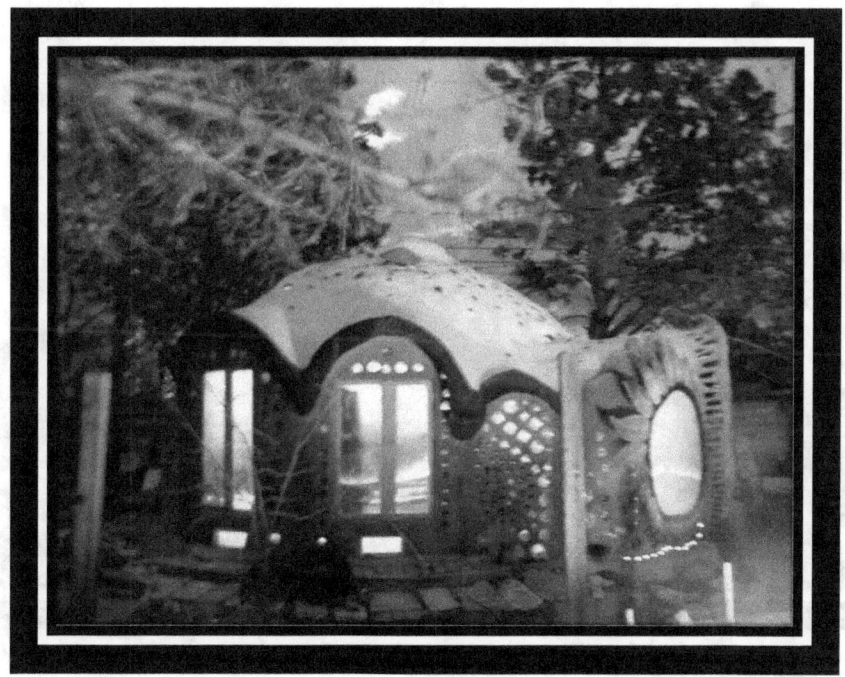

Check my website for specific details if you want to support me on my personal quest to build Unity Play Stations/Sustainability Community Centers. Sign up to support me on one of the many social platforms I am on. Get in touch with me or someone on my team and let me know if this resonates with you or aligns with your own goals, dreams, and visions for the future. Share my story, my videos, my books, and play every day!

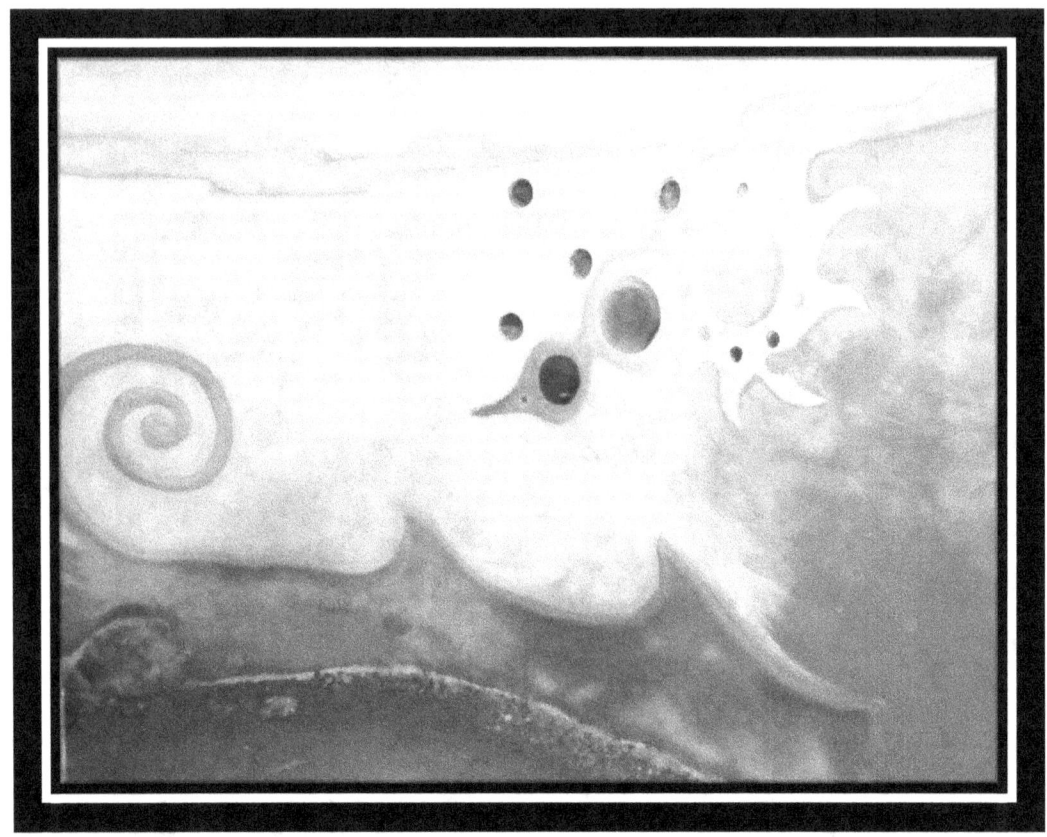

"No matter how isolated you are and how lonely you feel, if you do your work truly and conscientiously unknown friends will come and seek you" ~ Carl Yung

Special thanks to Khalid, Adam, Thomas, Jordan, Liam, George, Spirit, Harmony, Justice, Jacob, Gail, Mark, and everyone else who lent a helping hand or cheered me on during the long construction of The Head Hutt. Thank you.

www.ingramcontent.com/pod-product-compliance
Lightning Source LLC
Chambersburg PA
CBHW082244220526
45469CB00009B/2871